TME 30-420

HANDBOOK
ON THE
ITALIAN MILITARY FORCES

2 AUGUST 1943

MILITARY INTELLIGENCE SERVICE

The Naval & Military Press Ltd

Published by

The Naval & Military Press Ltd
Unit 10 Ridgewood Industrial Park,
Uckfield, East Sussex,
TN22 5QE England

Tel: +44 (0) 1825 749494
Fax: +44 (0) 1825 765701

www.naval-military-press.com
www.military-genealogy.com

In reprinting in facsimile from the original, any imperfections are inevitably reproduced and the quality may fall short of modern type and cartographic standards.

TABLE OF CONTENTS

	Paragraphs	Page
Foreword	1-5	1
CHAPTER 1. Introduction:		
Section I. Distinctive Branches, or Specialties	6-11	5
II. Semimilitary Forces	12-19	7
CHAPTER 2. Recruitment and Mobilization:		
Section I. System of Conscription and Mobilization	20-27	18
II. Professional Cadre and Officers	28-30	28
III. Training, Efficiency, and Morale	31-35	30
IV. Pay and Emoluments	36-38	37
CHAPTER 3. Organization:		
Section I. Command and Staff	39-44	39
II. Administration	45-46	44
III. Higher Units	47-62	45
IV. Infantry	63-77	57
V. Cavalry	78-82	71
VI. Land Reconnaissance Units	83-86	74
VII. Field Artillery	87-97	76
VIII. Antiaircraft Artillery	98-100	88
IX. Coast Artillery	101-102	91
X. Armored Troops	103-117	92
XI. Engineers	118-120	99
XII. Signal Communications	121-132	103
XIII. Chemical Troops	133-137	109
XIV. Motor Transport Agencies	138-140	112
CHAPTER 4. Services, Supply, and Transportation:		
Section I. Central Organization	141-144	114
II. Services	145-152	116
III. Particular Services	153-169	123
IV. Transportation	170-173	145
CHAPTER 5. Ranks, Uniforms, and Insignia and Identification:		
Section I. Ranks	174-179	157
II. Uniforms and Insignia	180-194	159
III. Decorations, Medals, and Awards	195-203	175

RESTRICTED

TABLE OF CONTENTS

	Paragraphs	Page
CHAPTER 6. ARMAMENT AND EQUIPMENT:		
SECTION I. Infantry	204–213	179
II. Cavalry	214–221	210
III. Antiaircraft and Antitank	222–230	212
IV. Artillery	231–234	230
V. Armored Vehicles	235–238	251
VI. Engineers	239–247	269
VII. Signal Communications	248–258	325
VIII. Chemical Warfare	259–269	343
CHAPTER 7. AIR FORCE	270–279	367
CHAPTER 8. TACTICS:		
SECTION I. Doctrine	280–284	401
II. Principles of Employment	285–288	405
CHAPTER 9. PERMANENT FORTIFICATIONS	289–294	408
CHAPTER 10. CAMOUFLAGE	295–305	417
CHAPTER 11. ABBREVIATIONS	306–310	422
CHAPTER 12. MISCELLANEOUS:		
SECTION I. Road Spaces	311–313	461
II. Flags and Insignia of Certain Units		465
III. Coinage, Weights, and Measures	314–319	468
INDEX		475

RESTRICTED

LIST OF ILLUSTRATIONS

Figure		Page
1	Map of Italy, showing principal cities	3
2	Map of Italy, showing regions	4
3	Typical organization of a depot command (*reparto depósito*)	22
4	Organization of the High Command in war	41
5	Organization of the infantry division (*d visione binária*)	49
6	Organization of the mobile (cavalry) division (*divisione célere*)	55
7	Organization of the normal type of infántry regiment (*binary division*)	61
8	Organization of the Grenadier type of infantry regiment	63
9	Organization of the assault and landing type of infantry regiment	65
10	Organization of the Alpine regiment	67
11	Organization of the Bersaglieri cyclist regiment in the mobile (cavalry) division (*divisione célere*) or an army corps	69
12	Organization of a divisional Black Shirt legion	70
13	Organization of the cavalry brigade in the mobile (cavalry) division (*divisione célere*)	71
14	Organization of the normal cavalry regiment	72
15	Organization of the artillery regiment in the infantry division	82
16	Organization of the artillery regiment in the mobile (cavalry) division (*divisione célere*)	83
17	Organization of the artillery regiment in the armored division	84
18	Organization of the artillery regiment in the Alpine division	85
19	Organization of the artillery regiment in an army corps	86
20	Organization of the antiaircraft regiment	89
21	Organization and assignment of 20-mm antiaircraft batteries	90
22	Organization of the light tank regiment	90
23	Organization of principal engineer units	100
24	Organization of special engineer units	101
25	Organization of the assault pioneer battalion	102
26	Organization of the radiotelegraph battalion in an army	104
27	Organization of the radiotelegraph company in an army corps	105
28	Organization of the signal unit in the mountain division	105
29	Organization of the photographic company	109
30	Table of motor transport loads	131
31	Map of Italy, showing main railroad lines and highways	147
32	Water tank car	150

LIST OF ILLUSTRATIONS

Figure		Page
33	Freight car for transporting acids	151
34	Table of carrying capacity of rolling stock	152
35	Table of relative ranks	156
36	Commissioned officers in service dress uniforms. (The black collar on the brigadier general's uniform indicates the style of uniform prior to June 1940)	163
37	Group of Italian enlisted men	169
38	Identity plate (*Medaglioncino di riconoscimento*)	171
39	Individual record book (*libretto personale*)	173
40	Service revolver and pistols	180
41	9-mm automatic pistol, model 910 (Glisenti)	181
42	Service rifles and carbines	183
43	20-mm antitank rifle (Soluthurn)	187
44	6.5-mm light machine gun, model 30 (Breda)	189
45	8-mm medium machine gun, model 37 (Breda)	190
46	8-mm tank-mounted machine gun, model 38 (Breda)	192
47	8-mm medium machine gun, model 35 (Fiat-Revelli)	194
48	8-mm medium machine gun, model 07/12 (Schwarzlose)	195
49	9-mm machine carbine, model 38 (Beretta)	197
50	20-mm heavy machine gun, model 35 (Breda)	199
51	65/17 infantry gun	201
52	45-mm light mortar, model 35 (Brixia)	204
53	81-mm medium mortar, model 35	205
54	81-mm mortar squad	206
55	Firing the 81-mm mortar	207
56	Hand grenades	208
57	Characteristics of antiaircraft guns	215
58	75/27 (2.95-inch) AA gun	216
59	75/46 (2.95-inch) AA gun, model 34 (Ansaldo)	216
60	Detail of the 75/46 (2.95-inch) AA gun, model 34 (Ansaldo)	217
61	AA guns, model 1933 (Ansaldo)	218
62	20/65 (.79-inch) AA gun, model 35 (Breda)	219
63	20/65 (.79-inch) AA gun, model 35 (Breda), ready for transport	220
64	47/32 (1.85-inch) antitank gun, model 37	225
65	90-mm antitank gun, self-propelled model	227
66	102/35 (4.016) AA gun	230
67	Characteristics of artillery weapons	241
68	75/27 gun in traveling position	241
69	75/27 gun with shield raised	242

RESTRICTED   VI

LIST OF ILLUSTRATIONS

Figure		Page
70	90/53 AA and coast defense gun	243
71	149/35 gun	246
72	381/40 railway gun	246
73	305-mm howitzer	250
74	Characteristics of types of tanks	251
75	L 3/35 tank	253
76	Fiat-Ansaldo 3000 B tank (old model)	254
77	L 6/40 tank	255
78	Renault R 35 tank (French)	256
79	M 11/39 tank	257
80	M13 (formerly M11) tank	258
81	M13/40 tank	259
82	Cross section of the M13/40 four-man tank	260
83	S 35, Somua (French) medium tank	262
84	Characteristics of armored cars	263
85	Autoblinda 40	264
86	Italian motorized divisions showing *autocarrette*	265
87	S. P. A. Sahariano (Saharan) truck (Fiat)	268
88	Tabulation of bridge equipment	270
89	Girder bridge (*ponte metallico*) no. 1	271
90	Girder bridge no. 2 (*ponte metallico 2*)	272
91	Variations of girder bridge no. 2	273
92	*Passarella da montagna*	274
93	Cableway no. 3	274
94	Ponton and trestle bridges	275
95	Ponton and trestle bridges	276
96	Special raft (*Záttera*)	277
97	Friction igniter (*miccia da 40*)	278
98	Time-delay igniter	280
99	Cross section of antipersonnel mine B4	283
100	Antipersonnel mine B4	284
101	Antipersonnel mine B4 (top view)	285
102	Bomb 4AR	286
103	Antitank mine B2	289
104	Antitank mine B2 (cross section)	289
105	Antitank mine B2 (S. C. G.)	291
106	B2 mine (hinged-lid type)	293
107	Type D mine	295
108	Antitank mine N5	297
109	Antitank mine N5	298
110	Metal tube mine	301

LIST OF ILLUSTRATIONS

Figure		Page
111	Railway mine (old pattern)	303
112	Railway mine (new pattern)	304
113	Antipersonnel (2-kg) pressure mine	305
114	Antipersonnel trip mine, type 2	307
115	Electrical mine, type 2 (B)	308
116	Antipersonnel trip mine, type 9	309
117	Pressure mine, type 9	311
118	Antitank mine, type 9	313
119	Mine, type N	315
120	Road and field mine	316
121	Road and field mine (details)	317
122	Shell mine	319
123	Pressure mine with grenade exploder	321
124	Items of camouflage equipment	324
125	Searchlight unit (120-cm)	324
126	Types of radio	327
127	Type O. G. M. rotary key telephone switchboard (with circuit diagram for 10 lines)	328
128	Characteristics of the various types of telephone wire	329
129	Circuit diagrams of Morse telegraph set. (The black holes indicate the positions of the plugs.)	331
130	Repeating coil for simultaneous phantom telephony and simplex telegraphy, model O. G. M. (1928) (with circuit diagram)	335
131	Heliograph rectifier of 80-mm optical signaling apparatus	336
132	Generator of 80-mm optical signaling apparatus	337
133	Showing use of the converter of the 180-mm phototelephonic set	338
134	List of radios	339
135	Types, numbers, characteristics, and applications of storage batteries	340
136	Diagrams of communication nets	342
137	List of gas bombs	349
138	List of Italian incendiary bombs	351
139	Portable flame thrower, model 35	352
140	Portable flame thrower, model 35, showing nozzle	353
141	Portable flame thrower, model 40	355
142	Italian flame-thrower tank, L 3/35, with trailer	356
143	Military gas mask, M31. (The separate type canister is attached.)	357
144	Protective clothing	361

LIST OF ILLUSTRATIONS

Figure		Page
145	Organization of the Air Ministry	368
146	Territorial organization of the Air Force	372
147	Tactical organization of the Air Force	374
148	Strength report of Italian Air Force, April 1943	375
149	Aircraft in operational use	376
150	SM-82 transport planes in flight	377
151	Markings of Italian aircraft	378
152	P-108, long range bomber	379
153	Cant. Z-1007 Bis, *Alcione* (Kingfisher), medium bomber	380
154	BR-20, *Cicogna* (Stork), medium bomber	381
155	SM-79, *Sparviero* (Hawk), medium bomber	382
156	CA-310, *Libéccio* (Southwest Wind), reconnaissance bomber	383
157	CA-311, reconnaissance bomber	384
158	SM-82, *Canguru* (Kangaroo), transport	385
159	SM-85, dive bomber	386
160	Cant. Z-506B, *Airione* (Heron), flying boat	387
161	Cant. Z-501, flying boat	388
162	RE-2001, *Falco II* (Falcon), fighter	389
163	RE-2000, *Falco I* (Falcon), fighter	390
164	MC-200, *Saetta* (Thunderbolt), fighter	391
165	MC-202, *Saetta II* (Thunderbolt), fighter	392
166	MC-205, fighter. (This fighter resembles the MC-202 in appearance.)	393

RESTRICTED

COLOR PLATES

Plate
I. Army service dress and field uniforms: commissioned officers
II. Army field uniforms: noncommissioned officers and enlisted men
III. Army tropical uniforms: officers and men
IV. Miscellaneous Army and Black Shirt uniforms
V. Air Force uniforms: commissioned officers
VI. Insignia of rank of general officers
VII. Insignia of rank of company and field officers
VIII. Insignia of rank of noncommissioned officers and enlisted men
IX. Collar patches of infantry regiments and divisions
X. Collar patches and devices of arms and services (other than infantry of the line)
XI. Insignia of arm or service
XII. Insignia of arm or service (continued)

PLATE 1

HANDBOOK ON THE ITALIAN MILITARY FORCES

ARMY SERVICE DRESS AND FIELD UNIFORMS
Commissioned Officers

INSIGNIA ON HEADGEAR
General officer

COLLAR PATCH
1st Cavalry

BRIGADIER GENERAL

SECOND LIEUTENANT, INFANTRY

LIEUTENANT COLONEL, CAVALRY

INSIGNIA OF RANK

SERVICE CAP BAND
Brigadier general

SLEEVE INSIGNIA
Brigadier general

INSIGNIA OF RANK

INSIGNIA ON GARRISON CAP
Captain

INSIGNIA ON
ALPINE TYPE OF CAP
Major

FROM J.A.N. NO. 1

PLATE II

ARMY FIELD UNIFORMS
Noncommissioned Officers and Enlisted Men

INSIGNIA OF RANK

SHOULDER STRAP
*Marshals
(Ordinary marshal)*

CHEVRONS
*Noncommissioned officers
(Sergeant)*

BERSAGLIERI
Marshal, old-style coat

HEADGEAR

FEZ OF BERSAGLIERI

HAT OF BERSAGLIERI

SUMMER UNIFORM
Private, Infantry

ALPINI
Sergeant-major, new-style coat

HEADGEAR

CAP OF FRONTIER GUARDS

HAT OF CARABINIERI

FROM J.A.N. NO. 1

PLATE III

ARMY TROPICAL UNIFORMS
Officers and Men

INSIGNIA
ON TROPICAL HELMET
15th Infantry

CAPTAIN, INFANTRY

INSIGNIA OF RANK

SHOULDER STRAP
Captain, 15th Infantry

INSIGNIA ON GARRISON CAP
Second lieutenant

PRIVATE, ARTILLERY

LANCE-CORPORAL

INSIGNIA OF RANK

SHOULDER STRAP
Ordinary marshal

CHEVRON
Lance-corporal

FROM J A N. NO. 1

PLATE IV

MISCELLANEOUS ARMY AND BLACK SHIRT UNIFORMS

CRASH HELMET
Tank troops

GAS MASK
With canister

COLLAR PATCH
Tank troops

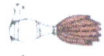
COLLAR PATCH
Chemical troops

UNIFORM OF TANK CREWS
Private, leather coat

BLACK SHIRT INSIGNIA

BLACK SHIRT COLLAR PATCH

SERVICE CAP BAND
Brigadier general

SLEEVE INSIGNIA
Brigadier general

FROM J.A.N. NO. 1

FASCIST MILITIA
Private

PROTECTIVE SUIT
Private, chemical troops

BLACK SHIRT INSIGNIA

INSIGNIA ON GARRISON CAP
Captain

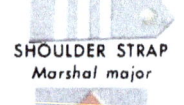
SHOULDER STRAP
Marshal major

SLEEVE INSIGNIA
Lance-corporal

PLATE V

AIR FORCE UNIFORMS
Officers and Men

MILITARY PILOTS' INSIGNIA

SLEEVE INSIGNIA
Major

SERVICE DRESS
Major

PARACHUTIST
Second lieutenant

FLYING UNIFORM
Captain

PARACHUTISTS' COLLAR PATCH

PARACHUTISTS' SLEEVE INSIGNIA

FROM J.A.N. NO. 1

PLATE VI

INSIGNIA OF RANK
OF
GENERAL OFFICERS

L = (Land) Army   N = Navy   A = Air Force   M = Militia

U.S. Army equivalent	Rank		Headgear	Army	Insignia worn on cuffs Navy	Air Force	Militia
Commander-in-Chief	Maresciallo d'Italia	L					
	Grande Ammiraglio	N					
	Maresciallo dell' Aria	A					
General	Generale d'Armata	L					
	Ammiraglio d'Armata	N					
	Generale d'Armata	A					
	Comandante Generale	M					
	Gen designato d'Armata	L					
	Ammiraglio des. d'Armata	N					
	Gen designato d'Armata	A					
Lieutenant general	Gen di Corpo d'Armata	L					
	Ammiraglio di Squadra	N					
	Generale di Squadra	A					
	Luogotenente Gener. Capo di S.M.	M					
Major general	Generale di Divisione	L					
	Ammiraglio di Divisione	N					
	Generale di Divisione	A					
	Luogotenente Generale	M					
Brigadier general	Generale di Brigata	L					
	Contrammiraglio	N					
	Generale di Brigata	A					
	Console Generale	M					

PLATE VII

INSIGNIA OF RANK
OF
COMPANY AND FIELD OFFICERS

L = (Land) Army   N = Navy   A = Air Force   M = Militia

U.S. Army equivalent	Rank	Headgear	Army	Navy	Air Force	Militia
FIELD OFFICERS (Ufficiali superiori)				Insignia worn on cuffs		
Colonel	Colonnello / Capitano di Vascello / Colonnello / Console	L N A M				
Lieutenant Colonel	Tenente Colonnello / Capitano di Fregata / Tenente Colonnello / Primo Seniore	L N A M				
Major	Maggiore / Capitano di Corvetta / Maggiore / Seniore	L N A M				
COMPANY OFFICERS (Ufficiali inferiori)						
	Primo Capitano / Primo tenente di Vascello	L N				
Captain	Capitano / Tenente di Vascello / Capitano / Centurione	L N A M				
	Primo tenente	L				
Lieutenant	Tenente / S. Tenente di Vascello / Tenente / Capo Manipolo	L N A M				
Second Lieutenant	Sotto tenente / Guardiamarina / Sottotenente / Sotto Capo Manipolo	L N A M				
Officer candidate	Aspirante / Asp. Sotto Capo Manipolo	L M				

PLATE VIII

INSIGNIA OF RANK
OF
NONCOMMISSIONED OFFICERS AND ENLISTED MEN

L = (Land) Army   N = Navy   A = Air Force   M = Militia

With the exception of the grades of *marescialli*, all insignia appear on the sleeves and headgear. *Marescialli* wear the insignia of rank on the shoulder straps.

	U.S. Army equivalent	Rank		Headgear	Army	Navy	Air Force	Militia
NONCOMMISSIONED OFFICERS (Sottufficiali)		Maresciallo Maggiore Capo di Prima Classe Maresciallo di 1ª Classe Primo Aiutante	L N A M	—				Shoulder straps
		Maresciallo Capo Capo di 2ª Classe Maresciallo di 2ª Classe Aiutante Capo	L N A M	—				
		Maresciallo Ordinario Capo di 3ª Classe Maresciallo di 3ª Classe Aiutante	L N A M	—				
	Sergeant-major	Sergente Maggiore Secondo capo Sergente Maggiore Primo Capo Squadra	L M A M					
	Sergeant	Sergente Sergente Sergente Capo Squadra	L N A M					
ENLISTED MEN (Truppa)	Corporal	Caporale Maggiore Sotto Capo Primo Aviere Vice Capo Squadra	L N A M					
	Lance-corporal	Caporale Aviere Scelto Camicia Nera Scelta	L A M					
	Private 1st class	Appuntato Comune di 1ª Classe Camicia Nera	L N M					
	Private	Soldato Comune di 2ª Classe Aviere	L N A					

PLATE IX

COLLAR PATCHES OF INFANTRY REGIMENTS AND DIVISIONS

I. R. — Infantry regiment S. M. R. — Semimotorized regiment I. D. — Infantry division
M. I. R. — Motorized infantry regiment A. R. — Airborne regiment M. I. D. — Motorized infantry division

Divisions usually have the same names as their component regiments. Only in cases where names differ are they shown on this plate.

1st–2d I. R. Re¹ 13th I. D.	59th–60th I. R. Calabria 31st I. D.	129th–130th I. R. Perugia 151st I. D.	223d–224th I. R. Etna
3d–4th I. R. Piemonte 29th I. D.	61st–62d M. I. R. Sicilia 102d M. I. D. Trento	131st–132d I. R. Lazio	225th–226th I. R. Arezzo 53d I. D.
5th–6th I. R. Aosta 28th I. D.	63d–64th I. R. Cagliari 59th I. D.	133d–144th I. R. Benevento	227th–228th S. M. R. Reviga 105th I. D.
7th–8th I. R. Cuneo 6th I. D.	65th–66th M. I. R. Valtellina 101st M. I. D. Trieste	135th–136th I. R. Campania	229th–230th I. R. Campobasso
9th–10th I. R. Regina 50th I. D.	67th–68th I. R. Palermo 58th I. D. Legnano	137th–138th I. R. Barletta	231st–232d I. R. Avellino 11th I. D.
11th–12th I. R. Casale 24th I. D.	69th–70th I. R. Ancona 61st I. D. Sirte	139th–140th I. R. Bari 47th I. D.	233d–234th I. R. Lario
13th–14th I. R. Pinerolo 24th I. D.	71st–72d I. R. Puglie 38th I. D.	141st–142d I. R. Catanzaro 64th I. D.	235th–236th I. R. Piceno
15th–16th I. R. Savona 55th I. D.	73d–74th I. R. Lombardia¹ 57th I. D.	143d–144th I. R. Taranto	236th–238th I. R. Grosseto
17th–18th I. R. Acqui 33d I. D.	75th–76th I. R. Napoli 54th I. D.	145th–146th I. R. Catania	239th–240th I. R. Pesaro
19th–20th S. M. R. Brescia 27th I. D.	77th–78th I. R. Toscana 7th I. D. Lupi di Toscana	147th–148th I. R. Caltanissetta	241st–242d I. R. Teramo
21st–22d I. R. Cremona 44th I. D.	79th–80th S. M. R. Roma 9th M. I. D. Pasubio	149th–150th I. R. Trapani	243d–244th I. R. Cosenza
23d–24th I. R. Como¹ 14th I. D. Isonzo	81st–82d S. M. R. Torino 52d I. D.	151st–152d I. R. Sassari 17th I. D.	245th–246th I. R. Siracusa
25th–26th I. R. Bergamo 15th I. D.	83d–84th I. R. Venezia 19th I. D.	153th–154th I. R. Novara 157th I. D.	247th–248th I. R. Girgenti
27th–28th S. M. R. Pavia 17th I. D.	85th–86th I. R. Verona 80th I. D. Sabratha	155th–156th I. R. Alessandria	249th–250th I. R. Pollanza
29th–30th I. R. Pisa 26th I. D. Assietta	87th–88th I. R. Friuli 20th I. D.	157th–158th I. R. Liguria 63d I. D. Cirene	251st–252d I. R. Massa Carrara
31st–32d I. R. Siena 51st I. D.	89th–90th I. R. Salerno 5th I. D. Cosseria	159th–160th I. R. Milano	253d–254th I. R. Porto Maurizio
33d–34th I. R. Livorno 4th I. D.	91st–92d I. R. Basilicata 1st I. D. Superga	161st–162d I. R. Ivrea	255th–256th I. R. Veneto 159th I. D.
35th–36th S. M. R. Pistoia 16th I. D.	93d–94th I. R. Messina 18th I. D.	163d–164th I. R. Lucca	257th–258th I. R. Tortona
37th–38th I. R. Ravenna 3d I. D.	95th–96th I. R. Udine 46th I. D.	201st–202d I. R. Sesia	259th–260th I. R. Murge 154th I. D.
39th–40th I. R. Bologna 25th I. D.	97th–98th I. R. Genova	201st–204th I. R. Tanaro	261st–262d I. R. Elba
41st–42d I. R. Modena 37th I. D.	111th–112th S. M. R. Piacenza 103d I. D.	205th–206th I. R. Lambro	263d–264th I. R. Gaeta
43d–44th I. R. Forlì 36th I. D.	113th–114th S. M. R. Mantova 104th I. D.	207th–208th I. R. Taro	265th–266th I. R. Lecce
45th–46th I. R. Reggio 30th I. D. Sabauda	115th–116th I. R. Treviso 622 I. D. Marmarica	209th–210th I. R. Bisagno	267th–268th I. R. Caserta
47th–48th I. R. Ferrara 23d I. D.	117th–118th I. R. Padova	211th–212th I. R. Pescara	269th–270th I. R. Aquila
49th–50th I. R. Parma 49th I. D.	119th–120th I. R. Emilia 155th I. D.	213th–214th I. R. Arno	271st–272d–273d I. R. Potenza
51st–52d I. R. Alpi¹ 22d I. D. Cacciatori delle Alpi	121st–122d I. R. Macerata 153d I. R.	215th–216th I. R. Tevere	274th–275th–276th I. R. Belluno
53d–54th I. R. Umbria 2d I. D. Sforzesca	123d–124th I. R. Chieti	217th–218th I. R. Volturno	277th–278th–279th I. R. Vicenza 156th I. D.
55th–56th I. R. Marche 32d I. D.	125th–126th A. R. 80th I. D. Spezia	219th–220th I. R. Sele	280th–281st–282d I. R. Foggia
57th–58th M. I. R. Abruzzi 10th M. I. D.	127th–128th I. R. 41st I. D. Firenze	221st–222d I. R. Ionia	Machine-gunners

¹ May wear a red necktie. ² May wear a blue necktie.

PLATE X

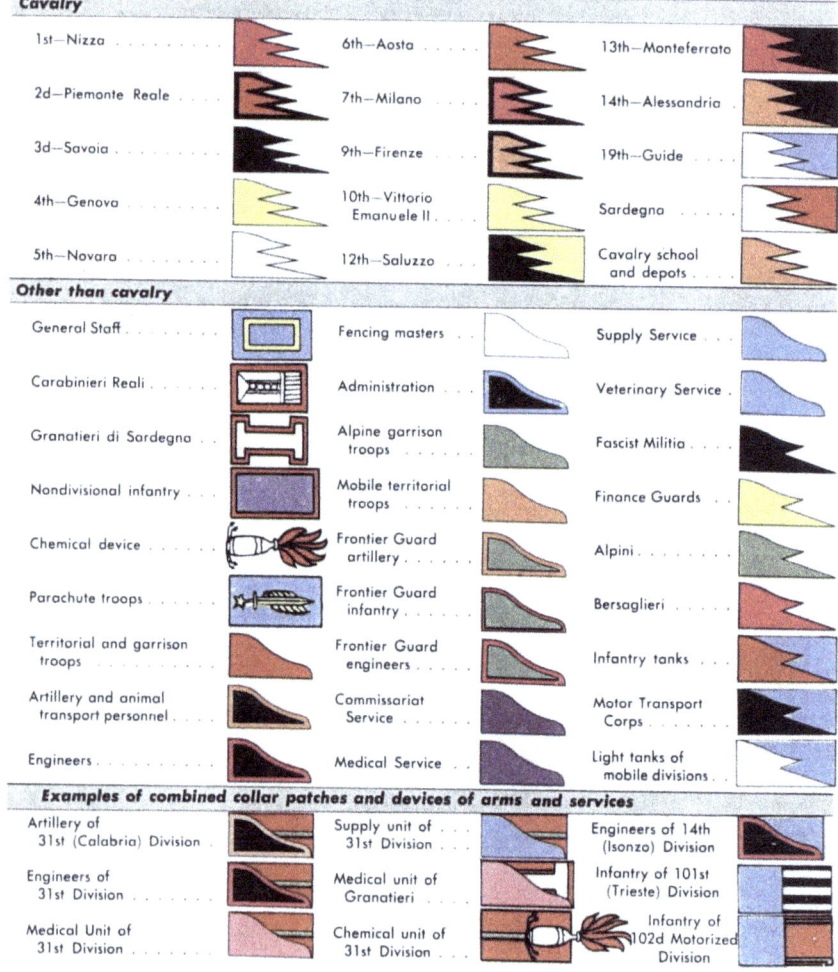

PLATE XI

INSIGNIA OF ARM OR SERVICE

The eagle is worn on all headgear of Army generals and officers of the General Staff. It is silver on the service dress cap and black on the garrison cap and steel helmet, except for General Staff officers, who wear the eagle in gold.

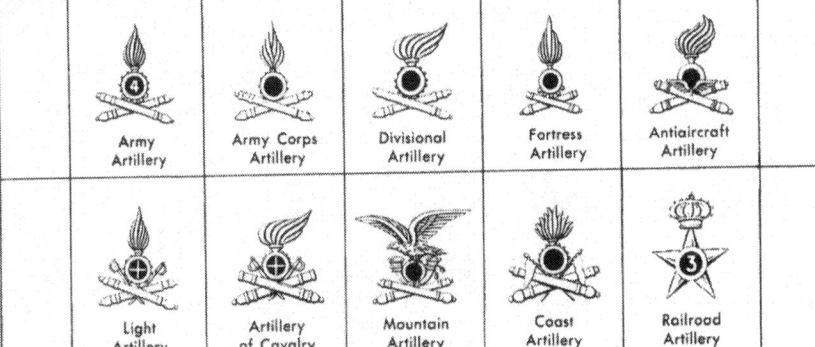

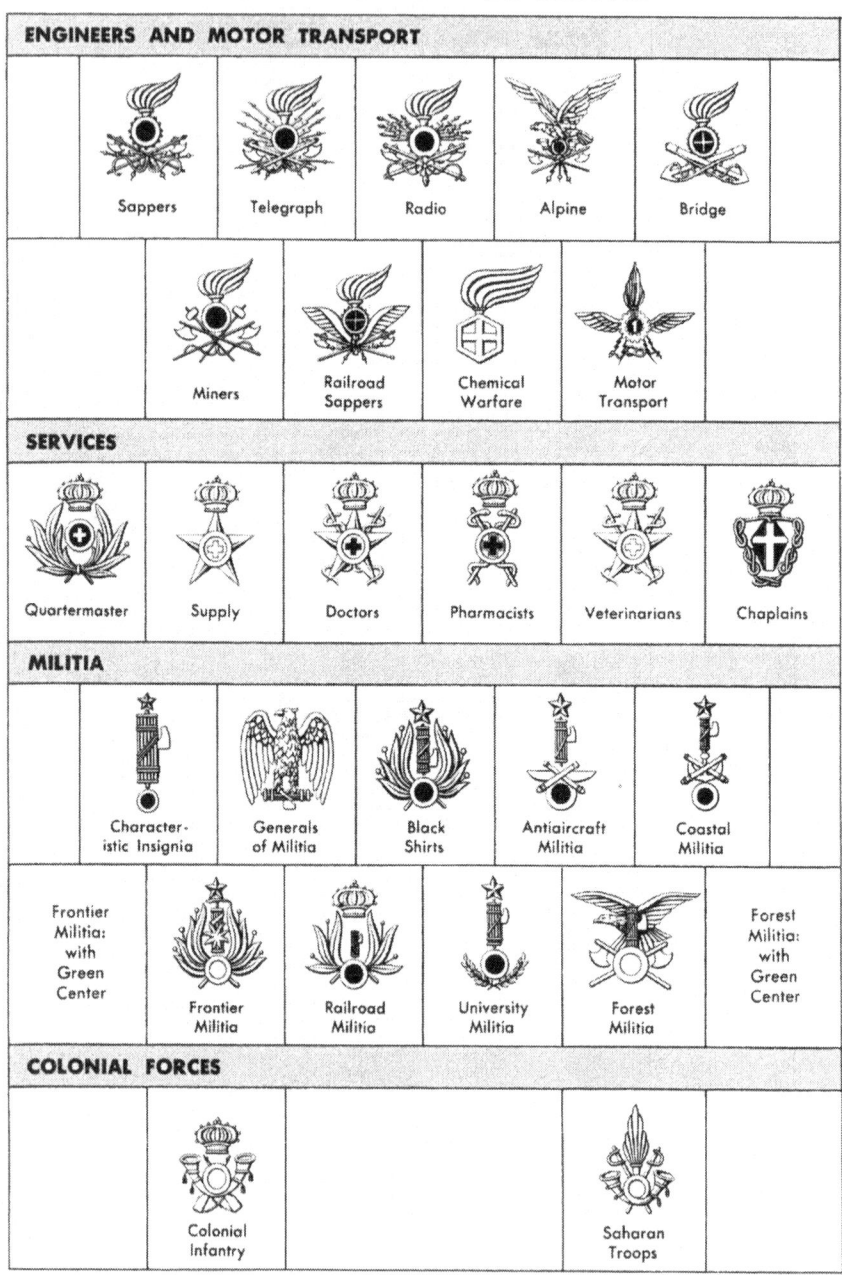

FOREWORD

	Paragraph
Purpose	1
Scope and limitations	2
Inclusion of Air Force	3
Difficulties of terminology and pronunciation	4
Revisions	5

1. Purpose.—The purpose of this handbook is to give United States military personnel a better understanding of the principal characteristics of the Italian Army.

2. Scope and limitations.—No attempt has been made to give complete details of any subject discussed in this handbook, a balanced, general picture of the Italian Army being considered of paramount importance. More detailed information regarding individual units, campaign, and commanders is provided in a special study of the Order of Battle of the Italian Army. On the other hand, Fascist as well as military elements are set forth. The effects of 20 years of Fascist organization of the social, industrial, and economic structure of Italy cannot be expected to disappear at once with the dissolution of the Party. A considerable part of the Italian armed forces bears the stamp of Fascist education and training. It is therefore imperative, regardless of recent events, that the Fascist Militia and its component services, which for so long have dominated the life of the Italian people, be given an integral place in the text.

3. Inclusion of Air Force.—A discussion of the Italian Air Force is included in this handbook, for no adequate idea of a modern Army can be given without recognizing the close cooperation of all arms. The Italian Air Force must therefore be considered an integral part of a single military organization.

4. Difficulties of terminology and pronunciation.—*a. Terminology.*—On its first (and sometimes later) use, any im-

RESTRICTED

FOREWORD

portant Italian term or name is usually followed in the text by the English equivalent in parentheses. Likewise, in cases where the Italian equivalents might be helpful, they are also given in the same manner. Certain Italian terms and names, such as *raggruppamenti*, *célere*, *Bersaglieri*, and *Alpini*, which are in common use in their Italian forms, are generally used in this form throughout the handbook. There is often no exact English or American equivalent, as, for instance, for the ranks of *marescialli*. In these cases translations are sometimes given, but not used throughout the text, as they would be more misleading than helpful.

b. Pronunciation.—The following general principal of pronunciation will serve as a rough guide for those Italian sounds that vary from the English:

a	*ah* as in f*a*ther
c before *e* or *i*	*ch* as in *ch*in
ch	*k* as in *k*ill
g before *e* or *i*	*j* as in *j*et
gl	*ly* as in schoo*ly*ard
gn	*ny* as in ca*ny*on
gu	*gu* as in *Gu*am
i	*ee* as in b*ee*t
j	*y* as in *y*es
o	*o* as in n*o*t
qu	*qu* as in *qu*een
sci	*sh* as in *sh*ow
u	*oo* as in r*oo*m

Throughout the text, accent marks are placed on Italian words whenever the accent does not fall on the last syllable but one.

5. Revisions.—All errors or suggested changes and additions to this handbook should be reported to the Dissemination Unit, Military Intelligence Service, War Department, Washington, D. C.

FOREWORD

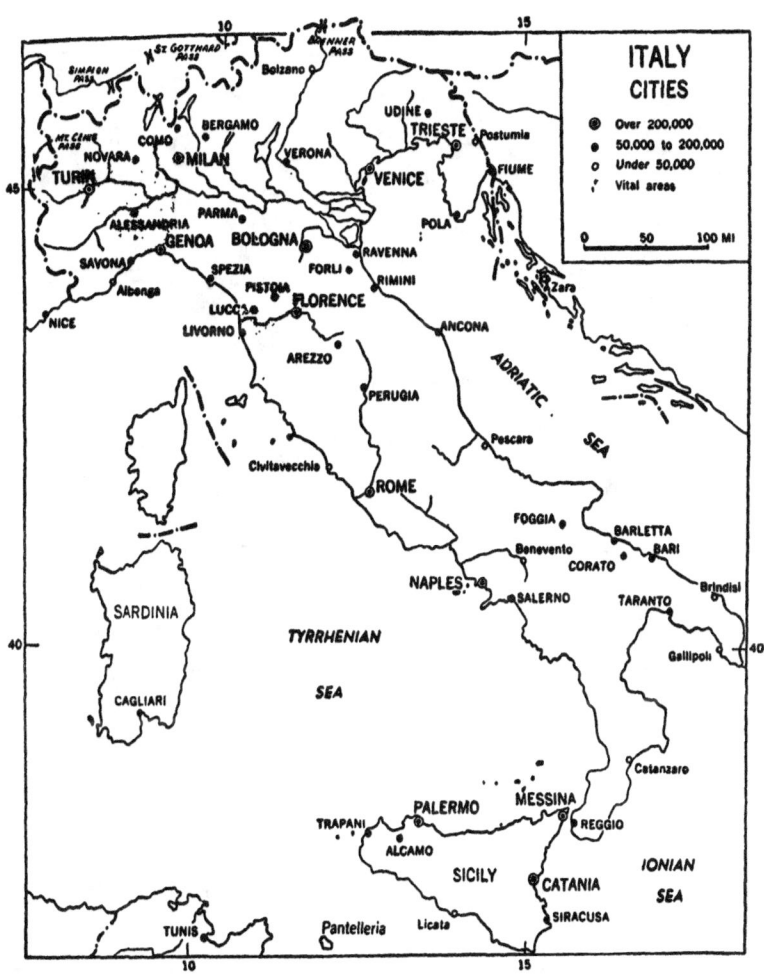

FIGURE 1.—Map of Italy, showing principal cities.

FOREWORD

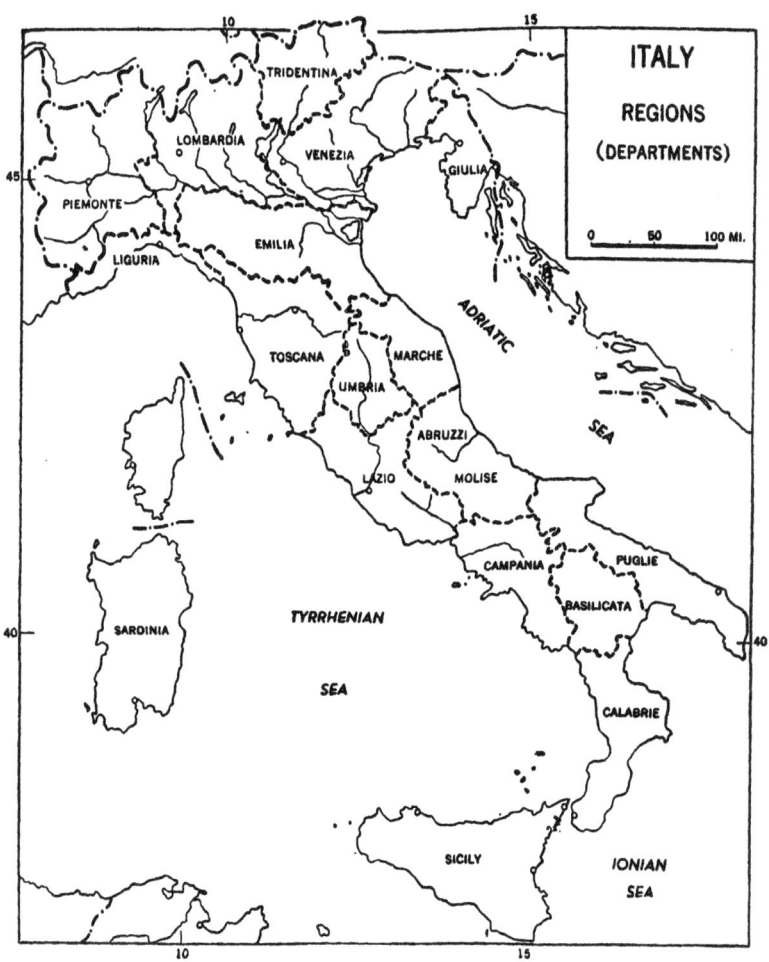

FIGURE 2.—Map of Italy, showing regions.

Chapter 1
INTRODUCTION

	Paragraph
SECTION I. Distinctive branches, or specialties	6–11
II. Semimilitary forces	12–19

SECTION I
DISTINCTIVE BRANCHES, OR SPECIALTIES

	Paragraphs
General	6
Royal Carabinieri	7
Grenadiers of Sardinia	8
Bersaglieri	9
Alpini	10
San Marco Marine Regiment	11

6. General.—The Italian Army contains certain distinctive branches, or specialities (*specialità*), an understanding of which is essential to an accurate conception of the organization as a whole. The most characteristic of these is the arm of the Royal Carabinieri (*Carabinieri Reali*). Certain specialties included in the infantry are also highly characteristic. Divisional infantry (*fanteria divisionale*), for example, includes the Grenadiers of Sardinia (*Granatieri di Sardegna*), who are differentiated from other troops only by their height and their reputed superior morale. Two other specialties, the *Bersaglieri* (Sharpshooters) and the *Alpini* (Alpine men), differ both in training and tactical employment from other infantry. The Frontier Guard (*Guárdia alla Frontiera*, or *G. a. F.*) (see par. 62), though not a special branch, performs a special function, being responsible for the fortress duties previously carried out by the army corps stationed in the frontier districts. A link between the Army and the Navy, similar to the U. S. Marine Corps, is provided by the San Marco Marine Regiment (*Il Reggimento di San Marco*).

RESTRICTED

7. **Royal Carabinieri.**—This arm is a semimilitary body (see par. 12), but it occupies historically the senior position in the Army. It originated as the Corps of Royal Carabineers, formed in Piedmont after the fall of the Napoleonic regime. At the time of the constitution of the Kingdom of Italy (1861), the Corps assumed the title of Arm and absorbed the units that had been exercising analagous functions in the annexed Italian states. It has always served as both a police and a combatant force, and is participating in large measure in the present war. The triangular hat, characteristic of the uniform when not in combat, recalls the original dress of the Corps of Royal Carabineers (see plate II, following p. 174).

8. **Grenadiers of Sardinia.**—The tradition of the Grenadiers dates back to the seventeenth century in Piedmont, where companies of Grenadiers were distributed among infantry regiments. Later a specialized regiment of Grenadiers was constituted, and finally all Grenadiers were united in a Brigade of Guards (*Brigata Guardia*). Since 1852 they have been called the Brigade of Grenadiers of Sardinia (*Brigata Granatieri di Sardegna*).

9. **Bersaglieri.**—The Bersaglieri were first employed in Piedmont in 1836 by General La Marmora when the advantages of a special light infantry, trained in marksmanship and experienced in operating with unusual agility, became apparent. .Even before World War I a part of the Bersaglieri had been mounted upon bicycles. After the war they were entirely transformed into a bicycle unit and later were equipped with motorcycles. To the Bersaglieri are assigned the drafted men of superior physical strength. The long plumes of black cock feathers worn on their headgear are similar to those worn by La Marmora's original marksmen (see plate II, following p. 174).

10. **Alpini.**—The Alpini are specialists in mountain warfare. In 1871 it was first realized that there would be a great advantage in uniting in special units the recruits from the same Alpine regions, instead of distributing them through the whole infantry. The first constitution of Alpine units was completed the follow-

ing year, when 15 companies were formed. The numbers were rapidly increased, and several Alpine regiments were formed before the outbreak of World War I. Between 1915 and 1918, owing to the predominance of mountain fighting, the number of Alpine battalions was increased to 88. After the war, Alpine brigades and their divisions were formed, with permanent assignments of mountain artillery and engineer units and matériel adapted for Alpine warfare. To the Alpini, as well as to Alpine artillery, are assigned drafted men born in mountain regions who are accustomed to living in high altitudes. The distinctive headgear of the Alpine soldier is a hat with a long feather resembling that of the Tyrolean mountaineer (see plate II, following p. 174).

11. **San Marco Marine Regiment.**—This independent command is organized in battalions which serve as assault units or, on the coast, as anti-invasion (*anti-sbarco*) detachments. Ranks in the San Marco Regiment correspond to those in the Army, though the commanding officer is a naval *capitano di vascello*. A naval officer commands each battalion, but an army liaison officer is attached to each for the purpose of coordinating the training of the companies with that of similar departments of the Army. The enlisted man of the Regiment is distinguished by a sailor's collar on his uniform and a beret.

SECTION II

SEMIMILITARY FORCES

	Paragraph
Royal Carabinieri (*Carabinieri Reali*, or *CC.RR.*)	12
Fascist Militia (*Milizia Volontária per la Sicurezza Nazionale*, or *M. V. S. N.*)	13
Special militias	14
Royal Finance Guard (*Régia Guárdia di Finanza*)	15
Special Division of Public Security (*Divisione Speciale Púbblica Sicurezza*)	16
Military Police	17
Civil and secret police forces	18
Other forces	19

**12. Royal Carabinieri *(Carabinieri Reali,* or *CC.RR.).*—*a. General.*—The Royal Carabinieri, commonly called the "first arm of the Army," actually compose a select corps of well-trained, well-equipped, and disciplined military police. The organization, training, equipment, and discipline of this arm are under the direct control of the Ministry of War, and it is the senior corps of the Italian Army. Peacetime functions are variously controlled by the Ministry of the Interior, the Ministry of the Navy, and the Ministry of Italian Africa.

b. Organization.—(1) The organization of the Royal Carabinieri, with an estimated strength of 1,400 officers, 11,550 noncommissioned officers, and 39,000 men, is as follows:

(*a*) GHQ at Rome, commanded by an army corps general.
(*b*) Three divisions.
(*c*) One high command for Albania.
(*d*) Seven brigades, or zone inspectorates.
(*e*) Twenty-eight territorial legions (*legioni territoriali*).
(*f*) A central training school.
(*g*) One cadet legion.

In addition, two battalions are attached to the Rome territorial legion and one each to the Bolzano and Palermo territorial legions. The Rome territorial legion also contains one group of squadrons and one squadron of mounted Royal Carabinieri. The latter form the King's bodyguard (*Carabinieri Guárdie del Re*), popularly known as cuirassiers (*corazzieri*). There is also an independent group of Royal Carabinieri for the Aegean Islands.

(2) The Royal Carabinieri are better paid than the personnel of the Regular army, and Carabinieri rank is senior to corresponding Army rank. A *carabiniere*, for example, is the equivalent in grade to a *caporale* (lance-corporal) in the other branches of the Army (see fig. 35.) Pre-war plans provided for the use of Carabinieri as regular combat units or picked infantry, as well as a military police force, but it is believed that they are so used only in time of emergency. For combat duty, they are organized into

units no higher than the battalion, and in mobile form are used for reconnaissance and liaison between operating units.

(3) All officers and higher noncommissioned officers of the Royal Carabinieri are designated as "judicial police officers"; corporals and enlisted men are "judicial police agents," being employed on detective duties (special squads do duty as plain-clothes men and political agents) and in assisting the regular police in tracing and arresting criminals. When Public Security police (see par. 16) and Carabinieri officers cooperate in the maintenance of public order, the latter take command.

  c. Function.—(1) The Carabinieri have a dual role:

  (*a*) They are the military and field security police of the Army, and are also responsible for the registration of the annual conscript classes and the smooth working of mobilization.

  (*b*) They perform the duties of a civilian police force except in the larger towns, where the Public Security police (see par. 16) or municipal police operate. Other peacetime functions are attendance at law courts, and the providing of guards of honor, escorts, and special guards at docks, railroads, etc.

  (2) Military police duties of the Carabinieri in wartime include—

  (*a*) Traffic control.
  (*b*) Escorting prisoners of war.
  (*c*) Administration of prisoner of war camps.
  (*d*) Security of communications zones and base areas, and guarding of vulnerable points.
  (*e*) Supervision of population in occupied areas.
  (*f*) Counterespionage through an agency known as the *Centro Statistico.*

  NOTE.—For special militias which have police functions in the rear areas, see paragraph 14.

13. Fascist Militia *(Milizia Volontária per la Sicurezza Nazionale,* or *M. V. S. N.).*—*a. General.*—(1) The Fascist Militia, popularly known as the Black Shirts (*Camicie Nere*, or *CC.NN.*), is a purely Fascist organization which originated in the bands of ex-service men (*squadristi*) formed by Mussolini after World War I, in opposition to the Communists. In 1923, on the accomplishment of the revolution, the Fascist Militia was declared an integral part of the armed forces of the State, while retaining its identity as an independent force.

(2) Typical Fascist terminology aims to recall imperial Rome by its Latin association. For example, the *fascio* (*fasces*), the bundle of rods signifying unity to the ancient Romans, has been adopted as the symbol of the Fascist Party (*Partito Nazionale Fascisti*, or *P. N. F.*, or *P. N.*). The elementary or local unit of the Party is called a *Fascio*, and all the units collectively form the *Fasci*. Fascisti may be defined as "adherents to the *fascio*." *Duce* is the Italian form of *dux* (leader). In several instances the ranks of the Fascist Militia are called by the Italian version of the Latin names (see fig. 35).

b. Organization.—The organization of the Fascist Militia centers in the GHQ in Rome, which was under the Commanding General, Mussolini, with a Chief of Staff as the executive commander. This militia is now reported to have been merged into the regular Army. In war time the Chief of Staff of the militia is under orders of the Chief of the General Staff. The ordinary Militia, apart from the special militias, is organized as follows: 14 zone commands (roughly corresponding to army corps areas of the Regular Army); 33 groups of legions (*legioni*); 133 legions; and a few autonomous cohorts (*coorti*) and smaller units. The estimated strength of the Militia, including both permanent forces and reserves mobilized for war, is 340,000.

c. Function.—The primary function of the Fascist Militia is political, that is, the defense and strengthening of the present regime. It is also entrusted with important police duties, mainly in Government services at home and in the colonies. These duties are undertaken by the special militias. The main military tasks of the Militia are as follows: raising of combatant Black Shirt battalions for service with regular divisions; provision of personnel for antiaircraft defense (except in field units) and coast defenses; post-military training (see par. 32e); and training of complementary (reserve) officers (*ufficiali di complemento*) in the universities.

14. Special militias.—*a. General.*—These are technical in character and have an organization entirely separate from that of the Fascist Militia, although all are controlled by the GHQ of the Black Shirts. The respective Ministries are, however, responsible for their training, employment, and supply of technical equipment. In most cases service counts as military service.

b. Railway Militia.—The Railway Militia (*Milízia Ferroviária*), with an estimated strength of 29,500, functions under the Ministry of Communications. In peacetime its duties are the maintenance of order and punctuality on the railroads, the prevention of frauds and theft, and the discharge of railroad police duties. During wartime it is probably used for the protection of railroads, and possibly functions as railroad-operating troops. The personnel is drawn from the staff of the State Railways, and members may enlist for permanent service or for specified periods. The organization consists of a headquarters, 14 legions, and 49 cohorts. (There was an additional legion for service in Italian East Africa.)

c. Port Militia.—The Port (Harbor) Militia (*Milízia Portuaria*), with an estimated strength of 1,000 men, functions under the Ministry of Communications. It is charged with police and guard duties in all the principal ports of Italy, and in those coastal sections where such service is a recognized necessity. The organization consists of a headquarters, a training school, and 4 legions. (Detachments existed in some colonial ports.)

d. Post and Telegraph Militia.—The Post and Telegraph Militia (*Milízia Postatelegráfica*), with an estimated strength of 1,500, functions under the Ministry of Communications. It safeguards the financial interests of the State by preventing fraud and other dishonesty in the postal, telegraph, and telephone services. In wartime it forms the nucleus of a military censorship department, as well as the Field Postal Service. The personnel is drawn from officials and employees of the postal, telegraph, and telephone services.

e. Forestry Militia.—The Forestry Militia (*Milízia Forestale*), with an estimated strength of 400 officers and 4,600 enlisted men, functions under the Ministry of Agriculture and Forests. It exists for the protection and exploitation of forests, fisheries, and game. Some of the units are given special military training, and several served as combatant troops in the Ethiopian and Greek wars. The Forestry Militia cooperates with the Army for supplies of timber, and is employed in the preparation of camp and bivouac sites, water arrangements, etc. The organization consists of a headquarters, 9 territorial legions, several motorized legions, 3 independent cohorts, the Academy of Forestry Militia, a school for noncommissioned and enlisted personnel, and 1 Albanian legion. (There was an additional legion for service in Libya.)

f. Highway Militia.—The Highway Militia (*Milízia Stradale*), with an estimated strength of 65 officers and 1,185 noncommissioned officers and men, functions under the Ministry of Public Works. It is responsible for road police duties generally. In wartime it cooperates with the Carabinieri in traffic control; it also performs special services assigned to it by the headquarters of the General Staff Corps, but is used as a combat force only in emergency. Its organization consists of a headquarters, 5 inspectorates, 4 groups of departments, 19 departments, and 47 detachments.

g. Antiaircraft and Coast Defense Artillery Militia.—Units of the Antiaircraft and Coast Defense Militia (*Milízia Artiglieria Controaérea*, or M. A. C. (formerly known as *DICAT*) and *Milízia Artiglieria Maríttima*, or *M. A. M.* (formerly known as *MILMART*)) have an estimated combined strength of 90,000 men. Although administered from a single headquarters, the units of each body are normally separate. During wartime units of both bodies operate under the control of the local territorial defense head-

RESTRICTED

INTRODUCTION

quarters. Personnel is drawn from those who are between 18 and 20 years old, or over 37, or who are unfit for active service, and from men living in the vicinity of the batteries. A small cadre of officers, noncommissioned officers, and specialists are on permanent assignments to the units.

(1) *Antiaircraft.*—The antiaircraft defenses of the Army and of the country itself are separate organizations, the Antiaircraft Militia being responsible only for the latter. It mans fixed antiaircraft defenses, as opposed to the mobile units which are operated by the Army. The organization consists of 16 territorial defense commands, 5 groups of legions, 22 legions, and a central training school. This militia also provides the personnel for searchlight units and for the Observation Service. It was reported that, in March 1941, the antiaircraft protection of the country was transferred from the Ministry of War to the Ministry of the Interior. However, this change does not include the militia units assigned to the defense of Navy installations, which are presumably still under the control of the Navy.

(2) *Coast Defense.*—This militia is responsible for manning coast defense batteries, and functions under the General Staff of the Navy. Its organization consists of a headquarters, 3 groups of legions, 14 legions, and a central training school. (Coast defense batteries of defended ports and bases are for the most part manned by naval personnel.)

h. University Militia.—The University Militia (*Milízia Universitária*), with an estimated peacetime strength of 29,000 men, is roughly comparable to the R. O. T. C. in the United States. It is composed entirely of university students who have reached the age of 18, and its members normally become complementary (reserve) officers on leaving the service. Its organization consists of a headquarters under an Inspector General; 9 legions; 14 independent cohorts for administration; and 69 school detachments, organized by battalions, companies, and platoons for training. (A legion of the University Militia fought in the Ethiopian war, and some of its members served in Spain.)

RESTRICTED

i. Frontier Militia.—The Frontier (Border) Militia (*Milizia Confinária*), with an estimated peacetime strength of 2,400, is composed of "special detachments" of the ordinary Fascist Militia legions located in the vicinity of the frontier. It cooperates with the Frontier Guard (par. 62) in guarding frontiers against illegal crossings of the border. It also has a cooperative function with the Royal Finance Guard (see par. 15) in the suppression of smuggling and with the Royal Carabinieri (see par. 12) in making investigations. Its members must be mountaineers with an intimate knowledge of the frontier districts. The organization consists of a headquarters (at Turin), a school (at Tolmezzo), and 4 legions.

15. **Royal Finance Guard (*Régia Guárdia di Finanza*).**—*a. General.*—The Royal Finance Guard is an integral part of the armed forces of the State, its members being recruited largely from mountaineers with an intimate knowledge of the frontier districts of Italy. It operates under the Ministry of Finance except in wartime, when it is transferred to the Ministry of War; its adequacy for combat duty is a result of its thorough elementary military training. Because its armament is unequal to that of a normal infantry battalion, its use in the field is limited tactically.

b. Organization.—The organization of the Royal Finance Guard, with a strength of about 1,000 officers and 30,000 enlisted men, is on a territorial basis and is as follows:

(1) GHQ at Rome, commanded by an army corps general (assisted by a divisional general of the Finance Guard as second in command, and two general officers from the Regular Army).

(2) Three groups of legions (each group commanded by a brigadier general of the Finance Guard and comprising four legions).

(3) Twelve territorial legions.

(4) Three or more *círcoli* (equivalent to battalions).

(5) Company commands.

(6) Lieutenant commands.

(7) Noncommissioned officer commands.

All units are known by the names of the localities in which they are stationed.

c. Function.—The Royal Finance Guard is stationed along the land and sea frontiers of Italy, and also at important commercial centers throughout the country. Its main functions in peacetime are to prevent smuggling and to assist in the collection of taxes, but it is also responsible for the suppression of attempts at espionage across the frontier, and for the collection of intelligence reports on adjacent countries. During war it places all its forces distributed along the land frontiers and coast at the disposal of the Army, and in cooperation with the Frontier Militia (see par. 14*i*) and the Frontier Guard (see par. 62), it provides a covering force during the period of mobilization and concentration. In addition, it performs certain duties for the Navy and assists in police work, requisitioning, and industrial mobilization. Throughout the country it continues to carry out its normal duties for the Ministry of Finance. In the Albanian campaign a few battalions were formed and used as ordinary fighting troops.

16. Special Division of Public Security *(Divisione Speciale Púbblica Sicurezza)*.—One of the armed forces of the State, the Public Security police, is a hand-picked body of men operating under the Ministry of the Interior. It functions purely in the interest of public security, in which it receives the cooperation of the Royal Carabinieri (see par. 12*c* (1) (*b*)), the Fascist Militia (see par. 13), and the special militias (see par. 14), as indicated above. The estimated 2,000 officers and 23,000 enlisted men are exempt from all manner of military service, including call for mobilization or instruction.

17. Military Police.—*a. Organization.*—In addition to the military police activities of the Royal Carabinieri (see par. 12*c*), traffic control in the Army area, with the exception of the immediate vicinity of divisions, is coordinated and handled by an office at Army Headquarters called the Transportation and Movement Office. Under the control of this office a traffic control battalion (*battaglione movimento stradale*) of specially selected men is

RESTRICTED

organized for the control of the road net. To cover an 886-kilometer road net during the annual maneuvers of the Army of the Po in August 1939, the traffic-control battalion (equipped with 424 kilometers of telephone wire) operated the following stations:

(1) One central control station.
(2) Four control sections.
(3) Seventeen control subsections.
(4) One hundred and seventy-two control posts.
(5) Fifty-seven control patrols.
(6) Three emergency wrecking and aid groups.
(7) Twenty-two radio stations (including eight mobile stations).

b. Control of traffic.—In the organization and control of traffic, the following details are considered by the officers in charge of sections:

(1) Seeking out routes for diversion and expansion.
(2) Distribution of control personnel and strength of the control posts and of the traffic patrols.
(3) Road and direction signs.
(4) Liaison between the sections and control posts.
(5) Regulations for cross roads.
(6) Traffic regulations in towns and cities in the localities where loading and unloading are being done, and at the fuel stations.

18. Civil and secret police forces.—The regular civil police functions under the Ministry of the Interior, with the Chief of Police appointed by Mussolini. In addition to this regular police system, there are the *SIM* (*Servizio Informazione Militare*), and the *OVRA* (*Organizzazione Volontária per la Repressione dell'Antifascismo*). The *SIM* is a military intelligence organization which functions directly under the Chief of the Supreme General Staff. It has its branches in the Army, Navy, and Air Forces, and in the Royal Carabinieri. It is exceedingly well-organized, and controls especially the movement and supervision of all foreign military attachés in Italy, and all other foreigners insofar as their activities may touch the military security of the country. The

OVRA is a widespread surveillance agency of the Fascist Party, consisting of a well-organized, permanent professional police force, augmented by a large number of volunteer informers. Its purpose is to protect the Fascist Party from any subversive influence, whether among the people or within the Government.

19. Other forces.—*a. Military-Political Fascist Organization.*—There are 140 legions of Military-Political Fascists, including a legion of disabled war veterans, which are under the direction of the 14 zone commands and the 33 group commands of the Fascist Militia. Their military training is limited, and it is believed that they function for the most part solely as ceremonial and demonstrative units.

b. Young Fascists.—The Young Fascists (*Gióvani Fascisti*) comprise groups of young men (approximately 1,000,000) of the ages of 18, 19, and 20 who are serving their periods of compulsory military training. The conscript training program is sufficiently complete for these young men to be used in the field with virtually no further instruction (see par. 32c).

c. Merchant Marine Service.—The 318 officers who perform the duties of port captains are organized into the Merchant Marine Service under the direction of the Ministry of Communications.

Chapter 2
RECRUITMENT AND MOBILIZATION

	Paragraphs
SECTION I. System of conscription and mobilization	20–27
II. Professional cadre and officers	28–30
III. Training, efficiency, and morale	31–35
IV. Pay and emoluments	36–38

SECTION I

SYSTEM OF CONSCRIPTION AND MOBILIZATION

	Paragraph
Period of service	20
Exemptions from active service	21
Mobilization areas	22
Expansion of existing units	23
Creation and designation of units	24
Other classes of military service	25
Development of manpower	26
Available manpower	27

20. **Period of service.**—*a. General.*—All Italian male citizens between the ages of 18 and 54, inclusive, are legally liable to military service. This service is divided into periods as follows:

(1) Premilitary training (18 to 20, inclusive).

(2) Conscript service (18 months beginning after the 21st birthday).

(3) Postmilitary training (from the completion of service with the colors until the 33d birthday).

(4) Reserve status, subject to call in time of war (33 to 54, inclusive).

(For details of training, see sec. III below.)

b. Classes.—Men are divided into classes according to year of birth. For example, the class normally entering premilitary

RESTRICTED

(Young Fascist) service in 1941 and military service in 1943 is known as the class of 1923. Under present wartime conditions, youths are conscripted for service with the colors at the age of 18 and do not go through normal premilitary training. The full period of active service is 18 months, but the Minister of War is empowered to authorize the premature dismissal on leave of conscripts who may be surplus to requirements or who may be in certain family categories. These categories vary from year to year. After service in the Army, voluntary enlistment is encouraged.

o. Enlistment.—(1) *General.*—There is provision for 3-, 2-, and 1-year enlistments.

(2) *Three-year.*—The 3-year enlistments are as follows:

(*a*) Soldiers of certain arms and services reenlisting after completion of service.

(*b*) Volunteers or transfers to the Carabinieri.

(*c*) Corporals in remount service.

(*d*) Musicians on active service (not noncommissioned officers).

(3) *Two-year.*—The 2-year enlistments are as follows:

(*a*) Volunteers in arms and corps, exclusive of Carabinieri.

(*b*) Volunteers in auxiliary Carabinieri (excluding transfers from other arms).

(*c*) Corporals and soldiers reenlisting after completion of service.

(4) *One-year.*—The 1-year enlistments are as follows:

(*a*) Soldiers in all arms and services may be retained in service for 1 or more years if necessary.

(*b*) Specialists who receive a bonus of 2 or more lire a day.

(*c*) Certain headquarters troops may reenlist for a period of 1 year with or without a bonus or 3 years with a bonus.

21. Exemptions from active service.—Exemptions from active service for reasons other than physical disability are as follows: penal offenses, deprivation of political rights, previous enrollment in the various militias, and mental deficiency. Length of service may be reduced because of family need. Thus, for example, reduction may be granted to "the only brother of an orphan sister," "the only child of a widow over 64," "the first-born of a family of 10 sons," etc. Students may have their service deferred until completion of their education, but not later than the end of their 26th year. Italians born or residing in foreign countries are liable for military service, but, in practice, the majority are exempted during their period of residence abroad or, under certain circumstances, serve for only 6 months. In 1942, persons having dual nationality were exempted from military service, if, in addition to Italian nationality, they possessed the nationality of a state at war with Italy. Italian citizens of the Aegean Islands, citizens of Libya, and subjects of Italian East Africa are not required to perform military service. Foreigners who become naturalized citizens are exempt from service only if over 32 years old.

22. **Mobilization areas.**—*a. Territorial commands.*—To facilitate mobilization and to free army, corps, and division commanders from territorial responsibility in matters of mobilization, a system of territorial commands (*enti territoriali*) has been established. Each corps area is a territorial command; each division area is a military zone command; and the military zones are further divided into military districts, of which there are one hundred and six.

b. Military districts.—The military districts (*distretti militari*), in addition to headquarters and general offices, are organized in two sections. One handles routine procurement and registration of personnel; the other, war planning for mobilization of reserve manpower. The districts are based on the communes (*comuni*), which are roughly equivalent to townships in the United States. Early each year, civil authorities must furnish the district command a list (*lista di leva*) of all males who reach the age of 18 years during the calendar year just opening. In the late spring, conscripts are called up for medical examination, leaving their identity cards and statements of premilitary service. Examinations are made in the various communes by "mobile commissions" (*commissioni mobili*) sent out from the district office and draft boards (*consigli di leva*), which then make disposition of the enrollees.

c. Depots.—Recruits are assigned by the districts to depots (*depósiti*), each of which equips and trains a regiment. When regiments move into the theater of operations, the personnel of the depot commands (*reparti depósiti*) (see fig. 3), which are distinct from those of the field armies, remain at their posts to equip and train other regiments. Depots and their regular regiments have the same numbers. Regiments subsequently organized receive new numbers.

d. Officers of commands.—Officers of the commands are secured on request from the over-age in grade and are promoted by seniority without examination, in order to relieve the younger and more active officers of the Army from the promotion hump due to World War I. The commander of each military district is responsible for the registration and drafting of conscripts and their assignments to units. He likewise maintains a list of all men furloughed to the reserves, that is, assigned to the district company until called to active duty.

e. Unit recruitment.—In general, divisions are recruited from their own divisional districts, and army corps from their own corps areas. Alpine divisions are invariably recruited from the mountaineers of their own locality. There is a separate system for the Royal Carabinieri and another for the Fascist Militia.

23. Expansion of existing units.—Upon mobilization, each corps area command brings its combat troops within its area to strength and equips them for initial employment in the theater of operations.

24. Creation and designation of units.—*a.* Immediately upon the departure of combat units for the theater of operations, the corps area command forms new units. In some cases, the formation of these new units has been completed, but in other cases losses to the original unit have necessitated replacements which have exhausted the available trained manpower. These new units do not appear to be named and numbered in any definite relationship to the units which were originally at the depots. It is impossible to determine any definite system for the designa-

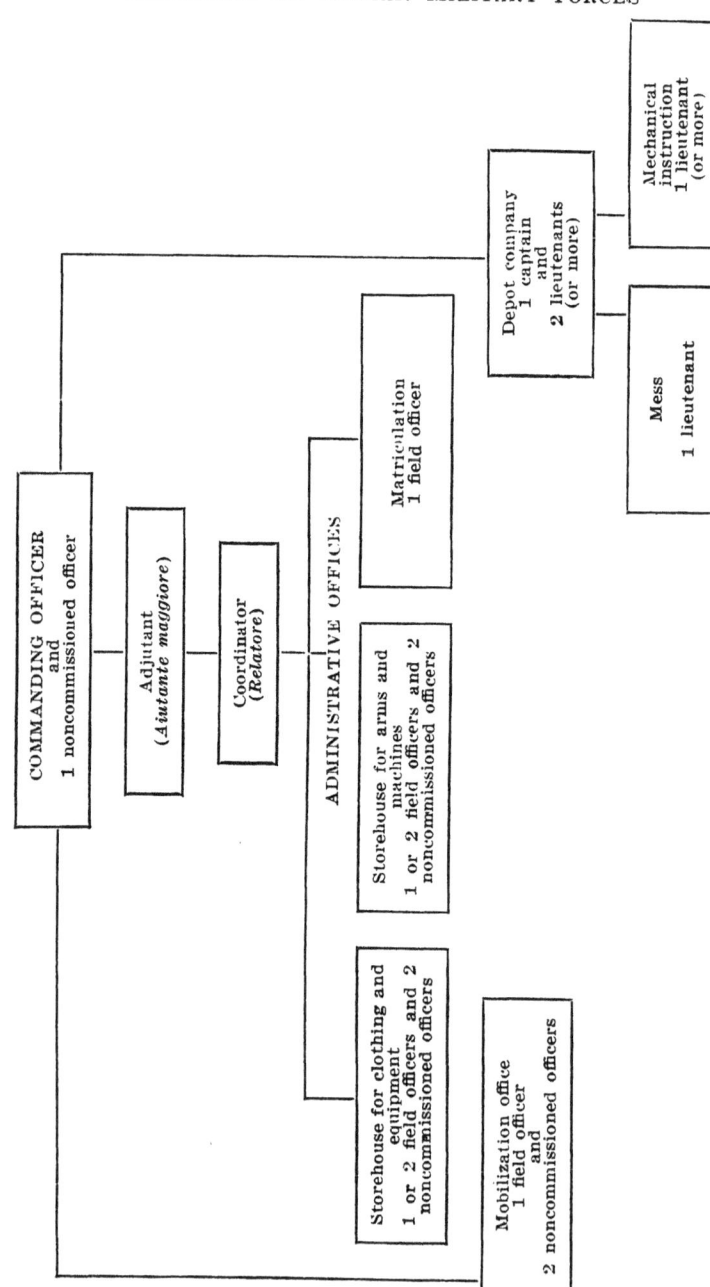

FIGURE 3.—Typical organization of a depot command (*reparto deposito*).

tion of Italian units, as the method is elastic and frequently changed.

b. Divisions and, occasionally, regiments are known by geographical and historical names, sometimes by the names of their commanders, by nicknames, or by a combination of nickname and geographical name (for example, *Lupi di Toscana* (Wolves of Tuscany) or *Cacciatori delle Alpi* (Alpine Hunters). Regiments may take the name of their division or, having had long service such as the three regiments of the Grenadiers of Sardinia, may give their names to the divisions.

c. The two infantry regiments in the present "binary" division (*divisione binária*) have successive numbers (as 55th and 56th Infantry) and are both called by the same name, which is usually (but not always) the name of the division. All other units of the division, except the artillery regiment, take the divisional name. New artillery regiments usually adopt the number of the new division to which they are to belong, so that the number of the new division can usually be predicted from a knowledge of the new artillery regiment number. Confusion results from the use of regimental and divisional names rather than numbers, even in official reports.

d. Sometimes, when three battalions are with an infantry regiment in the field, a fourth battalion is formed at the depot in Italy. On the other hand, when it was necessary to reinforce Italian units during the North African campaign, a large number of independent replacement companies were created in Italy, which, on arrival in Africa, were absorbed into existing units. It is also a frequent practice, particularly in the case of nondivisional troops, to form second-line units which are given the number of the first-line unit with an additional "0" (thus the 4th Corps Artillery Regiment may form a new regiment numbered 40), or with 1, 2, or 3 prefixed (thus both the 10th and the 110th Machine Gun Battalion exist). In some cases, depot units of a division in Italy have been sent out to reinforce a similar division in the field; this results in considerable confusion, as they continue to wear the collar patches of their original unit.

e. Every field unit in the Italian Army is normally reinforced as necessary from the depot of the unit in Italy. Thus the 3d Infantry Regiment in Greece is reinforced from the depot of the 3d Infantry Regiment at Messina. The battalions and companies of the depot regiment have the same numbers as those of the first-line regiment. Therefore, confusion may arise, since the 1st Battalion of the 3d Infantry Regiment may be the depot unit in Sicily or the first-line unit in Greece. Occasionally, but not very often, the depot regiment is referred to as *bis* (repeated).

25. Other classes of military service.—*a. Combat elements.*—(1) *Fascist Militia.*—The Fascist Militia (*Milízia Volontária per la Sicurezza Nazionale*, or *M. V. S. N.*), popularly known as the Black Shirts, is composed of men who volunteer for 10 years after the completion of their 18 months service. In theory, the 10 years service is compulsory, but because of the lack of trained instructors in the ranks of the Militia, the law has, for the most part, remained a dead letter. Training of Militia reservists is mainly carried out by periodical recall to the colors.

(2) *Colonial troops.*—Colonial troops have now (1943) been wiped out or captured. They were formerly officered by Italians, with natives in the noncommissioned grades. Officers were required to be at least 5 feet 8 inches tall. They were chosen from the Army, the Royal Carabinieri, the Royal Finance Guards, the Civil Police, or the Fascist Militia. After selection, they attended a special course at the Tivoli Training School before going out to the colonies for 3 years service. There was also a recruiting and training center for natives in each province of the colonies.

b. Semicombat elements.—(1) *Royal Carabinieri (Carabinieri Reali).*—Although the Royal Carabinieri are probably nearly as good combat troops as most other Italian organizations, they are in time of peace primarily concerned with police duties. Some officers are obtained by transfer from the Army, but roughly two-

tion of Italian units, as the method is elastic and frequently changed.

b. Divisions and, occasionally, regiments are known by geographical and historical names, sometimes by the names of their commanders, by nicknames, or by a combination of nickname and geographical name (for example, *Lupi di Toscana* (Wolves of Tuscany) or *Cacciatori delle Alpi* (Alpine Hunters). Regiments may take the name of their division or, having had long service such as the three regiments of the Grenadiers of Sardinia, may give their names to the divisions.

c. The two infantry regiments in the present "binary" division (*divisione binária*) have successive numbers (as 56th and 56th Infantry) and are both called by the same name, which is usually (but not always) the name of the division. All other units of the division, except the artillery regiment, take the divisional name. New artillery regiments usually adopt the number of the new division to which they are to belong, so that the number of the new division can usually be predicted from a knowledge of the new artillery regiment number. Confusion results from the use of regimental and divisional names rather than numbers, even in official reports.

d. Sometimes, when three battalions are with an infantry regiment in the field, a fourth battalion is formed at the depot in Italy. On the other hand, when it was necessary to reinforce Italian units during the North African campaign, a large number of independent replacement companies were created in Italy, which, on arrival in Africa, were absorbed into existing units. It is also a frequent practice, particularly in the case of nondivisional troops, to form second-line units which are given the number of the first-line unit with an additional "0" (thus the 4th Corps Artillery Regiment may form a new regiment numbered 40), or with 1, 2, or 3 prefixed (thus both the 10th and the 110th Machine Gun Battalion exist). In some cases, depot units of a division in Italy have been sent out to reinforce a similar division in the field; this results in considerable confusion, as they continue to wear the collar patches of their original unit.

e. Every field unit in the Italian Army is normally reinforced as necessary from the depot of the unit in Italy. Thus the 3d Infantry Regiment in Greece is reinforced from the depot of the 3d Infantry Regiment at Messina. The battalions and companies of the depot regiment have the same numbers as those of the first-line regiment. Therefore, confusion may arise, since the 1st Battalion of the 3d Infantry Regiment may be the depot unit in Sicily or the first-line unit in Greece. Occasionally, but not very often, the depot regiment is referred to as *bis* (repeated).

25. Other classes of military service.—*a. Combat elements.*—(1) *Fascist Militia.*—The Fascist Militia (*Milizia Volontária per la Sicurezza Nazionale*, or *M. V. S. N.*), popularly known as the Black Shirts, is composed of men who volunteer for 10 years after the completion of their 18 months service. In theory, the 10 years service is compulsory, but because of the lack of trained instructors in the ranks of the Militia, the law has, for the most part, remained a dead letter. Training of Militia reservists is mainly carried out by periodical recall to the colors.

(2) *Colonial troops.*—Colonial troops have now (1943) been wiped out or captured. They were formerly officered by Italians, with natives in the noncommissioned grades. Officers were required to be at least 5 feet 8 inches tall. They were chosen from the Army, the Royal Carabinieri, the Royal Finance Guards, the Civil Police, or the Fascist Militia. After selection, they attended a special course at the Tivoli Training School before going out to the colonies for 3 years service. There was also a recruiting and training center for natives in each province of the colonies.

b. Semicombat elements.—(1) *Royal Carabinieri (Carabinieri Reali).*—Although the Royal Carabinieri are probably nearly as good combat troops as most other Italian organizations, they are in time of peace primarily concerned with police duties. Some officers are obtained by transfer from the Army, but roughly two-thirds come from the military academies and one-third from the ranks. Officers have a 6-month course at the Central Carabinieri School at Florence. Noncommissioned officers are appointed from Carabinieri who have completed an 8-month course at the same school. Enlistment is voluntary for other ranks. Men between the ages of 18 and 26 who have not yet done their military service, and reservists of the Carabinieri, Army, or Navy, up to the age of 30, are eligible. Carabinieri are of two classes: "effective" (*Carabinieri effettivi*) and "auxiliary" (*Carabinieri ausiliari*). The former enlist for 3 years, normally, with the idea of making the service their profession. The latter, who may after a year become "effective" Carabinieri, are men who do the whole or part of their 2 years conscript service in the Carabinieri. In addition, regular soldiers are often added to the Carabinieri with the title of *Carabinieri aggiunti* (attached). On enlistment, all recruits, except those who have had at least 6 months service in the Army, Navy, or Carabinieri are sent for a 6-month course at the Cadet Legion (*Legione Allievi*) in Rome.

(2) *Royal Finance Guard* (*Régia Guárdia di Finanza*).—Officers are recruited from noncommissioned officers of the Guard not below the rank of brigadiere (equivalent of sergeant major) or over 30 years of age, and from men between the ages of 18 and 23 with secondary-school education. Both categories take a 3-year course at the school for cadet officers at Rome before appointment. Young men who have not done military service, and reservists of the Finance Guard, the Army, or Navy, are eligible for enlistment. All categories are sent for a 6-month course at the Cadet Legion. On completion of the course, cadets (*allievi*) are promoted to *guárdie comuni* (the equivalent of corporals). Men with special qualifications are sent for a 9-month course at a school for noncommissioned officers at Caserta. Enlistment at first is for 3 years, until they have completed 20 years' service, after which they may reenlist only for 1 year at a time.

RESTRICTED

c. Volunteers.—Italian nationals and those who have the right to become such by performing military service may enlist if they are—

(1) Over 17 and under 27 years old.
(2) Bachelors or widowers without children.
(3) Physically fit to perform service in corps for which they volunteer, as well as military service in general.
(4) Of good character and morals, that is, not guilty of certain enumerated crimes.
(5) Able to show parental consent.
(6) Able to read and write.

The Fascist Militia, the Carabinieri, the Royal Finance Guard, and the special noncombatant organizations included in the armed forces are supported by voluntary enlistment. In time of war, voluntary enlistments for the duration may be accepted.

26. Development of manpower.—*a. First phase.*—Plans for the first phase of mobilization provided for five field armies, together with zones of the interior troops and services. This phase was completed by 1 November 1939.

b. Second phase.—Plans for the second phase provided for a force greater than that mobilized in the first. The special corps were not duplicated as contemplated in the peacetime plan. The character of the theaters of operations in Albania and Greece required duplication or expansion of certain Alpine and mountain units. Units in this phase were 8 field armies, 24 army corps, and 68 daivisions. These included certain armored, motorized *celeri*, and Alpine divisions, proportionate corps, army, GHQ troops, and services. The second phase of mobilization had been accomplished in part by the end of 1939, and was completed by the end of May 1940. It was retarded chiefly by lack of equipment and armament. Most of the men mobilized must have received weapons of the older type, at least at the beginning.

RESTRICTED

c. Third phase.—Plans for the third phase called for the mobilization of all available manpower within the limitations imposed by shortage of equipment. The peak of mobilization for the present war was reached in September 1942, when the Italians had 11 armies and 27 corps. In all, they are believed to have put 91 divisions in the field, though not necessarily all at one time. Perhaps 30 divisions had been destroyed by the middle of 1943. These figures include the so-called "coastal divisions," developed from "coastal militia" and not attached to corps.

27. Available manpower.—*a. First phase.*—Although Mussolini has referred to the "eight million bayonets" he could raise, this figure somewhat exaggerates the Italian military manpower available and grossly exaggerates the number of men that he can equip. Armament and equipment have always been the limiting factors in the Italian Army. Mobilization in the first phase reached only about 2,240,000 men. This included the regular forces of approximately 1,657,000, the Black Shirt battalions for service with the Army, and the various special militias and other forces for duty in the zone of the interior and in the colonial possessions.

b. Second phase.—In the second phase, Italian forces reached about 2,467,000 men. This included regular forces, which then had reached a figure of approximately 1,885,000, and replacements for the existing forces, new combat units, and requisite additional zone-of-the-interior elements.

c. Third phase.—(1) The peak of mobilization in September 1942 may have reached as high as approximately 3,000,000. This included regular forces of about 2,564,000, all classes of military age having been mobilized, including the 18-year-old class, which reached that age during the third phase. In July 1943, there were about 1,180,000 first-line troops, 600,000 second-line troops, and 200,000 depot troops—a total of 1,980,000. The decline was due to heavy losses in Russia, North Africa, and the Balkans. Additional Italian manpower includes approximately the following numbers:

Total reserve	2,765,000
Partially trained and available for service	1,250,000
Trained but needed for industry	1,300,000
Additional but untrained (mainly from 45 to 55 years old)	1,293,000
Total	6,608,000

(2) Italy cannot mobilize her maximum strength unless the necessary equipment is made available from the supplies of some other nation, either by gift or capture. There being little prospect of either under present conditions, the present mobilized forces probably represent her maximum capacity. Given a sufficient supply of industrial raw material, Italy can probably maintain her forces at about the present strength.

SECTION II

PROFESSIONAL CADRE AND OFFICERS

	Paragraph
Active (regular) officers (*ufficiali in servizio permanente effettivo*)	28
Complementary (reserve) officers (*ufficiali di complemento*)	29
Noncommissioned officers	30

28. Active (regular) officers (*ufficiali in servizio permanente effettivo*).—Permanent second lieutenants are drawn mainly from graduates of the military academies at Turin (artillery and engineers) and Modena (other arms) and from noncommissioned officers who have completed a special course for applicants of this class. There is a certain intake from complementary (reserve) officers who, after completing their ordinary training, decide to adopt the army as a profession. A small percentage of marescialli (see par. 175) may also become regular officers. A corps cadet school is maintained in each of the territorial corps areas. All conscripts with a high school diploma are required to attend these schools, unless the necessary quota of officer students has been filled for that year. After graduation from these schools, and with not less than 3 months service with a regiment, they may become applicants for appointment as permanent second lieutenants. Applicants possessing such qualifications are sent to one of the military academies. There are three military colleges, one, each, at Rome, Naples, and Milan, which are preparatory to the military academies at Turin and Modena. As soon as the regular officers are commissioned, they spend from 1 to 2 years (according to arm) at training school. Officers are promoted by arm or branch to include certain grades of general officers. Promotion takes place by seniority up to the rank of colonel and by selection according to a merit list for the higher ranks.

29. **Complementary (reserve) officers** *(ufficiali di complemento).*—Youths who attain a certain standard of education are compelled by law to carry out their conscript service as complementary, or reserve, officers. These reserve officers form the main source from which junior officers are provided on mobilization. They do 7 months service as cadets in "school units" and the remainder of their conscript service as officers in service units. Subsequently they are liable for a certain amount of post-military training. Conscripts who successfully complete the course in a corps area cadet school may be commissioned as complementary second lieutenants without going to a military academy. The system of promotion for these officers is definitely prescribed. However, social position sometimes has a good deal to do with appointment, and in many cases reserve officers are wretchedly trained.

30. **Noncommissioned officers.**—All noncommissioned officers of the rank of sergeant and above are known as under-officers *(sottufficiali)* and are volunteer, long-service, professional soldiers. Ranks below that of sergeant are found from the short-

service conscripts. Hence the percentage of well-trained, long-service, noncommissioned officers is lower in the Italian Army than in most other armies.

Section III

TRAINING, EFFICIENCY, AND MORALE

	Paragraph
General	31
Training of citizens	32
Training of soldiers	33
Efficiency	34
Morale	35

31. **General.**—The training of the Italian Army is the outgrowth of intensive pre-war compulsory training in various organizations, schools, and maneuvers, and of the participation of Army units in the Ethiopian Campaign (1935–36), the Spanish Civil War (1936–39), the Greek Campaign (1940–41), and the Libyan Campaign, which began in 1940. The prolonged but unsuccessful fighting in Ethiopia, ending in 1941, provided no training of importance.

32. **Training of citizens.**—*a. Citizen-soldier.*—In the Fascist State the functions of the citizen and soldier are regarded as inseparable. Military training is an integral part of national education. It begins as soon as the citizen is capable of learning, and continues as long as he is capable of carrying arms. The military training includes three phases, as follows:

(1) Premilitary instruction with the object of preparing the citizen morally, physically, and militarily in the period previous to his joining the armed forces of the State;

(2) Military instruction, with the object of improving and completing the military training of the citizen;

(3) Further military instruction, with the object of keeping the reservist an efficient soldier.

RESTRICTED

RECRUITMENT AND MOBILIZATION

b. Coordinating bureau.—A special bureau directly under the head of the Government is responsible for coordinating the efforts of all political, scholastic, and military organizations of the State. This coordinating bureau includes—

(1) The Chief Inspector (a corps general), assisted by two secretaries (Army officers) and seven members (civilians).

(2) Four representatives of the armed forces (Army, Navy, Air Force, and Fascist Militia) with the rank of colonel or general.

(3) Two representatives of the *Balilla* (see *c*(2) below) and the Young Fascists (see *c*(4) below).

c. Premilitary training.—The Italian Youth of the Lictor's Rod (*Gioventù Italiana del Littòrio*, or *G. I. L.*) is responsable, under the auspices of the Fascist Militia, or Black Shirts, and the National Fascist Party, (*Partito Nazionale Fascista*, or *P. N. F.*, or *P. N.*) for the premilitary training of Italian youth. This training and inculcation in the principles of the Party is conducted through successive organizations, as follows:

(1) *Children of the She-Wolf.*—The Children of the She-Wolf (*Figli della Lupa*), for boys and girls from 6 to 8 years of age, provides an introduction to Fascist and military doctrines.

(2) *Balilla.*[1]—The *Opera Nazionale Balilla*, or *O. P. N.*, for boys from 8 to 14 years of age, continues the moral preparation to develop a military spirit in the nation. Enthusiasm for a military life is encouraged in the boys, and they are kept in contact with the armed forces of the State.

(3) *Members of the Vanguard.*—The Members of the Vanguard (*Avanguardisti*), for boys from 14 to 18 years of age, intensifies the military and physical preparation for service in the Army.

(4) *Young Fascists.*—The Fascists (*Gióvani Fascisti*), for boys

---

[1] "Balilla" is the nickname of Giovanni Battista Perasso, a boy who, in the middle of the eighteenth century, refused to help the Austrians who were impressing the inhabitants of Liguria to work on fortifications. His action of defiance (hurling a stone at his oppressors) communicated a rebellious spirit which was the cause of revolt against the invaders.

from 18 to 21 years of age, provides a technical professional preparation designed to make a finished soldier.

d. Military Service.—In peacetime, young men from 21 to 22 years of age are conscripted to serve 18 months in the Army (see par. 20).

e. Post-military training.—This is entrusted to the Fascist Militia, and is compulsory to the age of 32.

f. Theoretical instruction.—Theoretical military instruction in the schools completes the practical training given by premilitary training organizations. This instruction aims to make good citizen-soldiers by the development of military spirit, patriotism, and character in young men. Military instruction in the schools includes thirty 2-hour lessons annually for 5 scholastic years, spread out from the last year of grammar school to the second year of college. Military training in the schools is divided into 3 grades:

(1) The first course, lasting 1 year, covers the final year of grammar school, and gives an elementary military knowledge (organization of the Italian Army, interpretation of topographic maps, etc.) to boys who, not continuing their academic course, will be enlisted as noncommissioned officers and specialists. Use is made of moving pictures, photography, drawings, diagrams, etc., in instruction.

(2) The second course, lasting 2 years, covers the final 2 years of high school, and gives military knowledge (organization of the armed forces of different nations, elementary knowledge of arms and fire, etc.) to boys who may become complementary (reserve) officers without attending the universities. Its purpose is to complete the first-grade course, to show the close connection between the military and the social and economic life of the nation, and to give the boys a warlike spirit, and a sense of discipline, comradeship, and sacrifice.

(3) The third course, lasting 2 years, covers the first 2 years of college, and presents material on the military preparation of a modern nation, the theory of modern warfare, with discussion

of missions of the various armed forces, separately and jointly. The mass of the officers for the armed forces is later obtained from graduates of this course.

g. Other training.—The pre-military training in schools and in special organizations like the *Avanguardisti* and Young Fascists emphasizes the individual training of the soldier. Special training in marksmanship is afforded by enrollment in the Italian Target Practice Union, which is under the control of the Chief Inspector of Pre- and Post-Military Training.

33. Training of soldiers.—*a. General.*—The training of the Army emphasizes operation of units. In the past, regular maneuvers have been held. The Army of the Po, for example, participated in large-scale maneuvers in northern Italy in the summer of 1939, and Alpine units have frequently held winter maneuvers in the frontier mountains. In addition to the training periods, maneuvers, and simulated warfare, most of the units of the Italian Army have gained military experience under actual combat conditions in Ethiopia, Spain, Albania, Greece, North Africa, and Russia.

b. Arms and service schools.—In addition to the practical military training of the field, the personnel of the Italian Army have attended schools of the various arms and services. These include the following:

(1) Military colleges, preparatory to military academies, at Rome, Naples, and Milan.

(2) Infantry and Cavalry Military Academy (Modena).

(3) Artillery and Engineers Military Academy (Turin).

(4) School of Application for Infantry (Parma).

(5) School of Application for Cavalry (Pinerolo and Tor di Quinto).

(6) School of Application for Artillery and Engineers (Turin).

(7) School of Application for Medical Corps (Florence).

(8) Central School for Carabinieri (Florence).

(9) Central School for Infantry.

(10) Central School for Artillery.
(11) Central School for Engineers.
(12) Central School for Alpine troops.
(13) Central School for Céleri ("rapid" or mobile (cavalry), troops).
(14) Artillery School of Fire (including antiaircraft) (Nettuno).
(15) School of Assault Engineers (Civitavecchia).
(16) Superior of War Institute (Turin).
(17) Superior Technical Course for Artillery (Turin).
(18) Superior Technical Course for Engineers (Turin).
(19) Superior Motor Transport Course (Turin).
(20) Four schools for student noncommissioned officers (two for infantry, one for artillery, and one for engineers).
(21) Eleven schools for student reserve officers (five for infantry, five for artillery, and one for engineers).
(22) One School for Fascist Militia (Mirandola).
(23) Military Geographic Institute (Florence).
(24) One Commissary Finishing School.

c. Nature and objective of training for officers.—Training is progressive, and in peacetime all officers were required periodically to take short practical courses in tactics. Considerable effort was made to impart to individuals the ability to handle troops in all phases of combat.

d. Nature and objective of training for enlisted men.—As far as time permits, enlisted men are given thorough individual and unit training and training in the technique of combat. In peacetime, wherever possible, they were trained for service in the type of terrain in which they were most likely to serve in the event of war. Men who possessed a high school diploma, or the equivalent, were required to attend the Reserve Officers' Training Schools in the Corps Area Schools, unless those so qualified exceeded in number the required number of student officers to be enrolled for that year.

e. Unit and combined training.—The aim of each unit is to reach a degree of training that will enable it to meet successfully the tactical and logistical problems of the battlefield. In peacetime, special emphasis was placed on mountain warfare, particularly during winter. Great stress was laid on cooperation of the different arms, especially between infantry and artillery. Great stress was laid also on training for war of movement. For the infantry and *céleri* ("rapid" or mobile (cavalry) troops), the fundamental combat unit is the platoon, and only when the training of the platoon was perfected was the training of larger units undertaken. Infantry command is greatly decentralized, with platoons and even squads acting largely on their own initiative during offensive movements.

f. Training of reserves.—(1) *Officers.*—In peacetime a portion of the reservoir of reserve officers was recalled each year for duty and training, usually during the summer months, the number of these often reaching 20,000 to 30,000 annually. Reserve officers also underwent theoretical instruction during the winter months. Whenever the Army was augmented by the recall of previously trained classes, a proportionate number of reserve officers was ordered to active duty.

(2) *Specialists.*—In addition to officer personnel, a large number of specialists and technicians were recalled annually for training and for participation in maneuvers. Under normal conditions this number often reached 250,000. The requirements of trained specialists were also met by premilitary training. Young men 18 and 19 years of age, who had not yet been called up for regular military service, were trained as mechanics, electricians, radio and telegraph operators, chauffeurs, motorcyclists, etc. Courses were and still are given in the universities and high schools, in which enrollment in the past has reached 750,000. In normal times a large number were called to active duty with the armed forces.

34. Efficiency.—*a. Officers.*—The military education of Italian officers is, on the whole, considered fairly good. Prior to the war, inefficient officers were eliminated, usually in the lower grades. The War College is an excellent institution for advanced training, and, partly as a result of the work there, the general fitness for high command and staff greatly improved.

b. Career enlisted personnel.—(1) The Army has a professional cadre of noncommissioned officers corresponding in general to United States noncommissioned officers of the first four grades. These career soldiers are carefully selected, and are promoted or eliminated by competitive examination under a combined selective and seniority system. They are trained at special service schools as well as with troops. In general, they are well equipped for their jobs of training continuous levies of conscript troops.

(2) In wartime all junior noncommissioned officers and the majority of senior noncommissioned officers come from the ranks of conscript troops. Their military education is not at all comparable to that of the career noncommissioned officers. The dearth of able, adequately trained, and experienced noncommissioned officers is one of the chief weaknesses of the Italian army.

c. Other enlisted personnel.—The training of the conscript masses follows a set routine that turns out soldiers of a fixed military standard. This training is necessarily limited and rather superficial, but its effectiveness is somewhat increased by pre-military training, and by frequent recall to duty. While the individual initiative of the Italian soldier is not remarkable, he has been raised under a type of government that makes discipline seem simple and natural. He is tough and hardy, and is able to endure cold, exposure, and insufficient food. He is an extremely good worker, who will lay aside his arms and do 14 hours of hard labor a day without complaint.

d. Combat efficiency.—Before the present war, Fascist Militia combat elements were rated as second-line troops, and their record to date places them in an even lower category. Also based on its record to date, the efficiency of the Regular Army combat units must likewise be rated as poor. This showing may be partially due to the fact that Italy's entry into the war on 10 June 1940 was not a popular move. Moreover, the unprovoked and completely unprepared attack on Greece on 28 October 1940 was even more unpopular. The basic reason probably goes deeper, for despite Fascist efforts to create in the Italians a spirit of indomitability, the Italians are not a warlike people and never will be. In justice to the Regular Army, it can only be said that it was unprepared for a real war and apparently has never had its heart in the task before it. However, when bolstered by the German military, there is a marked increase in the efficiency of the Italian Army, as has been demonstrated in North Africa and Russia.

35. Morale.—Italian defeats in Africa have naturally caused a lowering in the morale of the Italian Army. Owing to past defeats and the general unpopularity of the war, morale cannot be considered better than satisfactory.

Section IV

PAY AND EMOLUMENTS

	Paragraph
General	36
Rates of pay by rank	37
Special considerations	38

36. General.—All finance of the Italian Army is handled by the Administrative Service (*Servizio Amministrazione*), which is headed by a colonel. As of 1940, this Service totaled 1,470 officers.

37. Rates of pay by rank.—The rates of pay by rank have steadily increased since the beginning of the war. As of 1940, these rates, with maximum allowances, are estimated as follows:

a. Officers (per year).

Marshal of Italy	$3,802.00
Army general	2,932.00
Corps general	2,582.00
Division general	2,282.00
Brigadier general	1,854.00
Colonel	1,471.00
Lieutenant colonel	1,359.00

Major	1,159.00
Captain	1,050.00
First lieutenant	876.00
Second lieutenant	699.00
Second lieutenant (band and fencing masters)	851.00

b. *Noncommissioned officers and enlisted men* [2] (*per month*):

Maresciallo maggiore	$27.99 to $29.51
Maresciallo	27.57 to 29.60
Sergente maggiore	18.98 to 25.71
Corporal	1.85 to 2.21
Private, 1st class	1.60
Private	1.51

38. Special considerations.—*a.* In addition to the maximum allowances, the married enlisted man receives an allotment of $12.80 per month for his wife and $4.80 for each child.

b. All soldiers who are killed are considered for 12 months thereafter as "present with the colors," and their families receive the pay.

c. According to report, Mussolini ordered, effective from 28 October 1942, that the allowances of the mobilized be doubled, but that the increases, together with interest for the delay, will be paid after the war.

---

[2] See paragraph 175.

Chapter 3
ORGANIZATION

	Paragraph
SECTION I. Command and staff	39-44
II. Administration	45-46
III. Higher units	47-62
IV. Infantry	63-77
V. Cavalry	78-82
VI. Land reconnaissance units	83-86
VII. Field Artillery	87-97
VIII. Antiaircraft artillery	98-100
IX. Coast artillery	101-102
X. Armored troops	103-117
XI. Engineers	118-120
XII. Signal communications	121-132
XIII. Chemical troops	133-137
XIV. Motor transport agencies	138-140

SECTION I

COMMAND AND STAFF

	Paragraph
High Command	39
Supreme Commander	40
Supreme General Staff (*Stato Maggiore Generale*)	41
Chief of Army General Staff (*Capo di Stato Maggiore dell' Esército*)	42
Army General Staff (*Stato Maggiore dell'Esército*)	43
Advisory councils	44

39. High Command.—*a.* Under the Italian constitution the King is commander of the armed forces of the State (*Comandante Supremo delle Forze Armate dello Stato*). In time of peace he delegates his powers to the Ministers of War, Navy, and Air; in time of war, to a Supreme Commander appointed by Royal decree with the advice of the Council of Ministers. Under the Fascist regime, Mussolini, being simultaneously the Head of the Government (*Capo del Governo*) and Minister of War, Navy, and Air, was actually in complete control of all armed forces and determined the appointment of the Supreme Commander. (See fig. 4.) In addition, he was chairman of the Supreme Commission of Defense (*Commissione Suprema di Difesa*), an interministerial council working with the armed forces, and was responsible for its coordination of all policies and practices of total war. Its membership, which comprises the highest officials of the State and the ranking members of the armed forces, is as follows:

(1) Chairman—Head of the Government.
(2) Members—Ministers, Secretaries of State.
(3) Members with consulting vote, as follows:
(*a*) Under Secretaries of State for Armed Forces.
(*b*) Under Secretary of State to the Presidency of the Council of Ministers.
(*c*) Under Secretary of State for Albanian affairs.
(*d*) Marshals of Italy.
(*e*) Grand Marshals.
(*f*) Air Marshals.
(*g*) Chief of the Supreme General Staff.
(*h*) Chief of the Army Staff.
(*i*) Chief of Staff for the Navy.
(*j*) Chief of Staff for Fascist Militia.
(*k*) Inspector of Overseas Troops.
(*l*) Under Secretary of State for the Manufacture of War Materials.
(*m*) Secretary of the Supreme Commission of Defense.

b. The following advisory bodies handle matters that come especially under their jurisdiction:
(1) Army Council.
(2) Admiralty Committee.

ORGANIZATION

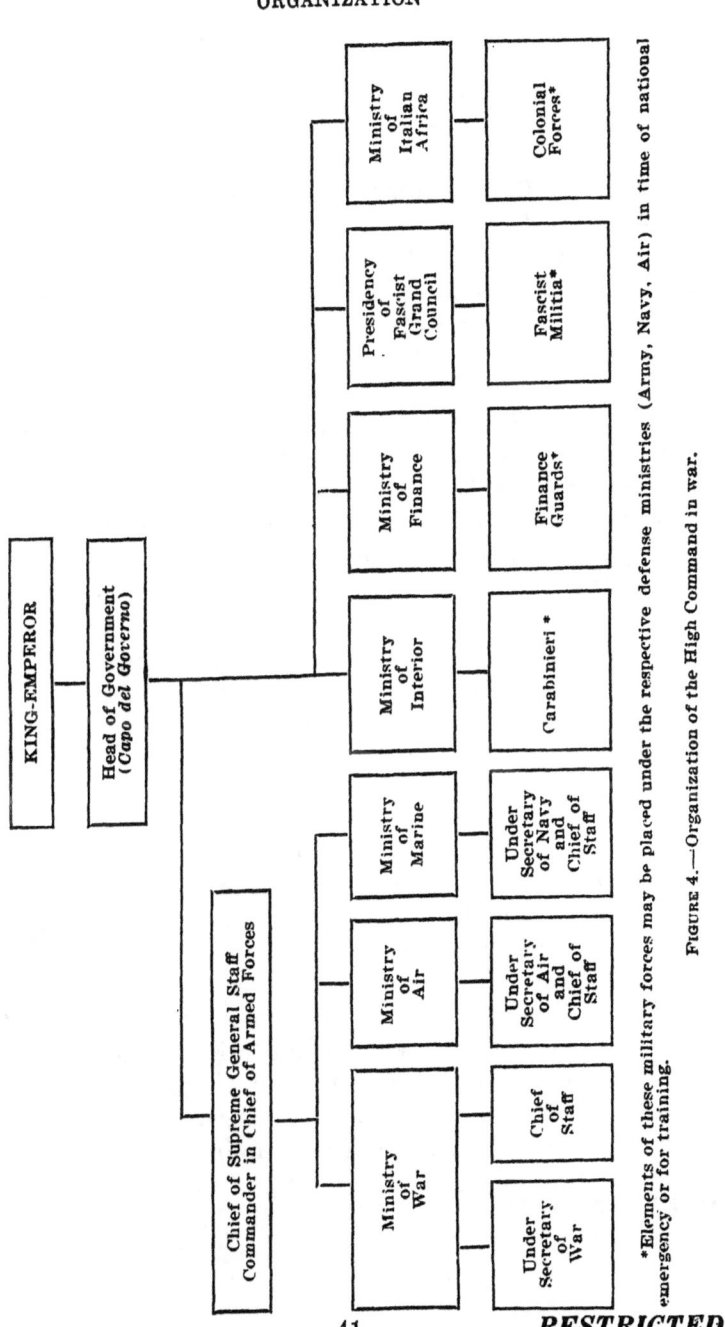

FIGURE 4.—Organization of the High Command in war.

*Elements of these military forces may be placed under the respective defense ministries (Army, Navy, Air) in time of national emergency or for training.

(3) Air Council.
(4) National Fascist Party's Civil Mobilization Center.
(5) National Research Council.
(6) General Commissariat for Manufacture of War Materials.

40. **Supreme Commander.**—The Supreme Commander is the Chief of the Supreme General Staff (*Capo di Stato Maggiore Generale.*) He is selected from the ranking officers of any of the armed forces. Theoretically, he is responsible only to the Head of the Government, and is his technical advisor in all matters concerning the coordination of defense and the conduct of land, sea, and air operations.

41. **Supreme General Staff** *(Stato Maggiore Generale).*—The Supreme General Staff is selected by the Supreme Commander from officers of the Army, Navy, and Air Force. It is his organic staff, and functions through the respective Ministries as liaison between him and the various services. It is composed of the General Staff Corps (*Corpo di Stato Maggiore*) and the General Staff Service (*Servizio di Stato Maggiore*). The head of the General Staff Corps is the Chief of the Army General Staff (*Capo di Stato dell'Esercito*) in the case of the Army. After a 3-year course at the Staff College and upon recommendation of a board from the General Staff Corps, officers selected for the Supreme General Staff are reassigned for 1 year to the headquarters of a line unit. Upon successful completion of this assignment they are sent to the General Staff Service and serve as heads of the various staff departments of a unit headquarters, where they are assisted by attached and reserve officers who may be temporarily employed. An officer must serve with a unit of his own arm for 2 years after promotion, after which he is again assigned to the General Staff Service. Upon promotion to the rank of lieutenant colonel, subject to his having satisfactorily fulfilled his duties, an officer is transferred to the General Staff Corps. There are normally 48 colonels and 178 lieutenant colonels in the Corps, while the number of officers in the Service is unlimited. All Chiefs of

Staffs in higher units are members of the General Staff Corps. Since these officers remain in close collaboration with the parent body, the Chief of the Army General Staff (and through him the Chief of the Supreme General Staff and the Head of the Government) is kept in close touch with the daily conduct of the war.

42. Chief of Army General Staff *(Capo di Stato Maggiore dell'Esército)*.—The Chief of the Army General Staff, appointed by royal decree on approval of the Council of Ministers, is professional advisor to the Council of Ministers of War, and is in actual control of the Army. He communicates directly with army and field commanders, commanders of corps areas, and inspectors of the various arms and services. He is under the orders of the Chief of the Supreme General Staff and is assisted by a Deputy Chief of Staff.

43. Army General Staff *(Stato Maggiore dell'Esército)*.— The Army General Staff consists of a secretarial office and three sections. The secretarial office handles general administration and General Staff personnel. Each section is administered by an Assistant Chief of Staff nominated by royal decree, as follows:

a. Assistant Chief of Staff for Operations *(Sottocapo di Stato Maggiore per le Operazioni)*, who supervises territorial and colonial operations, training, records, and intelligence.

b. Assistant Chief of Staff for "Intendance" *(Sottocapo di Stato Maggiore Intendente)*, who supervises organization, mobilization, transportation, and services.

c. Assistant Chief of Staff for Territorial Defense *(Sottocapo di Stato Maggiore per la Defesa Territoriale)*, who directs all defense (including coast defense, as far as it concerns the Army, but excluding frontier defense). Officers of the General Staff are rarely delegated to this section staff, which normally consists of specialists in the various branches within whose jurisdiction defensive measures fall.

44. Advisory councils.—*a. General.*—In addition to the Supreme Commission of Defense, certain councils act in an advisory capacity.

b. Committee for Civil Mobilization.—This committee studies all questions relating to the resources necessary for the conduct of war, and to the organization, disposition, and utilization of all national activities. It is composed of a president selected by the Head of the Government, a representative from each of the three defense Ministries, and eight members representing commerce, industry, agriculture, and the professions.

c. Superior Technical Committee for Arms and Munitions.—This committee coordinates all studies and experiments of common interest to the Army, Navy, and Air Force.

d. Superior Technical Committee for Military Electrical Services and Communications.—This committee has functions similar to those of the Superior Technical Committee for Arms and Munitions.

SECTION II

ADMINISTRATION

	Paragraph
Administrative offices	45
Inspectorates (Ispettorati)	46

45. Administrative offices.—These offices consist of the following:

a. Private Secretary of the Under Secretary.

b. Cabinet of the Under Secretary, which generally administers the War Ministry and has direct charge of the following offices:

(1) Office of the Generals.

(2) Office of Military Publications.

(3) War Ministry Headquarters Command.

(4) Special Company Carabinieri.

(5) Foreign Liaison Section.

c. General Directorates of—

(1) Office Personnel (both active duty and reserve).

(2) Civilian Personnel and General Affairs.

(3) Artillery.

(4) Engineers.

(5) Logistic Services.
(6) Medical Services.
(7) Administrative Services.
(8) Chemical Services.

d. Superior Directorate of Studying and Testing Engineer Equipment.

e. Office of Administration of Various Military Personnel.

f. General Accounting Office.

g. General Inspectorate of Drafting of Noncommissioned Officers and Enlisted Men.

46. Inspectorates (*Ispettorati*).—An "inspector" corresponds in general to the former U. S. chief of an arm or service. There are Inspectorates of Artillery, Infantry, Engineers, Motorization, Animal and Veterinary Service, Commissary Service, Alpini, and *Céleri* (mobile) troops, which include the cavalry. There is an Inspector of Overseas Troops, who has a consulting vote in the Supreme Commission of Defense. These inspectorates are consulting offices for the Under Secretary for War and the Chief of Staff on matters of administration, training, organization, armament, and equipment affecting their respective arms and services.

Section III

HIGHER UNITS

	Paragraph
General	47
Army group (*gruppo d'armata*) and army (*armata*)	48
Army corps (*corpo d'armata*)	49
Corps headquarters (*comando di corpo d'armata*)	50
Infantry division (*divisione fanteria*)	51
Assault and landing division (*divisione d'assalto e da sbarco*)	52
Infantry division headquarters (*comando di divisione fanteria*)	53
Truck-borne infantry division (*divisione fanteria autotrasportábile*)	54
Mountain infantry division (*divisione fanteria da montagna*)	55

Motorized division (*divisione motorizzata*)	56
Alpine division (*divisione alpina*)	57
Mobile (cavalry) division (*divisione célere*)	58
Armored division (*divisione corazzata*)	59
Parachute division (*divisione paracadutista*)	60
Coastal division (*divisione costiera*)	61
Frontier Guard (*Guardia alla Frontiera*, or *G.a.F.*)	62

47. General.—Units of the Italian Army are modeled to a considerable extent on those of the German Army. In contrast to the German units, however, their organization is extremely fluid. Tables of organization are seldom followed in practice and are often entirely abandoned. Improvised units called regroupments (*raggruppamenti*) are common. In general, the three highest units may be defined as follows:

a. Army group—any unit larger than an army.

b. Army—two or more army corps.

c. Army corps—two or more divisions.

48. Army group *(gruppo d'armata)* and army *(armata)*.—*a.* In time of peace, army groups and armies (with the exception of the Army of the Po) were represented only by the headquarters of the army generals designated to command them in war.

b. In time of war, the composition of an army group and of an army varies according to circumstances. So far as is known, at present, army groups vary from one army, with two attached corps, to five armies. The number of army corps in any army will not normally exceed four. Army troops include heavy artillery and mechanized field artillery (*artiglieria suppletiva*), mining, sound-ranging, meteorological, and survey units.

c. There are ten field armies, each commanded by an army general or an army general designate.

49. Army corps *(corpo d'armata)*.—*a.* The composition of an army is very flexible. Divisions are frequently transferred from one corps to another, and an army corps overseas will usually be found to contain different divisions from those which it would normally contain in Italy. The Italians have now created 27 army corps, but a considerable number of these are believed to contain only home defense or communications zone troops. Though the following, therefore, is the theoretical constitution of an army corps, it is rarely attained in practice:

(1) Headquarters (see par. 50).
(2) Two, three, or four infantry divisions.
(3) One motorized machine-gun battalion (eventually to be enlarged to a regiment.)
(4) One artillery regiment.
(5) One engineer regiment.
(6) One chemical company.
(7) One flame-thrower company.
(8) One mortar battery (chemical warfare).
(9) One medical company.
(10) One supply company.
(11) A motor transport center.

b. Theoretically, in time of war each corps has reconnaissance groups (*nuclei esploranti*) attached to it. These are Military (mobile and infantry) and Air Force Reconnaissance Groups; but it is very doubtful whether they exist in practice, except, occasionally, as improvised units.

c. Some army corps have had tank battalions attached, and special units, such as Alpini, Bersaglieri, etc., may be added if available.

50. Corps headquarters *(comando di corpo d'armata).*—Corps headquarters consists of the following components:

a. General Staff (*Stato Maggiore*).
(1) Department of the Chief of the Army General Staff:
(*a*) Operations and Intelligence Service.
(*b*) Discipline.
(*c*) Personnel and Administration.
(2) Corps artillery headquarters.
(3) Corps engineer headquarters.

(4) Intendance:
(a) Corps Transport Directorate.
(b) Corps Medical Directorate.
(c) Corps Commissariat Directorate.
(d) Corps Veterinary Directorate.
(5) Military tribunal.

b. Headquarters personnel (*quartiere generale*):
(1) Headquarters infantry unit.
(2) Photography section.
(3) Staff-car unit (*autodrappello*).
(4) Horsed Carabinieri section.
(5) Aircraft signaling station.
(6) Survey section.
(7) Post office.
(8) Two topographical sections.
(9) Two mixed Carabinieri sections.

51. Infantry division *(divisione fanteria)*.—*a*. The infantry division is called "binary" (*divisione binária*) owing to the incorporation of two infantry regiments instead of the old three-regiment (*ternária*) organization. As from 1 March 1940, a Fascist Militia legion of two battalions was attached to infantry divisions, partly, it is believed, to increase the number of infantry in the division and partly to include Black Shirt troops with Regular Army units. The legion is, however, described as an independent mobile unit to be used as shock (*assalto*) troops.[1] During the Albanian campaign the weakness of the binary division became evident. Divisions which had suffered heavy losses had to be reformed with whatever infantry was available or even by merging with another division. Now that infantry divisions in the Balkans have been brought up to strength, some have been given a third infantry regiment. It is not yet clear whether this is a reverse or whether it means a change in the table of organization. (For the organization of the binary division, see fig. 5.)

---

[1] The Militia legion is in theory an integral part of a division, but is ordinarily mobilized only when operations are in view. Many divisions have lost their legion.

ORGANIZATION

b. The table of organization of an infantry division provides for two reserve battalions. In practice, however, reinforcement is from reserve units which are held under **GHQ** in the theater of operations for allotment to units as required, or from the depot of the division.

Units	O	EM	LMG	MG	45-mm Mort	81-mm Mort	20-mm AA/AT guns	47/32 guns	Arty (guns and How)	MT	Anl	Mtcl
Hq	34	302	8							15	23	10
Two Inf Regts	234	6,416	234	54	108	18		16		110	600	24
Arty Regt	82	2,687		20			8		36	159	896	20
AT Co	6	222						8		10	76	
Mort Bn	21	508				18				16	80	3
Pion Co	6	200								8		2
Tg and Rad Co	6	269								12		
Med Sec	7	133								17		
Supply and MT Secs	8	127								10		
Total, without Militia legion	404	10,864	242	74	108	36	8	24	36	357	1,735	59
Militia legion	51	1,305	48	12	18					6	202	2
Total for division	455	12,169	290	86	126	36	8	24	36	363	1,937	61

FIGURE 5.—Organization of the infantry division *(divisione binária)*.

c. The latest table or organization for the 81-mm mortar battalion of an *autotrasportábile* (truck borne) division (see par. 54) is twenty-seven 81-mm mortars (three companies of nine 81-mm mortars each). It is probable that the infantry division also will eventually be given a mortar battalion of this type.

d. A few divisions have been given machine-gun battalions.

e. Engineers in the infantry division are often organized in an engineer battalion.

52. Assault and landing division *(divisione d'assalto e da sbarco).*—*a.* The assault and landing division assumes a special

RESTRICTED

organization different from that of the ordinary infantry division. Increased mobility is obtained by the decentralization of heavy support weapons (antitank guns and 81-mm mortars) from regimental to battalion control and of light support weapons (machine guns and 45-mm mortars) from battalion to company control. Certain special units such as assault engineers and rock-climbers were added to fit this type of division for combined operations.

b. An assault and landing division compares with an ordinary infantry division as follows:

Assault and Landing Division	*Ordinary Infantry Division*
Two infantry regiments (new organization).	Two infantry regiments.
Artillery regiment (new organization).	Artillery regiment.
81-mm mortar battalion.	81-mm mortar battalion.
Engineer battalion.	Pioneer company.
Assault engineer battalion.	Signal company.
Rock-climbers battalion.	
	Supply and motor transport sections
Motor-tricycle group.	Black Shirt legion
Chemical warfare company.	
Medical section	
Supply and motor transport sections	

This reorganization was effected in the latter part of 1941 and is believed to have affected three ordinary infantry divisions.

53. Infantry division headquarters *(comando di divisione fanteria).*—Division headquarters, with a strength of 34 officers and 302 enlisted men, consists of the following components:

 a. Commanding General and aides.
 b. Chief of Staff.
 c. General Staff.

RESTRICTED

(1) Operations and Services.
(2) Information.
(3) Personnel and Administration.
d. Artillery officer (commanding officer, artillery regiment).
e. Engineer officer.
f. Medical officer.
g. Commissary officer.
h. Veterinary officer.
i. Headquarters and General Staff.
j. Headquarters troops:
(1) Headquarters company.
(2) Topographic section.
(3) Motor pool.
(4) Three sections of military police.
(5) Post officer.

54. Truck-borne infantry division *(divisione fanteria autotrasportábile).*—There used to be two types of truck-borne divisions: "European" and "North African." The European type is the latest development of the infantry division, from which it differs little except that it may have mechanized artillery, no Black Shirt legion, and two divisional mortar battalions in the field if not on paper. The motor transport needed to carry it entirely is not allotted to the division, but is drawn when required from the Intendance. The division retains a good proportion of animal transport which enables it to operate, when grounded, in "horsed" columns. The animal transport, which can be lifted and transported by rail or motor transport, is sometimes referred to as a pack train.

55. Mountain infantry division *(divisione di fanteria da montagna).*—Certain infantry divisions are known as mountain infantry. These differ from Alpine divisions (see par. 57) and are infantry divisions specially adapted for mountain warfare. They have the ordinary composition of an infantry division, but have more animal transport. The total strength is reported to be about 14,500 men and 4,000 animals. All the guns of the artillery regiment can be transported in horse-drawn wagon loads or on pack animals. Personnel is not specially trained in mountain warfare, but is for the most part recruited from mountain districts in Italy (other than Alpine regions). It is believed that the division is not designated to operate at a higher altitude than 2,000 meters (about 6,500 feet).

56. Motorized division *(divisione motorizzata)*.—Each of these divisions was originally designed to operate with an armored division.

a. Composition.—The composition of the motorized division has been given as follows: divisional headquarters, two motorized infantry regiments, a Bersaglieri regiment, a support and antitank battalion, an artillery regiment, an engineer battalion, and services.

b. Approximate strength.—The strength of the motorized division has been estimated as follows:

Officers and enlisted men	9,500
Antitank guns	48
Field and medium guns	36
Light machine guns	199
Heavy machine guns	109
81-mm mortars	57
Motor transport (mixed medium and heavy trucks)	850
20-mm dual-purpose guns	40

57. Alpine division *(divisione alpina)*.—*a. General.*—The Alpine division is different from the infantry division, that is, specially adapted for mountain warfare (par. 55), its personnel being drawn from Alpine regions. The standard of physique and training is high and the artillerymen are expert in the manhandling of pack artillery. The regiments have their own detachments of artillery, engineers, and auxiliary services permanently attached. This makes the regiment self-supporting and capable of independent action for a considerable period. Decentralization does not stop at regiments; Alpine battalions and companies are detached from their parent units and regrouped with artillery units into regroupments (*raggruppamenti*). This procedure is made easier by the existence of independent transport right down to company organization.

b. Composition.—The Alpine division consists of a headquarters, two Alpine regiments, one Alpine artillery regiment, one mixed engineer battalion, one chemical warfare company,[2] and one supply section and one medical section, decentralized to regiments. The table of organization provides for two reserve battalions (*battaglioni di complemento*) (one for each infantry regiment). In practice replacements are drawn from the depot of the division as required. No allowance is therefore made for reserve battalions.

c. Approximate strength.

Officers and enlisted men	13,000
Light machine guns	[3] 162
Machine guns	66
Light mortars	54
Heavy mortars	[3] 24
Artillery (75/13 howitzers)	24
Animals	5,400
Bicycles	53
Motorcycles	22
Motor transport	50

58. Mobile (cavalry) division *(divisione célere).*—The main components of the mobile (cavalry) division are two horsed cavalry regiments and one cyclist Bersaglieri regiment. The cavalry regiments are virtually mounted infantry. The Bersaglieri

---

[2] No chemical warfare company has been identified with any Alpine division.

[3] According to a captured document, there are 250 light machine guns and 36 heavy mortars in the division. The same document, however, shows the infantry regiment as having 12 mortars and 81 light machine guns; that is, the divisional total should be as shown above. It is possible that the figures for the division represent a proposed increase in the table of organization which has not yet been carried into effect, and is therefore not given in the figures for the regiment.

regiment has collapsible bicycles and could be truck-borne if necessary. The artillery regiment has two motorized batteries and one pack battery. The division includes a support group of light tank squadrons. This semimotorized division was designed primarily for warfare in terrain which, though mountainous, permits the use of semimotorized units in a reconnaissance or support role. Armament has been sacrificed to this end, and the division is not designed for defense. There are indications that efforts have been made to motorize these divisions completely, but this has been hindered by shortage of trained personnel and equipment, and by demands being made on the divisions. Some mobile divisions are now probably converted into armored divisions. (For the organization of the mobile (cavalry) division, see fig. 6.)

59. Armored division *(divisione corazzata).—a. General.—* The armored division, as designed before the war, was a mixture of light and medium tanks, none heavier than 11 tons and the majority 3½ and 5 tons. It was incapable of more than light assault. The Italian armored division has changed radically in composition under German influence, with an improved type of medium tank and the introduction of self-propelling (*semovente*) guns and heavier divisional supporting weapons. In addition to a tank regiment of at least three battalions, the division now has a Bersaglieri truck-borne regiment, a divisional artillery regiment of six batteries (two self-propelling), and probably an armored car unit. Three Italian armored divisions were destroyed in North Africa. Mobile (cavalry) divisions are being converted into armored divisions. At present, however, these converted divisions probably have only two mechanized cavalry regiments containing armored cars, light tanks, and perhaps some self-propelled artillery (75-mm and 90-mm guns mounted on the chassis of medium tanks). It is not known whether these converted divisions will eventually conform to the normal type of armored division.

ORGANIZATION

Unit	O	EM	LMG	MG	20-mm AA and AT Guns	47/32-mm Guns	Arty (Guns and How)	MT	Mtcl	Bcl	Anl
Hq	28	196						24	12	58	28
Two Cav Regts	74	1,682	72	24				34	12	78	1,030
Bersaglieri Cyclist Regt	106	2,799	93	40				43	298	2,304	
AT Co	6	149				8		17	4		
L Tk Gp	23	289						¹50	32		
Div Arty Regt	69	1,454		14	8		24	172	30	53	348
Mixed Engr Co	7	359						40	23	10	
Med Sec	7	103						12	1	2	
Sup Sec	3	34						5	1		
MT Gp	11	340						201	18		
Total	334	7,405	165	78	8	8	24	598	431	2,565	2,012

¹ There are also 35 tank-carrying motor vehicles, 13 trailers, and 8 tractors in the group.

FIGURE 6.—Organization of the mobile (cavalry) division (*divisione célere*).

b. Composition.—The composition of the armored division has been reported as follows: a headquarters, one tank regiment, one Bersaglieri regiment, one support and antitank battalion, one armored division artillery regiment, one mixed engineer battalion, one supply section, and one medical section.

c. Approximate strength.—The strength of the armored division has been estimated as follows:

Officers and enlisted men__ 6,000 to 7,000
Light machine guns_____ 64
Machine guns _____ 632 (including tank-mounted)
20-mm antiaircraft and antitank guns _____ 40
37- or 47-mm guns_____ 198 (including tank-mounted)
Field artillery_____ 36
75-mm self-propelled guns_ 20
90-mm self-propelled guns_ 8
Medium tanks_____ 165
Armored cars _____ ?
Motor transport_____ 750 (mixed heavy and medium truck)

60. Parachute division *(divisione paracadutista).*—Another parachutist division has been formed in Italy to replace the Folgore division, which was destroyed while fighting as infantry in Egypt. According to report, it consists of a headquarters, two parachute regiments, a parachute artillery regiment, parachute guastatori battalion, and a parachute signal company.

61. Coastal division *(divisione costiera).*—Little is known concerning the coastal division. The organization of these troops does not appear to be fixed, although recent evidence indicates that they are gradually approaching the form of an ordinary field division. Analysis of locations of coastal units suggests that a coastal division may have under its command all or some of the following units: a headquarters; 2 to 5 coastal regiments, containing from 6 to 18 coastal battalions; 1 antitank battalion; 1 or 2 machine-gun battalions; 3 or 4 coast defense battalions; 1 mortar company; 1 or more motorcycle companies; 1 engineers attached from field forces; and services.

62. Frontier Guard *(Guardia alla Frontiera, or G. a. F.).*— *General. a.*—The Frontier Guard is responsible for the fortress duties previously carried out by the army corps stationed in the frontier districts. Frontier Guard headquarters are attached to the headquarters of 11 army corps and are allotted a certain length of frontier divided into sectors, which are further subdivided into subsectors containing a varying number of fortified positions (*caposaldi*). Personnel is provided mainly by the army corps, but infantry are also drawn from the Frontier Guard infantry regiment. The regiments and *raggruppamenti* of Frontier Guard artillery are under the command of army corps Frontier Guard headquarters and reinforce as required the artillery units permanently allotted to sectors and subsectors. A large part of the Frontier Guards in Northern Italy have been taken from frontier defense and are now used for coast defense in southern Italy and the islands. Others are employed on garrison duties in occupied territories in the Balkans. For this purpose a large number of rifles and machine-gun battalions have been created.

ORGANIZATION 62

b. Composition.—The Frontier Guard consists of the following components:

(1) Eleven Frontier Guard Commands, commanded by a brigade general assigned to the headquarters of the corps areas touching the frontier.

(2) A varying number of covering sectors commanded by colonels.

(3) One Frontier Guard infantry regiment for training and replacements.

(4) Nine Frontier Guard artillery regiments and one independent Frontier Guard group.

c. Sectors of defense.—Each covering sector includes a varying number of subsectors and minor units of the various arms and specialties, including infantry, artillery, and engineers. As a rule, each sector has a sector depot. The members of the Frontier Guard man the fixed defenses of the frontier. The strength of the command varies with the requirements of the particular frontier. The artillery regiment assigned to a Frontier Command furnishes personnel for the guns of the fixed defenses of the subsectors and also furnishes general artillery support for the sector or sectors.

Section IV

INFANTRY

	Paragraph
General	63
Motorized units	64
Fascist Militia	65
Normal type of infantry regiment (binary division)	66
Assault and landing type of infantry regiment	67
Truckborne (*autotrasportábile*) infantry regiment	68
Mountain infantry regiment	69
Motorized infantry regiment	70
Alpine regiment	71
Bersaglieri (cyclist) regiment	72
Motorized Bersaglieri regiment	73
Bersaglieri motorcycle company	74

RESTRICTED

	Paragraph
Black Shirt legion	75
Black Shirt battalion in truck-borne regiment	76
Black Shirt battalion in Bersaglieri (bicycle or motorized) regiment	77

63. General.—*a.* The prolonged reorganization of the Italian Army since World War I has resulted in a new conception of the infantry arm (*arma della fanteria*). Maneuverability has been sacrificed in an effort to develop proficiency in attack and capacity to make deep penetration of the enemy position. In contrast, however, to the German system of selecting first-class personnel for infantry units to make this arm the mainstay of forces in the field, the Italians appear to have subordinated infantry to other arms. It has therefore become a sort of pool into which are directed all those men not particularly fitted for one of the more highly regarded arms. The infantry of the Italian Metropolitan Army (*Esército Metropolitano*) is under the control of the Inspectorate of the Infantry Arm.

b. Heavy infantry weapons (that is, cannon designed to furnish the equivalent of artillery fire power) are an integral part of the Italian infantry regiment. As in the case of the new (binary) division, which comprises approximately 7,000 fewer men than the old type, the new regiment is much more easily maneuvered than its predecessor. At the same time, the assault troops have been increased to about 61 percent of the command, a 12-percent increase.

c. The infantry platoon has been reduced to 2 sections. Increased fire power in the section has been achieved by increasing the number of men from 11 to 18 and arming them with 2 machine rifles instead of 1 as previously.

d. The number of animals in infantry units has been reduced to the absolute minimum necessary for movement of supplies.

64. Motorized units.—*a.* Motorized units draw upon the Army for necessary vehicles, since they do not have their own motor-transport agencies. It should be noted that the bicycle is a characteristic means of transport, being substituted in many cases for the motorized transportation used in the U. S. Army. It is not limited in its allocation to the Bersaglieri commands, but is frequently used in other units. The vehicle itself differs materially from the U. S. machine, in that it is a purely utilitarian affair. Its primitive mechanical nature perhaps insures its long life. Comfort is sacrificed to sturdiness, solid rubber tires being used instead of the familiar U. S. pneumatic cushioning.

b. It is prescribed that the sergeants will be mainly concerned with the rifle group, and the corporals with the light machine-gun group. Two members of the rifle group are trained in patrol duties. The rifle group will not necessarily be trained to fire the light machine gun.

65. Fascist Militia.—A certain division of command exists within the divisions because of the incorporations into the Regular Army of 132 Black Shirt battalions on the basis of one combat legion (comprising two battalions) to each division. Many of the administrative details of the Black Shirt units, such as rank, promotion, and assignment of personnel, are administered by the Fascist Militia headquarters rather than by the Ministry of War. Mussolini first announced in October 1939 that 142 Black Shirt combat battalions would be incorporated into the Regular Army. The War Ministry was reluctant to take action or even to discuss the ultimate use of the units and, in April 1940, Mussolini learned that his instructions were being passively contravened. Immediately he issued peremptory orders that his original intent be followed and the process was subsequently carried through. Actually the absorption was not completed until late in 1942, and then it was as a result of a critical need for military manpower that the incorporation was effected.

66. Normal type of infantry regiment (binary division).—*a. General.*—Ordinarily, a territorial depot is assigned to each regiment. The regiment includes communications and some supply facilities, but its lack of integral combat engineers and antitank defense reduces its effectiveness. Its normal total war strength is estimated at 117 officers and 3,161 enlisted men, although there is considerable variation in these figures. (For an organization chart of the normal type of infantry regiment, see fig. 7.) The number of battalions varies in other types of the infantry regiment. (For the Grenadier type, which may have as many as five battalions, see figs. 8.)

b. Composition.—The normal type of infantry regiment (binary division) consists of a headquarters; a headquarters company; an 81-mm mortar company (of six mortars); a 47-mm accompanying battery (of eight guns); three battalions; an accompanying arms company (of eighteen 45-mm mortars and eight machine guns).

c. Battalion.—(1) Each normal type of battalion consists of a headquarters, a headquarters company, and three rifle companies, with a headquarters platoon and three rifle platoons each.

(2) Italian rifle companies are numbered consecutively throughout the three battalions of the regiment. Every fourth company is a machine-gun company.

d. Accompanying arms company.—The accompanying arms company consists of a headquarters platoon, two machine-gun platoons (of four machine guns each) and two 45-mm mortar platoons (of nine mortars each).

RESTRICTED

ORGANIZATION

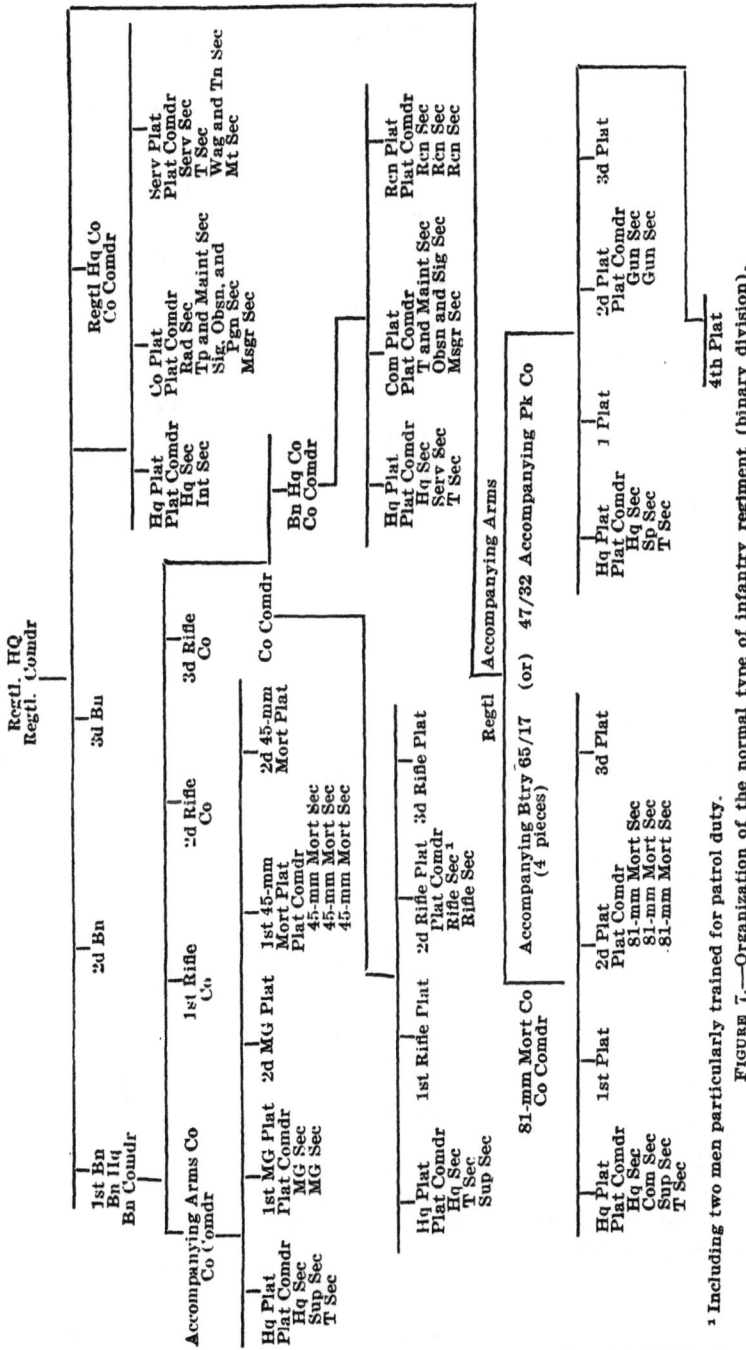

FIGURE 7.—Organization of the normal type of infantry regiment (binary division).

[1] Including two men particularly trained for patrol duty.

HANDBOOK ON ITALIAN MILITARY FORCES

Unit and composition	O	NCO	EM	LMG	MG	45-mm Mort.	81-mm Mort.	47-mm guns
Regt:								
Hq Co	16	22	232					
Three Bns	90	132	2,406	117	27	54		
47-mm Gun Co [3]	6	7	222					8
81-mm Mort Co	5	9	185				9	
Total	117		3,045	117	27	54	9	8
Rifle Bn								
Hq Co	9	10	109					
Three Rifle Cos	15	21	438	39				
One Sup Co	6	13	261		9	18		
Total	30	44	802	39	9	18		
Rifle Co.:								
Hq Plat	2	1	29					
Three Rifle Plats	3	6	[3] 117	12				
Total	5	7	146	12				
Rifle Plat:								
Two Secs [4]	1	2	38	4				
Runner			1					
Sup Co:								
Hq Plat	2	3	107					
Two MG Plats	2	4	72		[3] 8			
Two 45-mm Mort Plats	2	6	82			18		
Total	6	13	261		8	18		
MG Plat:								
Two Secs [5]	1	2	34		4			
Runner			1					
Signaler (with lamp apparatus)			1					
45-mm Mort Plat:								
Three Secs [6]	1	3	39			9		
Runner			1					
Signaler (with flags)			1					
47-mm Gun Co: [7]								
Hq Plat	2		54					
Four gun Plats	4		168					8
47-mm Gun Plat:								
Two Secs	1	2	38					2
Runner			1					
Signaler			1					
81-mm Mort Co:								
Hq Plat	2		50					
Three 81-mm Mort Plats	3	9	135				9	

See footnote at end of table.

RESTRICTED

Unit and composition	O	NCO	EM	LMG	MG	45-mm Mort.	81-mm Mort.	47-mm guns
81-mm Mort Plat:								
Three Secs	1	3	42				3	
Runner			1					
Signaler (with lamp apparatus)			1					
Range-taker			1					

¹ NCO is used for the Italian *sottufficiali*, that is, noncommissioned grades of sergeant and above.
² The obsolescent 65/17-mm close-support gun may still sometimes be found in place of the 47/32-mm antitank close-support gun.
³ One in reserve.
⁴ Each section (2 noncommissioned officers, 18 enlisted men, and 2 light machine guns) is commanded by a *sottufficiale* with a corporal-major as second in command. The section is divided into 2 groups: a light machine-gun group of 9 men and a rifle group of 11 men. The light machine-gun group is composed of the following personnel: a commander, 2 men in charge of the machine guns, and 4 men carrying ammunition.
⁵ Each machine-gun section (2 noncommissioned officers, 16 enlisted men, and 2 machine guns) is commanded by a *sottufficiale* and is divided into a firing group of 9 men and an ammunition group of 9 men. The firing group is composed of the following personnel: a commander, 2 men in charge of the machine guns, 2 men carrying the tripods, 2 men carrying the spare parts, and 2 men carrying the ammunition. The machine guns allotted are theoretically the new Breda 37 model, but it is probable that the majority of infantry regiments are still equipped with the old Fiat 35.
⁶ Each 45-mm mortar section (1 noncommissioned officer, 13 enlisted men, and 3 mortars) is commanded by a *sottufficiale* and is divided into a firing group of 10 men and an ammunition group of 4 men. The firing group is composed of a commander, 3 corporals or corporal-majors in charge of the mortars, 3 men carrying mortars, and 3 men carrying ammunition.
⁷ The organization of the regimental 47-mm gun company is identical with that of the divisional 47-mm company. The only difference is that the ammunition of the regimental company is two-thirds ordinary and one-third armor-piercing, whereas in the divisional company the proportion is one-third ordinary and two-thirds armor-piercing; that is, the role of the regimental company is mainly close-support while that of the divisional company is mainly antitank.

FIGURE 8.—Organization of the Grenadier type of infantry regiment.

67. Assault and landing type of infantry regiment.— The assault and landing division type of infantry regiment (see fig. 9) differs from an ordinary infantry regiment (par. 66) in the following important respects:

a. The regimental 47-mm gun company and the 81-mm mortar company are eliminated, with these weapons decentralized to the battalion support companies.

b. The light support weapons (machine guns and 45-mm mortars) of the battalion support company are assigned to the rifle companies.

RESTRICTED

c. The new regiment has a platoon of three sections, each armed with one light machine gun in place of the former platoon of two twin sections, each armed with two light machine guns. The war strength of the new regiment is estimated at 118 officers and 3,281 enlisted men.

68. Truck-borne *(autotrasportábile)* **infantry regiment.**—The normal type of truck-borne infantry regiment consists of a headquarters; a headquarters company; 3 battalions; an 81-mm mortar company (of 18 mortars); a 47-mm accompanying battery (of 8 guns); and an accompanying arms company (of eight machine guns and eighteen 45-mm mortars). The regiment has an estimated total strength of 117 officers and 3,078 enlisted men. Its chief difference from the normal infantry regiment (par. 66) is in the number of *autocarrette* (four-wheeled truck), of which it has 78.

69. Mountain infantry regiment.—The mountain infantry regiment differs from the normal type of infantry regiment (par. 66) only in the detail of a small pack train, the strength of which is 3 officers and 205 enlisted men, which is added to the mountain operating unit.

Unit and composition	O	EM	LMG	MG	45-mm Mort	81-mm Mort	47-mm Guns	Flame throwers
Regt:								
Comdr	1							
Hq Co	15	254						
Three Bns	102	3,027	81	36	27	18	12	12
Total	118	3,281	81	36	27	18	12	12
Bn:								
Comdr	1							
Hq Co	9	150						
Three Rifle Cos	18	633	27	12	9			
One Support Co	6	226				6	4	4
Total	34	1,009	27	12	9	6	4	4

ORGANIZATION

Unit and composition	O	EM	LMG	MG	45-mm Mort	81-mm Mort	47-mm Guns	Flame throwers
Rifle Co:								
Comdr	1							
Hq Plat	1	45			3			
Three Rifle Plats	3	120	9					
One MG Plat	1	46		4				
Total	6	211	9	4	3			
Rifle Plat:								
Comdr	1							
Three Secs		39	3					
Runner		1						
Total	1	40	3					
MG Plat:								
Comdr	1							
Four MG Secs		44		4				
Runner		1						
Signaler		1						
Total	1	46		4				
Support Co:								
Comdr	1							
Hq Plat	1	31						
Two 47-mm Gun Plats	2	84					4	
Two 81-mm Mort Plats	2	96				6		
Flame-thrower Sec		15						4
Total	6	226				6	4	4
47-mm Gun Plat:								
Comdr	1							
Two 47-mm Gun Secs		40					2	
Runner		1						
Signaler		1						
Total	1	42					2	
81-mm Mort Plat:								
Comdr	1							
Three 81-mm Mort Secs		45				3		
Runner		1						
Signaler		1						
Range-taker		1						
Total	1	48				3		

FIGURE 9.—Organization of the assault and landing type of infantry regiment.

RESTRICTED

70. Motorized infantry regiment.—The motorized infantry regiment consists of a headquarters; a headquarters company, including a mortar platoon (of six 81-mm mortars) and two battalions, each consisting of a headquarters: and a headquarters company, including a mortar platoon (of nine 45-mm mortars) and three rifle companies, each of which includes three rifle platoons and one machine-gun platoon. The estimated war strength of the motorized infantry regiment is 70 officers and 1,765 men.

71. Alpine regiment.—*a. General.*—(1) The battalion is the highest Alpine unit which has a fixed organization. A regiment may contain two, three, or four battalions, though three is the normal number. In addition, each regiment has formed at its depot a number of second-line battalions which may be distinguished by the fact that their names always begin with *Val* or *Monte*. These battalions normally operate with Alpine artillery units, in independent regroupments (*raggruppamenti*), and groups of varying sizes, but may also be used to supplant battle casualties of the parent regiment, since the reserve battalion, which is provided for in the table of organization of the regiment, does not usually exist.

(2) This flexibility of organization, which is necessitated by the difficulty of employing large units in mountain conditions, is made possible by the existence of independent supply and transport services within all units down to and including companies. The Alpine division is, therefore, often only an administrative headquarters. Regiments, as in the Greek campaign, normally operate as independent units, with a full complement of supporting arms and services, and battalions, and even companies, may frequently be employed on independent missions. However, organic relations with each other and with their parent organization are usually maintained.

b. Normal composition.—The normal Alpine regiment (see fig. 10) consists of a headquarters, a headquarters company, three

ORGANIZATION

Unit and composition	O	EM	LMG	MG	45-mm Mort	81-mm Mort	75/13-mm Pk How	Narrow-track Mtr Trk	Bcl	Carts	Mtcl	Anl
Regt:												
Hq		700 (estimated)							3	7	7	5	420
Hq Co												
Med Sec												
One Hosp												
One Sup Det												
T Det												
Three Bns		3,800	81	27	27	12			15	6	54		981
Total		4,500	81	27	27	12			18	13	61	5	1,400
One Arty Bn Atchd		850 (estimated)		6			12				12		408
Bn:												
Hq	5												1
Hq Co	5	231				4			5		3		62
Three Cos	21	1,005	27	9	9						15		264
Total	31	1,236	27	9	9	4			5	2	18		327
One Arty Btry Atchd	2	200 (estimated)		2			4						116
Co:												
Hq	2												
Hq Plat	1	69											2
Three Rifle Plats	3	135	9										9
One MG Plat	1	59		3	3								12
T Det		72									5		65
Total	7	335	9	3	3						5		88
Plat:												
Three Secs	1	45	3										3
MG Plat:												
Three MG Secs		39		3									6
One 45-mm Mort Sec	1	20			3								6

FIGURE 10.—Organization of the Alpine regiment.

battalions, and a service, comprising a medical section, a field hospital, a supply detachment, and a transport detachment. Each battalion consists of a headquarters, a headquarters company, and three rifle companies, each including a machine-gun platoon (of three 45-mm mortars). The estimated total war strength of the normal Alpine regiment is 4,500 officers and enlisted men.

72. Bersaglieri (cyclist) regiment.—The Bersaglieri cyclist regiment is normally attached to the mobile (cavalry) division (*divisione célere*) (par. 58) or to army corps. The Bersaglieri cyclist regiment (see fig. 11) consists of a headquarters, a headquarters company, a motorcycle company, and three battalions, each consisting of a headquarters, a headquarters company, three bicycle companies, and one machine-gun company (of twelve machine guns). The regiment has an estimated war strength of 106 officers and 2,799 enlisted men.

73. Motorized Bersaglieri regiment.—The motorized Bersaglieri regiment consists of a headquarters, a headquarters platoon, and two battalions, each consisting of a headquarters platoon, two companies (of nine machine rifles and three machine guns), and a heavy truck company. The regiment has an estimated total strength of 35 officers and 775 enlisted men.

74. Bersaglieri motorcycle company.—In the mobile (cavalry) division (*divisione célere*), the motorcycle company is detached and is directly under the divisional commander. Unattached Bersaglieri cyclist regiments also have a motorcycle company. This Bersaglieri motorcycle company (see fig. 11) consists of a headquarters (of three machine rifles and one machine gun); three rifle platoons (of four machine rifles each); and a machine-gun platoon (of four machine guns). The company has an estimated total strength of 6 officers and 172 men.

75. Black Shirt legion.—The Black Shirt legion (see fig. 12) consists of a headquarters, a headquarters platoon, and two battalions, each consisting of a headquarters company and three companies, each comprising a headquarters platoon and three rifle platoons (of nine machine rifles). The estimated strength of the legion is 44 officers and 1,354 enlisted men.

Unit [1] and composition	O	EM	LMG	MG	Bcl	Mtcl	MT
Regt:							
Hq Co	13	167			78	37	6
Three Bcl Bns	87	2,460	81	36	2,286	153	33
One Mtcl Co	6	172	12	4		108	4
Total	106	2,799	93	40	2,364	298	43
Bcl Bn:							
Hq Co	8	127			58	51	11
Three Bcl Cos	15	507	27		516		
One MG Co	6	186		12	190		
Total	29	820	27	12	764	51	11
Bcl Co:							
Hq Plat	2	34					
Three Bcl Plat	3	135	9				
Bcl Plat:							
Three Bcl Secs	1	45	3				
Bcl MG Co:							
Hq Plat	2	66					
Four MG Plats	4	120		12			
Bcl MG Plat:							
Three MG Secs	1	30		3			
Mtcl Co:							
Hq Plat	2	36					
Three Mtcl Plat	3	96	12				
One Mtr MG Plat	1	40		4			
Mtcl Plat:							
Four Mtcl Secs	1	32	4				
Mtr MG Plat:							
Four MG Secs	1	40		4			

[1] Figures for company and platoon strengths are approximate only. Bersaglieri also supply the 47/32-mm antitank company in these divisions. This company consists of 6 officers and 149 enlisted men, and has 17 motor vehicles, 4 motorcycles, and 8 antitank guns.

FIGURE 11.—Organization of the Bersaglieri cyclist regiment in the mobile (cavalry) division (*divisione célere*) or an army corps.

Unit and composition	O	NCO	EM	LMG	MG	45-mm Mort	Bcl	Mtcl	Carts	Cars	LTk	Anl
Black Shirt legion: [1]												
Hq	9		1				2	2	?			
Hq Plat	1	8	83							1	1	9
Two Black Shirt Bns	36	58	948	48		18	10		10		4	152
One MG Co	5	9	198		12		1		4			41
Total	51	75	1,230	48	12	18	13	2	14	1	5	202
Black Shirt Bn:												
Hq	4											1
Hq Plat	1	5	59				5		5		2	15
Scout Plat	1	3	37									
Three Rifle Cos	12	21	378	24		9	3					60
Total	18	29	474	24		9	8		5		2	76
Black Shirt Co:												
Hq and Hq Plat	2	3	58				1					20
Two Rifle Plats	2	4	68	8		3						
Total	4	7	126	8		3	1					20
Black Shirt Plats: Two Secs	1	2	34	4								
Black Shirt MG Co:												
Hq and Hq Plat	2	3	96						4			41
Three MG Plats	3	6	102		12							
Total	5	9	198		12				4			41
Black Shirt Mtcl Plat: Two Secs	1	2	17		4							

[1] A few legions, particularly in Sardinia, have an 81-mm mortar company and a 47-mm antitank close-support battery.

FIGURE 12.—Organization of a divisional Black Shirt legion.

76. Black Shirt battalion in truck-borne regiment.—The Black Shirt battalion in the truck-borne regiment consists of a headquarters, a headquarters company, and three rifle companies (of nine machine rifles). The estimated strength of the battalion is 20 officers and 550 enlisted men.

77. Black Shirt battalion in Bersaglieri (bicycle or motorized) regiment.—The Black Shirt battalion in the Bersaglieri (bicycle or motorized) regiment consists of a headquarters, a headquarters company, and three companies (of nine machine rifles). The estimated strength of the battalion is 21 officers and 593 enlisted men.

SECTION V

CAVALRY

	Paragraph
General	78
Composition	79
Identification of units	80
Employment	81
Cavalry horses	82

78. General.—The cavalry arm (*arma della cavalleria*) of the Italian Army consists of brigades and regiments, as well as squadrons of autonomous troops, but it is not organized into divisions. The *célere* ("rapid," or mobile) division (par. 58) is designed to carry out the role of cavalry in maneuvers and combat, and includes elements of varying fighting power and mobility. One cavalry brigade is attached to each of these divisions. Cavalry regiments are also attached to corps troops as required. In 1939 cavalry amounted to about 1.6 percent of the armed forces.

79. Composition.—*a. Brigade.*—The cavalry brigade (fig. 13) consists of a headquarters and 2 regiments, with an estimated strength of 81 officers and 1,695 enlisted men.

Units	O	EM	Saddle Horses	Pk Anl	Machine Rifles	MG	Bcl	Mtcl	Auto	Cargo Trk
Brig Hq	7	75	50	14			3	8	2	3
1st Regt	37	810	758	52	36	12	31	12		15
2d Regt	37	810	758	52	36	12	31	12		15
Total	81	1,695	1,566	118	72	24	65	32	2	33

FIGURE 13.—Organization of the cavalry brigade in the mobile (cavalry) division (*divisione célere*).

b. *Regiment.*—The cavalry regiment (fig. 14) normally consists of a headquarters, a headquarters troop of two platoons, and two squadrons of two troops each (or one cavalry troop and one machine-gun troop each). The troop consists of a headquarters platoon and 3 rifle platoons of three sections each. The headquarters platoon is made up of the necessary personnel for the administrative functioning and the internal liaison of the troop, and other necessary personnel, such as a horseshoer and medical personnel, cooks, orderlies, etc. The machine-gun troop (of twelve machine guns) consists of a headquarters and four platoons of three sections each, and in other respects differs in organization from the regular cavalry troop.

Units	O	EM	Saddle horses	Pk Anl	Machine rifles	MG	Bcl	Mtcl	Cargo Trk
RHQ:									
Hq Tr (2 Plats)	12	110	66	14			10	12	15
1st Sq Hq	2	10	10	1			3		
1st Tr Hq Plat	1	32	27				3		
1st Plat (3 Secs)	1	36	37		3				
2d Plat	1	36	37		3				
3d Plat	1	36	37		3				
Total, 1st Tr	4	140	138		9		3		
Total, 2d Tr	4	140	138		9		3		
Total, 1st Sq	10	290	286	1	18		9		
Total, 2d Sq	10	290	286	1	18		9		
Total Regt	32	690	638	16	36		28	12	15
MG Tr:									
Four Plats (3 Secs each)	5	120	120	36		12	3		

FIGURE 14.—Organization of the normal cavalry regiment.

c. *Autonomous troops.*—Autonomous cavalry troops are usually assigned to training schools, the War College, and the Capital. Although no breakdown of the normal squadron is available, it has been reported to consist of a headquarters, a headquarters platoon, two troops, and a machine-gun platoon of three sections. Its strength is estimated at 18 officers and 445 enlisted men.

80. Identification of units.—*a. Regiment.*—The names and numbers of the known cavalry regiments are as follows:

1st—Nizza	9th—Firenze
2nd—Piemonte Reale	10th—Vittorio Emanuele II
3rd—Savoia	12th—Saluzzo
4th—Genova	13th—Monferrato
5th—Novara	14th—Alessandria
6th—Aosta	19th—Guide
7th—Milano	

b. Autonomous troops.—The two known squadrons of autonomous troops are the *Cavaleggieri di Sicilia* and the *Cavaleggieri di Sardegna.*

81. Employment.—*a. General.*—The principal mission of the Italian cavalry is that of reconnaissance, and, in case of necessity, to exploit advantages, close gaps, etc. It maneuvers mounted and fights mounted or dismounted. Horse cavalry frequently acts as mounted infantry or as dismounted machine-gun squadrons, in support of other units. Most cavalry depots have formed dismounted squadron groups which are employed on coast or home defense, mainly in southern Italy and the Islands. Its fire power has been lessened by the withdrawal of the squadron of light tanks from the regiment and the transfer of this squadron to the light tank regiment of the armored division.

b. In Albania and Greece.—Although there were three cavalry regiments in Albania at the beginning of hostilities, their use was limited. A very limited secondary use of the Italian cavalry was evident during the first phase of the Italian penetration. The same inactivity was noted during the period of Italian retirement. During the period of Italian defense, the presence of cavalry was established only in mountainous regions.

82. Cavalry horses.—*a. General.*—Italian cavalry horses are among the finest in the world. Italian cavalry officers are generally of the wealthy and socially prominent classes, and horsemanship is more than a military interest. Hence, the training of cavalry horses is uniformly excellent. In spite of this, ordinary troop horses do not meet U. S. Army standards. Government breeding stations are maintained in the country.

b. Forage.—Green forage is used to some extent in summer months, but in general a synthetic forage known as *energon* is used. The normal ration is about $6\frac{1}{2}$ pounds of hay and $8\frac{1}{2}$ pounds of *energon*.

SECTION VI

LAND RECONNAISSANCE UNITS

	Paragraph
General	83
Mobile (cavalry) division	84
Motorized and armored divisions	85
Infantry division	86

83. General.—*a.* As a rule, reconnaissance detachments of the mobile (cavalry) division (*divisione célere*) (par. 58) furnish the tactical ground reconnaissance on the front of the large units of the first echelon. If these are lacking, or if special conditions prevail as to terrain or climate, these missions are entrusted to reconnaissance detachments of the infantry division.

b. The motorized division (*divisione motorizzata*) (par. 56) may cooperate with the mobile (cavalry) division in strategical reconnaissance or in general advance guard action. It is preceded by a light and very fast advance guard (of motorcyclists, tanks, or other units) for observation.

c. In Spain the armored division (*divisione corozzata*) (par. 59) cooperated with the motorized infantry to perform advance guard, reconnaissance, and exploitation missions.

84. Mobile (cavalry) division.—The reconnaissance detachments of the mobile (cavalry) division are units of Bersaglieri regiments, light tank battalions, and cavalry regiments. The Bersaglieri are light, fast troops mounted on motorcycles and motortricycles and armed with machine guns. The light tank battalions consist of light tanks (armed with 2 Fiat machine guns), machine guns, and machine rifles. In reconnaissance, tanks conform to the action of the mobile troops, the cavalry, and Bersaglieri. The cavalry regiment (horse) (2 regiments in each *célere* division) is armed with 36 machine rifles and 12 machine guns. The cavalry regiment may act alone as a reconnaissance regiment or may be incorporated as part of a large mobile, or close-reconnaissance, unit.

85. Motorized and armored divisions.—The motorized division includes one Bersaglieri regiment. The armored division has one Bersaglieri regiment, four battalions of light tanks, and armored cars.

86. Infantry division.—The size of the reconnaissance detachment of the infantry (binary) division will depend on the width of the sector to be reconnoitered and on the missions with which the force is charged. As a rule, it consists of a battalion reinforced by a 47-mm gun unit and signal communications, and at times, also, by machine-gun units, mortars, light tanks, and artillery. The action of the infantry reconnaissance detachment is planned by the command of the army corps, except whenever special conditions exist, such as terrain or extension of the front, and large units advance in broken formations. Tactical ground reconnaissance is then organized and directed by commanders of the individual columns, and the infantry reconnaissance unit is broken up to form reconnaissance patrols, as a rule, reconnaissance rifle squads. The infantry reconnaissance detachment provides for signal communications. All means from the messenger to the airplane are employed. Aviation, of course, cooperates with the infantry in reconnaissance missions.

Section VII

FIELD ARTILLERY

	Paragraph
General	87
Organization	88
Regiment in infantry division	89
Regiment in mobile (cavalry) division (*divisione célere*)	90
Regiment, North African type (1942)	91
Regiment in armored division	92
Regiment in Alpine division	93
Regiment in army corps	94
Regiment in an army	95
Regiment in Frontier Guard	96
Antitank units	97

87. General.—The artillery arm (*arma dell'artiglieria*) of the Italian Army is under the Inspectorate of Artillery, which is a consulting office for the Under Secretary for War and the Chief of Staff on all matters of administration, training, organization, armament, and equipment affecting the artillery. Antiaircraft and coast artillery are also under control of this office.

88. Organization.—*a. Staffs.*—Each army corps headquarters includes a corps of artillery headquarters commanded by a major general of artillery, under whose orders all the artillery in the corps area is controlled except divisional artillery. The corps artillery commander consults the Inspectorate of Artillery on technical matters. His staff includes one ordnance officer and three or four survey officers.

b. Main components.—(1) The Italians classify artillery as divisional, corps, and army. These roughly correspond to field, medium, and heavy, respectively, but artillery classified by the Italians as "corps" is included in the artillery regiments of some divisions, particularly armored divisions, whereas much of the equipment of corps and army artillery regiments is of calibers classified by the Italians as "divisional" and "corps," respectively.

ORGANIZATION

(2) The artillery arm consists of the following main components:

- 44 infantry divisional artillery regiments.
- 3 truck-borne divisional artillery regiments.
- 2 motorized divisional artillery regiments.
- 1 armored divisional artillery regiment.
- 3 Alpine divisional artillery regiments.
- 1 mobile (cavalry) divisional artillery regiment.
- 18 army corps artillery regiments.
- 17 army corps artillery regroupments (*raggruppamenti*).
- 11 frontier guard artillery regiments (including 1 autonomous group) and 6 regroupments (*raggruppamenti*).
- 5 army artillery regiments.
- 4 army artillery regroupments (*raggruppamenti*).
- 5 antiaircraft mechanized field artillery regiments.

c. Recent developments.—(1) Italian artillery has always been deficient by modern standards. Improvement is difficult owing to the low capacity of the Italian arms industry, and shortage of artillery has probably been the main factor in limiting expansion of the Army. Notable weaknesses are the retention of obsolete types both of home and foreign (mainly Austrian) makes of guns, and the slow progress of mechanization, particularly of field artillery. The Italians, however, have made great efforts to improve their artillery. Thus considerable progress had been made in production of the Italian 90-mm antiaircraft gun, which, like the German 88-mm gun, is used in an antitank role. Artillery of calibers that have hitherto been classified as "corps" is included in the table of organization of at least the armored divisions, and is often allotted to other divisions in place of their normal equipment. Self-propelled artillery (usually the 75/18 gun-howitzer on the chassis of the M13 tank) has been developed, and two batteries are included in the artillery regiments of the armored divisions.

(2) Also, a certain amount of assistance has been forthcoming from the Germans, who provided some of their 88-mm guns for use

RESTRICTED

in Libya, and also a considerable number of 100/22 Skoda howitzers, which are employed either on coast defense in southern Italy and the Islands or to equip the new infantry divisions. It must be remembered, moreover, that obsolete types of guns are not necessarily inefficient, and that in many parts of Italy pack or horse-drawn artillery is more suitable than mechanized.

d. Mechanization.—All corps and army artillery is motorized. The artillery of the ordinary infantry division is either pack or horse-drawn, but certain pack types can be horse-drawn or tractor-drawn in weapon loads on a type of gun carrier known as a *carrello*. All motorized artillery is theoretically tractor-drawn, but there is a shortage of tractors. Trailing vehicles are sometimes improvised. There are three known methods of moving artillery mechanically:

(1) *Tractor-drawn.*—*Carrello* with solid rubber tires which raises the equipment off its own wheels, giving a 15-inch clearance. The *Pavesi* (light and heavy), the *Breda*, and the 708-cm, which has been specially designed for pulling the 75/18 gun-howitzer. They have cleated wheels, and are not track-laying vehicles.

(2) *Carriage.*—By truck or trailer.

(3) *Haulage.*—By tractor or by a light truck which carries a few men.

e. Numbering.—(1) Artillery regiments of infantry divisions, except regiments of more recently created divisions (those with higher numbers), do not bear the same number as the division.

(2) Corps artillery regiments bear the same number as the corps.

(3) The numbering of army artillery regiments has no connection with armies of the same number.

(4) Battalions and batteries of divisional artillery are normally numbered throughout the regiment.

(5) Corps, army, and Frontier Guard artillery battalions and batteries are numbered in sequence throughout the arm, with many

ORGANIZATION

gaps. The numbering of battalions in regiments is most eccentric, though pairs of battalions tend to be allotted to the same regiment.

f. Fire control and registration.—Methods are similar to those in use in the U. S. Army, except that targets are normally areas instead of definite points, and the battalion fire-direction technique is neither common nor very effectively used.

g. Method of employment.—The employment of artillery by the Italians is quite normal, and the only feature worthy of note is the tendency to site the bulk of their artillery well forward. Artillery personnel have earned a reputation for good shooting and have displayed considerable courage under heavy fire or in direct attack. In many cases artillery firing over open sights has been used against attacking tanks or infantry. Alpine artillerymen are highly skilled in the manhandling of pack artillery.

h. Regimental specialists.—(1) *General.*—Gunnery specialists and visual signal personnel are allotted to all battalions and batteries. Radio personnel are alloted to battalions, but not to batteries.

(2) *Gunnery specialists.*—Gunnery specialists are allotted as follows:

	Officers	Noncommissioned officers	Men
Battalions			
All battalions (except those given below)	5	1	9
152/45 gun, 260/9 mortar, 305/8 mortar, and 305/17 howitzer (army artillery)	6	2	8
Antiaircraft battalions	2	1	6
Batteries			
65/17 howitzer (replaced in part by the 47/32 gun)	1	1	5
All other batteries except antiaircraft		1	4
Antiaircraft batteries		1	13

RESTRICTED

(3) *Visual signal personnel.*—Visual signal personnel are allotted as follows:

	Noncommissioned officers	Men
Battalions		
All battalions except antiaircraft	1	14
Antiaircraft battalions	1	15
Batteries		
65/17 howitzer		6
All other batteries except antiaircraft	1	12
Antiaircraft batteries	1	10

(4) *Radio personnel.*—Radio personnel are allotted as follows:

	Noncommissioned officers	Men
Battalions		
65/17 and 75/13 howitzers, 75/27 gun, and 100/17 howitzer (divisional artillery)	1	6
Alpine artillery	1	15
All other battalions up to 149/19 howitzers (corps artillery)	1	15
Heavier battalions (army artillery)		3
Antiaircraft battalions		6

(5) *Spare personnel.*—All battalions and batteries of Alpine and army artillery have a varying number of spare personnel for allotment to headquarters observation and liaison patrols.

i. Ammunition and supplies.—Every artillery battalion has its own ammunition and supply unit which comprises a unit headquarters and as many ammunition and supply sections as there

RESTRICTED

are batteries in the battalion, the second day's rations and forage, and the reserve rations. This organization exists for all batteries up to army artillery batteries of 149-mm guns and 152-mm howitzers.

j. Artillery survey.—For the corps artillery there is a survey unit composed of 2 topographical sections, a sound-ranging section, and a flash-spotting section. In divisional artillery there is a party of 1 officer and 4 enlisted men with a plane-table in each group, and, with the regiment, a survey party of 2 officers and 12 enlisted men with a truck. For sound-ranging a hand-operated or an automatic instrument is used.

k. Depots.—The regimental headquarters of every type of artillery regiment has a depot battery (which has a strength equal to the personnel of regimental headquarters), a mobilization office, and an administrative office. The Alpine artillery depot has in addition mobilization stores for detached battalions.

89. Regiment in infantry division.—*a.* The artillery regiment in the infantry division (fig. 15) consists of a headquarters, a 100/17 howitzer battalion, a 75/27 gun battalion, a 75/13 howitzer battalion, and a 20-mm. antiaircraft battery.

b.. In 1939 the 100/17 howitzer battalion and the 75/27 gun battalion were officially motorized, but captured documents show that the normal organization remains two horse-drawn and one pack battalion. It is believed that the artillery regiment with two motorized battalions and one pack battalion contains 2,203 officers and enlisted men, 217 motor vehicles, and 358 animals.

c. The 75/27 gun and the 75/13 howitzer have been replaced in part by the 75/18 gun-howitzer.

d. The artillery regiment of the mountain infantry division has two battalions of 75/13 pack howitzers, one battalion of 100/17 howitzers (wagon- or horse-drawn) and one 20-mm antiaircraft battery (which may be transported by pack). It is estimated that this regiment consists of 2,791 officers and enlisted men, 142 motor vehicles, and 910 animals.

89   HANDBOOK ON ITALIAN MILITARY FORCES

e. The artillery regiment of the truck-borne division (*divisione trasportabile*) division may contain three motorized battalions (two of 75/27 guns and one of 100/17 howitzer) and a 20-mm antiaircraft battery (motorized). The regiment contains about 3,000 officers and enlisted men, and 400 motor vehicles.

Unit	Composition	O	EM	100/17 How	75/27 Guns	75/13 How	20-mm AA/AT Guns	MG	Trk	An
Regt	Hq	13	125						17	75
	100/17 How Bn	21	808	12				6	46	269
	75/27 Gun Bn	21	808		12			6	46	269
	75/13 How Bn (Pk)	22	829			12		6	29	283
	20-mm AA Btry	5	117				8	2	21	
	Total	82	2,687	12	12	12	8	20	159	896
100/17 How Bn	Hq	7	71						4	29
	Three Btrys	12	597	12				6	18	240
	Am and Sup Unit (Three Secs, one per Btry)	2	140						24	
100/17 How Btry	Hq	2	46							
	Four Secs	2	104	4				2	6	80
	T Ech (baggage and rations)		49							33
75/27 Gun Bn	(Same as 100/17 How Bn)	21	808		12			6	46	269
75/13 How Bn (Pk)	Hq	7	69							
	Three Btrys	12	651			12		6	29	283
	Am and Sup Unit (Three Secs, one per Btry)	3	109							
75/13 Pk How Tr.	Hq	2	55							
	Four Secs	2	116			4		2	?	?
			46							
20-mm AA Tr.	Hq	1	19							
	Four Gun Secs	4	76				8	2	21	
	Am Sec T Unit		22							

FIGURE 15.—Organization of the artillery regiment in the infantry division.

f. It will be found that few divisional artillery regiments conform exactly to a table of organization. Many recently created divisions have at least one battalion of Czech 100/22 Skoda guns. Some divisions have been given battalions of what is normally classified by the Italians as corps artillery; a few divisions, particularly in Russia, have motorized regiments similar to those of the truck-borne divisions.

90. Regiment in mobile (cavalry) division (*divisione célere*).—*a.* The artillery regiment in the mobile (cavalry) division (fig. 16) consists of a headquarters, two 75/27 gun battalions (motorized), a 75/27 gun battalion (horse-drawn), and a 20-mm antiaircraft gun troop (motorized). The regiment includes 69 officers, 1,454 enlisted men, 172 motor vehicles, 30 motorcycles, 53 bicycles, and 348 animals.

b. The 75/27 gun has been replaced in part by the 75/34 gun.

c. The mobile (cavalry) artillery regiments which were sent to Libya had 12 gun batteries, that is, a total of 36 guns.

Unit	Composition	75/27 Guns	MG	20-mm AA/AT Guns
Regt	Hq			
	Two 75/27 Gun Bns (Mtz)	16	8	
	One 75/27 Bns (H-Dr)	8	4	
	20-mm AA Tr (Mtz)		2	8
	Total	24	14	8
75/27 Gun Bn	Hq			
	Two (or three) Btrys	8(12)	4(6)	
	MT Unit			
75/27 Gun Btry	Hq			
	Four Secs	4	2	
	MT Unit			
20-mm AA Btry	(As in Inf Div)		2	8

FIGURE 16.—Organization of the artillery regiment in the mobile (cavalry) division (*divisione célere*).

91. Regiment, North African type (1942).—*a.* The artillery regiment, North African type (1942), consists of a headquarters, two battalions of 75/27 guns, two battalions of 100/17 howitzers, and two batteries of 20-mm antiaircraft guns.

b. In the field each battalion has an ammunition and supply train. With these the approximate total of personnel in the regiment is 1,800 officers and enlisted men.

c. The regiment is entirely motorized and requires a total of about 225 heavy and light vehicles.

d. To some of these regiments have been added a battalion of German 88/55 dual-purpose guns, thus increasing the regimental total by 12 guns, 500 officers and enlisted men, and approximately 50 vehicles.

92. Regiment in armored division.—*a.* The artillery regiment in the armored division (fig. 17) consists of two 75/27 gun battalions of three batteries (motorized), one 105-mm gun battalion of two batteries (motorized); one 90/53 gun battalion of two batteries (motorized); two 75/18 self-propelled howizer battalions; 47-mm antitank gun batteries; and three 20-mm antiaircraft-antitank gun batteries.

Unit	Composition	75/27 Guns	105-mm Guns	90/53 Guns	75/18 Guns	47-mm AT Guns	20-mm AA/AT Guns	MG
Regt	Hq							
	Two 75/27 Gun Bns of three Btrys (Mtz)	24						12
	One 105-mm Gun Bn of two Btrys (Mtz)		8					2
	One 90/53 Gun Bn of two Btrys (Mtz)			8			8	2
	Two 75/18 SP Bns				20			12
	47-mm AT Btrys					8		
	Three 20-mm AA/AT Btrys						24	6
	Total	24	8	8	20	8	32	34

FIGURE 17.—Organization of the artillery regiment in the armored division.

b. The 75/18 self-propelled (*semovente*) howitzer equipment is a 75/18 howitzer on an M 13/40 tank chassis.

c. It is believed that the 90/53 gun will eventually be self-propelled on an improved M 13 tank chassis.

d. The 75/27 gun has been in part replaced by the 75/34 gun.

93. Regiment in Alpine division.—*a.* The artillery regiment in the Alpine division (fig. 18) normally consists of a headquarters and two 75/13 pack howitzer battalions. It is estimated that this regiment contains 1,700 officers and enlisted men, 848 animals, and 11 vehicles.

Unit	Composition	75/13 Pk How	MG
Regt	Hq, Two 75/13 Pk How Bns (normal)	24	12
75/13 Pk How Bn	Hq, Three (or two) Btrys	12 (8)	6 (4)
75/13 How Btry	Hq, Four Secs vehicles and Am Tn	4	2

FIGURE 18.—Organization of the artillery regiment in the Alpine division.

b. Each artillery regiment in the Alpine division allots one battalion to each Alpine regiment in the division, and each battalion contains one battery for each battalion in the Alpine regiment. These artillery regiments may be issued 65/17 guns.

c. Each battalion is distinguished by a name, as opposed to a number, in the same way as the Alpine infantry battalions.

94. Regiment in army corps.—*a.* The artillery regiment in an army corps (fig. 19) consists of a headquarters and four (or three) battalions, each uniformly armed, and one antiaircraft battalion. The peacetime strength of such a regiment is estimated to be 80 officers and 2,200 enlisted men.

b. In wartime a regiment may have as many as eight battalions of three or more batteries each. It is probable that the antiaircraft battalion, provided for in peacetime, is no longer included.

c. Most army corps artillery regiments have formed regroupments (*raggruppamenti*) which bear the same number as the parent regiment. In North Africa the *raggruppamento* is the corps artillery pool; in the case of some corps artillery overseas, the parent regiment exists only at the depot in Italy; whereas in other cases the *raggruppamento* has been detached from its corps and sent to a different theater. There are also a number of

RESTRICTED

raggruppamenti which have no corresponding corps artillery regiments.

Unit	Composition	Guns and How	75/46 AA Guns	MG
Regt	Hq			
	Four (or three) Bns	32(24)		16(12)
	AA Bns		12	6
Bn	Hq			
	Two Btrys	8		4
Btry	Hq			
	Four Secs	4		2
AA Bn	MT Hq			
	Three Btrys		12	6
AA Btry	Hq			
	Four AA guns		4	2

FIGURE 19.—Organization of the artillery regiment in an army corps.

d. Weapons include 105/22 and 105/32 guns, and 149/13 and 149/19 howitzers, but the actual allocations of these weapons to battalions is not known.

95. Regiment in an army.—*a.* The artillery regiment in an army consists of a headquarters, four battalions, one tractor unit, a depot, and a workshop. Battalions are very frequently detached and operate independently. Each battalion consists of a headquarters and two or three batteries of uniform armament. Each battery consists of a headquarters and four sections (except if armed with the 305/8 or 305/10 mortar, where there are two sections). There are also four army artillery *raggruppamenti*. The total strength of this regiment is estimated to be approximately 2,000 officers and enlisted men.

b. The tractor unit is responsible for the training of all the driver personnel in the regiment. The material issued to a tractor section is sufficient to move a heavy battery.

c. Weapons include 149/35, 149/40, 152/37, and 152/45 guns; 152/13, 210/22, and 305/17 howitzers, and 210/8, 260/9, 305/8, and 305/10 mortars.

96. Regiment in Frontier Guard.—*a.* Each of the 11 regiments of artillery in the Frontier Guard consists of a headquarters, a varying number of battalions, a varying number of batteries, and a depot. Other battalions and batteries of Frontier Guard artillery belong to the various covering sectors and are independent of the regiments except concerning technical matters. Nothing is known about the organization of the *raggruppamenti* of Frontier Guard artillery which have been identified.

b. A suitable number of tractor units are available for requisition by regimental or battalion headquarters as required.

c. The regiments are equipped with all types of guns, howitzers, and mortars.

97. Antitank units.—The basic antitank unit is the battery; each division has one battery assigned, and sometimes two or even three are assigned. There are many variations in the organization of these units. The following shows a typical allotment of antitank units and 47-mm AT guns to the various types of divisions:

a. Infantry division (binary).	2 Rgts of Inf (of 8 guns each), 1 AT Btry (of 16 guns).
b. Truck-borne infantry division (Libyan type).	1 Bn (of 12 guns).
c. Motorized infantry (Metropolitan type).	1 Btry (of 12 guns).
d. Motorized infantry division (North African type).	2 Rgts of Inf (of 16 guns each), 1 Bn (of 8 guns).
e. Mountain infantry division (binary).	2 Rgts of Inf (of 8 guns each), 1 Btry (of 16 guns).

f. Célere, or mobile (cavalry), division. — 1 Btry (of 8 guns).

g. Armored division — 1 Btry (of 6 guns).

SECTION VIII

ANTIAIRCRAFT ARTILLERY

	Paragraph
Mobile	98
Fixed	99
Warning system	100

98. Mobile.—The artillery arm mans all mobile antiaircraft units, which may be allotted to armies and lower units as required. Regiments, which are for training and administrative purposes, are composed of a varying number of battalions. Battalions, which in practice are the highest operational units, are normally assigned to corps, and batteries to divisions. Battalions normally are composed of a headquarters, three batteries, a searchlight and sound-locator section, and an ammunition and supply section. The strength of the battalion is estimated at 18 officers and 541 enlisted men (including specialists). It is equipped with 78 motor vehicles and 30 bicycles, and 1 with 2 light machine guns for local protection. (For organization of the antiaircraft regiment, see fig. 20; for that of the battery, see fig. 21.)

99. Fixed.—*a. General.*—The Antiaircraft Artillery Militia (*Milízia Artiglieria Controaéri*, or *M. A. C.*) mans all fixed antiaircraft units. This Militia, together with the Coast Defense Artillery Militia (*Milízia Artiglieria Maríttima*, or *C. A. M.*), functions under the command of a lieutenant general of the combined Militias. There is a headquarters of the Antiaircraft Artillery Militia and Coast Defense Artillery Militia, and a central training school. The antiaircraft militia is responsible to the Ministry of Interior with two exceptions: for recruiting, training, discipline, administration, and mobilization of personnel, the militia is under militia headquarters; and it is assumed that the Navy still controls the militia units assigned to the defense of Navy installations. Personnel of both of the militias must be physically fit for the special duties of the Army but unfit for general military duties or first-line duty. Officers and men of the Army assigned to the Militia must be not less than 37 years old; men 30 years old and over, however, if they are specialists, may be assigned to these Militias.

Unit	O	EM	MG	75-mm AA Guns	Bcl	Mtcl	Auto	Auto-carrette	Cargo Trk	Sp Trk
RHQ and Hq Btry	7	65			7	3	3		5	[1] 2
75/27-mm Gun Bn:										
Bn Hq and Hq Btry	3	55			4	6	2		5	
S-L Sec		29								[2] 2
1st Btry	4	130	2	4	8	1	1		7	[3] 3
2d Btry	4	130	2	4	8	1	1		7	[3] 3
3d Btry	4	130	2	4	8	1	1		7	[3] 3
C Tn	3	85			2	1				[4] 15
Total Bn	18	559	6	12	30	10	5		31	26
75/46 Gun Bn:										
Bn Hq and Hq Btry	3	55			4	6	2		5	
S-L Sec		29								[2] 2
4th Btry	4	135	2	4	8	1	1		7	[5] 11
5th Btry	4	135	2	4	8	1	1		7	[5] 11
6th Btry	4	135	2	4	8	1	1		7	[5] 11
C Tn	3	90			2	1			5	[6] 18
Total Bn	18	579	6	12	30	10	5		31	53
Total Regt	43	1,203	12	24	67	23	13		67	81

[1] One radio and communication truck; one machine-shop truck.
[2] Sound locators and trucks.
[3] Two motor caissons; one fire-control truck.
[4] Including ammunition trucks and one machine-shop truck.
[5] Two motor caissons; four tractors; one fire-control truck; four ammunition trucks with trailers.
[6] Including 12 ammunition trucks and 1 machine-shop truck.

FIGURE 20.—Organization of the antiaircraft regiment.

Type of Division	Q	EM	Wpn	Bcl	Mtcl	Saddle Horses	Draft Anl	Pk Anl	Auto	Auto-carrette	Cargo Trk	Wag
Inf Div (binary)	5	117	8	2	7				1	2	18	
Trk-borne Inf Div	5	117	8	2	7				1	2	18	
Mtn Inf Div (binary)	5	272	8	6		1	8	110				4
Mtz Inf Div [1]	8	190	12	4	12				2		34	
Célere Div	5	110	8	2	7				1		9	
Armd Div [1]	8	190	12	4	12				2		34	

[1] Two batteries.

FIGURE 21.—Organization and assignment of 20-mm antiaircraft batteries.

Unit	Composition	Tanks	Men
Regt	Hq and 3 (or 5) Trk Bns	156 or 260	1,450 or 2,350.
Bn	Hq (4 tanks) and 3 Cos	52	450 average.
Co	Hq (1 tank) and 3 Secs	16	150 average.
Sec	5 tanks	5	50 average.

FIGURE 22.—Organization of the light tank regiment.

b. *Organization.*—(1) The Antiaircraft Artillery Militia consists of five headquarters of groups of Antiaircraft Militia legions and 22 headquarters of Antiaircraft Militia legions. Its strength is about 60,000 officers and enlisted men.

(2) The territory of a legion (*legione*) may be divided, depending upon its size, into subordinate areas manned by a command of cohorts (*comando di coorti*). This is composed of men who live in the vicinity of their batteries. Each unit has a small cadre of officers, noncommissioned officers, and specialists who are assigned permanently to it.

(3) Each defense command may have one or more localities (important cities or installations) for which antiaircraft must be provided. Some 450 batteries of 75-mm antiaircraft guns are known to exist. These are mostly old models with relatively short range and with an antiquated system of fire control. But some of

these batteries have gradually acquired modern armament of the types issued to mobile forces or have special types under development. These special types include the 37/54, 76/40, 102-mm, and 105-mm antiaircraft guns, and others. There are also some 540 machine-gun sections, mostly of old model machine guns. The old guns have been gradually replaced by the 12.7-mm machine guns.

100. Warning system.—The Antiaircraft Artillery Militia operates the warning service, which includes a complete system of observation posts along the coast and on islands off the coast and along the land frontiers. The service also includes a communication net connecting the observation posts with information centers, from which it is disseminated to the active and passive antiaircraft defense. The Antiaircraft Artillery Militia is concentrated near more important and vulnerable industrial targets and the larger cities and communication centers. There is no pursuit aviation especially assigned to antiaircraft territorial defense, and Italy has no balloon barrages.

SECTION IX

COAST ARTILLERY

	Paragraph
General	101
Organization	102

101. General.—The coast defense of Italy is under the Coast Defense Artillery Militia (*Milizia Artiglieria Maríttima*, or *M. A. M.*) which, together with the Antiaircraft Artillery Militia (*Milizia Artiglieria Controaéri*, or *M. A. C.*) (see sec. VIII) is under the command of a lieutenant general of the combined militias.

102. Organization.—*a.* The Coast Defense Militia consists of 3 headquarters of groups of Coast Defense Artillery Militia legions, and 14 headquarters of Coast Defense Artillery Militia legions. The strength of this militia is about 30,000 officers and enlisted men. Personnel wear anchors on the sleeve of their uniform, indicating they are under naval command.

b. For organic, disciplinary, and administrative matters, it is responsible to Militia headquarters. For technical matters and those connected with training and employment, it is responsible to the office of the Navy General Staff. The territorial distribution of the Coast Defense Artillery Militia is established by Militia headquarters in agreement with the Ministry of Marine.

c. At each naval zone, sector, or command, the command of a group of artillery units of the Navy for the defense against ships and aircraft, when all units of the group are manned by personnel of the Coast Defense Artillery Militia, is assumed by the highest ranking or senior officer from among the commanders of the units concerned. These tactical commands come directly under their respective Navy headquarters.

d. The Coast Artillery Militia employs equipment furnished by the Navy for antiship and antiaircraft defense of localities, in accordance with instructions issued by the office of the Navy General Staff.

SECTION X

ARMORED TROOPS

	Paragraph
General	103
Organization	104
Classification of tanks	105
Armored division (*divisione corazzata*)	106
Tank regiment	107
Tank battalions	108
Bersaglieri regiment	109
Antitank company	110
Artillery regiment	111
Antiaircraft-antitank battery	112
Mixed engineer and communications battalion (*battaglione del génio e di collegamenti*)	113
Light tank battalion of *célere*, or mobile (cavalry), division	114
Light tank battalion of motorized infantry division	115
Corps or army tank battalions	116
Miscellaneous tank units	117

103. General.—The organization, equipment, and tactics of Italian armored troops have been influenced by the German direction and domination of the Italian military system.

104. Organization.—*a.* Three known armored divisions, plus two motorized divisions, originally made up the Army of the Po and as such were under the direct supervision of the Italian Chief of Staff. In all, the Italians are known to have organized 3 or 4 armored divisions. These *célere*, or mobile (cavalry) divisions have 1 tank regiment each, consisting of 5 battalions of medium tanks. The battalion has a nominal strength of 46 tanks. In addition, there are a number of tank units with infantry divisions. There is also an undetermined number of light tank squadrons (U. S. company) with the 13 cavalry regiments of the Army. Lack of equipment and battle losses have undoubtedly weakened the Italian tank units considerably.

b. The Inspector of Motorization is believed to have control of Italian armored forces in technical and training matters, the operational control being delegated to the army group commanders to which armored divisions are assigned.

c. The armored units of the Italian Army fall into the following categories:

(1) Armored division (*divisione corazzata*).

(2) The so-called tank infantry (*fanteria carrista*).

(3) Groups of light tanks supplied to mobile divisions (personnel drawn from the cavalry).

(4) Tanks in varying numbers to be found within the Frontier Guard and with the Carabinieri.

(5) Independent tank battalions for assignment as corps or army troops.

105. Classification of tanks.—The Italians classify tanks as light (*leggiero*, or *L*), medium (*medio*, or *M*), and heavy (*pesante*, or *P*). The first category includes vehicles up to about 8 tons; the second, those between 8 and 15 tons; and the third, those over 15 tons. The last mentioned are projected only. Types are designated by the appropriate letter followed by the weight figure. The addition of the last two figures of the year of adoption is a further conventional distinguishing mark: for example, L 6/40 or M 11/39.

106. **Armored division** *(divisione corazzata)*.—*a. Composition.*—The Italian armored division, a mechanized force of all arms, normally consists of the following:

(1) Division headquarters.
(2) One Bersaglieri regiment (infantry).
(3) One battery of 47-mm antitank guns (motorized).
(4) One tank regiment.
(5) One artillery regiment.
(6) Two 20-mm antiaircraft batteries (motorized).
(7) One mixed engineer company (artificers and communications).
(8) One medical company.
(9) One commissary company.
(10) Gasoline and oil supply platoon.

b. Theory of employment.—The original tactical concept of the armored division was considered to be that of a mobile reserve to be used in the exploitation of success or to counter enemy penetration. It may also engage in reconnaissance with mobile units, or in wide envelopment of an enemy flank, infiltration through gaps, or assault against a hastily prepared defensive position. This cautious conception of the functions of an armored division, has, no doubt, undergone some modification as a result of the lessons of the present war. The fact remains, however, that Italian tank tactics and training were somewhat rudimentary until the armored divisions came under German command and German training and tactical doctrines were introduced. Since it is weak in inherent infantry, the armored division is organized and trained primarily to operate in conjunction with infantry, motorized, or *célere*, or mobile (cavalry) divisions. It is not designed to operate ahead of the army in the seizure of important terrain, as the Italians assign such missions to the motorized or *célere* divisions. The

ORGANIZATION

armored division is designed for the exploitation of a breakthrough, and also to function as a mobile reserve to be thrown in to use its shock action and fire power to obtain a decision.

c. Subordinate units.—(1) *Personnel.*—The following tabulation shows the estimated strength of the subordinate units of the division:

	Officers	Enlisted men
Headquarters	15	163
Tank regiment	84	1,040
Bersaglieri regiment	53	1,556
Antitank company	6	130
Mixed engineer company	3	155
Artillery regiment	55	1,165
Two 20-mm antiaircraft-antitank batteries	8	190
Division services	12	223
Medical company.		
Commissary company.		
Gas and oil supply platoon.		

(2) *Summary of personnel, armament, and equipment.*—The following tabulation shows the estimated strength of the armored division in personnel, armament, and equipment:

Personnel	4,858
Light automatic weapons	54
Machine guns (exclusive of tanks)	36
47-mm antitank guns (exclusive of tanks)	6
Tank guns (47-mm)	214
20-mm antiaircraft-antitank guns	58
Flame throwers	16
Artillery pieces	24
Tanks	230
Motor transport vehicles	1,534
Automobiles	32
Cargo trucks	220

RESTRICTED

Tractors	54
Special trucks	84
Autocarette (four-wheeled trucks)	67
Motorcycles	[4] 1,077

[4] This is probable only where a fully motorcycle-mounted Bersaglieri regiment is present.

107. Tank regiment.—*a. Composition.*—The tank regiment consists of a headquarters company and five battalions of medium tanks. The total personnel of each regiment is 84 officers and 1,040 enlisted men.

b. Armament and equipment.—The armament and equipment of the tank regiment is as follows:

Machine guns	460
Flame-throwers	16
Tank guns	214
Motorcycles	53
Light tanks	16
Medium tanks	214
Automobiles	6
Cargo trucks	45
Special trucks	64

The Italians have found their light tank unsatisfactory in combat and as rapidly as possible they are supplanting light tanks (Italian designation) with medium tanks, and medium tanks with heavy tanks. Home forces and auxiliaries, presumably, will be furnished with the light tanks.

108. Tank battalions.—It is believed that the Italians are intending to make the fifth battalion a heavy tank battalion when production permits. The basic organization of this heavy battalion will probably be the same as that of the medium. The medium tank battalion consists of a headquarters company and two medium tank companies, with a headquarters platoon and three medium platoons each.

109. Bersaglieri regiment.—*a. Composition.*—The Bersaglieri regiment of the armored division consists of a headquarters and three battalions. The battalion consists of a headquarters, a headquarters platoon, and three companies, each including a headquarters platoon, three rifle platoons (of three sections each), and a machine-gun platoon. Some sources give the Bersaglieri regiment organization as three motorcycle battalions. In Libya this organization was highly flexible and largely dictated by the availability of equipment. It is believed that German influence on Italian organization has resulted more in the truck-motorcycle type of regimental organization.

b. Summary of armament and equipment.—The aggregate strength of the Bersaglieri regiments in armament and equipment is as follows:

Machine rifles	54
Machine guns	24
Motorcycles (for truck-motorcycle type of regiment; 871 motorcycles for all-cycle regiment)	400
Automobiles	3
Autocarette (four-wheeled trucks)	41
Machine-shop trucks	2

110. Antitank company.—*a. General.*—Tables of organization show only one antitank, or support companies per armored division, but two or even three companies have been known to be assigned according to the situation and the material available.

b. Compositions.—The antitank company, with a strength of 6 officers and 130 enlisted men, consists of a headquarters platoon and 3 platoons. Headquarters platoon consists of a headquarters section, a specialist section, and an ammunition section. The regiment has 6 truck-drawn 47-mm guns.

111. Artillery regiment.—*a.* The artillery regiment of the armored division, with a strength of 55 officers and 1,165 enlisted men, consists of a headquarters, a headquarters battery, and two battalions.

b. The battalion consists of a headquarters, a headquarters battery, 3 batteries, and a combat train. The exact composition ot the combat train is not known, but the trains of an army corps artillery regiment are divided into groups of 10 trucks and 20 trailers each, as well as other types of trucks. There is also a depot and a workshop group. A variant of this may be used with the armored division. The battalion has 12 75-mm truck-drawn guns and 6 machine guns. The batteries have 4 guns each.

112. **Antiaircraft-antitank battery.**—Each AA/AT battery consists of a headquarters, 3 platoons (of 2 guns each), and a combat train. The strength of each battery is 4 officers and 95 men. The batteries are motorized, and have twelve 20-mm AA/AT guns, 12 motorcycles, 2 automobiles, and thirty-four cargo trucks.

113. **Mixed engineer and communications battalion** *(battaglione del génio e di collegamenti).*—Its unit strength is as follows:

Officers	3
Enlisted men	155
Motorcycles	11
Automobile	1
Cargo trucks	4
Special trucks	14

114. **Light tank battalion of the *célere*, or mobile (cavalry), division.**—There are three *célere* divisions, each having a light tank battalion of 61 tanks. It is probable that the tanks are of the L 3/35 type, mounting two light machine guns. Its unit strength is as follows:

Officers	21
Enlisted men	270
Machine rifles	16
Machine guns	122
Light tanks	61

Automobile _____ 1
Cargo trucks _____ 4
Special trucks _____ 10

115. Light tank battalion of motorized infantry division.—The organization of this battalion is similar to that of the tank battalion in the armored division. Its unit strength is as follows:

Officers and enlisted men _____ 236
Light tanks (probably L 3/35's) _____ 46
Machine guns _____ 92
Motor vehicles _____ 65
Motorcycles _____ 11

116. Corps or army tank battalions.—As the situation dictates, tank battalions, whenever available, will undoubtedly be attached as corps or army troops. As an example of this, it is known that a battalion of medium (11- to 13-ton) tanks was attached to the truck-borne corps sent to Libya. It is not definitely known how many independent battalions exist, or how many, if any, are in the process of formation in Italy.

117. Miscellaneous tank units.—As obsolete tanks are replaced by the improved models manufactured both in Italy proper and in the captive factories of France, the older models will probably be relegated to home defense units such as the Finance Guard, Frontier Guard, and Royal Carabinieri. Light tank units have already been identified as part of the Frontier Guard organization.

Section XI

ENGINEERS

	Paragraph
General	118
Function	119
Pioneer battalion (*battaglione guastatori*)	120

118. General.—The engineer arm (*arma del génio*) of the Italian Army is under the control of the Inspectorate of Engineers. In peacetime it consisted of an Inspectorate of Engineers, 18 engineer corps headquarters, 18 engineer corps regiments, 2 mining regiments, 2 ponton regiments, 1 railway regiment, 2 workshop units, and 29 pigeon lofts. The most important units are listed in figures 23 and 24.

Unit	Components	O	EM	Remarks
Composite Co, Inf Div	Hq and 5 Secs	6	350	Engineer and communication functions.
Composite Co, Armd Brig	Hq and 4 Secs	3	155	Engineer and communication functions.
Composite Co, Mtz Div	Hq and 4 Secs	7	345	Engineer and communication functions.
Composite Bn, Mtz Div	Hq. 2 Cos, and 1 Sec.	17	505	Engineer and communication functions.
Mtz Bn (*autocarreggiata*)	Hq and 2 Cos	16	465	
Mtz and wagon-transported Bn (*autocarreggiata e carreggiata*).	Hq and 2 Cos	18	485	
Mtz and Pk Bn (*autocarreggiata e someggiata*).	Hq and 2 Cos	18	545	
Wagon-transported Bn (*carreggiata*).	Hq and 2 Cos	16	525	
Wagon-transported and Pk Bn (*carreggiata e someggiata*).	Hq and 2 Cos	18	585	
Pk Bn (*someggiata*)	Hq and 2 Cos	18	725	

FIGURE 23.—Organization of principal engineer units.

119. Function.—Under Italian doctrine, engineers are considered to be technical, rather than combat, troops. Engineer functions are conventional: work communications zones, erection

ORGANIZATION

of obstacles, clearance of obstacles, laying of minefields, water supply, and supply of engineer materials. Also, in the Italian Army, the providing of signal communications and the supplying of hydrogen for captive balloons are engineer functions.

Unit	Components	O	EM	Remarks
Bdg Co (Light bridges)	4 Secs	2	133	
Bdg Co (No. 1 metal bridge).	2 Secs	1	50	
Pon Bn (Light bridges)	Hq and 2 Cos	22	770	16 ponton trucks and 8 trestle trucks.
Pon Bn (Light bridges with Bdg hauling unit).	Hq and 3 Cos	21	695	
Pon Bn (Heavy bridges)	Hq and 2 Cos	18	800	
Pon Bn (metal bridges)	Hq and 2 Cos	25	556	
Aerial ropeway Bn	Hq and 2 Cos	15	474	Aerial ropeway, type A-1, carried on heavy truck.
Bln Sec	1 anchored balloon.	6	100	
Cam Co	8 Secs	7	265	
Electrical Mechanics' Co	Hq and 4 Secs; Co Park and 5 Secs.	7	285	
Fire-fighting Co	Hq and 4 Secs	6	285	
Mining Bn	Hq and 2 Cos	16	505	
Photo Co	1 Sec and 2 Sqds	7	65	
Searchlight operators	3 Secs	6	168	50-cm, 75-cm, and 90-cm searchlights.
W Sup Co	Hq and 5 Secs	7	255	

FIGURE 24.—Organization of special engineer units.

RESTRICTED

Unit and composition	O	EM
Bn:		
Hq		
2 Cos		
Co:		
Hq	2	19
1 Lbr Plat	1	47
3 Pion Plat	3	144
1 Prk		
MT Prk:		
Hq		
1 Sec for Co Hq		
1 Sec for Lbr Plat		
1 Sec for each Pion Plat		

FIGURE 25.—Organization of the assault pioneer battalion.

120. **Pioneer battalion *(battaglione guastatori)*.**—The pioneer battalion (fig. 25) consists of three pioneer shock units (*reparti d'assalto*). The shock units are formed into the following: a wire destruction section, a smoke section, a close-combat section (with light flame-throwers) and a light machine-gun section. The attacks by pioneers (*guastatori*) are nearly always carried out at dawn, the objective having been approached during the night. Assault engineers have been used against tanks at night. Personnel do not lay mines but are trained in removing them should they impede their progress. An Assault Engineer School (*Scuola Guastatori del Génio*) exists at Civitavécchia. It was instituted at the end of March 1940 and organized by Colonel Steiner of the German Army. The Navy has similar shock units which are designated as *semoventi* and *somozzatori*. These naval units work under water.

ORGANIZATION 121-122

Section XII

SIGNAL COMMUNICATIONS

	Paragraph
General	121
Radiotelegraph battalion in army	122
Radiotelegraph company in army corps	123
Signal unit in motorized division	124
Signal unit in mountain division	125
Radiotelegraph battalion in infantry division headquarters	126
Signal units in binary infantry division and in truck-borne infantry division (Metropolitan type)	127
Signal units in *célere*, or mobile (cavalry), division	128
Radiotelegraph battalion in *célere*, or mobile (cavalry), division	129
Signal units in armored brigade	130
Telephone, telegraph, and phototelegraph units	131
Photographic company	132

121. General.—Tables of organization indicate that the Italians depend to a great extent on radio communications, employing them even between the headquarters of higher units. They also make a considerable use of a recently developed optical means of communication, the so-called phototelegraph apparatus. Pigeons and dogs serve as emergency means of communication. But in the Italian Army there is no signal corps as such, signal communications being a part of the engineers, headed by an Inspector, who corresponds to the former Chief of Engineers in the U. S. Army. The engineers, who function as both an arm and a service, in addition to purely engineering functions, provide signal equipment for all arms. The Superior Technical Committee for Military Technical Services and Communications coordinates all studies and experiments relating to communications which are of common interest to the Army, Navy, and Air Force.

122. Radiotelegraph battalion in army.—*a. Organization.*—The organization of the radiotelegraph battalion in an army is shown in figure 26.

Unit	O	EM	Bcl	Mtcl	Mtrcl	Auto	Cargo Trk
Hq	3	15	2			1	2
Rad Tg Ln Co (5 Plats)	4	250	2	1	8	1	[1] 27
Sp Co (5 Plats)	4	200	2	1	9	1	[2] 20
Total	11	465	6	2	17	3	49

[1] Twenty-four of which are special vehicles.
[2] Eleven of which are special vehicles.

FIGURE 26.—Organization of the radiotelegraph battalion in an army.

b. Radiotelegraph liaison company.—The radiotelegraph liaison company has the following equipment:

Platoon	Radio sets
No. 1 (4 sections)	1 type R6
No. 2 (4 sections)	1 type R4
No. 3 (4 sections)	1 type R3
No. 4 (4 sections)	1 type R2
No. 5 (10 sections)	1 type R4–A

c. Special company.—The special company has the following equipment:

Platoon	Radio sets
No. 1 (3 sections)	1 type R. I. 3
No. 2 (3 sections)	1 type R. I. 2
No. 3 (6 sections)	1 type R. A. 2
No. 4 (3 sections)	1 type R. G.
No. 5 (12 sections)	1 (type unknown)

123. Radiotelegraph company in army corps.—*a. Organization.*—The organization of the radiotelegraph company in the army corps is shown in figure 27.

Unit	O	EM	Bcl	Mtcl	Mtrlcl	Auto	Trk
Hq	4	35	2	1	18	3	3
6 Plats		165				¹26	
Total	4	200	2	1	18	29	3

¹ Including 13 special automobiles.

FIGURE 27.—Organization of the radiotelegraph company in an army corps.

b. Signal equipment.—The signal equipment of the company is distributed as follows:

Platoon	Radio sets
No. 1 (4 sections)	1 type R4
No. 2 (6 sections)	1 type R3
No. 3 (6 sections)	1 type R2
No. 4 (8 sections)	1 type R4A
No. 5 (2 sections)	1 type RC-2
No. 6 (4 sections)	1 type RA-2

124. Signal unit in motorized division.—*a.* Communications in the truck-borne infantry division (Libyan type) and in the motorized infantry division are provided by the communication company of a composite engineer battalion for a motorized division. This battalion, with a strength of 5 officers and 225 enlisted men, is divided into a telegraph section, a telegraph section (motor-transported), and a radiotelegraph section.

Unit	O	EM	Pk Anl	Mtcl	Auto-carrette
Tg Sec	1	70	11	3	6
Rad Tg Sec	1	80	21	2	4
Composite Engr Sec	1	75	36	1	33
Total	3	225	68	6	43

FIGURE 28.—Organization of the signal unit in the mountain division.

b. Signal equipment.—The radiotelegraph section is equipped with the following radio sets:

    1 type R5   9 type RF3C
    2 type R4   2 type RI2
    2 type R4–A   2 type RA2

c. General equipment.—The radiotelegraph section also has the following general equipment.

    3 bicycles   1 automobile
    1 motorcycle   8 trucks
    13 motor tricycles   6 special radio trucks

125. Signal unit in mountain division.—*a. Organization.*—Communications in the binary infantry division and in the Alpine division are provided by the telegraph, radiotelegraph, and composite engineer sections of a composite engineer company for mountain divisions, the strength of which unit is shown in figure 28.

b. Radiotelegraph section.—The radiotelegraph section is equipped with the following radio sets:

    2 type R4A   1 type RI2
    8 type RF3A   1 type RAI

c. Composite engineers section.—The composite engineer section is equipped with six 180-mm phototelephones and three searchlights.

126. Radiotelegraph battalion in infantry division headquarters.—*a. General.*—It is believed that a supplementary unit is attached or assigned to division headquarters, according to the practice in the German Army, to provide communications between headquarters and the various units of the division in the event of the failure of the composite engineer company assigned to the division to do so. It has a total strength of 2 officers and 120 enlisted men.

ORGANIZATION   126-129

b. Signal equipment.—The battalion consists of three platoons and two radio posts equipped with he following radio sets:

    1st platoon (2 sections) ---------------------- 1 type RC2
    2d platoon (3 sections) ----------------------- 1 type R3
    3d platoon (10 sections) ---------------------- 1 type R2
    2 radio posts --------------------------------- 1 type RI2
    2 radio posts --------------------------------- 1 type RA2

c. General equipment.—The battalion also has the following transport:

6 pack animals	1 wagon
2 draft animals	1 automobile
2 bicycles	2 radio trucks
17 motor tricycles	

127. Signal units in binary infantry division and in truck-borne infantry division (Metropolitan type).—The exact organization of signal units in binary and motor transportable divisions is not known. The binary division is served by a composite engineer company comprising 6 officers and 133 enlisted men while the motor transportable division is served by a company with 6 officers and 268 enlisted men.

128. Signal units in *célere*, or mobile (cavalry), division.—Communications in this type of division are provided by the telegraph and radiotelegraph sections of the composite engineers company for the *célere* division. The composite company, which includes 2 engineer sections and headquarters, comprises 7 officers and 345 enlisted men. The radio telegraph section is equipped with 12 mobile radiotelegraph stations and 9 radiotelegraph trucks.

129. Radiotelegraph battalion in *célere*, or mobile (cavalry), division.—*a. General.*—There is no positive information as to the exact function of the radiotelegraph battalion in the

107   **RESTRICTED**

célere division. It seems probable, however, that it must serve essentially the same purpose as the similar battalion in the infantry division, referred to in paragraph 7. That is, it provides communication when the composite engineer company fails to do so. It has an estimated strength of 2 officers and 140 enlisted men.

b. Signal equipment.—Radio sets for this battalion are distributed among the four platoons and five radiotelegraph posts as follows:

1st platoon	1 type RS (in automobile)
2d platoon (3 sections)	1 type R4
3d platoon (2 sections)	1 type R4A
4th platoon (8 sections)	1 type RF3C
1 radiotelegraph post	1 type RI3
2 radiotelegraph posts	1 type RA2
2 radiotelegraph posts	1 type RI2

c. General equipment.—The battalion has the following transport:

16 pack animals
2 bicycles
12 motor tricycles
1 automobile
13 trucks (9 of which are special automobiles)

130. **Signal units in armored brigade.**—In the armored division, communications are provided by the radiotelegraph squad which has 32 enlisted men. It is equipped with 1 motorcycle, 2 trucks, and 8 special trucks.

131. **Telephone, telegraph, and phototelegraph units.**—For information regarding the organization of the telephone, telegraph, and phototelegraph units, see

132. **Photographic company.**—The organization of the photographic company is shown in figure 29.

ORGANIZATION

Unit	O	EM	Pk Anl	Bol	Trk	Spec Trk
1 Photo Sec	5	40		2	4	[1] 1
1 Photo Sqd	1	10			1	[2] 1
1 Telephoto Sqd	1	15	5		1	[2] 1

[1] Laboratory truck with trailer.
[2] Photographic laboratory truck.

FIGURE 29.—Organization of the photographic company.

SECTION XIII

CHEMICAL TROOPS

	Paragraph
General	133
Peacetime organization	134
Chemical regiment	135
Mixed chemical group	136
Regimental antigas units	137

133. General.—No doubt the almost total unpreparedness of the Italians for gas warfare in the last war, which resulted in many thousands of deaths and casualties, prompted them to establish a Military Chemical Service (*Servizio Chimico Militare*) in July 1923. Serving both the Navy and Air Force as well as the Army, this service is responsible for chemical warfare in all its forms. A directorate was set up at the Ministry of War, and a number of experimental centers established. Later developments included establishment of the chemical regiment and the mixed chemical group.

134. Peacetime organization.—*a. General.*—The peacetime organization of chemical troops called for a chemical regiment, and a number of separate chemical companies and platoons assigned to army corps and divisions as follows:

b. One mixed chemical company to each army corps, composed of headquarters, one flame-thrower platoon, and as many chemical platoons as there are divisions in the corps.

RESTRICTED

c. One chemical platoon to each mobile (cavalry) division (*divisione célere*), Alpine division, and motorized division. It is considered doubtful that each corps and division had a chemical company or platoon attached, but at least 11 chemical companies have been definitely identified.

135. Chemical regiment.—An official Italian publication in 1940 stated that the chemical regiment, commanded by a colonel, consisted of a headquarters; one chemical battalion, composed of three chemical companies; one mixed battalion, composed of two chemical companies, one officers' training company, and one noncommissioned officers' training company; one flame-thrower battalion, composed of two flame-thrower companies; and one chemical depot. It is uncertain whether this peacetime organization still exists intact, inasmuch as the chemical regiment has been reported, since 1938, to have assumed the functions of a central training school for chemical troops. In wartime the regiment (or parts of it) presumably operates as GHQ or army troops, and it may provide the chemical battalion of the mixed chemical group.

136. Mixed chemical group.—*a. General.*—The nucleus of the war organization appears to be the mixed chemical group, assigned to GHQ, which is reported to consist of one chemical battalion, several chemical company battalions, several flame-thrower battalions, and one chemical mortar group.

b. Chemical battalion.[5]—This battalion, only one of which is known to exist, consists of two heavy companies and one light company. The heavy companies are said to be provided with large stocks of toxic gases, together with the equipment and protective clothing necessary for their dispersion, as well as meteorological apparatus. The light company, on the other hand, is provided with a large stock of toxic smoke and teargas generators. It is possible that this battalion could function as a depot for

---

[5] Some documents refer to this battalion as *nebu*, but this may possibly be a typographical error for *nube* (smoke—literally, "cloud").

issuing and filling chemical weapons, but from the nature of its equipment, it appears more likely that it is an offensive unit.

c. Chemical and flame-thrower battalions and chemical mortar group.—The chemical and flame-thrower battalions provide companies, and the chemical mortar group provides batteries on the scale of one for each army corps. Thus, whereas in peacetime each army corps possessed a mixed chemical company composed of chemical, smoke, mortar, and flame-thrower sections, in wartime it possesses one chemical company, one flame-thrower company, and one mortar battery. These units presumably may be assigned to divisions as required.

d. Chemical company.—Chemical company is believed to consist of two platoons, one of which is trained and equipped for both contamination and decontamination, the other for smoke generation. Apparently, these chemical companies have replaced the smoke companies described in the Italian *Smoke Training Manual* (1933), inasmuch as enemy documents examined in January 1941 contain no mention of the existence of any smoke other than the smoke platoons of the chemical companies.

e. Alpine chemical company.—Little is known of the Alpine divisional chemical company, except that it has 4 platoons, with a total strength of 5 officers and 223 enlisted men, and carries larger stocks of mustard gas and chemical mines than the ordinary chemical company.

137. Regimental antigas units.—*a. General.*—The existence of regimental antigas platoons and sections, which may or may not be special chemical units has been determined, but it is certainly probable that they consist of regimental personnel who have received special training in antigas duties.

b. Antigas platoons.—Antigas platoons are provided on the scale of one per regiment in peacetime and one per battalion in wartime. The platoon, composed of 1 officer and 46 enlisted men, is organized in sections, which can be assigned to companies.

They are equipped to assist in antigas measure, and to carry out immediate repairs to gas masks and protective clothing.

c. Decontamination sections.—Decontamination sections are allotted on the scale of one to each GHQ, army, corps, and division. Each section consists of a headquarters platoon (of 1 officer and 12 enlisted men), two decontamination platoons (each of 1 officer and 18 enlisted men), and one repair and supply platoon. The personnel of the section are equipped with protective clothing for their task of protecting and decontaminating headquarters and other important areas.

SECTION XIV

MOTOR TRANSPORT AGENCIES

	Paragraph
General	138
Automobile Corps (*Corpo Automobilistico*)	139
Automobile Service (*Servizio Automobilistico*)	140

138. General.—The Italians follow the practice of keeping motor transport under corps or army control. The size and composition of motor transport units are dictated by the situation rather than by any hard and fast organization.

139. Automobile Corps (*Corpo Automobilistico*).—Supervision of mechanical transport comes under the Automobile Corps, which comprises motor transport centers (*autocentri*), made up of a depot, a stores office, and one or two motor transport groups (*autogruppi*). There are smaller sections (*autosezione*) consisting of 24 vehicles in four squads (*squadre*). Organization is extremely elastic. This organization is general throughout the Army, and is not designed especially for any higher unit.

140. Automobile Service (*Servizio Automobilistico*).—Recently there has been formed an Automobile Service to provide for the supply, evacuation, and repair of motor transport vehicles, which are numerous and of wide variety.

ORGANIZATION 140

a. Supply.—The supply of gasoline comes from central depots to army automobile parks, and from these to the divisional fuel section (*sezione carburanti*). These sections carry a variable number of fuel and oil units. A fuel and oil unit is one sufficient to run a vehicle 50 km (about 31 miles).

b. Evacuation and repair.—The responsibility for the evacuation and repair of motor vehicles is the concern of the automobile park, which establishes forward mobile workshops, fixed workshops in the communications zone, and a workshop at army headquarters for major repairs.

Chapter 4

SERVICES, SUPPLY, AND TRANSPORTATION

	Paragraphs
SECTION I. Central organization	141-144
II. Services	145-152
III. Particular Services	153-169
IV. Transportation	170-173

SECTION I

CENTRAL ORGANIZATION

	Paragraph
Assistant Chief of Staff for Intendance	141
Inspectorates	142
Territorial and field administration	143
Procurement	144

141. Assistant Chief of Staff for Intendance.—One of the three sections into which the Italian General Staff is divided comes under the Assistant Chief of Staff for "Intendance" (*Intendenza*). In Italian parlance, "Intendance" signifies all departments of supply and transport. The Assistant Chief of Staff for Intendance controls organization, mobilization, transportation, and the Services. The Intendant General's Office is designed to combine in one body the functions of procuring and issuing ordnance stores, and storing and issuing supplies, and to provide for certain phases of their transportation. On all such matters, the Intendant General is directly responsible to the Supreme Command.

142. Inspectorates.—In the Italian Army, an "inspector" corresponds roughly to the chief of an arm or service in the U. S. Army. Inspectors are consulting officers for the Under Secretary of War and the Chief of Staff on matters pertaining to the administration, training, organization, armament, and equipment of their arms and services. There are Inspectorates of Artillery, Infantry, Engineering, Motorization, Animal and Veterinary Service, Commissary Service, Alpini, and *Céleri*, or mobile (cavalry), troops.

143. Territorial and field administration.—The Italian Army maintains a system of territorial commands in order to facilitate mobilization and to free the commanders of armies, corps, and divisions from administrative responsibility. Personnel of the territorial commands are distinct from the field armies and remain at their posts when the latter move to a theater of operations. The Italian supply services are organized to function both in the territorial corps areas and with the forces in the field.

144. Procurement.—*a. General.*—Procurement of supplies is the responsibility of the General Commissariat for War Manufacturers and not that of any commander of an area. This Commissariat was instituted under the direct control of the Head of the Government (*Capo del Governo*) for the purpose of regulating and directing activities relating to the manufacture of war supplies and equipment. It coordinates all procurement for the three armed services (Army, Navy, and Air Force) and is responsible for developing the supply resources of the country. Each of the armed services has its own service for the distribution of its supplies.

b. Method of purchase.—The usual method for the purchase of military supplies is by negotiated contract. Before the institution of the General Commissariat for War Manufacturers, there existed a Central Purchasing Board in the Ministry of War which determined the specifications, quality, quantity, and methods of purchase of supplies; these were common to all branches of the armed forces—food, forage, etc. Actual purchases were then made through the local organizations of the Commissariat Corps. Purchases of materials not common to all branches were made directly from the manufacturers by the different branches and by the supply services within the branches. At present it is not known how much these methods have been changed by the new system or how much the responsibility for individual purchases has been shifted from the various branches to the central organization.

SECTION II

SERVICES

	Paragraph
Chief Services	145
Other Services	146
Mission of Services and their fields of activity	147
Field Services	148
Territorial Services	149
Control of Field Services	150
Control and allotment of Services within different types of units	151
Scheme of supply	152

145. Chief Services.—*a.* The chief Services of the Italian Army are as follows:

(1) Commissariat Service (*Servízio di Commissariato*).
(2) Transport Service (*Servízio di Trasporto*).
(3) Lines of Communication Service (*Servízio delle Tappe*).
(4) Automobile Service (*Servízio Automobilístico*).
(5) Administrative Service (*Servízio d'Amministrazione*).
(6) Artillery Service (*Servízio d'Artiglieria*).
(7) Engineer Service (*Servízio del Génio*).
(8) Chemical Service (*Servízio Chímico*).
(9) Medical Service (*Servízio Sanitário*).
(10) Veterinary Service (*Servízio Veterinário*).

b. Each of these Services has one Inspectorate or Directorate at the Ministry of War and others in the territorial corps headquarters which are to serve all troops, territorial districts, and units within the particular area.

146. Other Services.—*a.* In addition to the above, the following Service organizations exist:

(1) Chaplains' Service (*Servízio dell'Assistenza Spirituale*).

(2) Geographical Service (*Istituto Geográfico Militare*).
(3) Water Service (*Servízio Idrico*).
(4) Timber Service (*Servízio di Legnami*).
(5) Road and Water Service (*Servízio delle Strade e Servízio dell'Acque*).
(6) Postal Service (*Servízio Postale e Telegráfico*).
(7) Judge Advocate's Service (*Servízio della Giustízia Militare*).

147. Mission of Services and their fields of activity.—The principal task of the Services is to supply the fighting forces with the necessary means for living, moving, and fighting. They must also remove from the zone of operations all that becomes unnecessary, unserviceable, or burdensome to combat. In order to perform this function, the Services are subdivided into Field Services, which are under the military authorities and operate within the zone of operations, and Territorial Services, which remain under the territorial authorities.

148. Field Services.—These constitute a part of the army of operations, generally disposed in the zone where it operates, and join the Territorial Services to the fighting units through supplies and evacuations.

a. First-line units.—These are assigned to army corps, to divisions, and to the Alpine regiments. They provide for the more direct and urgent needs of the troops. They may be divided into smaller units and are characterized by mobility.

b. Second-line units.—These are assigned to the army. They consist in particular of army stores and the means of transport by road. They supply the first-line units, and may supply the troops directly where this seems necessary or advantageous. They receive personnel and materials to be evacuated, provide repairs, and carry out major salvaging operations.

c. Reserve units.—Reserve units are either directly subordinate to the high command or are assigned to armies. They consist of central depots (dumps). They furnish supplies and make evacuations for the units in front of them only in unexpected cases, or, in the case of the territorial units, where there is an interruption in the supply operations of the army stores.

149. Territorial Services.—The territorial Services procure, collect, and forward to the Field Services the means for conducting operations. Field Services form the link between the Territorial Services and the operating troops; they must supply the troops with materials obtained from the Territorial Services and not obtained in the zone of operations.

150. Control of Field Services.—The Services are organized and administered through a triple organization: "coordinative," "directive," and "executive."

a. Coordinative organization.—This is represented in every unit by the unit commander. For this purpose the Commander-in-Chief makes use of the Intendant General, while in each army the commander makes use of the army Intendant. The coordinative organization is charged with—

(1) Acquiring knowledge of operations being carried out or planned, in order to be able to organize the necessary services.

(2) Being informed of the efficiency and location of the means assigned to the unit.

(3) Preparing ahead of time the necessary means in order that the Services can meet the exigencies of the operation.

(4) Maintaining contact with the commander (coordinative organization) of the next higher unit and always keeping him informed of the condition of the Services.

(5) Issuing orders concerning all Services in the unit and their coordination.

(6) Subdividing the available services within the unit.

b. Directive organization.—In the large units each Service comes under a separate directive organization (headquarters, office of inspectors, service director, assigned officers), which is charged with the efficiency of the Service.

SERVICES, SUPPLY, AND TRANSPORTATION 150-151

c. Executive organization.—Executive organizations are variously assigned to the units and are charged with execution of orders received concerning the functioning of the Services. These executive organizations include—

(1) Headquarters of the supply stores assigned to large units and to Alpine regiments.
(2) Headquarters of specialist sections.
(3) Specialist sections.

d. Command.—Both the directive and executive organizations come under a double subordination:

(1) The headquarters of the unit to which they are assigned, for employment and discipline.
(2) The directive organization of the same Service within the higher unit, for employment and administration.

In case of disagreement, the command subordination always takes precedence.

151. Control and allotment of Services within different types of units.—*a. Army.*—Being the large unit of logistical importance, the army must achieve complete independence, and consequently has all the Services complete within itself. At army headquarters there is an Intendant who represents the Intendant General and controls all the Services, including the Artillery and Engineer Services. His office is the center which handles the organization and distribution of all means for life and combat. The army receives supplies directly from the territorial area and possesses all kinds of transportation means. Resources are kept pooled as much as possible; all transport, except unit transport, remains within the Transport Service and is allotted to units and other Services only for specific tasks. Under the Intendant's control, each Service estabilshes supply depots (magazines) in the army area; additional reserve depots insure the logistic freedom of the army. The Intendant does not normally exercise direct control within corps areas, but as the amount of transport allotted to each corps is entirely at his discretion, his control is practically effective up to delivery points.

b. Corps.—(1) The Services assigned to the corps are of considerable size, but are highly mobile because of the tactical character of the unit. As a rule, the corps has the personnel and means necessary for daily life and for the first necessities of combat, in addition to a small reserve of foodstuffs and materials. For those materials (for example, artillery and engineer) which may be required in carrying out tactical operations, a number of distributing points are organized, and additional services are assigned whenever necessary.

(2) The Chief of Staff of the corps is also the director of certain Services (Chemical, and Postal, etc.), but he is assisted by the chiefs of other Services who are on the corps staff. Each corps has the following units which operate under the chief of the respective service on the staff:

(*a*) One artillery technical section, including a mobile repair shop.

(*b*) One engineer park and mobile repair shop.

(*c*) One medical company.

(*d*) One commissary company, with as many sections as there are divisions of the corps, plus a section for corps troops.

c. Division.—The division is the smallest of the large units. It has a tactical character and is normally *encadrée* within the corps. Services are limited to those necessary for daily life, since the division must be highly maneuverable.

(1) The Chief of Staff of the division is charged with the direction of part of the Artillery Service (small arms and ammunition), and with Chemical, Transportation, and Postal Services. Special chiefs may be assigned to the division in case Services of a technical character (Medical, Commissariat, and Veterinary) are needed, or else divisional headquarters of the army (artillery and engineers) take care of them. Additional means can be assigned whenever necessary. The *célere*, or mobile (cavalry), division has a motor truck section.

(2) The Services assigned to the division are one medical section, one supply section, and one chemical warfare section. To these may be added field hospitals, infirmaries for men and animals, and distributing posts for ammunition and engineer material.

d. Alpine regiment.—The Alpine regiment has its own artillery and all necessary Services, so that from a logistic point of view it closely resembles a small division. It is normally under the direct orders of the corps and in certain cases comes under those of the army, and it possesses sufficient agencies for contact with the Services of the large units. To it are assigned such elements of the Services as are necessary for daily life, particularly Medical, Commissariat, Artillery, Transportation, and Postal. In certain cases the Services of the Alpine regiment are more extensive than those of the division: a section of the Transport Service comprising a column of pack animals and wagons, as well as a motor truck section, is assigned to the Alpine regiment but not to the division; field hospitals, which are not normally assigned to divisions, are also assigned to the Alpine regiment.

152. Scheme of supply.—*a. General.*—Supplies come from the rear or are obtained from local resources. Those coming from the rear are distributed through supply stores.

b. Stores.—The supply stores assigned to large units are classified as first-line stores, second-line stores, and reserve stores.

(1) *First-line stores.*—First-line stores must statisfy the immediate needs of fighting troops. They are assigned to Alpine regiments, corps, and divisions. Their characteristics are mobility and the possibility of being divided, so that the parts can follow the troops in their movements.

(2) *Second-line stores.*—Second-line stores must supply the first-line stores, and, if necessary, must supply the troops directly. They also receive the material to be removed and are charged with repairs. They are assigned to armies, and include army supply stores and various transportation means. These army supply stores with limited mobility may be divided, and

their parts sent to different localities. Their location depends on the character of the operation, and on the availability of railroads and roads. As a rule, they are established neither too close to the first-line units (which might impede their action) nor too far away (which would render more difficult the daily supplying of first-line stores). Whenever possible, they are close to a railroad station and to good roads. These stores are supplied by territorial stores directly, but in exceptional cases can be supplied from reserve stores.

(3) *Reserve stores.*—Reserve stores may be assigned to armies, or remain under the Supreme Command, in which case they serve two or more armies. They are central supply stores and are located at important railroad centers. They are supplied from territorial stores and return old material to the territorial stores. In general, the material in each supply store is divided into small lots which are assigned to the mobile sections following the troops.

c. Requisitions.—(1) Requisitions for materials are made in each unit by the directive organization of the particular service, which orders what is needed both by the troops and by the supply stores. The requisitions are forwarded, through channels, to the army directive organization, which issues orders for the filling of requisitions from the army supply stores (second-line stores).

(2) Supplies for the army stores are requested by the army Intendant from the Intendant General or from the territorial authorities.

d. Local resources.—Decisions regarding the exploitation of local resources are made by the Intendant General or by the army Intendants, whose decisions are enforced by special boards appointed in each case. The resources requisitioned or purchased are collected at special centers or at first-line supply stores.

SERVICES, SUPPLY, AND TRANSPORTATION

SECTION III
PARTICULAR SERVICES

	Paragraph
Commissariat Service (*Servizio di Commissariato*)	153
Transport Service (*Servizio di Trasporto*)	154
Lines of Communication Service (*Servizio della Tappe*)	155
Automobile Service (*Servizio Automobilistico*)	156
Administrative Service (*Servizio di Amministrazione*)	157
Artillery Service (*Servizio d'Artiglieria*)	158
Engineer Service (*Servizio del Génio*)	159
Chemical Service (*Servizio Chimico*)	160
Medical Service (*Servizio Sanitário*)	161
Veterinary Service (*Servizio Veterinário*)	162
Spiritual Assistance, or Chaplains' Service (*Servizio dell' Assistenza Spirituale*)	163
Geographical Service (*Istituto Geográfico Militare*)	164
Road and Water Services (*Servizio della Strado e Servizio dell'acque*)	165
Water Service (*Servizio Idrico*)	166
Timber Service (*Servizio di Legnami*)	167
Postal Service (*Servizio Postale e Telegráfico*)	168
Judge Advocate's Service (*Servizio della Guistizia Militare*)	169

153. Commissariat Service *(Servizio di Commissariato).*
a. Functions.—This Service provides rations, forage, clothing, equipment, barracks, and fuel to troops, and handles the removal and recovery of these materials when damaged or unserviceable. In the Italian Army, the Commissariat Service performs the functions of the U. S. Quartermaster Corps. It distributes supplies in bulk to the tactical organizations, where the storage and issue is handled by line troops. The administrative services, including the Commissariat Service organization, remain in the zone and continue to function under the territorial organization which takes over when the combat troops move to the theater of operation.

b. Organization.—(1) *Directorate General (Direzione generale dei servizi logistici) and Inspectorate at the Ministry of War.*— The Inspector General of the Commissariat Service is a counselor

RESTRICTED

for the War Ministry in all executive matters concerning the Service, and for the Chief of Staff of the Army in all questions concerning the organization and functioning of the Commissariat Service and the training of personnel. As regards studies and advisory functions, he submits plans and opinions on the organization of the Service and the training of personnel; reports on the requirements of the Service, necessary purchases and costs; establishes rules for technical operation and upkeep of establishments; makes suggestions for new matériel and supervises tests of matériel; takes part in the compilation and revision of regulations and technical instructions concerning the service; makes directive rules regarding the work of the commissary personnel and advises the Minister on questions of the distribution of personnel: and supervises tests of the technical abilities of civilians to be employed in the service.

(2) *Zone inspectors.*—In 1940 there were two zone inspectors. They assist and take orders from the Inspector General, make inspections of the Commissary Services, supervise and check on supplies, and coordinate the work in their zones.

(3) *Directorates at corps headquarters.*—These are responsible for supervising the organization and functioning of the Service in their area in accordance with orders from higher authority; they insure the supply of foodstuffs and materials; request necessary transportation means for supplies and removals; make recommendations as to variation in rations according to the availability of foodstuffs, etc.; make recommendations for the best use of local resources; organize and direct the salvage service; forward through channels requests for personnel; recommend officers for assignments, and inspect the commissary service within the unit.

(4) Supply companies (*sezioni sussistenza*).—These are executive organizations with divisions, Alpine regiments, corps headquarters, base railheads, etc.

(5) *Other units.*—These include organizations and detached sections which are determined by Royal decree upon recommen-

dation of the Minister of War in agreement with the Finance Minister. Still other organizations include—

(*a*) Military bakeries and mills located with all army corps and with most divisions.

(*b*) Military hardtack units produce all hardtack for the army for war needs.

(*c*) Military rations depots with all army corps and divisions.

(*d*) Military port and interior refrigerator plants for storing imported meats.

(*e*) Plants for preserved foodstuffs. (These units have turned out tinned meat, *Chiarizia* soups, condensed broth, and sauces in tins.)

(*f*) Plants for the production of concentrated forage. (These plants were created to eliminate the importation of foreign oats for storage.)

(*g*) Military forage and fuel depots at the sites of army corps and divisions.

(*h*) Military salvage depots, located with army corps and divisions and at all garrisons. (These repair cloth, wooden and iron articles, remake mattresses, etc.)

(*i*) Military clothing and equipment units, for studying military uniforms and uniform models for distribution to regimental tailors and for manufacturing considerable numbers of shoes for troops.

(*j*) Central military clothing and equipment depots for testing and distributing to all regiments material required for clothing and equipment stocks.

(*k*) Wool requisition service.

c. Supply media.—The location of plants, centers of production in the territorial zone, storehouses for foodstuffs, forage, etc., and the possibility of using local resources make the system very elastic. As a rule, however, territorial authorities forward supplies from production plants to central reserve depots or to army storehouses. When army stores must be supplied from central depots, special trains are organized, each train carrying a day's ration for the total strength of the army. The central stores are used only in exceptional circumstances, however, and must be replenished immediately. Supply depots (*magazzini*) are formed in accordance with instructions from the army Intendant. If the situation is stable, supplies are sent forward daily from the supply depots under arrangements made by the army Intendant, who establishes the hours and order of issues and determines the roads to be followed to distributing posts, transport being provided by the Transport Service. The supply column proceeds to divisional distribution posts (*posti di distribuzione ed avviamento*) fixed by the corps offices of the Transport Service. Here the supplies are handed over to the supply sections which break bulk and issue to lower echelons. Beyond the distributing posts, supplies are transported by the receiving units. If a line of communications is too long to make this system workable, advance supply depots will probably be formed on the scale of one per army corps.

d. Ration situation in the field.—The normal ration situation in the field is—

(1) Unexpired portion of day's ration with unit.
(2) Two reserve (iron) rations on the man.
(3) One day's ration in divisional supply section.

There are thus 3 to 4 days' rations within the division. Alpine regiments carry another 2 days' rations in a special supply column.

e. Stationary situations.—When stationary for long periods, temporary foodstuff stores may be organized within corps and divisions. The organization, size, and functioning of these stores is determined by headquarters. When corps and units remain stationary for long periods, the supply sections build up a supply of materials sufficient for a long period, and the supply may be repeated once a week instead of daily.

f. Rations on the march.—On the march, the troops normally receive food and forage at the end of each march, from supply sections. When local resources are used, the supply sections or the troops themselves are charged with slaughtering cattle.

g. Uniforms and equipment.—In the case of uniforms and equipment for the troops, of materials for supply sections and of the means for making camp, transporting water, and clerical work, the supply is handled somewhat differently. The central military clothing and equipment depots or the arm stores are supplied by the territorial plants as in the case of food and forage. The army Intendant is responsible for distribution on the basis of requisitions submitted by the units. Supplies are either sent to selected localities where units may call for them or they are delivered directly to the units. This service also takes care of the salvage of old uniforms and equipment. Special centers are organized where units can forward all salvaged uniforms and equipment. These centers send them to the army depots which take care of disinfection, washing and repairing, etc., if facilities are available. Otherwise the centers send everything direct to territorial plants designated by the Intendant General.

h. Local Resources.—Headquarters of large units may authorize the requisition and purchase of linen, shoes, and other materials from local resources. Only in special cases may smaller units be authorized to secure the same objects locally.

154. Transport Service *(Servizio di Trasporto).*—*a. Function.*—This service is charged with the transportation of troops and matériel and includes air transport, rail and water transport, motor transport, and animal transport. The intendant General and the army Intendants must decide as to the coordination between these different methods of transportation. Headquarters of large units decide as to the transportation which is necessary. The Transport Service furnishes the data on which the decisions are based.

b. Subdivisions.—The Service is subdivided into rail and water transport, air transport, and ordinary transport, which includes motor transport, wagon transport, pack transport, and cable railways. The different branches come under the same directive organizations (military transportation delegations) but have different executive organizations.

(1) *Rail and water transport (trasporti ferroviari e per via acquea).*—(*a*) This Service is controlled by general headquarters through the Directorate of Rail and Water Transport, the territorial executive organs being military commands at railroad stations, embarkation officers at ports, military ticket offices, and the railway regiment of engineers.

(*b*) This Service controls the employment of railroad lines, the means for river and canal navigation, and the means for sea navigation furnished by the Ministry of Communications, in accordance with military demands. It is also in charge of the maintenance and improvement of rail and water communications and the erection of military field railroads.

(*c*) After mobilization is completed the railroad net is subdivided into—

> *1.* The net within the zone of operations, including all lines within the zone and those in the territorial zone which have a very great importance for war operations;
> *2.* The net within the territorial zone, including all other lines.

(*d*) The dividing line between the two nets is determined by the Supreme Command. The stations on the boundary belong to the net within the zone of operations, where the net is controlled by the Supreme Command, the army Intendants, and the army transport directorates.

(2) *Air Transport Service (trasporti per via aerea).*—This Service has the tasks of carrying personnel, material, and stores and of evacuating casualties. In practice it is probably very loosely organized.

(3) *Ordinary Transport Service (trasporti per via ordinária).*—(*a*) This Service is responsible for the transportation of troops, services, and matériel. It directs the coordination of

SERVICES, SUPPLY, AND TRANSPORTATION   154

all means of transport, including rail, and water transport, and organizes the transhipment and unloading of matériel. The basic principles on which it is organized are "central control" and "pooling of resources." There is little decentralization below the Army Transport Directorates. Corps have a definite allotment of motor transport which may be withdrawn and replaced by other transport as required.

(*b*) Mechanical transport is provided by the Motor Transport Corps, which includes:

1. Motor transport centers, consisting of a headquarters, a depot, and a stores office. One center is assigned to each corps.
2. A variable number of motor transport groups, each consisting of 2 or more companies which in turn are divided into 3 or 4 motor transport sections (*autosezione*), light or heavy, each of 24 vehicles.
3. An independent group for every motorized and mobile division. Under the peacetime organization a motor transport workshop of the Army and an independent office for motor transport supplies were also included. In wartimes, the units above the *autosezione* are elastic and have no definitely fixed organization; sections are combined into *autoreparti*, *autogruppi*, and *autoraggruppamenti* according to requirements. There is no specific divisional motor transport unit or controlling organ, except in motorized and mobile divisions; at corps headquarters there is a unit called *autodrappello*. Control is exercised from army headquarters as in the other services.

(*c*) The Transport Service also provides for road organization and discipline by means of road movement battalions and light aid detachments assigned to armies.

(d) The Technical Service comprises—

1. A superior directorate of the Technical Service and Motor Transport Corps;
2. A center for the studying of motor transportation problems.

(4) *Moving of units by motor transport and motor transport loads.*—(a) *Moving of units.*—The motor transport assigned to units is for the transport of matériel. Extra motor transport needed to move troops is supplied in the case of motorized, mobile, and armored divisions, from the divisional motor transport detachment or group, and in the case of truck-borne divisions from the corps motor transport center.

In calculating the amount of motor transport needed to move a given unit or formation it is estimated that the material-carrying trucks will each carry in addition 5 men. Pack animals are carried in heavy trucks with two-wheeled trucks attached, at the rate of 4 to 5 animals per truck. Troop-carrying trucks have an average capacity of 25 men. Thus the total motor transport required to move an infantry division is estimated to be approximately 1,250.

(b) *Motor transport loads.*—Motor transport loads are shown in figure 30.

155. Lines of Communication Service (*Servízio della Tappe*).—This Service is concerned with the maintenance of the lines of communication, the protection of vulnerable points, and the evacuation and recovery of material.

156. Automobile Service (*Servízio Automobilístico*).—*a.* This provides for the supply, repair, and evacuation of motor transport Service and its technical care.

b. Gasoline and oil are supplied from the central depots to army automobile parks and from these to the divisional "fuel and oil unit." The quantity provided is that needed to allow each type of vehicle or formation to travel 50 km.

SERVICES, SUPPLY, AND TRANSPORTATION

Type of truck	Load		Speed in kilometers per hour	
	Men	Material (kg)	Single vehicles	Columns (average)
Light:				
Infantry Truck	10 to 12	1,000	40	25
OM4 OMF	12 to 15	1,200	60	30
Fiat 618 CM	12 to 15	1,250	65	30
Spa 25 C 10	16 to 20	1,800	50	25
Fiat 612 P	20 to 25	2,500	43	25
Spa 38 R	20 to 25	2,500	52	25
Ceirano 47 CM	20 to 25	3,000	45	25
Bianchi Mediolanum 36	20 to 25	3,000	55	25
OM, CRD	20 to 25	3,000	51	25
Isotta Fraschini D 70 NM	20 to 25	3,000	56	25
Heavy:				
Ceirano 50 CM	20 to 25	5,000	25	18
Lancia RO.NM	24 to 30	5,000	32	20
RO BM	24 to 30	5,000	39	22
Fiat 633 NM	24 to 30	5,000	30	20
Fiat 633 GM	24 to 30	3,500	28	18
Isotta Fraschini D 80 NM	24 to 30	5,000	34	20
OM 3 BOD	24 to 30	5,000	51	23
Giant:				
Fiat 634 N	28 to 32	7,000	40	20
3 RO Lancia	28 to 32	6,500	43	22

FIGURE 30.—Table of motor transport loads.

c. For evacuation and repair the automobile park establishes forward mobile workshops, fixed workshops on the line of communications, and a central workshop for large scale repairs at army headquarters. Army Intendance is responsible for control of the repair organization and replacement of motor transport in units as necessary, but the actual work is done by the Automobile Service.

RESTRICTED

157. Administrative Service (*Servízio di Amministrazione*).—This Service is responsible for the administration and account of higher units. It has a Directorate General at the Ministry of War and administrative offices at corps headquarters. Its principal functions are—

a. To direct and coordinate the administration of all mobilized units.

b. To provide for pay and accounts and the control of expenditure.

c. To keep the civil and criminal records of soldiers.

This Service was constituted to obviate the inconvenience of treating units in the field as administratively dependent on their territorial depots, to relieve the Commissary Service of the responsibility for accounts and to control expenditure.

158. Artillery Service (*Servízio d'Artiglieria*).—*a. Function.*—This Service is charged with the study, production, supply, maintenance, storage, and distribution of arms, ammunition, armored vehicles, explosives, and harness needed by the Army. It includes two branches: the territorial branch and the technical branch.

b. Organization.—The Artillery Service is organized as follows:

(1) The Directorate General of the Service functions under the operational control of the Intendant General.

(2) Within each army, the army Intendant is responsible for the coordination of the Service. He has operational control and issues instructions for the establishment of supply depots. At army headquarters the directive organization is the superior Artillery Service Directorate. Supplies from the Army depots are issued by the Directorate upon requisition from other units.

(3) At corps headquarters there is no directorate as for other Services, the corresponding duties being carried out by corps artillery headquarters and the corps Chief of Staff. Artillery headquarters supervises the supply of artillery ammunition, and the Chief of Staff is in charge of the supply ammunition for small

automatic arms. Through these organizations the allotment of available ammunition among dependent units and the order of distribution is determined.

(4) An army artillery service depot consists of a department for arms and equipment, an ammunition department, and a workshop. It normally has on hand 4 days' supply of ammunition for all weapons within the army, and draws on a Central depot (*depósito centrale d'artiglieria*) for replenishments.

(5) The Technical Branch (*Servizio Técnico Armi e Munizioni*) is charged with the study, selection, and manufacture of guns and other artillery matériel. It includes the following installations (as of in 1939):

(*a*) Three Army arsenals (located at Naples, Turin, and Piacenza) for the manufacture and repair of guns, carriages, projectiles, harness, and ordnance equipment.

(*b*) One small arms manufacturing plant at Terni with a subsidiary plant at Gardone.

(*c*) Two small arms ammunition plants at Capua and Bologna.

(*d*) One fuze manufacturing plant at Rome, with a subsidiary plant at Torre Annunziata.

(*e*) One powder plant at Fontana Liri.

(*f*) One plant at Rome for the manufacture of optical and fire control instruments.

(*g*) One laboratory at Piacenza for loading artillery projectiles.

(*h*) One projectile plant at Genoa.

(*i*) One plant at Pavia for the manufacture and repair of engineer supplies.

(*j*) One plant for manufacture and repair of radio and communication equipment at Rome.

c. Method of supply.—Requisitions for ammunition supplies are made as follows:

(1) For small and automatic arms, for infantry accompanying guns, and for hand grenades, requisitions are submitted by regimental headquarters through divisional headquarters to corps

headquarters, where they are consolidated by the the corps General Staff and forwarded to the Army Directorate.

(2) For artillery, requisitions are forwarded from batteries through regimental headquarters to corps artillery where they are consolidated and forwarded to the army Intendance, which arranges for supply. Demands are based on the basis of a day's fire (250 rounds for small calibers, 150 for medium, 100 for heavy, and 50 for super-heavy) or a portion of a day's fire.

d. Distribution posts and points.—(1) The army Artillery Directorate supplies the distributing posts of the corps, divisions, etc., from its own depot, from the central ammunition depot, or from supplies arriving from territorial arsenals or depots.

(2) The distributing points are determined by the army Intendant but are organized by the Chiefs of Staff and artillery headquarters of the smaller units. They should be located within a convenient distance of the army depot, close to good roads so that they can be reached by truck columns. Transport is provided by the Transport Service Directorate at army headquarters acting in accordance with instructions from the army Intendance staff. Transportation from the distributing posts is supplied by the divisions and other units requiring it.

e. Supplies from territorial zones.—Supplies from the territorial zone to the war zone are forwarded by the territorial authorities. As a rule, ammunition is forwarded to central artillery depots or to army depots, but where railroad communications permit, supplies may be forwarded directly to the distributing posts or even nearer to the point of use. The central depots usually keep trains in readiness to be sent immediately upon request.

f. Ammunition reserves.—When high consumption of ammunition is foreseen, headquarters of large units and artillery headquarters create an ammunition reserve at each distributing point.

g. Elasticity.—The system described above is elastic, and in advanced lines, where consumption is likely to be variable, commanders of first-line troops can request ammunition from any nearby posts. Headquarters of the large units can request supplies directly from the army Directorate without passing through channels.

h. Repair.—Maintenance and minor repairs are carried out by workshops (*officini campali*). Heavier repairs are done by base workshops.

159. Engineer Service *(Servizio del Génio).*—*a. Function.*—The Engineer Service is responsible for the plans, organization and maintenance of all military buildings and fortifications, the supply of engineer stores and heavy engineer equipment and of signal equipment and stores.

b. Organization.—It has a Directorate General at the Ministry of War and an engineer headquarters and works office at corps headquarters. Its organization in war resembles that of the Artillery Service.

160. Chemical Service *(Servizio Chimico).*—The Chemical Service is concerned with offensive and defensive gas measures and flame-throwers. It serves the Navy and the Air Force as well as the Army.

161. Medical Service *(Servizio Sanitário).*—*a. Function.*—The Medical Service is responsible for enforcing the rules of hygiene and prophylaxis and protecting the troops from epidemic and infective diseases. Also, it supplies sanitary and medical materials and takes care of their removal from battlefields, and handles the evacuation and treatment of the sick and wounded, the identification of the dead, burials, and the reclamation of battle fields.

b. Organization.—The Medical Service is controlled by a—

(1) General Directorate for the Military Medical Service in the Ministry of War. It controls the following technical bodies.

(*a*) Board of legal medicine, for medical-legal advice and for effecting medical visits requested by the Comptroller's Office to ascertain cases of disability incurred in the line of duty.

(b) Scientific laboratories, which carry out experiments and research in all medical and surgical fields.

(c) The military chemical pharmaceutical institute, a great organization, with modern equipment for the technical and industrial work. It provides the supply of medicines and medical material for the Army, Navy, and Air Forces.

(2) Zone Medical Inspectorates, for inspective duties. The medical inspectors (major generals) are directly under the Ministry of War (General Directorate) for technical duties, and under corps headquarters for disciplinary duties. These inspectors perform the following functions:

(a) Study technical matters concerning the functioning of the Medical Service in their respective territories.

(b) Keep informed of studies and proposals advanced by the Medical Directors of the zone, as regards the mobilization of the Medical Service, and study special questions concerning the organization and functioning of the mobilized Medical Services.

(c) Make medical-legal decision on wounds or disabilities as provided by law.

(d) When authorized by the Ministry of War, make inspections of Medical Directorates and establishments in the zone of their jurisdiction.

(e) Promote the technical-professional culture of medical officers in active service, and give orders to the Medical Directorates of the zone.

(f) Cordinate the work of Medical Directors in the zone in maintaing liaison with the medical services of other armed forces, hospital centers, etc.

(3) Army corps Directorates, which perform directive functions within their units, as follows:

(a) Supervise the organizations and functioning of the Medical Service in the zone assigned to the unit in compliance with orders and instructions received from higher authority.

(b) Issue orders concerning hygiene and prophylaxis.

SERVICES, SUPPLY, AND TRANSPORTATION

(*c*) Organize and direct the service for the search and the treatment of sick and wounded and their transportation, when necessary, to hospitals in the rear.

(*d*) Insure immediate treatment of gassed soldiers.

(*e*) Requisition from higher authorities the necessary supplies and transportation which will be required in the operations planned, and make arrangements for distribution.

(*f*) Insure supplies for all the organizations in the unit.

(*g*) Forward through channels requests for medical personnel and recommend medical officers for assignments.

(*h*) Inspect the Medical Service within the unit.

(4) Medical companies assigned to each corps.

(5) Medical sections (*sezioni di sanità*), an integral part of the division, which are organized as follows: headquarters; a vehicle detachment (*reparto carreggiato*); a pack detachment (*reparto sommeggiato*); and a litter-bearer detachment (*reparto portaferiti*). The Alpine regiment has a medical section consisting of headquarters and pack and bearer detachments.

(6) Other medical units.—(*a*) Casualty clearing stations (*centri di smistamento*) are designed for sorting wounded and distributing them to field hospitals, and do not retain cases for treatment. They are established under the corps Medical Directorate.

(*b*) Field hospitals (*ospedali da campo*) are allotted as required to corps, divisions, and Alpine regiments, under the orders of the army Medical Directorate. The standard field hospital is designed for 50 beds, but can be enlarged to 100. It has no transport of its own, and transport is provided by the army Intendance when required.

(*c*) Specialist ambulances (*ambulanze specializzate*) and certain specialized field hospitals in the rear areas are established as required. The specialist ambulances for X-ray and dental treatment are attached to corps field hospitals. Surgical ambulances are attached to armies as available. Special field hospitals for infectious diseases, special treatment, etc., are organized from specially trained medical personnel when required.

(d) Base hospitals (*ospedali di riserva*) situated within the war zone.

(e) Army medical depots (*magazzini di sanità di armata*) keep the forward medical units supplied with the necessary medical stores.

(f) A disinfecting section (*sezione di disinfezione*) is attached to each corps.

(g) Decontamination sections (*sezioni bonifiche*) are under the army Medical Directorate, and are allotted to units as required. They deal primarily with gas casualties but are also available for providing ordinary baths.

(h) A chemical laboratory is allotted to each corps and a chemical-bacteriological-toxicological laboratory to each army.

c. *Operation.*—The system of operation of the Medical Service depends upon whether the troops are stationary, on the march or in combat.

(1) *Stationary troops.*—(a). In each unit, a medical examination takes place daily.

(b) During short stops, men of divisional troops needing hospital attendance are concentrated at given localities from which they are transported to hospitals by means of motor ambulances. Men of corps and armies are transported to hospitals directly.

(c) During extensive stops, men needing only a short hospital attendance are housed at emergency infirmaries within the unit. When the unit advances, the infirmary is discontinued and the men are transported to hospitals.

(2) *Troops on march.*—(a) A medical examination is made before the beginning of the march. Sick men are sent to hospitals. Those not feeling well but not actually sick follow on vehicles which march with the unit.

(b) During the march, men becoming sick are picked up and transported by vehicle. Those in bad shape remain on the road,

SERVICES, SUPPLY, AND TRANSPORTATION

assisted by a soldier of the Medical Corps, and are picked up by the ambulances which follow the troops.

(*c*) At the end of the march, a second medical examination is made.

(3) *During combat.*—(*a*) Doctors assigned to units organize first-aid posts (as a rule, one to each battalion), close to the line of combat, but well protected. Wounded men are carried to the post by men of the Medical Corps assigned to the unit.

(*b*) The medical section is located at places selected by the division headquarters, which takes into consideration the front occupied by the division, the intensity of the action, the opportunity of being close to first-aid posts, the communication service, and good protection. The medical section must be in close communication with first-aid posts and is charged with the transportation of wounded from the posts to its own organizations.

(*c*) In certain cases, in the mountains, for example, the distance between posts and medical section may be very considerable, and it is then advisable to organize a number of intermediate posts.

(*d*) Transportation of wounded to field hospitals (organized by corps headquarters) is entrusted to the medical section with its own motor ambulances.

(*e*) While the action progresses, the medical section must be capable of following the troops. To this end, all wounded must be evacuated to the rear, except those who cannot be transported, and these remain with only a few medical officers and men while the main body of the section advances.

(*f*) In case of withdrawal, the medical section transports to the rear the wounded who can be removed, but leaves on the spot those who cannot be transported, together with the necessary personnel and medical materials. Troops not included in the division are cared for by the medical section or field hospital closest to the place where they fight.

(*g*) The surgical units assigned to corps are sent to the medical sections of the divisions whenever necessary, upon orders issued

RESTRICTED

by the medical director of the corps. Field hospitals (50 beds, standard type) assigned to armies or corps may, in case of absolute necessity, be temporarily assigned to divisions. They are erected in places well protected against enemy fire. If possible, existing buildings are used. If roads are good and motor cars available, these field hospitals will be located at a certain distance from the medical sections. When advanced hospitals are full of wounded, medical officers of the Alpine troops and of divisions and other units will notify the medical director of the army, who will either remove the wounded to other hospitals to the rear or assign to the units additional field hospitals.

(*h*) In case of advance, field hospitals will not move, but will be assigned to the last rear unit in the zone of operations. This unit, in turn, will give to the advancing units its field hospitals which have not yet been used.

(*i*) Whenever necessary, upon request by the division headquarters, the section handling gassed men is sent by the corps medical director to the medical sections of the divisions.

(*j*) For the removal of wounded and sick behind the medical sections, there are three zones—

> 1. *First zone of removal.*—The zone included between the medical sections up to and including corps hospitals.
> 2. *Second zone of removal.*—The zone included within army hospitals. This zone is located on the boundary line between the zone of operations and the territorial zone.
> 3. *Territorial zone.*—The zone which includes territorial hospitals and other territorial medical establishments.

From the medical sections, sick and wounded are removed directly to hospitals in the first and second zones of removal. The selection of men to be treated within the zone of operations or in the territorial zone takes place in the second zone of removal. Those to be treated in the territorial zone are transported by railroad trains especially equipped and by hospital trains of the Red Cross or of the Order of Malta, or, in certain cases, river ambulances are used.

(*k*) The army Medical Directorates issue orders for the organization of temporary infirmaries for the removal of wounded, in localities close to railroad stations or embarkation posts on rivers, provided no other infirmary is available in the same locality.

162. Veterinary Service *(Servízio Veterinário).*—*a. Function.*—The Veterinary Service is responsible for the supervision of the health of animals and the institution of preventive measures against disease; for the collection, evacuation and treatment of wounded and sick animals; to insuring the good quality of meat on the hoof, and forage intended for distribution to the troops and to animals; and for the provision of veterinary and blacksmith's equipment and stores. The Remount Service (*Servízio dei Centri Rifornimento Quadrupedi*) provides centers for the furnishing of horses and mules.

b. Organization.—(1) *General.*—The Veterinary Service has an Inspectorate at the Ministry of War, as well as zone inspectors and officers with corps and divisions. Representatives of the Service are located with the headquarters of higher and subordinate units. It is entirely independent of the Medical Service. Mounted troops have veterinary infirmaries in each regiment.

(2) *Duties.*—The duties of the directive organizations are as follows:

(*a*) To issue instructions for hygiene and prophylaxis and supervise their enforcement, making sure that animals belonging to the Army are not infected by sick animals belonging to the civilian population.

(*b*) To recommend changes in the forage ration for animals.

(*c*) To isolate sick and wounded animals, and take care of their treatment if possible or send them to hospitals designated by higher authority.

(*d*) To issue instructions for the killing of animals no longer suitable for service.

(*e*) To recommend to headquarters the organization for temporary infirmaries.

(*f*) To supply materials for veterinary and horseshoeing.

(*g*) To forward through channels the request for personnel and to recommend officers for assignment.

(*h*) To ascertain the quality of meat and forage.

(*i*) To inspect the operation Service within the unit.

(3) *Remount Service.*—The Remount Service administers six remount centers (five to cavalry and one for artillery) and three remount squadrons which train horses between the ages of 2 and 4 years. Officers of cavalry and artillery units are attached to the remount service, which is administered by the Ministry of Agriculture and Fisheries.

c. Operation.—(1) All sick and wounded animals are visited daily by veterinary officers. Units which have no veterinary officer send the animals to the nearest unit having an officer, or request a visit from the officer. When troops remain stationary, animals may be assembled in a temporary infirmary. When the unit moves on, sick animals are removed to corps and army infirmaries, which also handle animals requiring long treatment and are equipped with special cars for their transportation. Special isolated infirmaries are organized in case of epidemic diseases. When the unit to which an infirmary belongs advances, the infirmary remains and a pack infirmary is assigned to the unit. Special depots may be organized for the convalescence of animals.

(2) After treatment, animals are either returned to their units or sent to the army depots.

(3) Veterinary materials and materials for horseshoeing are supplied from territorial depots to the army veterinary depot, which supplies the army infirmaries. Troops of the corps receive the supplies from the corps infirmaries, which obtain them from army infirmaries.

163. **Spiritual Assistance, or Chaplains' Service *(Servizio dell'Assistenza Spirituale).*—*a. Function.*—The Spiritual Assistance, or Chaplains' Service, is responsible for the spiritual welfare of the Army, the Navy, and the Air Force. The Service consists of military chaplains and civilian priests.

b. Organization.—(1) The Chief of Chaplains has the title of Military Ordinary for Italy and is commonly called "the Bishop of the Army." He is assisted by a Vicar, or Assistant Chief Chaplain, and two Inspectors, one for the Army and the other for the Navy and Air Force.

(2) In peacetime 27 chaplains stationed at hospitals are authorized for the Army. In wartime a great many more are necessary and acting chaplains are appointed upon recommendation by the Military Ordinary. During World War I there were more than 2,000 chaplains, or approximately 1 per 2,800 men.

164. Geographical Service *(Istituto Geográfico Militare)*.—This service compiles and issues maps and monographs concerning military studies and operations.

165. Road and Water Service *(Servizio delle Strade e Servizio dell'Acque)*.—*a. Function.*—This Service is responsible for the maintenance and improvement of roads in the rear of the zone of operations and the maintenance of canals, river banks, and hydraulic works. Maintenance of roads must be continuous. Other works are carried out only when necessary.

b. Organization.—(1) The Road and Water Services make use of the road, port, water, electric, and other technical organizations belonging to the Ministry of Public Works and local authorities. They have no representation lower than army headquarters. Personnel and means for work, when sufficient, are obtained through the Intendant General, by whom depots and storehouses are organized.

(2) The Service distributes work to its own offices or to the offices assigned to the various armies: when territories occupied by more than one army are concerned, as in the case of canals and rivers, the work is handled by the offices of the Road Service; when only the territory occupied by an army is concerned, it is taken care of by the office assigned to the army.

(3) The work is done by civilian workmen obtained locally, and with materials from the depots and storehouses of the road service or obtained from the engineers service.

166. Water Service (*Servízio Ídrico*).—*a.* This Service, which is manned by the engineer arm, supplies water to troops, animals, and Services. The direction of the Service is entrusted to headquarters of each large unit, assisted by the directive organizations of the Medical, Commissariat, Engineers, Road and Water, and Transport Services, which, in turn, also assist with executive duties.

b. The directive organizations are responsible for ascertaining the water resources in the zone; determining the potability of the water and condition of pumps and installations for conveying it from sources to reservoirs and tanks; furnishing the necessary means for the transportation of water and means for its storage; reporting excess or deficiencies of water resources in the zone; and organizing its distribution.

c. Executive duties are performed by the related Services as follows:

(1) The Medical Service takes care of disinfection.

(2) The Commissariat Service issues to headquarters and units the means for storage and distribution.

(3) The Engineer and Road and Water Services ascertain water resources and plants and make recommendations of projects in order to insure adequate supply. When authorized, they carry out the necessary works, supply the necessary equipment (pumps, pipes, etc.) and order the employment of water sections or civilians.

(4) The Transport Service furnishes the necessary vehicles for the transportation of water from the sources to the places of distribution.

167. Timber Service (*Servizio di Legnami*).—*a.* This Service is responsible for the supply of forage, timber, and firewood. Personnel is supplied by the Forest Militia.

168. Postal Service (*Servizio Postale e Telegráfico*).—*a. Function.*—This Service is responsible for the distribution and collection of all official and private correspondence, for savings bank and money order services, and for the dispatch and receipt of private telegrams for the Field Army.

b. Organization.—There is a Directorate for the Postal Service at army headquarters. In corps and divisions the directive functions are performed by the Chief of Staff.

169. **Judge Advocate's Service** *(Servizio della Guistizia Militare).*—This Service is responsible for the application of military penal law.

SECTION IV

TRANSPORTATION

	Paragraph
Estimate of Italian transportation facilities	170
Railroads	171
Highways	172
Water transportation	173

170. **Estimate of Italian transportation facilities.**—*a. Effect of war on transport.*—The means of transport in Italy include railroads, highways, coastwise shipping, inland waterways, and airlines. Before the war the system was sufficient for domestic commerce, but it has been much disrupted in recent years. Coastwise shipping has been interrupted, the inland waterways have been inadequate, and the commercial airlines have been taken over for military purposes.

b. International traffic.—(1) Since Italy entered the war, railroads and highways have been obliged to carry a much increased volume of traffic. The northern distribution centers—including Milan (the most important commercial distribution point in all Italy), Turin, Genoa, Bologna, and Trieste—are reasonably well served by rail and highway facilities. In the central part of the country the facilities are less extensive; in this area, cities are commercially of less importance, with the exceptions of Rome, Leghorn, and Civitavecchia. In the south, except in the chief cities of Naples, Bari, Brindisi, and Reggio Calabria, commercial transportation service is limited.

(2) The effort to solve the transportation problem by recourse to inland waterways and railroads has been hampered by delay in transshipping and by the difficulty of handling by rail such bulky commodities as crude oil, rubber, and cotton. Italy has discovered no adequate substitute for the sea route to Germany.

171. Railroads.—*a. Railway net.*—Italian railways (see fig. 31) provide the major means of transport for troops and war materials inside Italy. Before the war, the most strategic railways were those which connected the inland cities of Turin, Milan, Bologna, Florence, and Rome with the great seaports of Genoa, Naples, and Trieste. Since the interruption of sea-borne traffic, Italian trade has been forced to deal with markets accessible by land, and consequently the railways connecting Italy with the rest of Europe have become strategically and economically indispensable. Of these, the most important are along the northwestern, northern, and northeastern frontiers.

b. Strategic rail net.—The strategic rail net, defined by areas, is as follows:

(1) *French frontier.*—This area contains three railway lines, listed in the order of their importance:

(*a*) A four-track line from Genoa to Arquata via the Giove Pass.

(*b*) A single-track line from Turin to Nice which traverses the Tenda Pass and crosses the French frontier at Ventimiglia.

(*c*) A line from Savona to Turin which crosses into France over the San Giuseppe Pass.

All these railways became important carriers of raw materials and commodities from France and Spain to Italy within 2 months after Italy's declaration of war.

(2) *Swiss frontier.*—Two lines cross the Alps between Switzerland and Italy, furnishing important connections with Germany: one by the St. Gothard Pass, which is the more important because it is shorter and has fewer and less difficult grades, and the other

SERVICES, SUPPLY, AND TRANSPORTATION 171

by the Simplon Tunnel. The latter is double-tracked between Milan-Gallarate and Arona-Domodóssola.

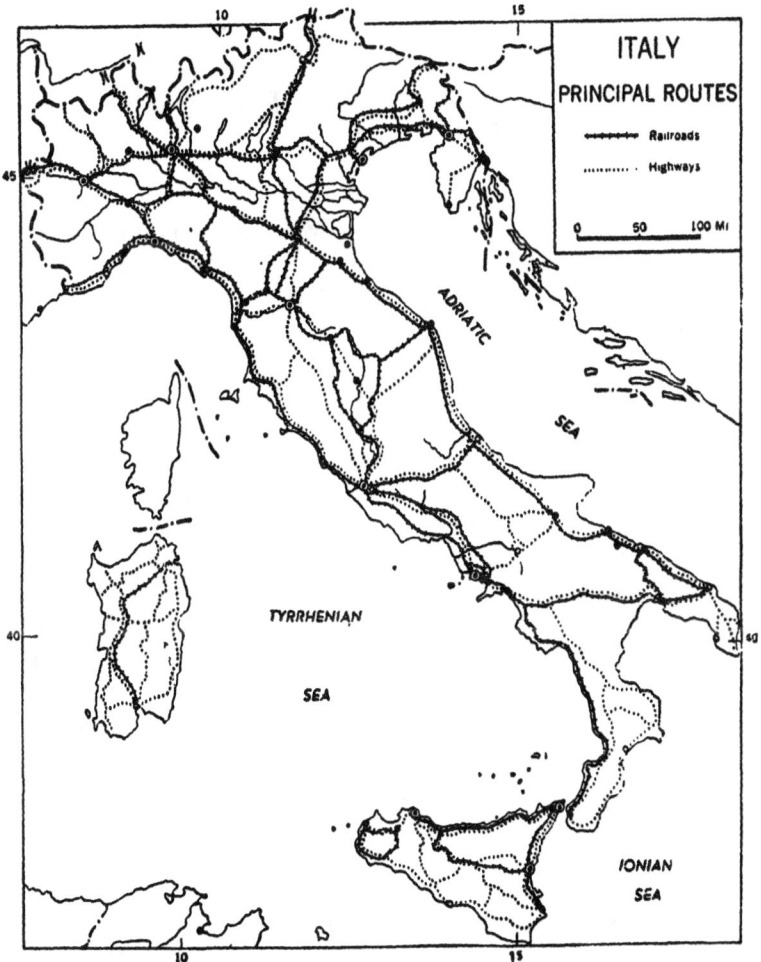

FIGURE 31.—Map of Italy, showing main railroad lines and highways.

(3) *German-Austrian frontier.*—This area has three railways: a single-tracked line which crosses the Italo-German border at Saint Candido; a single-tracked line which crosses at Tarvisio; and a double-tracked line leading through the Brenner Pass. The Brenner Pass line is the most important, having a daily capacity of 128 trains of from 20 to 40 cars each. It was a principal means of transport for German troops passing through Italy en route to Libya. It also carries a good deal of northbound freight.

(4) *Yugoslav frontier.*—Because of destruction resulting from the campaign in Yugoslavia, the only rail connection across the Italo-Yugoslav border, is by the partially restored Fiume-Zagrab railway, by way of Susak (called Borgonovo since the Italian annexation) and Ogulin. Pending further reconstruction, this railroad is available only to traffic moving between Germany and Italy and between Rumania and Italy. It involves many detours and much delay.

(5) *Italian peninsula.*—With the exception of Brindisi and Bari on the heel of the Italian boot, all important centers in Italy are connected by double-track railways. Some are electrically operated. The most important strategic railroads are the completely electrified lines on the Tyrrhenian coast. These transport the bulk of northbound and southbound traffic moving through Italy. Beginning at Reggio Calabria, almost at the southernmost tip of the peninsula, one railroad follows the coast by way of Naples, Rome, Spezia, and Genoa, crossing the French frontier at Ventimiglia. A second, beginning at Rome, goes north to Milan by way of Florence and Bologna. From Bologna a branch line goes to Ancona and Venice. A third, beginning at Genoa, consists of two principal routes, one of which leads northeast to Turin and the other, by the way of Milan and Verona, to the Brenner Pass and to Venice and Trieste.

c. Vulnerability.—(1) The most vulnerable spots in the Italian railway net are the northern passes. The railroads run through

SERVICES, SUPPLY, AND TRANSPORTATION 171

many tunnels and over many bridges, all of which are relatively unprotected from attack by air. So far as is known, however, none of these has yet been subjected to bombing. The Reggio Calabria-Ventimiglia railroad line, in addition to crossing numerous bridges, skirts the Tyrrhenian coast almost the whole length of the Italian peninsula, thus offering many opportunities for naval bombardment.

(2) Since Italy's most strategic railways are electrically operated, hydroelectric-power and power-transmitting stations offer natural targets for bombing. Such operations, in order to be effective, would have to be carried out on an extensive scale, because the Italian system of power distribution is so organized that a number of stations can be made to serve the same line.

d. Operation.—There are about 14,500 miles of railway lines in Italy, approximately one-fourth of which are electrically operated, and most of which are adequately equipped with sidings, loading platforms, repair shops, and station installations. Virtually all Italian railroads are owned by the State and at present are under the authority of a central technical commission directly responsible to the General Staff of the Italian armed forces.

e. Rolling stock.—Italian rolling stock is inadequate to meet the needs of the now abnormal traffic with Germany. Furthermore, a substantial portion of the equipment has been appropriated by Germany. Italian freight cars are smaller than United States cars (see figs. 32 and 33), and have had to be supplemented by many German tank and coal cars. Italy's total rolling stock in June 1940 consisted of—

Locomotive or rail motorcars:

Steam	4,117
Electric	1,602
Diesel	776
Passenger and mail cars	8,074
Baggage and freight cars	135,005

RESTRICTED

FIGURE 32.—Water tank car.

f. New railway construction.—(1) The current Italian railroad building program contemplated the electrification of a number of existing railways and the building of new electric lines. Railroad lines built since Italy's entry into the war include:

>Navara-Biella (near Milan in the north).
>Castellamare di Stabia—Le Terme (south of Naples on the Bay of Naples).
>Fano—Fossombrone section (16 miles long) of the Fano—Fermignano line (near Ancona, on the Adriatic coast).
>Grisignano di Zocco—Treviso (single-track, 72 miles long), an alternative through-route between Tarvisio and Bologna, avoiding Venice.
>Electrification of 205 km of the Bologna-Verona-Trento line.

(2) In May 1941 the following railroad projects were under construction:

SERVICES, SUPPLY, AND TRANSPORTATION

FIGURE 33.—Freight car for transporting acids.

Alessandria (north Italy, near Turin): 15-mile double-track circular railway.

Bologna: enlargement of the Lavino Station.

San Donato (outskirts of Bologna): overhead bridge.

Rome: 27-mile circular railway connection the Tiburtino, San Pietro, and Maccaresa stations.

Sicily: 6½-mile circular railway at Palermo.

(3) In May 1942 the following lines were being electrified:

Domodossola-Milan.
Rifredi-Empoli.
Ciampino-Velettri.

g. Transportation trends.—The maintenance of Italian railroads in recent years has become very lax, because of the following factors:

(1) Production has been directed almost entirely toward military equipment.

Type	Number	Capacity	Remarks
Coal car	6,000	16 to 20 metric tons.	At least 6,000, and possibly more, Italian coal cars were operating between Germany and Italy in the spring of 1941.
Tank car	3,000	15 metric tons (4,410 U. S. gallons).	The total known number of tank cars is about 3,000, but this figure does not include the tank cars used exclusively in the Government service before the war for the transport of petroleum products, or the tank cars, of which no estimate is available, used for the transport of chemical products and water.
Troop-carrying car.[1]	144,500	40 men or 8 horses.	The capacity of the average Italian freight car for military transport is approximately the European standard, that is, 40 men or 8 horses to each car. However, it is possible that this figure is too large, in view of the many small two-axle, four-wheeled Italian freight cars. The carrying capacity of most passenger and baggage cars compares favorably with European and United States standards.

[1] All freight cars, exclusive of coal and tank cars, and all passenger and baggage cars are classified as troop-carrying cars.

FIGURE 34.—Table of carrying capacity of rolling stock.

(2) Terrific strain has been imposed on the railroads in moving troops and their equipment.

(3) Practically all imports have been handled by rail as a result of the United Nations' blockade.

(4) The heavy demands made by Germany on Italian exports necessitate the movement by rail of the largest part of these commodities.

(5) The sale of Italian rolling stock has caused the remaining trains to be loaded to maximum capacity, with a consequent lowering in operating efficiency.

h. Motive power.—With the exception of the Po Valley line, all the main lines now use electric traction. The Brenner line is double-tracked and electrified, but its electrification is of the tri-phase variety, which is particularly vulnerable. It is in use over most of the lines in Italy. Because of the vulnerability of this type, the lines that have been electrified since 1933 have been supplied with direct current. Both the direct current and the tri-phase use overhead wires, and both use about the same voltage (3,000).

172. Highways.—*a. Highway system.*—(1) The Italian highway system (see fig. 31) is not sufficiently extensive to relieve the railroads of any important part of the burden of foreign or domestic commerce. Nevertheless, practically all of peninsular Italy, as well as the islands of Sicily and Sardinia, is served by a network of main and secondary automobile roads which connect points of commercial and military importance. Their total mileage is 10 times that of the railroads, most of which they parallel.

(2) Judged by United States standards and considering the requirements of modern heavy transport vehicles, most Italian roads are very narrow. But many are macadamized and most are fairly well constructed.

(3) International highways leading across Italy's northern frontiers, most of which cross Alpine passes, include:

(*a*) Year-round roads by way of the Dobbiaco, Tarvisio, Brenner, Resia, Mount Maloja, Julien, and Tenda Passes, and a coastal road by way of Ventimiglia.

(*b*) Roads opened seasonally from May to November by way of the Argentiere, Mount Cenis, Saint Bernard, Little Saint Bernard, Simplon, Saint Gothard, Bernina, and Stelvio Passes, and some mountain roads in the Venetian Trident and the Dolomite Mountains.

(*c*) The important Susak-Zagreb-Belgrade Highway, which traverses the Italo-Yugoslav frontier.

(4) The important interior roads include:

(*a*) The west-coast highway, which links Reggio Calabria in the south with the Brenner Pass by way of Auletta, Salerno, Naples, Rome, Leghorn, Spezia, Genoa, Turin, and Milan, and with the French frontier by way of Genoa, Ventimiglia, and Monaco.

(*b*) The eastern highway, which links Galatone on the Gulf of Taranto with Trieste by way of Brindisi, Bari, Foggia, Ancona, Bologna, and Venice.

(*c*) The transpeninsular highways: two in northern Italy, one linking Genoa and Turin with Trieste by way of Milan, Brescia, and Venice, and the other linking Leghorn with Trieste by way of Florence, Bologna, and Venice; two in central Italy, one linking Rome with Ancona and the other linking with Pescara; and two in southern Italy, one linking Naples with Foggia, and the other connecting Reggio Calabria with Galatone by way of Taranto.

b. Automotive equipment.—The limitations of Italian automotive transport, especially freight transport, are indicated by the following list of registered motor vehicles in Italy as of 20 May 1940: 375,000 passenger cars; 113,000 commercial trucks; 2,000 petroleum and gasoline tank-trucks with trailers, which have an average capacity of 17 metric tons per truck and trailer; 1,000 petroleum and gasoline tank wagons, with an average capacity of 2 to 4 tons; 10,000 passenger busses; and 220,000 motorcycles. Doubtless United States troops will need to move in their own motor transport not only because captured Italian equipment will be in a run-down condition, but also because much of it will probably not be suitable for the use of United States forces.

c. New highway development.—During recent years most new road construction has been confined to northern Italy, where improvements have been made upon the approaches to a number of the trans-Alpine passes and upon the roads which transverse the passes. A new coastal road, to be named the Tyrrhenian highway, is under construction between Genoa and Savona, and will supplant the old one by way of Aurelia.

d. Transportation trends.—The large quantity of cement in Italy makes road building relatively simple. However, the scarcity of trucks for internal transportation purposes and the shortage of gasoline to operate them prevent the roads from relieving the transportation difficulties. Because of this shortage there has been a marked trend toward the use of oil engines and engines using a fuel, with an alcohol base, called *Robur*—a mixture of gasoline and ethyl and methyl alcohol.

173. Water transportation.—*a. Principal ports.*—The British blockade at Gibraltar and Suez has confined the effective operation of the Italian merchant fleet to the Mediterranean. The presence of the United States and British Navies in the Mediterranean has further restricted the movements of Italian ships. At present the only important areas are as follows: Genoa, which is the home port of ships plying between Italian, and French, and Spanish ports; Naples, which is the main port from which troops and supplies were sent to Tripoli and Libya; Brindisi and Bari, at the southeastern tip of the Italian peninsula, which are the first ports of entry for ships arriving from the Eastern Mediterranean and the Black Sea; and Venice and Trieste, which probably now accommodate the bulk of Italy's seaborne traffic because of their strategic location at the head of the Adriatic Sea. The last named ports, in addition to being in direct-rail communication with Germany, are relatively inaccessible to attack by air.

b. Inland water routes.—(1) Italy's inland waterways, which normally carry only about one percent of all commercial traffic, are of negligible strategic value. The important navigable rivers and canals are the Po River and its tributaries; the Milanese and Ferrarese Canals; the Adda and Adige Rivers; and the Venetian inland and coastal canals. These waterways extend through the relatively flat northern provinces of Lombardy, Veneto, and Emilia. Most navigable canals and the principal Italian rivers traverse the Italian peninsula from east to west; these include the Isonzo and its tributaries, which empty into the Gulf of Trieste; the Tagliamento, Piave, Brenta, Adige, Po, and their tributaries, which empty into the Gulf of Venice; the Reno and its tributaries, which empty into the Adriatic Sea; and the Arno and Tiber, which empty into the Tyrrhenian Sea. These rivers are, therefore, of little advantage, because the bulk of Italian commerce moves north and south.

(2) Out of a total of 1,309 miles of waterways open to commercial boat traffic in 1939 only about 248 miles of rivers and canals were accessible to vessels of 600 tons, while 300-ton vessels were limited to an additional 186 miles of inland navigation and the remaining 875 miles accommodated vessels of only 100 tons or less.

(3) During 1939 most commercial traffic on Italy's inland waterways consisted of a fleet of about 2,000 boats, nearly all constructed of wood. Approximately 60 had a gross weight of more than 200 tons and the remainder had an average weight of only 25 tons.

(4) Boat transportation on the Alpine lakes, including Maggiore, Como, Iseo, Garda, Lugano, and Orta, and on the waterways in central and southern Italy, is not important either commercially or strategically. Except during the rainy season, the only rivers that normally would obstruct military transport are the Isonzo, Piave, Adige, and Po.

RESTRICTED

	U. S. Army	Army	Carabinieri	Fascist Militia (ordinary, railroad, etc.)
		Regio Esercito	Reali Carabinieri	M. V. S. N. (ordinaria, ferroviaria, ecc.)
1	Commander in chief.	Maresciallo dell'Impero		
2		Maresciallo d'Italia		Primo caporale d'onore
3	General	Generale d'armata		
4		Generale designato d'armata.		
5	Lieutenant general	Generale di corpo d'armata.	Commandante generale dell'arma.	Commandante generale.
6	Major general	Generale di divisione or Tenente generale.	Commandante in secondo dell'arma.	Luogotenente generale.
7	Brigadier general	Generale di brigata or Maggiore generale.	Generale ispettore di zona.	Console generale
8	Colonel	Colonnello	Colonnello	Console
9	Lieutenant colonel	Tenente colonnello	Tenente colonnello	Primo seniore
10	Major	Maggiore	Maggiore	Seniore
11	Captain	Capitano	Capitano	Centurione
12	First lieutenant	Tenente	Tenente	Capo manipolo
13	Second lieutenant	Sotto tenente	Sotto tenente	Sotto capo manipolo
14		Maresciallo maggiore	Maresciallo d'allogio maggiore.	Prima aiutante
15		Maresciallo capo	Maresciallo d'allogio capo.	Aiutante capo
16		Maresciallo ordinario	Maresciallo d'allogio	Aiutante
17	(Sergeant-major)	Sergente maggiore	Brigadiere	Primo capo squadra
18	Sergeant	Sergente	Vice brigadiere	Capo squadra
19	Corporal	Caporale maggiore	Appuntato dei Carabinieri.	Vice capo squadra
20	(Lance-corporal)	Caporale	Carabiniere	Camicia nera scelta
21	Private first class	Appuntato		
22	Private	Soldato	Allievo Carabiniere	Camicia nera

Fugure 35. A - Table of relative ranks.

	U. S. Army	Fascist Militia (Forest) M. V. S. N. (Forestale)	Finance Guard Regia Guardia di Finanza	Special Division of Public Safety Divisione Speciale Pubblica Sicurezza
1	Commander in chief.			
2				
3	General			
4				
5	Lieutenant general			
6	Major general		Generale di divisione	
7	Brigadier general	Console generale	Generale di brigata	
8	Colonel	Console	Colonnello	Colonnello
9	Lieutenant colonel	Primo seniore	Tenente colonnello	Tenente colonnello
10	Major	Seniore	Maggiore	Maggiore
11	Captain	Centurione	Capitano	Capitano
12	First lieutenant	Capo manipolo	Tenente	Tenente
13	Second lieutenant		Sotto tenente	Sotto tenente
14		Maresciallo maggiore	Maresciallo maggiore	Maresciallo di prima
15		Maresciallo capo	Maresciallo capo	Maresciallo di seconda
16		Maresciallo	Maresciallo	Maresciallo di terza
17	(Sergeant-major)	Brigadiere	Brigadiere	Brigadiere
18	Sergeant	Vice brigadiere	Sotto brigadiere	Vice brigadiere
19	Corporal	Milite scelto	Appuntato	Guardia scelta
20	(Lance-corporal)	Milite	Guardia	Guardia
21	Private first class			
22	Private	Allievo	Allievo	Allievo

Fugure 35. B - Table of relative ranks.

	U. S. Army	Judge Advocate's Service	Air Force	Navy	U. S. Navy
		Guistizia Militare	Regia Aeronautica	Regia Marina	
1	Commander in chief.		Maresciallo dell'Impero.		Commander in chief.
2			Maresciallo dell'aria.	Grande ammiraglio	
3	General		Generale di armata aerea.	Ammiraglio d'armata	Admiral.
4				Ammiraglio designato d'armata.	
5	Lieutenant general	Regio avvocato generale militare.	Generale di squadra aerea.	Ammiraglio di squadra.	Vice admiral.
6	Major general	Regio sostituto avvocato generale militare.	Generale di divisione aerea.	Ammiraglio di divisione.	Rear admiral.
7	Brigadier general	Regio avvocato militare.	Generale di brigata aerea.	Contrammiraglio	Commodore.
8	Colonel	Regio vice avvocato militare e giudice relatore di 1a classe.	Colonnello	Capitano di vascello	Captain.
9	Lieutenant colonel	Regio vice avvocato militare e giudice relatore di 1a classe.	Tenente colonnello	Capitano di fregata	Commander.
10	Major	Regio sostituto avvocato militare e giudice istruttore di 2a classe.	Maggiore	Capitano di corvetta	Lieutenant commander.
11	Captain	Regio sostituto avvocato militare e giudice istruttore di 2a classe.	Capitano	Tenente di vascello	Lieutenant.
12	First lieutenant	Regio sostituto avvocato militare e giudice istruttore di 3a classe.	Tenente	Sotto tenente di vascello.	Lieutenant, junior grade.
13	Second lieutenant	Cancelliere di 3a classe.	Sotto tenente	Guardiamarina	Ensign.
14			Maresciallo di 1a classe.	Capo di 1a classe	Chief petty officer, 1st class.
15			Maresciallo di 2a classe.	Capo di 2a classe	Chief petty officer, second class.
16			Maresciallo di 3a classe.	Capo di 3a classe	Chief petty officer, third class.
17	(Sergeant-major)		Sergente maggiore	Secondo capo	Petty officer (upper half).
18	Sergeant		Sergente	Sergente	Petty officer (lower half).
19	Corporal		Primo aviere	Sotto capo	(Leading seaman).
20	(Lance-corporal)		Aviere scelto	(Funzionante sotto capo).	Seaman, first class.
21	Private first class			Comune di 1a classe	Seaman, second class.
22	Private		Aviere	Comune di 2a classe	Apprentice seaman.

Fugure 35. C - Table of relative ranks.

Chapter 5

RANKS, UNIFORMS, INSIGNIA, AND IDENTIFICATION

		Paragraph
Section	I. Ranks	174–179
	II. Uniforms and insignia	180–194
	III. Decorations, medals, and awards	195–203

Section I

RANKS

	Paragraph
Commissioned officers	174
Noncommissioned officers (*sottufficiali*) and enlisted men (*truppa*)	175
Officer candidates	176
Fascist Militia	177
Air Force	178
Navy	179

174. Commissioned officers.—*a. General.*—In the Italian Army, as in the U. S. Army, commissioned ranks are divided into three groups: general officers (*ufficiali generali*), field officers (*ufficiali superiori*), and company officers (*ufficiali inferiori*). Above the rank of general there are two grades of marshals (*marescialli*) which are not to be confused with the *marescialli* of the noncommissioned grades (see par. 2). Before the resignation of Mussolini, the King and he were the only two marshals of the Empire (*Marescialli dell'Impero*). There were six marshals of Italy (*Marescialli d'Italia*).

b. Variations.—Figure 33 indicates the relative ranks of various branches of the armed forces of Italy and of the U. S. Army and Navy. However, there are a few peculiarities in the Italian system not readily shown by means of a chart. For instance, the titles of lieutenant general (*tenente generale*) and major general (*maggiore generale*), equivalent to U. S. major general and brigadier general, respectively, are reserved for the artillery, engineer, and other branches. The titles of first captain (*primo capitano*) and first lieutenant (*primo tenente*) are given to captains and first lieutenants who have held their respective ranks for 12 years. Head chaplains (*cappellani capi*) have the rank of *capitano* in the Army and *tenente di vascello* in the Navy. Band leaders and fencing masters have the rank of *sottottenente*.

175. Noncommissioned officers *(sottufficiali)* and enlisted men *(truppa)*.—*a. Noncommissioned officers.*—There are five grades of noncommissioned officers:

(1) *Sergente* (sergeant).

(2) *Sergente maggiore* (sergeant major).

(3) *Maresciallo ordinário* (ordinary marshal).

(4) *Maresciallo capo* (chief marshal).

(5) *Maresciallo maggiore* (marshal major).

The *marescialli* form a separate category, and inasmuch as there is no equivalent of this group in the U. S. Army, these titles are not usually translated. A *maresciallo* is not the equivalent of U. S. warrant officer.

b. Enlisted men.—The corporal (*caporale*) in the Italian Army is not a noncommissioned officer, but is classed with the private, first class (*appuntato*), both grades being called *graduate*.

176. Officer candidates.—An officer candidate (*aspirante ufficiale*) has a recognized rank. In the Navy it corresponds to the grade of *maresciallo maggiore*, with precedence over the maresciallo maggiore of the Army and the Air Force.

177. Fascist Militia.—Certain ranks of commissioned officers in the Fascist Militia are called by the Italian form of the ancient Roman titles.

178. Air Force.—Although the official titles in the Air Force vary somewhat from those in the Army, the simpler Army form is commonly used.

RANKS, UNIFORMS, INSIGNIA, AND IDENTIFICATION 179-181

179. Navy.—Only line officers use the naval titles. All others use the equivalent Army title.

Section II
UNIFORMS AND INSIGNIA

	Paragraph
General	180
Normal field uniform (*divisa di campagna*)	181
Colonial, or tropical uniform	182
Uniform of Fascist Militia	183
Impermeable clothing	184
Uniform of Chaplains	185
Officer's service dress uniform	186
General insignia	187
Insignia of arm (*fregio*)	188
Regimental number	189
Collar patches and devices	190
Insignia of Fascist Militia	191
Insignia of rank (*distintivi di grado*)	192
Style of uniform prior to June 1940	193
Means of identification	194

180. General.—In the Italian Army considerable freedom is exercised in the observance of regulations on uniforms and insignia, the individual taste of the wearer or the manufacturer sometimes accounting for a noticeable variety.[1] In June 1940 special instructions were issued providing for the adoption of the same style of uniforms in the field for all ranks, including officers. Retention and use of the former distinctive and more conspicuous styles are permitted, however, until stocks are exhausted or uniforms worn out. (Inasmuch as the older are sometimes encountered, details are given in par. 193.)

181. Normal field uniform *(divisa di campagna)* (plate II).—*a. General.*—The color is gray-green (*grigio-verde*), although a medium gray color is worn for fatigue duties.

---
[1] All plates illustrating uniforms and insignia follow page 174.

b. Headgear (copricapo).—Gray-green garrison cap, or "envelope" (*beretto a busta,* or *bustina*) or steel helmet (*casco, elmo,* or *elmetto*). The Alpine, Finance Guards, pack artillery personnel, Bersaglieri, and some others wear their special headgear (plate II), and paratroopers are provided with blue berets or special crash helmets. The Regular Army helmet is composed of a special steel casque, termically treated, varnished with a gray-green varnish (plate I). The old type French helmet is also encountered.

c. Coat (giubba, or giacca).—Gray-green with open collar (with no piping or embroidery, and plain gray-green buttons (four for officers, three for lower ranks).

d. Shirt (camicia).—Gray-green, worn with collar and necktie. (Militia units wear black shirts.)

e. Necktie.—Gray-green except in certain specific cases worn by all personnel.

f. Breeches (pantaloni corti).—Gray-green without stripes, now replacing the officers' breeches with stripes.

g. Puttees (fasce gambiere).—Gray-green wrapped leggings. Noncommissioned officers and enlisted men, cavalry, and some artillery, tank, and motor transport personnel wear black leather leggings (*gambali*). Horsemen wear leather leggings with straps around them.

h. Boots (stivali).—Officers wear black boots.

i. Shoes (stivaletti).—Black, except for mountain troops.

j. Shoulder pack.—The shoulder pack is divided into compartments by means of cloth partitions. Externally, it has two pockets for cartridges, and is provided with rings on both sides to which two additional pockets for grenades may be attached. For closing, the pack has leather straps, which may also be used for attaching to the pack an overcoat or blanket, half of a camouflaged tent, and steel tent poles. Also, it has adjustable, rounded shoulder straps and hooks in order that it may be worn on the back, as the U. S. pack is worn. Ammunition carriers may wear it below their ammunition boxes (*giberne*) like a pack or else sling it from the shoulders like a haversack. In the pack there is a pocket for the mess kit, which may be detached when the pack is worn like a knapsack and carried on top of the ammunition. It is made of waterproof canvas.

182. Colonial, or tropical uniform.—*a. General.*—Cotton khaki of the same general design as the woolen uniform is worn (plate III). It is evident that considerable variation is practiced and permitted.

b. Headgear.—Khaki helmet made of cork and provided with tinted goggles (plate III). Other types of headgear may often be encountered. The Italian Army used white helmets in the Libyan desert. It is believed that the dull, grayish color which these assume reduces the visibility of infantry. Insignia are mounted one a red, white, and green cockade. Garrison caps with fixed visors are also worn.

c. Coat.—Cotton khaki, with turn-down collar buttoning up to the neck.

d. Leg-wear.—Cotton khaki trousers fitting tightly above the ankles. Breeches are also worn with puttees, leggings, or stockings. Shorts are likewise in evidence, though they are not authorized.

e. Shoes.—Black, and tan hobnailed.

183. Uniform of Fascist Militia.—In June 1940 orders were issued both to the Militia and to the Army, instructing all ranks to wear the same style of uniform. The Militia uniform is substantially that of the Army, normally gray-green, but includes black shirts and black ties. Cotton khaki may be worn in hot climates. The field cap is prescribed, although other types of headgear may be found, notably a fez or a hat similar to that of the Alpini. The *Moschettieri del Duce* wore special black-garrison cap.

184. Impermeable clothing.—Impermeable protective suits are supplied to certain special troops such as chemical companies, decontamination squads, and certain combat troops whose duties require them to remain in fixed positions. The suit consists of an overall which extends from the ankles up to the neck; draw-straps to close the openings; a hood which fits tightly over the neck; gloves; and boots. The suits are made of double-woven cloth of a gray or greenish color rubberized on the outside and treated on the inside with a special chemical substance (plate II).

185. Uniform of chaplains.—Army chaplains on duty with troops during maneuvers or in the field are authorized to wear the uniforms of officers of their assimilated rank, but are required to wear the same star as worn on their ecclesiastical cassock.

186. Officer's service dress uniform.—Material of a much lighter and grayer shade of the *grigio-verde* characterizes the officers' service dress uniform. (See plate I and fig. 36.)

187. General insignia.—A five-pointed star is the distinctive emblem of all personnel belonging to the regular armed forces. In the case of the Army, it is worn on each side (plate I) of the collar. When the collar patch is worn (plate I), the star is in the center of the rectangle close to the lower edge. When the flames are worn it is placed in the center below the point where flames separate. While usually of metal, it is sometimes merely embroidered. Stars in plastic materials are being introduced. In the case of Militia personnel, the Fascist symbol (plate XII) on the collar takes the place of the five-pointed star worn by the Army. Both are of gilded metal for general officers and of white metal for all other ranks. The chaplain's five-pointed star has a cross in the center.

188. Insignia of arm *(fregio).*—Insignia of arm is worn on the front of all types of headgear (stenciled in the case of helmets), and also on the shoulder straps of officers in tropical uniform. Whereas in peacetime officers' insignia were embroidered (usually in gold upon a black background), the soldier's insignia in metal are now prescribed for all ranks. The embroidered insignia are still found on the shoulder straps of officers in tropical uniform (plate III).

FIGURE 30.—Commissioned officers in service dress uniforms. (The black collar on the brigadier general's uniform indicates the style of uniform prior to June 1940.)

189. Regimental number.—The number of the regiment should appear in the boss, or center circle, of headgear insignia, and the boss may be colored as follows:

Grenadiers	Black.
Colonial troops	Bright green.
Other fighting arms of the Metropolitan Army	Gray, green.

Services_ _ _ _ _ _ _ _ _ _ _ _ _ _ _ _ _ _ _ Same color as the collar patch for example, maroon for medical, violet for commisariat, etc.).

A cross is substituted for the number in the case of the services, or for certain headquarters personnel.

190. Collar patches and devices.—*a. General.*—In addition, all infantry regiments of the line wear colored collar patches (*mostrine*) on each side of the coat collar just above the lapel, while other arms and services are distinguished by a variety of colored devices (called generically *mostreggiature*). Collar patches and devices may be absent on the tropical uniform. On the other hand, the insignia of arm or service is worn on the shoulder straps of officers. The collar patches take the following forms:

b. Rectangles (*mostrine*).—Plain or striped (plate IX). When used alone, they denote divisional infantry. On the other hand, when they carry a "flame" or other device, superimposed upon them they indicate the divisional unit of the arm or service characterized by that device. Plain green and plain blue rectangles, which characterize Alpini and armored troops, respectively, are used in this connection only as a background for other devices, but it so happens that these colors also denote infantry regiments. (Plain green rectangles denote the 51st and 52d Regiments, and plain blue rectangles the 23d and 24th Regiments.) Careful discrimination is necessary in these cases.

c. Braids (*alamari*).—Worn on a colored background by the Royal Carabinieri, the Grenadiers of Sardinia, and the General Staff. The Grenadier patches have precisely the same significance as the infantry rectangles, and may also be used in combination with another device (see plate X).

d. Single-pointed flames (*fiamme ad una punta*).—These denote artillery, engineers, various services, the Frontier Guard, geographical and garrison troops, and are either in plain colors or in black or green with a colored background or colored piping. As explained above, they may be superimposed upon rectangles or braid (see plate X).

e. Two-pointed flames (fiamme a due punte).—Worn by Alpini, Bersagliere tank units, motor transport corps, and finance guards (plate X).

f. Three-pointed flames (fiamme a tre punte).—Worn only by the cavalry (plate X).

g. Chemical device.—There is a chemical device for all chemical warfare and decontamination troops. It may be superimposed upon rectangles or braids to denote the unit belonging to a particular higher unit (plate X).

191. Insignia of Fascist Militia.—*a. General.*—Black shirts wear a two-pointed black flame as a collar device. The personnel of territorial cohorts wear this flame on a scarlet rectangle (yellow-orange rectangle for mobile territorial cohorts). Also, enlisted men of territorial units, from *primo caposquadra* downward, wear their unit number in Roman numbers (white on black on the shoulder strap).

b. Combatant branch.—The ordinary (that is, combatant) Militia trains only as infantry. Therefore, no insignia of arm or service in the accepted sense of the term are worn. All personnel of the Militia have a cap badge embodying the fasces (plate XII) in combination with other symbols. The number of a Black Shirt battalion may appear in the space in the circle (territorial cohorts will have a small black cross on a gray-green background in this space).

c. Other branches.—Branches of the force other than the ordinary Militia are distinguished, as far as is known, by colors on their facings as follows:

Antiaircraft and coast defense	Yellow.
Frontier	Green.
Forests	Green.
Railway	Crimson.

RESTRICTED

Roads _____ Bright blue.
Ports _____ Crimson.
Posts and telegraph _____ Crimson.
Medical service _____ Maroon.
Administration service _____ Blue.

192. Insignia of rank *(distintivi di grado).*—*a. Commissioned officers.*—On active service and with the gray-green uniform, officers' insignia of rank are worn as follows:

(1) *On sleeve of coat or overcoat just above cuff.*—They take the form of broad and/or narrow bands (called *galloni* and *galloncini*, respectively) with a loop (*occhiello*) similar to that worn by the British Navy (see plate VII). (On the officer's overcoat, insignia are sometimes sewed on patches that button to the sleeve.) Those worn by general officers are in white artificial silk and include an ornamental design (*greca*), below the bands. The King and the Head of the Government (*Capo del Governo*) wear a double *greca* (plate VI). Officers below the rank of general have insignia of yellow artificial silk. If the shirt-sleeve uniform is being worn, the insignia of rank may appear above the left pocket.

(2) *On headgear.*—(*a*) *Garrison cap.*—Here the system is one of rectangles and stars (see plates VI and VII). Field officers actually in command of units wear rectangles with a red background bordered with gold. The Militia and Air Force use bands instead of stars, as described below for the hat. These are worn diagonally in the Militia, horizontally in the Air Force.

(*b*) *Service cap.*—If a service cap is worn, the insignia consists of continuous bands around the cap, just as for the sleeves, but without the top loop (plates VI and VII).

(*c*) *Alpine type of cap.*—On the Alpine type of cap, the system of bands is formed into one of chevrons worn on the left side, point-up (see plate II). The feather worn in this chevron (*nappina*) is white for ranks of major and above, and black for all others.

(3) *On breast.*—When the coat is not worn, the officer's insignia of rank may be worn on the left breast, taking either the form of

RANKS, UNIFORMS, INSIGNIA, AND IDENTIFICATION

the garrison cap patch or that of the cuff insignia. (See plate I.)

(4) *Tropical uniform.*—A system of stars (with or without embroidery or braiding according to the rank) is adopted. The insignia are worn on the shoulder strap, on which the insignia of arm or service also appear, or on the left breast (see (3) above).

(5) *Rank insignia of Navy and Air Force officers.*—These are similar in every way to those of the Army except that the loop is replaced by a diamond in the case of the Air Force.

b. Noncommissioned officers.—(1) Insignia of noncommissioned officers are illustrated in plate VIII. They are the same for the gray-green and for the tropical uniform.

(2) *Marescialli* wear bands 6 mm wide in yellow artificial silk—twisted with black—on the shoulder strap of the coat and overcoat and one band on the service cap.

(3) Noncommissioned officers wear chevrons on the sleeve only. They are now worn, point-down, above the elbow, on both the coat and overcoat. The chevrons of the sergeant major (*sergente maggiore*) and sergeant (*sergente*) are in yellow artificial silk (silver for Carabinieri), the remainder in red artificial silk.

c. Insignia of rank of Fascist Militia personnel.—These may be taken as identical, for all practical purposes, with those worn by equivalent ranks in the Army, in accordance with the table given in plates VI, VII, and VIII. Note, however, that general officers wear red edging on their shoulder straps, and the *greca* is of a different design from that of general officers in the Army (plate VI). The loop formed on the sleeves of Army officers is substituted by a diamond in the case of the Militia. Noncommissioned officers wear silver chevrons, whereas those of the regular army wear yellow.

d. Insignia of rank of Royal Carabinieri.—These are identical with those worn by equivalent ranks in the Army, except that silver is used instead of yellow for the chevrons of the *brigadieri* and *vice-brigadieri* and for the braid of the shoulder straps of the *marescialli maggiori*. The single stripe of the *soldato scelto* is not worn by the Carabinieri, as the lowest rank is equivalent to that of *caporale*. Colonial uniforms of the Carabinieri have shoulder straps with a red background, silver braid, and a blue border.

e. Variations.—All officers charged with the duties of the rank above their commission wear a background of deep red in the loop of the insignia of rank. A colonel charged with the duties of a brigade general wears on his cuff the insignia of rank of a colonel (yellow, with red between the bars and within the loop). On his cap, however, he wears the general's eagle in black, bordered in red. His shoulder straps may have a red border. Generals charged with the duties of a higher rank add a small bar beneath the insignia on the cuff. A star worn in the loop of the officers' insignia of rank signifies that the wearer is an aide to a general. Colonels and lieutenant colonels in actual command of units wear the insignia of rank with a deep red background and border as well as a border of the same red around the insignia of arm on the cap. Officers of the Services wear between the bands of the insignia of rank, both on the cuff and on the service cap, the color of their service. (Medical, red; commissariat, violet; veterinary, light blue; administration, dark blue.) Members of the automobile corps, which is considered a combatant arm, wear no color between the bands.

193. Style of uniform prior to June 1940.—*a. Commissioned officers and marescialli.*—(1) *Headgear.*—Gray-green garrison cap with black patent leather peak, except the Alpini, customs guards, all pack artillery personnel, and the Bersaglieri (plate II).

(2) *Coat.*—Gray-green with black or colored collars according to the arm of service (see the brigadier general in fig. 36), colored piping according to the arm of service, and metal buttons.

(3) *Shirt.*—Gray-green, with collar and necktie.

(4) *Breeches.*—Gray-green, with stripes down each side and colored piping according to the arm of service.

RANKS, UNIFORMS, INSIGNIA, AND IDENTIFICATION

(5) *Shoes.*—Black with gray-green puttees or stockings. Cavalry, some artillery, tank, and motor transport personnel wore leggings.

b. Noncommissioned officers and enlisted men.—(1) *Headgear.*—Same as at the present time.

(2) *Coat.*—Gray-green, with black or colored collars, according to the arm of service.

(3) *Shirt.*—Gray-green, with collar and necktie or zipper fastener.

(4) *Breeches.*—Gray-green.

(5) *Puttees.*—Gray-green wrapped leggings. Cavalry, some artillery, tank, and motor transport personnel wore leather puttees.

(6) *Shoes.*—Black.

FIGURE 37.—Group of Italian enlisted men.

RESTRICTED

c. *Insignia of arm or service.*—Insignia of arm or service appeared on the front of all types of headgear (maintained); on the shoulder straps of officers, embroidered in gold thread (discontinued, except with tropical uniform); and embossed on the buttons (discontinued). In addition, black or colored collars denoted the arm or service as well as the colored collar patch (maintained) or device (modified) worn on each side of the collar. Colored piping at the cuffs and colored strips down the breeches of officers (both discontinued) and in the field uniform still further distinguished the arm or service.

d. *Regimental numbers.*—Regimental numbers were worn in the center of the boss on headgear insignia (maintained). Company numbers were worn by enlisted men on the shoulder strap (discontinued). Divisional escutcheons were worn on the left arm (discontinued).

e. *Collar patches of infantry line regiments.*—There has been no change in the designs of collar patches of infantry line regiments. The size prescribed was sligthly larger than at present, and moreover, the patch was worn on a black collar, around the outer edge of which officers had red piping. They had this same piping at the cuffs and also wore broad, black stripes with red piping in the center down each side of their breeches.

f. *Collar patches of cavalry regiments.*—The following more conspicuous marks were worn: By the Nizza, Genova, Novara, Aosta, and Vittorio Emmanuale II, regiments, complete collars, plain without device, in their respective colors; by the Piemonte, a complete scarlet collar with thin black edging; by the Savoia, a complete black collar with thin scarlet edging; by Saluzzo Monteferrato, Allesandria, Guide, and Sardegna, complete collars in the respective base colors instead of rectangles only, with three-pointed flames in the colors as shown for the present flames; for Milano, a complete crimson collar with thin black edging; by Firenze, a complete orange collar with thin black edging; by the Cavalry School depot a complete plain orange collar.

RANKS, UNIFORMS, INSIGNIA, AND IDENTIFICATION 193-194

g. Collar patches of other arms.—The characteristic colors were the same as at the present time. The flames had one or two points, as now, but were rather more elaborate. Furthermore, all patches and devices were worn upon a complete black or colored collar.

h. Insignia of rank.—Insignia of rank were substantially the same as now except that all insignia were larger than those prescribed in 1940; that silver and gold braid was used in place of white and yellow (for officers, warrant officers, and noncommissioned officers down to and including the grade of sergeants); and that black braid was used instead of red rayon (for the remaining grades.)

FIGURE 38.—Identity plate (*Medaglioncino di riconoscimento*).

194. Means of identification.—*a. Identity plate.*—This is called a *piastrina* (or *medaglioncino*) *di riconoscimento* (fig. 38). It is worn on a chain around the neck. It is made of cheap metal and records the name, number, religion, year of conscript class (that is, of birth), home town and province, all stamped in relief. With the aid of a penknife or similar instrument, its two sides can be spit apart into two identical plates. Variations in the order in which the particulars are recorded occur, but a typical specimen is shown above.

b. Record books.—(1) *General.*—The soldier-citizen is issued two books in which are registered from time to time records of his health, activities, and military preparation.

RESTRICTED

(2) *Evaluation book.*—The evaluation book (*libretto di valutazione*) is required to be kept from the eleventh to the thirty-second year. In addition to all information regarding the physical condition of the owner, it contains an evaluation of his intellectual, sporting, social, political, and military activities. No employment can be obtained without it.

(3) *Individual record book.*—(a) The soldier's individual record book (*libretto personale*) (fig. 39) records age, name, rank, number, and unit down to the company or equivalent level. It contains many other interesting particulars regarding the holder's civil and military history and accomplishments. It also gives details of the arms, equipment, and clothing on issue to him. It does not serve as a paybook. One *libretto personale* only is issued to cover the whole of a soldier-citizen's military career. The front cover of the soldier's book shows his name, number, regiment, and battery (the last two added by rubber stamp). Many personal particulars are recorded on pages 1 and 2 of the book; page 3 deals with various phases of conscription, promotion, and discharge; page 4 again shows the battery, and records the transfer to another battery; page 5 refers to vaccinations and inoculations.

(b) The book carried by officers and *marescialli* is almost exclusively a pay book and is renewed every year. Much less information is obtainable from it, but age, name, rank, and unit are recorded. The front cover of the officer's book gives no information. Page 1 shows the unit and various personal particulars. The book is not, however, of much practical use to an examining officer.

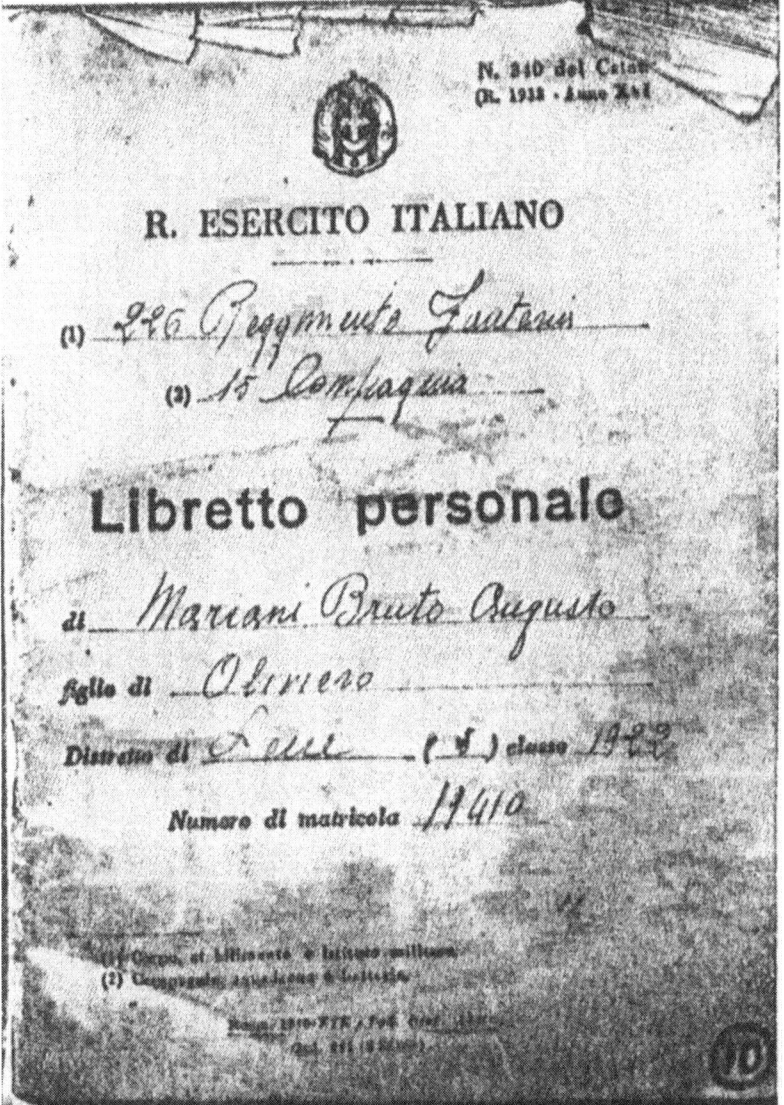

FIGURE 39.—Individual record book (*libretto personale*).

LIBRETTO PERSONALE

di Mariani Bruto Augusto

figlio di ... e di ...

nato addì ... 1922 nel Comune

di ... Provincia di Lecce

di religione (1) Cattolica

residente all'atto dell'arruolamento a

Via ... N. ...

Ufficio postale ...

inscritto nel Comune di ...

Provincia di Lecce Distretto militare

di Lecce (...) Classe 19...

Ammogliato con ...

il ... (2)

Rimasto vedovo ...

Professione o mestiere Bracciante

Grado d'istruzione e titolo di studio ...

(1) Cattolica, ...

(2) Con autorizzazione del Comandante ...

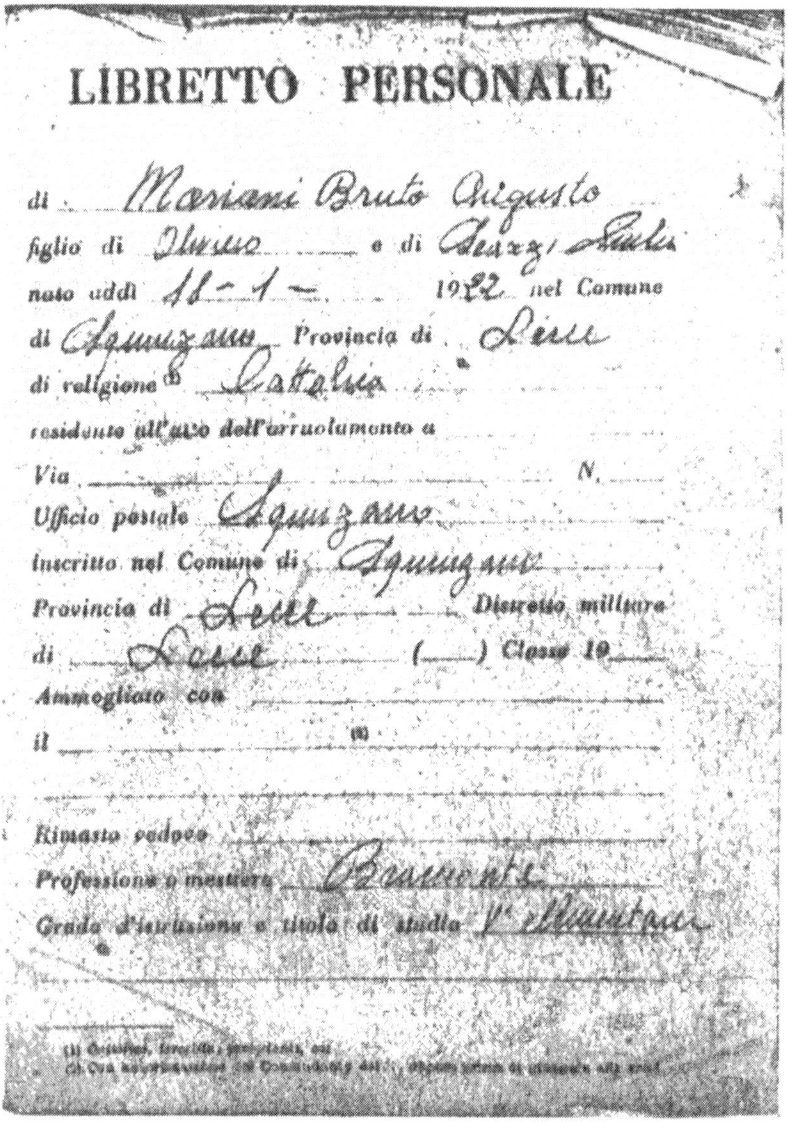

FIGURE 39.—Individual record book (*libretto personale*). ②

Section III

DECORATIONS, MEDALS, AND AWARDS

	Paragraph
General	195
Decorations	196
Grades of decorations	197
Medals for valor	198
Awards for long service	199
Crosses	200
Commemorative medals and ribbons	201
Recently instituted awards	202
Service ribbons	203

195. General.—Medals and decorations are freely given in the Italian Army and great emphasis is placed upon their importance. Military sentinels must salute persons in civilian clothes who have been decorated for valor or for wounds received in action, as well as mothers and widows wearing decorations of dead soldiers. Officers and soldiers who have not been decorated for valor or distinction in war must salute those men of the same grade who have these distinctions. There are more than 50 types of awards and medals, and of these a few entitle the recipient to an annuity.

196. Decorations.—There are the following orders of chivalry:

a. Supreme Order of the Most Sacred Annunciation (*Decorazione dell' Ordine della Santissima Annunziata*).—This order is the highest in rank of all Italian decorations. Persons upon whom it is bestowed automatically become honorary cousins of the King.

b. Order of Saint Maurice and Saint Lazarus (*Decorazione dell' Ordine de S. S. Maurizio e Lazzaro*).

c. Miltary Order of Savoy (*Decorazione dell' Ordine Militare di Savoia*).

d. Order of the Crown of Italy (*Decorazione dell' Ordine della Corona d' Italia*).

e. Colonial Order of the Star of Italy (*Decorazione dell' Ordine Coloniale della Stella d'Italia*).

f. The Equestrian Order of the Roman Eagle (*Ordine cavalleresco dell' Aquila Romana*).—This order was instituted in 1942 for non-Italians who have made valuable contributions toward Italy's consolidation and general development.

197. Grades of decorations.—The orders named above have five grades, that is, chevalier (*cavaliere*), officer (*cavaliere ufficiale*), commander (*commendatore*), grand officer (*grande ufficiale*), and grand cross (*gran croce*). The name of the grade becomes an honorary title: for example, *Cavaliere Carlo Annibile Manogallo, Tenente Colonnello di Fanteria.* If a person has an official title, or one of nobility, he is usually called by this title in preference to that of the order, although both may be used: for example, *Marchese Grand' Ufficiale Francesco Scema, Capitano di Frigata.*

198. Medals for valor.—So-called "Medals for Valor" (*Medaglie al Valore*) are popular awards in Italy. The Gold Medal (*Medaglia d'Oro*) corresponds to the U. S. Medal of Honor; the Silver Medal (*Medaglia d'Argento*) corresponds roughly to the U. S. Distinguished Service Cross; and the Bronze Medal (*Medaglia bi Bronzo*) corresponds roughly to the U. S. Silver Star citation. Holders of these decorations or their families receive annual pensions, as follows: Gold Medal, 1,500 lire (about $75); Silver Medal, 750 lire (about $38); Bronze Medal, 300 lire (about $15). The Gold Medal is usually awarded posthumously.

199. Awards for long service.—Length of service is rewarded with the Cross for Long Service (*Croce per Anzianità di Servizio*). This cross is awarded after 16 years of service and a gold star is added to the service ribbon after 25 years. There is also an award for long command (*Lungo Comando*), given after 16 years of active command and worn with a gold star after 25 years.

200. Crosses.—In addition to the Cross for Long Service, there is a Cross for War Merit (*Croce al Merito di Guerra*) and a War Cross for Military Valor (*Croce di Guerra al Valor Militare*).

201. Commemorative medals and ribbons.—Awards are given to all those who participate in campaigns and to soldiers stationed in war zones whether or not they have served in combat. The most common of these awards are the following:

  a. African Campaign Medal (*Medaglia a Ricordo delle Campagne d'Africa*).

  b. Commemorative medal for Campaigns in the Far East (*Medaglia Commemorativa delle Campagne nell'Estremo Oriente*).

  c. Service Medal for the Italo-Turkish War (1911–1912) and the Libyan campaigns (*Medaglia Commemorativa della guerra italo-turca 1911–1912 e delle Campagne di Libia*).

  d. National Commemorative Medal for the War of 1915–1918 (*Medaglia Commemorativa Nazionale della Guerra 1915–1918*).

  e. Medal for the Unity of Italy (*Medaglia a Ricordo dell'Unità d'Italia*).

  f. Medal of Merit for the Volunteers in the Italo-Austrian War of 1915–1918 (*Medaglia di Benemerenza per i Volontari della Guerra Italo-Austriaca 1915–1918*).

202. Recently instituted awards.—During the present war a number of awards have been added to the already long list. Among these are the following:

  a. Military Aeronautical Medal.—This medal is awarded to airplane and seaplane pilots, airplane and seaplane observers, dirigible commanders, and navigating officers, as follows:

  (1) First-grade medal for 25 years of flying service.
  (2) Second-grade medal for 15 years of flying service.
  (3) Third-grade medal for 10 years flying service.

  b. Medal for Aeronautical Bravery.—Gold, silver, and bronze medals are awarded to men who distinguish themselves for particular courage, or skill on board aircraft in flight. The gold medal is awarded by the King only when the Air Ministry attaches great honor to the deed.

c. Commemorative Medal of Aeronautical Feats.—Gold, silver, and bronze medals are awarded by the Air Ministry according to the importance of the feat itself or for the bold, intelligent, and efficient assistance of members of the crew of an aircraft in an emergency.

d. Russian campaign.—There is a special medal for men who participated in the Russian campaigns.

e. War zone ribbon.—A ribbon with alternating red and green vertical stripes is worn by soldiers present in the war zones of the present war for more than three months. A star is added for each year of service in these zones.

203. Service ribbons.—Awards are represented by ribbons worn as in the U. S. Army. Difference in rank does not affect the color, size, or manner of wearing these ribbons. The grade of an award may be indicated by a star, crown, laurel branch, palm, or sword worn on the ribbon. For example, the Medal for Valor, which is awarded in gold, silver, or bronze, is represented by a blue ribbon carrying a five-pointed star of gold, silver, or bronze, as the case may be. Without the star, the ribbon represents the cross awarded for bravery. Each star won on the ribbons for service in this war and the war of 1915–1918 represents 1 year of service.

Chapter 6

ARMAMENT AND EQUIPMENT

		Paragraphs
SECTION	I. Infantry	204–213
	II. Cavalry	214–221
	III. Antiaircraft and antitank	222–230
	IV. Artillery	231–234
	V. Armored vehicles	235–238
	VI. Engineers	239–247
	VII. Signal communications	248–258
	VIII. Chemical warfare	259–269

Section I

INFANTRY

	Paragraph
General	204
Pistols	205
Rifles	206
Carbines	207
Antitank rifle	208
Machine guns	209
Miscellaneous infantry guns	210
Mortars (*mortai*)	211
Hand grenades (*bombe a mano*)	212
Individual equipment	213

204. General.—In dealing with the subject of weapons in the Italian Army one is confronted with an extraordinary multiplicity of types and variety of employment. Many obsolete models in use, and the Italian aptitude for improvisation is reflected in the number of dual-purpose weapons. Classification is therefore difficult, and is necessarily somewhat arbitrary. Included in the discussion of infantry weapons are these that appear to be employed mainly in that arm.

205. Pistols.—*a. General.*—A revolver and two automatic pistols are standard issue in the Italian Army (see figs. 40 and 41).

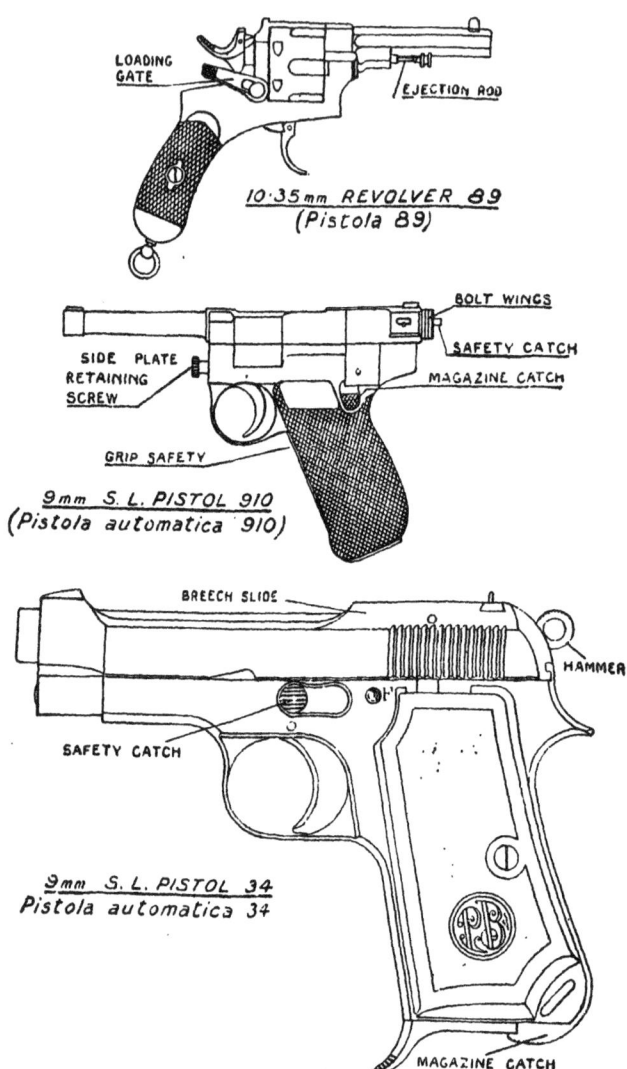

FIGURE 40.—Service revolver and pistols.

ARMAMENT AND EQUIPMENT

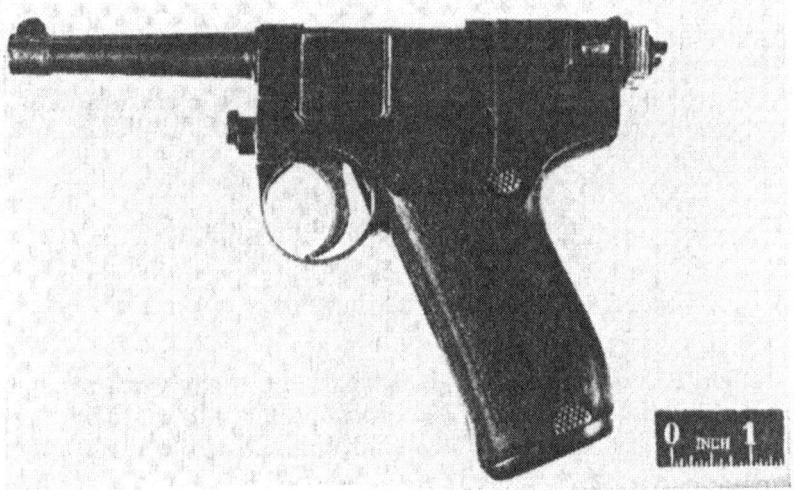

Figure 41.—9-mm automatic pistol, model 910 (Glisenti).

Noncommissioned officers and enlisted men of machine-gun and gun detachments and some other units carry the revolver. Commissioned officers and *marescialli* are armed with a pistol.

b. 10.35-mm revolver, model 89 (Bodeo).—This is a solid framed double-action revolver of old-fashioned design. The cylinder does not swing out, and empty cases can only be extracted one by one.

Caliber _____ 10.35 mm (0.41 inch).
Weight _____ 2 pounds.
Over-all length _____ 9¼ inches.
Cylinder capacity _____ 6 rounds.

c. 9-mm automatic pistol, model 910 (Glisenti) (fig. 41).

Caliber _____ 9 mm (0.35 inch).
Weight _____ 1 pound 12 ounces.
Over-all length _____ 8½ inches.
Feed _____ Removable 7-round magazine in butt.

RESTRICTED

d. 9-mm self-loading pistol, model 34 (Beretta).—This pistol has an external hammer, a fixed barrel, and a recoiling breech slide. The ammunition is the short 9-mm type which is interchangeable with the .38-inch ammunition used in the .38 Colt automatic pistol.

Caliber	9 mm (0.35 inch).
Weight	1 pound 7½ ounces.
Over-all length	6 inches.
Feed	Removable 7-round magazine in butt.

206. **Rifles.**—*a. General.*—Shortly before the present war the Italians decided to increase the caliber of the rifle and light machine gun from 6.5 mm. to 7.35 mm., and a new rifle and carbine of this caliber were actually introduced (see fig. 42). It seems, however, that the change-over has not yet progressed very far, and may even have been postponed, since rifles of the new 1938 pattern have been found to be fitted with a 6.5-mm barrel. Older models of both rifles and carbines of the Vetterli-Vitali type, which have been captured in North Africa, include a 10.35-mm rifle and a 10.35-mm carbine (musketoon). Some details of these older patterns are included, as they still appear to be used in large numbers.

b. 6.5-mm rifle, model 91 (Mannlicher-Carcano) (fig. 42).— The basic Mannlicher-Carcano design, which is embodied in all Italian rifles and carbines, combines the Mannlicher system of clip loading with a bolt action of the Mauser type developed by M. Carcano of the Turin Small Arms Factory. With the Mannlicher system of loading, each clip is inserted in the magazine together with the cartridges, and after all the cartridges have been forced up out of it by a spring-loaded lever known as the "elevator," the clip drops out through a hole in the bottom.

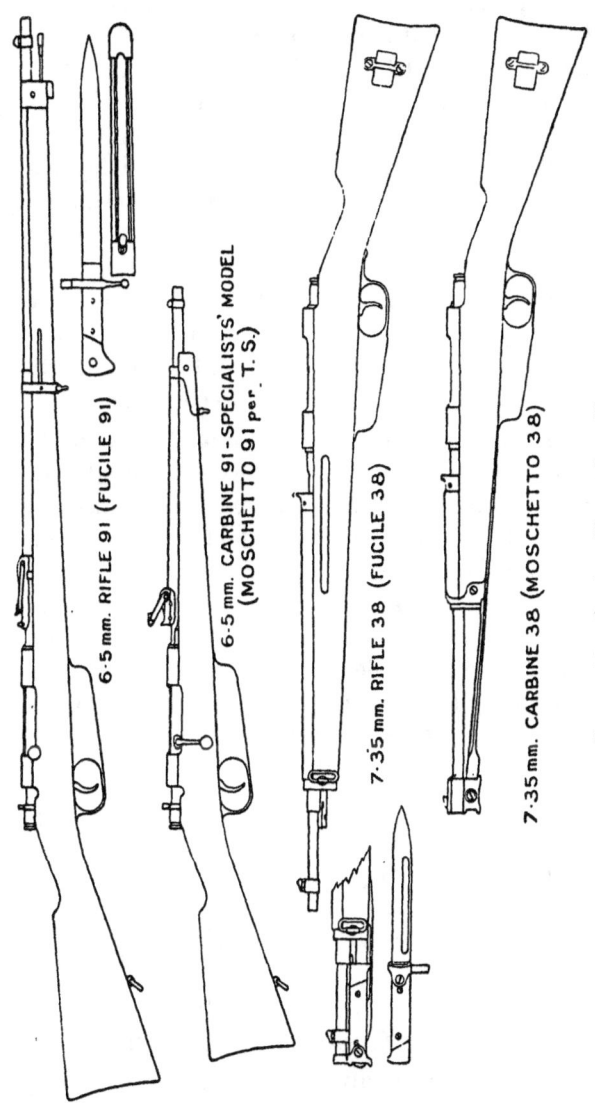

Figure 42.—Service rifles and carbines.

Caliber_____ 6.5 mm (0.256 inch).
Weight (without bayonet)_ 8½ pounds.
Length (without bayonet)_ 51 inches.
Rifling_____ 4 grooves (right hand, increasing twist).
Sight_____ V notch, barley corn, sighted 600 to 2,000 m.
Feed_____ Vertical box-magazine holding 6-round clip.
Safety_____ Catch on rear end of bulb engaged by pushing forward and to left and allowing it to come back.

c. 6.5-mm. rifle, model 70 (long) and 10.35-mm., P model 70 (long).—The two rifles are identical except for caliber. Both are fitted with a V back sight rising in steps up to 2,000 meters. The method of feed is the same as for model 91. The safety catch prevents the bolt from closing.

d. 7.35-mm rifle, model 38.—This rifle (fig. 42) is based on the model 91 rifle, the main differences being the increased caliber and reductions in weight and length. It has a light folding bayonet which is normally attached to the barrel but can be removed and used as a dagger. Some of these rifles are fitted with a 6.5-mm barrel.

Caliber_____ 7.35 mm (0.289 inch).
Weight (without bayonet)_ 7½ pounds.
Length (without bayonet)_ 40 inches.
Rifling_____ 4 grooves (right hand, constant twist).
Sight_____ Battle sight fixed for 300 m only.

e. Czech 7.92-mm self-loading rifle.—This rifle, fixed for a bayonet, is a gas-operated weapon fed by a 10-round magazine and sighted up to 1,400 meters.

ARMAMENT AND EQUIPMENT 206-207

f. 9-mm self-loading rifle (Pietro Beretta). This single-shot or automatic rifle is fitted to take a bayonet.

Caliber_____ 9 mm (0.35 inch).
Operation_____ Blowback.
Feed_____ Curved magazine holding 20 ounces.
Ejection_____ Underneath.
Sight_____ Fixed 200 m, offset to right.

g. 9-mm self-loading rifle (Beretta Gardine).—Earlier patterns of this single-shot rifle were fitted to take a bayonet. The cleaning rod is kept in the butt trap.

Caliber_____ 9 mm (0.35 inch).
Operation_____ Blowback.
Food_____ Magazine holding 10 rounds.
Ejection_____ Upwards.
Sight_____ Up to 500 m.
Safety_____ Catch on trigger guard.

207. Carbines.—*a. 6.5-mm carbine, model 91/24 (Mannlicher-Carcano).*

Caliber_____ 6.5 mm (26 inches).
Weight (without sling and_____ 4.270 kg (7 pounds).
  with bayonet).
Weight (without sling and_____ 3.900 kg.
  without bayonet).
Weight of bayonet_____ .37 kg.
Length without bayonet_____ 129 cm.
Length with bayonet_____ 159 cm.
Length of bayonet blade____ 30 cm.
Length of barrel_____ 78 cm.
Rifling_____ Constant progressive.
Total weight of cartridge__ 22.60 gr.
Weight of projectile_____ 10.35 gr.
Weight of case_____ 9.65 gr.

185   **RESTRICTED**

Weight of propellant
charge. 2.28 gr.
Length of projectile _____ 30.40 mm.
Pressure _____ 3.200 atmospheres.
Muzzle velocity_____ 700 meters per second.
Maximum ordinate at 300 120 cm.
m for the 500-m range.
Penetration _____ sufficient at 600 m range for putting out of action a man (or animal).

b. *6.5-mm carbine, model 91, "Per T. S."*—This carbine (fig. 42) is similar to the model 91 carbine, but has a separate bayonet like the model 91 rifle. "Per T. S." (*truppe speciali*) means "for special troops," that is, gunners and specialists.

c. *6.5-mm carbines, model 70, and 10.35-mm, model 70.*—These carbines are identical except for caliber. They are also identical with the model 70 rifles except that the magazine is of the pistol type.

d. *7.35-mm carbine, model 38.*—This carbine (fig. 42) compares with the model 91 carbine as the model 38 rifle compares with the model 91 rifle.

e. *8-mm. Steyr (Austrian) rifle, model 95 (long).*—Both the long and short patterns appear to have been used by the Italians in the Western Desert. They are distinctive in that the bolt is of the straight pull type very similar to that of the Canadian Ross.

Caliber _____ 8-mm (.315 inch).
Sight_____ 6 to 2,600 m. Fitted with 3 V's, one for use as a back sight when the leaf is down, giving approximately 200 m: one for use when leaf is raised, giving approximately 300 m; and one at

ARMAMENT AND EQUIPMENT 207–208

	the top of the leaf, giving 2,600 m. In addition, there is the V for use on the adjustable slide.
Feed	Magazine-fed by usual clip (5 rounds).
Ammunition	8-mm rim cartridge as for Schwarzlose.
Safety	Safety catch.

208. Antitank rifle.—The 20-mm Soluthurn antitank rifle (fig. 43) is a self-loading, single-shot weapon based on the Swiss 20-mm antitank rifle, model 18/100. It is fired normally from the shoulder on its bipod. The 1941 pattern can fire either single rounds or automatic, and a change lever is provided. In some cases, however, it has been observed that the change lever of some of the captured rifles had been fastened so that only single rounds could be obtained. A light two-wheeled carriage is provided for quick movement from one position to another. The rifle can be fired from this mount. The Soluthurn magazine on this rifle is easily confused with that of the 20-mm antiaircraft guns, but the weapons can be identified by the magazine positioning pieces on the front of the open end. In the Solu-

FIGURE 43.—20-mm antitank rifle (Soluthurn).

thurn magazine they are flat, and on the antiaircraft-gun magazines they are circular.

Caliber	20 mm.
Length	7 feet 1 inch (including muzzle brake).
Weight	Approximately 120 pounds.
Operation	Recoil.
Method of feed	Magazine capable of holding 10 rounds, normally filled with 8 rounds; on the last round's being fired, the magazine is ejected automatically.
Ejection	Right side.
Muzzle velocity	Varies according to type from 2,610 to 2,950 feet per second.
Locking	Rotating locking lugs.
Sighting	Telescope or open sight up to 1,500 m.
Single or automatic	Early models single only; model 1941 both.
State of chamber on "cease firing"	Clear.
Cyclic rate	Approximately 300 rounds per minute.
Safety:	
Applied	Catch on right side of pistol grip.
Mechanical	Usual.

209. Machine guns.—*a. 6.5-mm light machine gun, model 30 (Breda)* (fig. 44).—

Caliber	6.5 mm. (0.256 inch).
Length	48 inches.

ARMAMENT AND EQUIPMENT

FIGURE 44.—6.5-mm light machine gun, model 30 (Breda).

Weight	25½ pounds.
Operation	Recoil.
Feed	Magazine holding 20 rounds, fed by brass charger.
Ejection	To left.
Locked or unlocked	2,050 feet per second.
Sight	300 to 1,500 m battle sight for 300 m.
Barrel change	Quick.
Single or automatic	Automatic.
State of chamber on "cease firing."	Round in chamber.
Cyclic rate of fire	350 to 400 rounds per minute.
Safety:	
Applied	Safety catch on right side.
Mechanical	Round cannot be fired until chamber is sealed.

b. 8-mm medium machine gun, model 37 (Breda).—This weapon (fig. 45), reduction of the 20-mm heavy machine gun (see below), has certain special features of interest, as follows: empty

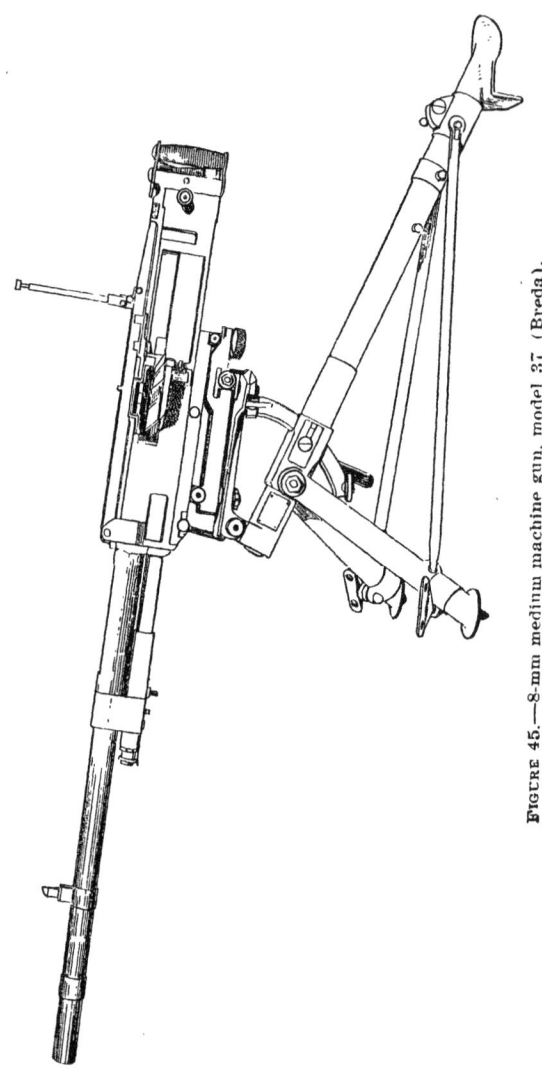

FIGURE 45.—8-mm medium machine gun, model 37 (Breda).

cases are returned to a tray; a special clamp is provided for quick changing of barrels; the piston head is changeable; and the gas regulator has 10 settings.

Caliber	8 mm (0.315 inch).
Length	50 inches.
Weight of gun without mounts)	42½ pounds.
Weight of tripod	41½ pounds.
Operation	Gas.
Method of feed	20-round strip (plate charger).
Ejection	Empty case returned to strip.
Locking	Locking lugs.
Muzzle velocity	Figures not published.
Sight	Tangent back sight up to 3,000 m, with wind gage.
Single or automatic	Automatic.
Barrel change	Fairly quick.
Cyclic rate	450 rounds per minute.
State of chamber on "cease firing."	Clear.
Safety:	
Applied	Safety catch on top of cross piece.
Mechanical	Chamber must be positively locked before firing.

c. 8-mm (0.315-inch) tank-mounted machine gun, model 38 (Breda).—Although this is usually a tank-mounted gun, the Italians have adapted it for use as an infantry gun (see fig. 46). When used as an infantry gun, a rough front sight is fitted on the right of the muzzle, as well as a rough rear sight on the right of the body. This gun, which is almost the same as the 13.2-mm Breda aircraft cannon (see 210*a*, below) has certain special features of interest, as follows: the cocking handle may be found on either side; when the magazine becomes empty it is thrown for-

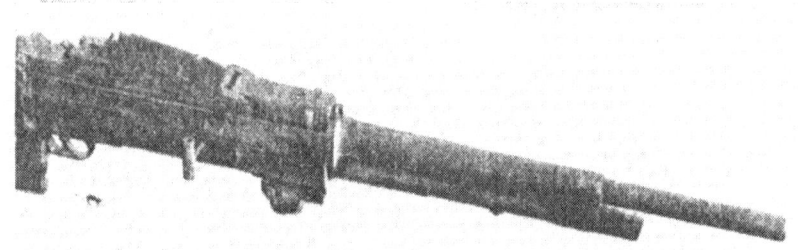

FIGURE 46.—8-mm tank-mounted machine gun, model 38 (Breda).

ward slightly; the gas regulator has 10 settings; the gun may be fitted with one plain or two twisted mainsprings; the gun has very pronounced muzzle flash.

Caliber	8 mm (0.315 inch).
Length	35½ inches.
Weight	34¼ pounds.
Operation	Gas.
Method of feed	Vertical box magazine (24 rounds).
Ejection	Locking lugs.
Muzzle velocity	No figures yet published.
Sight	Sighted co-axially with other gun.
Single or automatic	Automatic.
Barrel change	No quick change.
Cyclic rate	450 to 500 rounds per minute.
State of chamber on "cease firing"	Clear.
Safety:	
Applied	Safety catch at rear of body.
Mechanical	Usual.

d. 7.35-mm (0.285-inch) light machine gun, model 38 (Breda).—This gun is the same in all respects as the model 30, except for caliber. It fires the same ammunition as the model 38 rifle.

ARMAMENT AND EQUIPMENT

e. 6.5-mm (0.256-inch) light machine gun, model C (Breda).—
The 6.5-mm light machine gun, model C (or 5 C), is basically the same as the model 30. The model C, however, has a crosspiece with traversing handles instead of a butt and pistol grip. It is also provided with a tripod instead of a bipod mount. It weighs about 4 pounds more than the model 30.

f. 6.5-mm medium machine gun, model 14 (Fiat-Revelli).—
This is a water-cooled machine gun and is the pattern as used in World War I. It is now obsolescent but is still used for training purposes.

Calibre	6.5 mm (0.256 inch).
Length	46½ inches.
Weight (without water)	37½ pounds.
Operation	Recoil.
Feed	Magazine holding 50 rounds.
Ejection	Top and right.
Locking	Spring-loaded locking wedge.
Muzzle velocity	No figures available.
Sight	200 to 2,400 m.
Single or automatic	Both.
Barrel change	Not quick.
State of chamber on "cease firing."	Round in chamber parts forward.
Cyclic rate	500 rounds per minute.
Safety:	
Applied	Safety catch (upright).
Mechanical	Usual.

g. 8-mm medium machine gun, model 35 (Fiat-Revelli).—This machine gun (fig. 47) is a modification of the model 14, an air-cooled barrel and multiple-box magazine of the older model. Some, though not all, model 35 machine guns are actually converted from the model 14 type. There is no automatic lubricating of cartridge of chamber.

RESTRICTED

FIGURE 47.—8-mm medium machine gun, model 35 (Fiat-Revelli).

Caliber	8-mm (0.315 inch).
Length	49¾ inches.
Weight	39¾ pounds.
Operation	Recoil.
Feed	Metal belt in lengths of from 50 to 250 rounds.
Ejection	Right and top.
Locking	Spring-loaded locking wedge.
Muzzle velocity	(No figures available.)
Sight	200 to 2,400 m.
Single or automatic	Both.
Barrel change	Quick.
State of chamber on "cease firing"	Round in chamber, parts forward.

ARMAMENT AND EQUIPMENT

Cyclic rate_____ 250 or 500 rounds per minute (can be regulated on some guns).
Safety:
    Applied_____ Safety catch (upright).
    Mechanical_____ Usual.

FIGURE 48.—8-mm medium machine gun, model 07/12 (Schwarzlose).

h. 8-mm medium machine gun, model 07/12 (Schwarzlose).— This Austrian gun (fig. 48) is used extensively.

Caliber_____ 8-mm (0.315 inch) (rim cartridge).
Length_____ 37 inches (approximate).
Weight (without water or oil)_____ 44 pounds.
Weight of tripod_____ 35 pounds.
Operation_____ Recoil (single blowback).
Feed_____ Fabric belt of 250 rounds.
Ejection_____ Left side.
Muzzle velocity_____ (No figures available.)

RESTRICTED

Sight_____ 200 to 2,400 m.
Single or automatic_____ Automatic only.
State of chamber on
 "cease firing"_____ Round in chamber.
Cyclic rate_____ 400 rounds per minute.
Safety:
 Applied_____ Thumb-piece catch.
 Mechanical_____ Usual.

i. 7.7-mm machine gun (Scotti Isotta Fraschini).—This is an old type of Italian weapon used in aircraft.

Caliber_____ 7.7 mm (0.303 inch).
Feed_____ Belt.
Operation_____ Gas.
Rounds per minute_____ 1,100 (cyclic).

j. 9-mm machine carbine, model 38 (Beretta) (fig. 49).—Machine carbines have not been extensively used by the Italians; nevertheless, they possess in the model 38 Beretta a weapon which is considered above the average, both as regards functioning and convenience in handling. Earlier patterns were fitted to take a folding bayonet similar to that used with the model 38 rifle. Model 38 will fire 9-mm Parabellum ammunition of British, German, or Italian manufacture, and in this respect is similar to the Sten. A cleaning rod in three pieces is kept in the butt.

Caliber_____ 9 mm (0.35 inch).
Weight (without magazine) 9 pounds 1 ounce.
Length_____ 37½ inches.
Cyclic rate_____ 570 rounds per minute.
Sight_____ Radial leaf **V** sight from 100 to 500 m.
Feed_____ Box magazine fitted under body in three sizes: 10, 20, and 40 rounds.

ARMAMENT AND EQUIPMENT 209

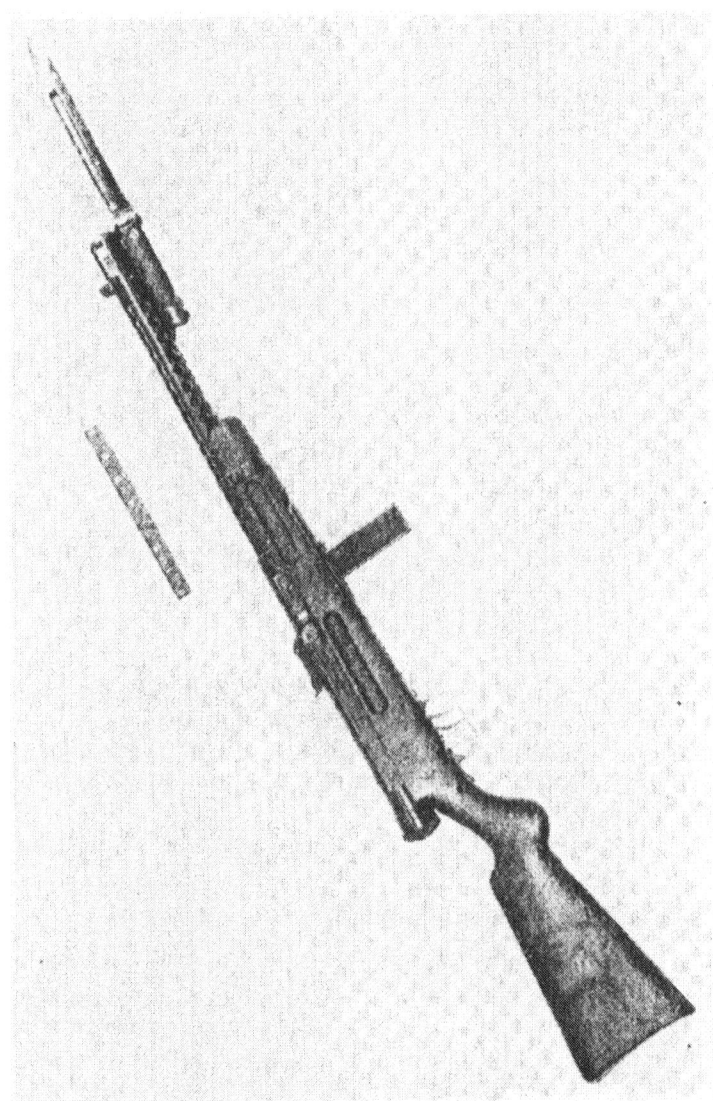

FIGURE 49.—9-mm machine carbine, model 38 (Beretta).

RESTRICTED

Operation	Blowback.
Safety	Lever on left of body.
Single or automatic	Both (two triggers, front for single rounds and rear for automatic; the automatic trigger is provided with a plunger which locks it when pressed in from left to right, thus preventing inadvertent automatic fire.

k. 20-mm heavy machine gun, model 35 (Breda).—This dual-purpose weapon (fig. 50) could be described as a heavier version of the 8-mm medium machine gun, model 37 (see *b* above).

Caliber	20 mm (0.79 inch).
Length of bore	65 calibers.
Weight	680 pounds.
Operation	Gas.
Feed	Strip containing 12 rounds.
Ejection	Into strip.
Locking	2,750 feet per second.
Sight	V sight, 3,000 m.
Single or automatic	Automatic.
Cyclic rate	120 rounds per minute.
Safety:	
Applied	Catch at rear.
Mechanical	Usual.
State of chamber on "cease firing."	Clear.

210. Miscellaneous infantry guns.[1]—*a. 12.7-mm. aircraft cannon (Breda).*—This gun is similar in design and operation to the 7.7-mm Breda Safat, and is difficult to adapt for ground use

---

[1] For 75/27-mm guns, 75/13-mm and 75/18 howitzers, and 100/17-mm howitzers, see section IV, paragraph 232. For 20-mm antiaircraft guns and the 47/32-mm (1.85-inch) antitank gun, model 37, see section III, paragraph 224c.

ARMAMENT AND EQUIPMENT

FIGURE 50.—20-mm heavy machine gun, model 35 (Breda).

although this has been done in at least one instance. A point worth noting is that it will not fire British or United States 0.5-inch ammunition.

Caliber	12.7 mm (0.5 inch).
Length	53¼ inches.
Weight	67½ pounds.
Operation	Recoil, assisted by gas.
Method of feed	Disintegrating metal link belt (.5 Vickers belt does fit).
Cyclic rate	650 rounds per minute.
Single or automatic	Automatic.
Muzzle velocity	2,430 feet per second.

b. 13.2-mm aircraft machine gun (Breda).—This machine gun is practically a stepped-up version of the 8-mm tank mounted model. It has a fixed pedestal mount for use as an antiaircraft and antitank weapon.

c. 7.7-mm aircraft machine gun (Breda Safat).—This gun will fire British 0.303-inch ammunition.

Caliber	7.7 mm (0.303 inch).
Length	44 inches.
Weight	27 pounds.
Operation	Recoil assisted by muzzle blast.
Feed	Disintegrating metal belt holding 250 rounds.
Ejection	Underneath.
Locking	Barrel and breechblock locked during first $3/16$ inch of recoil.
Muzzle velocity	2,440 feet per second.
Sight	Front sight $3/16$-inch ball in pillar; rear sight $1\,3/16$-inch ring with cross wires.
Single or automatic	Automatic.
Barrel change	No quick change.
Cyclic rate	800 rounds per minute.
State of chamber on "cease firing."	Clear.
Safety:	
Applied	Safety lever on top of feed cover.
Mechanical	Usual.

d. 65/17 infantry gun.—(1) *General.*—The 65/17 infantry gun (fig. 51) is an adaption of the Italian-made 65-mm mountain gun. It was superseded for use as a mountain gun by the 75/13 howitzer. For mobility the 65/17 is provided with a fore carriage.

Figure 51.—65/17 infantry gun.

(2) *Characteristics.*

Caliber	65 mm.
Length of bore	17 calibers.
Length of chamber	176.82 mm.
Length of rifling	905 mm.
Length from seating of cartridge case rim to muzzle.	1,082 mm (16.6 calibers).
Length from rear of breech to cartridge rim seating.	68 mm.
Total length	1,150 mm (17.5 calibers).
Volume of chamber	0.471 cm.
Rifling:	
Number of grooves	24.
Direction of twist	Left-handed.
Uniform twist for whole length.	1 in 1,950 mm (1 in 30 calibers).
Helix angle of rifling	5°58′42″
Weight of breech screw	7.500 kg.
Weight of barrel without breech screw.	92.500 kg.

Height of gun axis when horizontal.	671 mm.
Elevation	−7°30′ to +20°.
Traverse	8°.
Maximum width (to extremities of axle).	1,162 mm.
Over-all length (gun and trail).	3,570 mm.
Length of normal recoil	950 mm.
Diameter of wheels	700 mm.
Width of tire	50 mm.
Weight of wheel	25 kg.
Hydraulic buffer:	
Capacity	4.060 liters.
Mixture	37 percent water, 63 percent glycerine.
Density	22.50°.

(3) *Ammunition.*—This is of the fixed type. There are three kinds of projectiles: 65 (shell), 65 (armor-piercing shell), and 65/17 (case shot).

211. Mortars (*mortai*).—*a. General.*—The Italian Army has two standard mortars: a light mortar known as the 45-mm (1.77-inch), model 35 (Brixia), and a medium 81 (3-inch), model 35. The light mortar has a number of good points, including a high rate of fire, steadiness in action, and the fact that it folds conveniently for carrying; but these and other advantages, which have only been obtained at the expense of an unusually elaborate design, are largely offset by the poor fragmentation of the mortar bomb. The 81-mm mortar is a good weapon of conventional Stokes-Brandt design. Using a light 7¼ pound bomb, it has a high maximum range at full charge, mainly to the use of six large ballistite-filled secondaries. Fragmentation of both the light and heavy bombs is, however, relatively ineffective.

ARMAMENT AND EQUIPMENT 211

b. 45-mm light, model 35 (Brixia).—This is a breech-loaded trigger-fired weapon (fig. 52) which is capable of high-angle and low-angle fire (that is, it can fire at elevations above and below 45°). Only one charge is employed, but a reduced charge effect can be obtained by firing with ports in the barrel open. The cartridges are fed from a detachable box magazine fitted on top of the body, but the bombs have to be loaded singly by hand. The mount is a folding tripod, with a padded frame hinged to its rear leg. When the mortar is in the firing position, this padded frame acts as a cushion for the firer's chest, and when folded for transport, it eases the load on his shoulders. The safety lever, on the left of the body, is shifted back (exposing the letter S—*sicurezza*—for "safety") and forward (exposing the letter F—*fuoco*—for "fire").

Caliber	45 mm (1.77 inches).
Weight (with mount)	34 pounds.
Maximum range (ports closed)	586 yards.
Maximum range (ports open)	352 yards.
Magazine capacity	10 cartridges.
Weight of HE bomb	1 pound.
Sights	Pillar rear sight with vertical slot aperture; barleycorn front sight.
Rate of fire (without reaiming between rounds)	25 to 30 rounds per minute.

c. 81-mm medium, model 35.—(1) This mortar (figs. 53, 54, and 55) is of the same general type as the British 3-inch mortar. The chief differences are in the recoil gear and the cross-leveling gear. The recoil gear consists of two cylinders arranged side by side, each containing a recoil spring and a pneumatic buffer. The cross-leveling gear includes rough and fine adjustments. The rough adjustment is obtained by moving a sliding collar on the

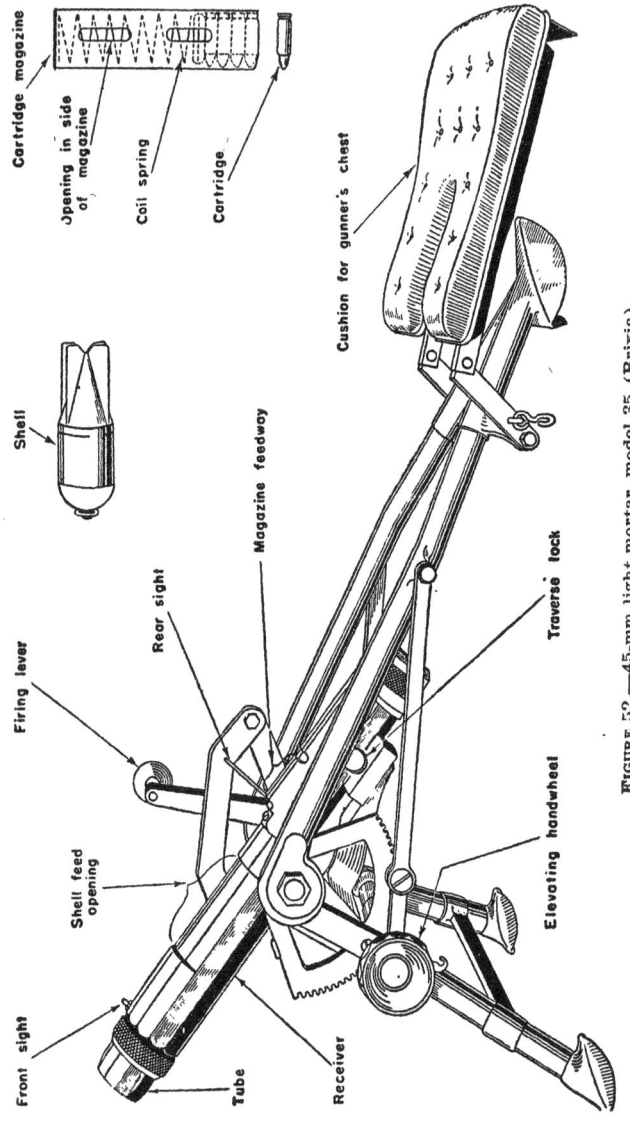

FIGURE 52.—45-mm light mortar, model 35 (Brixia).

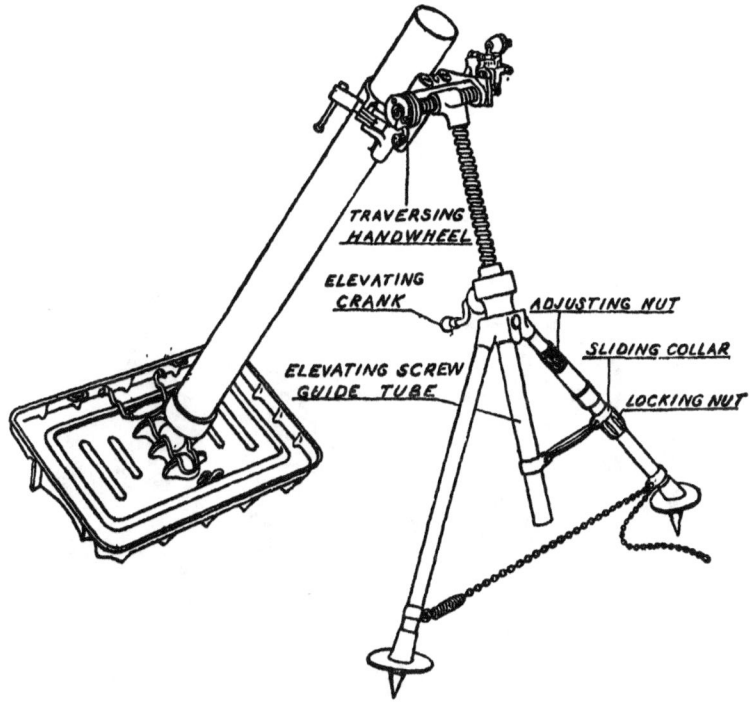

FIGURE 53.—81-mm medium mortar, model 35.

outer end of a connecting rod up or down the left leg and the fine adjustment by turning a milled nut near the top of the left leg. The mechanism is finally locked by means of a fluted clamping nut.

(2) German 8-cm mortar bombs 34 can be fired from this mortar, but British 3-inch mortar bombs are unsuitable, since the needle disk clip on the British bomb fouls the striker housing of the mortar and thus prevents a clean strike. When firing German bombs with a full charge, a maximum range of 2,250 yards can be expected at 45° elevation that is a slightly higher range than when fired from the German mortar 34.

FIGURE 54.—81-mm mortar squad.

Caliber_____ 81 mm (3 inches).
Total weight_____ 129 pounds.
Weight of light bomb_____ 7¼ pounds.
Weight of heavy bomb_____ 15 pounds.
Number of charges (light bomb)___ Seven (numbered 0–6).
Number of charges (heavy bomb). Five (numbered 0–4).
Maximum range (light bomb)_____ 4,429 yards.
Maximum range (heavy bomb)____ 1,640 yards.

ARMAMENT AND EQUIPMENT   211–212

FIGURE 55.—Firing the 81-mm mortar.

212. Hand grenades *(bombe a mano)*.—*a. General.*—Three models of hand grenades (fig. 56) are in service use. They are all very light grenades, functioned by "always" percussion fuzes and similar in general construction. Fragmentation is very poor and reliance is placed on blast for effect.

b. Model 35 (S. R. C. M.).—(1). *General.*—The S. R. C. M. grenade, model 35, is cylindrical in shape. It has an outer casing in top halves which screw together about the middle and an inner casing consisting of two metal cylinders. The striker and a spring which holds the striker away from the detonator are housed in the upper cylinder, while the lower cylinder contains the detonator and the explosive filling.

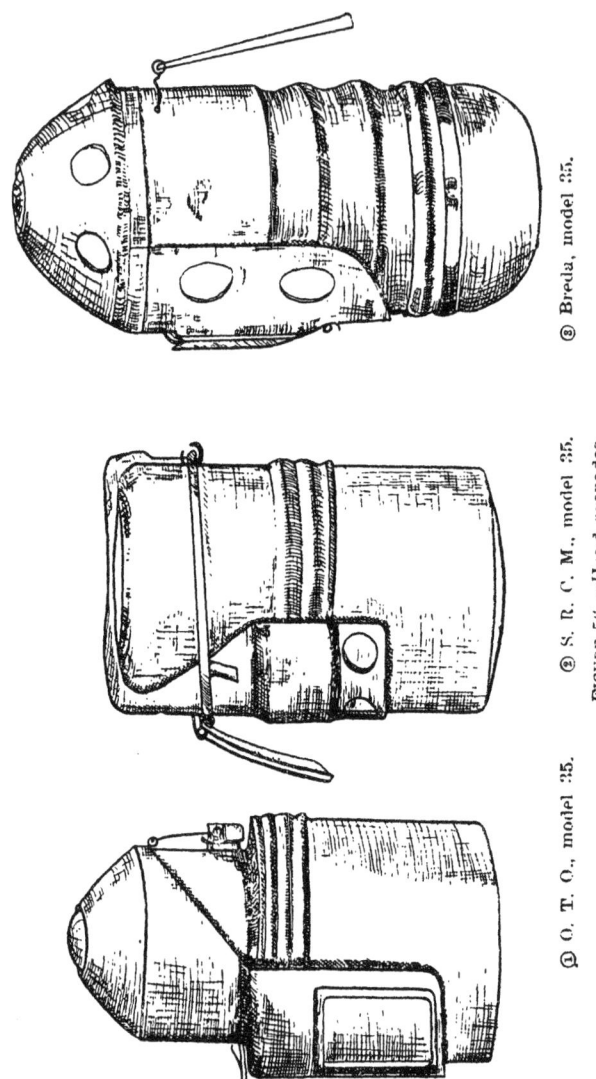

Figure 56.—Hand grenades.
① O. T. O., model 35.
② S. R. C. M., model 35.
③ Breda, model 35.

ARMAMENT AND EQUIPMENT

(2) *Characteristics.*

Weight	7 ounces.
Weight of explosive	1.5 ounces.
Over-all length	3.1 inches.
Maximum diameter	2.5 inches.

(3) *Safety.*—A large safety cap covers the top and part of the side of the grenade and is held in position by a metal strip, to which is attached a rubber tab. The safety cap is connected by a short chain to a safety bar. In addition, a shutter is fitted between the striker and the detonator which does not open until impact takes place.

(4) *To arm and fire.*—The grenade is grasped in the right hand and the rubber tab pulled away with the left hand. The grenade is then thrown in the usual manner. The safety cap comes away during flight and, after a short delay, pulls out the safety bar by means of the chain. On impact, the shutter moves and the striker can fire the detonator.

c. Model 35 (Breda).—(1) *General.*—The Breda grenade, model 35, is longer and thinner than the S. R. C. M. grenade, model 35, and has hemispherical ends.

(2) *Characteristics.*

Weight	7 ounces.
Weight of explosive	2.1 ounces.
Over-all length	3.8 inches.
Maximum diameter	2.1 inches.

(3) *Safety.*—The safety arrangements consist of a safety cap held in position by a brass strip with a rubber tab and a safety bar secured to the safety cap by a brass tape wound around the grenade.

(4) *To arm and fire.*—The grenade is held in the right hand and the brass strip pulled out by means of the rubber tab. In flight the safety cap falls off and, after a delay, pulls out the safety bar. The grenade is then armed.

RESTRICTED

d. Model 35 (O. T. O.).—The O. T. O. grenade is very similar to the model 35 Breda, and is armed and fired in the same way. It has a very light casing made in two parts, namely, a cylindrical lower part to which is screwed an upper part in the form of a cylinder of smaller diameter topped by a truncated cone.

Weight _____ 7.4 ounces.
Weight of explosive _____ 2.5 ounces.
Over-all length _____ 3.4 inches.
Maximum diameter _____ 2.1 inches.

213. Individual equipment.—In general, it may be said that the Italian infantry soldier is poorly equipped. During the present war the quality of clothing has rapidly deteriorated. There is an actual shortage of shoes, and troops are often without changes of stockings or underwear. The shortage of steel has also affected the issue of helmets and many other items. The personal equipment of the infantryman has been reduced to a minimum, primarily by the elimination of reserve articles of clothing from his pack. The articles listed for issue to the enlisted man include the following: haversack, belt and suspenders, canteen, mess kit, intrenching tool, shelter quarter, two reserve rations, and a minimum of clothing. The cape (*mantellina*), which proved during World War I to be an insufficient substitute for the overcoat, still appears, and quantities of other obsolete equipment have been brought back into use.

SECTION II

CAVALRY

	Paragraph
General	214
Pistols	215
Rifles	216
Saber	217
Lance	218
Machine guns	219
Ammunition supply	220
Individual equipment	221

RESTRICTED

ARMAMENT AND EQUIPMENT 214–220

214. General.—For more details on weapons used by the cavalry, see the discussion of infantry weapons (sec. I above).

215. Pistols.—Cavalry officers are armed with the pistol, usually the 9-mm, model 1910 or 1934 (Glisenti) or the 9-mm, model 34 (Beretta).

216. Rifles.—Each trooper usually carries a carbine or rifle (Mannlicher-Carcano).

217. Saber.—The saber carried by officers is similar to the field saber used by officers in the U. S. Army. There are also 92 sabers per squadron in addition to those used by officers. These are somewhat like the saber formerly used by the U. S. cavalry.

218. Lance.—Four regiments retain the lance for ceremonial purposes. It is made of steel, is about 8 feet long, and weighs about 10 pounds.

219. Machine guns.—The cavalry uses the following machine guns and carbines:

 a. 6.5-mm light machine gun (Breda).
 b. 8-mm medium machine gun (Breda).
 c. 6.5-mm medium machine gun (Fiat-Revelli).
 d. 8-mm medium machine gun (Fiat-Revelli).
 e. 9-mm machine carbine (Beretta).

220. Ammunition supply.—The allotment of ammunition is made by the headquarters of the superior large unit, generally the army. Plans for assuring supplies are made by the army commanders.

Weapon	*Day of fire*	*Maximum rapidity of fire*
Pistol	10 rounds per arm	14 rounds per minute
Hand grenades	4 per man	
Rifle or carbine	60 rounds per weapon	12 rounds per minute
Machine rifle	1,300 rounds per arm	150 rounds per minute
Machine gun "Fiat 35"	2,000 rounds per arm	600 rounds per minute
Machine gun "Breda 37"	2,000 rounds per gun	450 rounds per minute

221. **Individual equipment.**—In addition to rations, a grooming kit and nosebag, 280 rounds of machine-gun and 60 rounds of carbine ammunition, cavalry personnel carry the following items of personal equipment:

1 bandolier (36 rounds).
2 hand grenades.
1 water bottle.
1 gas mask.
1 steel helmet.
1 towel.
1 pair of socks.
1 overcoat.
1 waterproof sheet.

Section III

ANTIAIRCRAFT AND ANTITANK

	Paragraph
General	222
Mobile antiaircraft guns	223
Antitank guns	224
Antiaircraft guns for fixed defense	225
Intermediate small-caliber antiaircraft weapons	226
Special communication equipment assigned to antiaircraft batteries and groups	227
Antiaircraft fire control instruments (Galileo)	228
Searchlights	229
Sound locator (Galileo)	230

222. **General.**—The characteristics of antiaircraft guns are tabulated in figure 57.

223. **Mobile antiaircraft guns.**—*a. 75/27 (2.95-inch) AA gun (C. K.).*—In addition to its employment as an antiaircraft gun, this gun (fig. 58) is also employed against ground targets, particularly hostile mechanized and armored forces. It is used to supplement the fire of antitank weapons, but is unwieldly and poor in performance.

Caliber _____ 75 mm.
Length of bore _____ 27 calibers.

ARMAMENT AND EQUIPMENT

Muzzle velocity_____ 1,675 feet per second.
Maximum horizontal range_____ 6,600 yards.
Maximum effective ceiling_____ 13,150 feet.
Weight of projectile_____ 14.5 pounds HE.
Practical rate of fire_____ 15 rounds per minute.
Weight in action_____ 4.64 tons.
Elevation_____ 0° to 70°.
Traverse_____ 360°.
Method of transport_____ Truck.

b. 75/46 (2.95-inch) AA gun, model 34 (Ansaldo).—This mobile weapon (figs. 59 and 60) is the standard Italian heavy antiaircraft gun and performs well. It has a loose liner type of band, and the following special features of interest: variable recoil, a hydraulic brake, a hydro-pneumatic recuperator, spring equilibrators, a semi-automatic horizontal coil breechblock, and an aiming device with an independent line of sight and an independent angle of fire.

Caliber_____ 75 mm.
Length of bore_____ 46 calibers.
Muzzle velocity_____ 2,350 feet per second.
Maximum range_____ 17,000 yards.
Maximum horizontal range_____ 14,100 yards.
Effective ceiling_____ 27,200 feet.
Weight of projectile_____ 14.3 pounds.
Practical rate of fire_____ 20 rounds per minute.
Weight in action_____ 3.24 tons.
Weight in draft_____ 3.54 tons.
Elevation_____ 2° to 90°.
Traverse_____ 360°.
Width of carriage_____ 1,300 mm.

RESTRICTED

HANDBOOK ON ITALIAN MILITARY FORCES

Type of gun	Length in calibers	Muzzle velocity in feet per second	Maximum horizontal range (yards)	Maximum effective ceiling (feet)	Weight of projectile (pounds)	Practical rate of fire in rounds per minute	Weight in action	Weight in traveling position	Elevation	Traverse	Remarks
2-cm (0.79-inch) M/35 (Breda)	65	2,750	6,000	8,000	0.308 AP, 0.297 HE	120	677 lbs	781 lbs	−10° to 80°	360°	Dual-purpose AA/AT; course and speed sight fires HE tracer AP, or AP tracer; truck-drawn or 4 pack loads.
2-cm (0.79-inch) (Scotti)	70	2,720	5,900	7,000	0.275	120	501 lbs		−10° to 85°	360°	Mobile; course and speed sight; fires HE tracer.
37/54 (1.45-inch)	54	2,620	7,700	13,500	1.76	70			−10° to 90°	360°	Mobile; fires HE with time fuze or HE tracer with self-destroying percussion fuze; open sights. A twin-barrel (static) version is also in service.
75/27 (2.95-inch)	27	1,675	6,800	15,150	14.5	15	4.74 tons		0° to 70°	360°	A Krupp gun mounted on a truck.
75/46 (2.95-inch) model 34	46	2,350	14,100	27,200	14.3	20	3.24 tons	3.54 tons	−12° to 90°	360°	Mobile equipment.
75/50 (2.95-inch)	50	3,200	17,000	27,500	14.3	15	5 tons		0° to 90°	360°	Tractor-drawn.
76/40 (2.99-inch)	40	2,274	9,000	15,750	14.5	15			−3° to 80°	360°	Static; an old model.
76/45 (2.99-inch)	45	2,663	10,900	21,000	14.3		2.2	2.2	−5° to 73°	360°	Static.
77/28 (3.01-inch)	27.1	1,700	7,700	13,100	13.2		2.47			360°	Static.
88/56 (3.46-inch)	56	2,690	16,200	34,770	20.6	15 to 20	4.9	7.1	−3° to +85°	2 x 360°	Mobile; normal German Hv AA; much used for AT defense.

ARMAMENT AND EQUIPMENT

90/53	53	2,756	19,100	39,300	22.2	15 to 20	5.1	8.9	−2° to +85°	360°	Mobile; there is also a self-propelled (*semocente*) version.
100/60	60	2,590	19,000	36,725	33.2	8 to 10	11.56		−3° to +85°	360°	Both mobile and static versions exist.
102/35 (4.02-inch)	35	2,477	14,425	31,000	29	10 to 12			10° to 70°	360°	Static.
102/47 (4.02-inch)	47	2,950	16,500	32,800	33	8			0° to 80°	360°	Static.

FIGURE 57.—Characteristics of antiaircraft guns.

RESTRICTED

FIGURE 58.—75/27 (2.95-inch) AA gun.

FIGURE 59.—75/46 (2.95-inch) AA gun, model 34 (Ansaldo).

FIGURE 60.—Detail of the 75/46 (2.95-inch) AA gun, model 34 (Ansaldo).

c. *75/50 (2.95-inch) AA gun, model 1933 (Ansaldo).*—This is a good gun (fig. 61) but of shorter life than the L/46. It has a loose liner type of barrel.

Caliber	75 mm.
Length of bore	50 calibers.
Muzzle velocity	3,200 feet per second.
Maximum horizontal range	17,000 yards.
Maximum effective ceiling	27,500 to 34,000 feet.
Weight of projectile	14.3 pounds HE.
Practical rate of fire	15 to 20 rounds per minute.
Weight in action	5 tons.

FIGURE 61.—AA guns, model 1933 (Ansaldo).

Elevation_____ 0° to 90°.
Traverse_____ 360°.
Method of transport_____ Tractor-drawn.

d. 20/55 (0.79-inch) AA gun, model 35 (Breda).—(1) *General.*—This gun (figs. 62 and 63) is dual-purpose AA or AT with a course and speed sight. It is drawn by motor transport or in four pack loads, and is served by three gunners. It is designed on the gas-operated system and is fed by plate charges holding 12 rounds each. A continuous automatic rate of fire can be obtained by loading a further plate charger immediately after the preceding one. In Libya this gun was the most effective against low-flying aircraft. The telescopic sight serves for antiaircraft firing as well as for firing against ground targets, as it already takes account of the speed and the distance of the target.

(2) *Employment.*—The gun is normally employed for antiaircraft defense and occasionally as an antitank weapon. The contemplated employment laid down in regulations is as follows:

(*a*) *During movement.*—At the beginning of the march, for protecting the large unit (division) while it is breaking camp and getting into column.

ARMAMENT AND EQUIPMENT 223

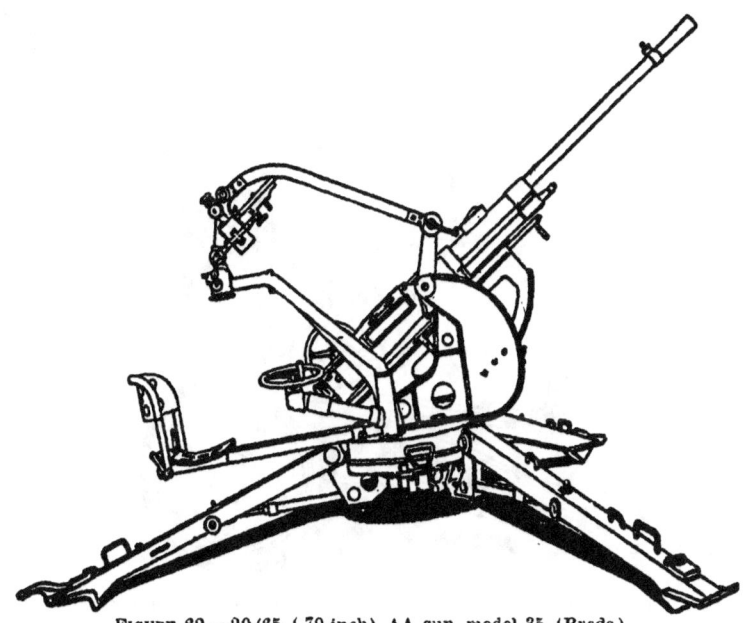

FIGURE 62.—20/65 (.79-inch) AA gun, model 35 (Breda).

(*b*) *During march.*—For protecting areas most vulnerable to attack from the air (passes, bridges, etc.).

(*c*) *During halt.*—For protecting thickly occupied areas or units especially exposed to aerial offense (artillery, trucks, carts, etc.).

(*d*) *During attacks.*—During the organization of the attack, for protecting movements and deployments of artillery and troops; during attack, for protecting deployed artillery and the principal attacking column, as well as the points selected for the attack.

(*e*) *In defense.*—For hindering enemy aerial reconnaissance flying at low altitude and for protecting movements of troops and artillery.

(*f*) *As antitank gun.*—At short distance, 500–600 meters.
   1. *During attack.*—To face enemy tank counterattacks.

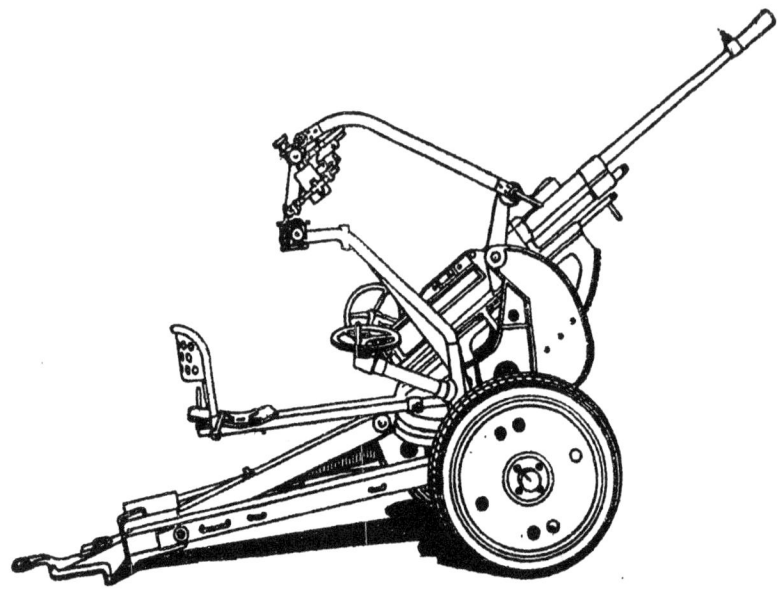

FIGURE 63.—20/65 (.79-inch) AA gun, model 35 (Breda), ready for transport.

2. In defense.—To augment from advanced positions the action of other antitank weapons, or to stop from rear positions enemy tanks which may have succeeded in breaking through the first lines.

(3) *Characteristics.*

Caliber	20 mm.
Length of bore	65 calibers.
Muzzle velocity	2,750 feet per second.
Maximum horizontal range	6,000 yards.
Maximum effective ceiling	8,200 feet.
Weight of projectile	(AP, 0.308 pounds) (HE 0.297 pounds).
Rate of fire	220 rounds per minute.
Practical rate of fire	120 rounds per minute.

ARMAMENT AND EQUIPMENT

Weight in action_____ 677 pounds.
Weight in draft_____ 781 pounds.
Elevation_____ −10° to +80°.
Traverse_____ 30° on wheels, 360° on tripod.
Depression_____ 10°.

(4) *Weights (approximate and without engagement).*

Barrel with muzzle tube_____ 27.7 kg.
Two wheels_____ 33 kg.
Bed platform_____ 60 kg.
Two lateral legs_____ 29.4 kg.
Rear leg_____ 16.9 kg.
Revolving platform_____ 63 kg.
Seat_____ 10.9 kg.
Direction and elevation gear columns with
  hand wheels_____ 10.6 kg.
Cradle_____ 28.9 kg.
Parallelogram arms_____ 9.3 kg.
Sight_____ 6 kg.
Three ground nails_____ 5.3 kg.
Hammer_____ 5.9 kg.
Thill (two shafts with U-shaped center
  piece)_____ 15.1 kg.
Weight of the gun on three legs carriage_____ 307.7 kg.
Weight of the gun on wheeled carriage_____ 355.8 kg.
Fire height from ground on three-leg car-
  riage_____ 780 mm.
Fire height from ground on wheeled carriage_ 885 mm.

e. 20/70 gun (2.79-inch) (Scotti).—(1) *General.*—This mobile gun, with the 20-mm Breda, is the standard light antiaircraft equipment in the Italian Army. The 20-mm HE shell has very little splinter effect. Aircraft have repeatedly been hit without being brought down. It is the British opinion that at least two

20-mm guns to one Bofors 40-mm are required to defend a locality. The 20-mm is comparable to a heavy machine gun. Although its rate of fire is greater, the maximum vertical range is about 7.000 feet, the remaining velocity at this height being considerably less than the 40-mm gun. Tracer is easy to observe at all ranges, according to British opinion. The equipment must be carried in a vehicle. It takes much longer to bring into action than a Bofors. Its advantages are simplicity of construction, ease of operation, and the convenience with which it is manhandled or concealed.

(2) *Characteristics.*

Caliber	20 mm.
Length of bore	70 calibers.
Muzzle velocity	2.720 feet per second.
Maximum horizontal range	5.900 yards.
Maximum effective ceiling	7,000 feet.
Theoretical rate of fire	250 rounds per minute.
Practical rate of fire	120 rounds per minute.
Weight in action	501 pounds.
Maximum elevation	+85°.
Maximum depression	−10°.
Maximum traverse	360°.
Weight of projectile	275 pounds.
Type of shell	HE tracer.
Type of fuze	Supersensitive percussion, self-destroying.
Breech mechanism	Automatic.
Recoil mechanism	Gas-operated.
Loading mechanism	Plate chargers.
Sights	Course and speed.

(3) *Ammunition—war types.*
Cartridge with tracer bullet.
Cartridge with armor-piercing bullet.

ARMAMENT AND EQUIPMENT

Cartridge with armor-piercing, explosive tracer bullet.
Cartridge with explosive extra-sensitive self-destructive, tracer bullet.
Cartridge with explosive extra-sensitive bullet.
Magazine contains 12 rounds.

The cartridge has an explosive, extra-sensitive bullet. This works with a fuze screwed on the nose which sets off the charge the moment the bullet hits an obstacle offering even very slight resistance. The bullet is also provided with a tracer. This is self-destructive, and is designed to explode in the air at the end of its tracing flight. This prevents the bullet's falling back to the ground and exploding among friendly troops. The armor-piercing bullet is provided with a percussion fuze. This does not explode until after the bullet has actually pierced its target.

f. 37/54 (1.45-inch) AA gun (Breda 39).—This gun was intended for position defense by the Antiaircraft Artillery Militia, but has been used by mobile units in Libya. It is air-cooled, and is equipped with an optical sight with automatic gun-laying.

Caliber	37 mm.
Length of bore	54 calibers.
Muzzle velocity	2,620 feet per second.
Maximum horizontal range	7,700 yards.
Maximum effective ceiling	13,500 feet.
Theoretical rate of fire	125 rounds per minute.
Practical rate of fire	70 rounds per minute.
Maximum elevation	+90°.
Maximum depression	−10°.
Maximum traverse	360°.
Weight of complete round	3.5 pounds.
Weight of projectile	1.76 pounds.
Type of shell	HE.
Type of fuze	Time or percussion, self-destroying.

Mounting_____ Mobile platform.
Breech mechanism_____ Automatic.
Loading mechanism_____ Loading tray of 6 rounds.

224. Antitank guns [2].—*a. 20-mm antitank gun (Breda).*—This is a dual purpose machine gun, wheel- or tripod-mounted with a muzzle velocity of 2,750 feet per second, a maximum rate of fire of 120 rounds per minute, and a range of 6,000 yards. It is transported on its own wheels (towed) or in a truck. It will penetrate 25 mm (0.983 inch) of armor at normal impact, and 15 mm (0.59 inch) at 30° at 500 yards. It weighs 680 pounds in action and 780 in transport.

b. 37/40 tank gun.—This gun has been found fitted to a M II Medium Tank and does not appear to have been used as a ground weapon. The performance is poor. Only AP ammunition has been found.

c. 47/32 (1.85-inch) antitank gun, model 37.—(1) *General.*—This weapon (fig. 64) is of Boehler design and was introduced in 1935. It is a good gun with a high rate of fire, and may be fired either on wheels or from its platform. It may be used as an infantry support gun in addition to its antitank role. Its disadvantages are that no protection is provided for the detachment, the traverse is limited, and the weapon's hitting power is inferior to that of the British 2-pounder. It fires HE or AP ammunition, but the former is very erratic in performance.

(2) *Characteristics.*

Caliber_____ 47 mm.
Length of bore_____ 32.5 calibers.
Length of gun_____ 3.35 meters (132 inches).
Length of barrel_____ 1.527 meters (60 inches).
Length of rifling_____ 1.312 meters (52 inches).

---

[2] For the Solothurn antitank rifle see paragraph 208, above.

ARMAMENT AND EQUIPMENT

FIGURE 64.—47/32 (1.85-inch) antitank gun, model 37.

Length of chamber	0.203 meter (8 inches).
Depth of breech opening	0.155 meter (6.092 inches).
Width of carriage	1.067 meters (42 inches).
Height on wheels	0.991 meter (39 inches).
Height on platform	0.813 meter (32 inches).
Rifling (24 grooves, plain section).	Uniform right-hand twist, 1 in 25.
Width of grooves	4 mm (0.158 inch).
Depth of grooves	0.55 mm (0.021 inch).
Weight of barrel	78.2 kg (172 pounds).
Weight of gun in draught.	299.5 kg (660 pounds).
Weight of gun in action	264.0 kg. (582 pounds).
Traverse on platform	70°
Traverse on wheels	40°
Maximum elevation	56°
Maximum depression	15°

Muzzle velocity (AP) ---- 630 meters per second (2,067 feet per second).
Muzzle velocity (HE) ---- 250 meters per second (820 feet per second).
Maximum range (HE) ---- 3,500 meters (3,800 yards).
Effective range (AP or HE) ---- 200 to 1,000 meters (220 to 1,100 yards).
Rate of fire (theoretical) -- 20 rounds per minute.
Rate of fire (practical) --- 7 to 8 rounds per minute.

(3) *Transport.*—The gun may be transported by man power, with the use of special ropes; drawn by one mule; carried by a truck; drawn behind a truck; or divided into five pack loads.

(4) *Ammunition.*

Type	Weight of projectile	Weight of HE filling	Fuze	Distinguishing marks
AP (tracer) shell	3 pounds, 4 ounces	1½ ounces	Base	Red nose, one white and one green band; gray projectile.
HE shell	5 pounds, 3 ounces	5¼ ounces	Nose	Aluminum nose fuze, green band, high ratio of length to diameter.
APBC (tracer shell).	3 pounds, 5 ounces	1 ounce	Base	Red nose, one white and one green band; gray projectile.

d. 90-mm antitank gun.—This AA/AT gun (fig. 65) which is frequently used for AT purposes, is a very effective gun, but is inclined to stoppage unless kept scrupulously clean. It is normally drawn on a four-wheeled *Lancia Ro* trailer. A self-propelled model is also reported, with the gun mounted on the chassis of a slightly heavier model of M 13/40.

Caliber ---------------------- 90 mm.
Length of bore -------------- 53 calibers.
Weight (in action) ---------- 11,220 pounds.

ARMAMENT AND EQUIPMENT

Weight of shell_____ 2,202 pounds.
Muzzle of velocity_____ 2,755 feet per second.
Maximum horizontal range___ 19,100 yards.
Maximum vertical range_____ 39,300 feet.
Rate of fire_____ 15 to 20 rounds per minute.
Elevation_____ $-2°$ to $+85°$.

225. Antiaircraft guns for fixed defense.—*a. 37/54 (1.45-inch) AA gun (Breda 39)*.—A twin-barreled static model is also in service.

Barrels_____ Cooled by water jackets (wear of barrel is negligible).
Sights_____ Open sights (two layers).
Firing_____ Can be fired by either layer with foot or hand-operated liner.

FIGURE 65.—90-mm antitank gun, self-propelled model.

b. 76/40 (2.99-inch) AA gun, model 1917.—This gun fires fixed ammunition. It has a spring recuperator, a glycerine and water buffer, and an interrupted thread breechblock with a removable firing case. The rifling is straight for about 50 cm., and then is progressive, left-hand twist. Laying for line and elevation is performed by one layer. It has a range disk, separate elevating gear, quadrant-elevation scale for indirect laying, and a hand fuze

227   **RESTRICTED**

setter. The lateral and vertical deflection scales are graduated in thousandths (*millésimi*). The vertical deflection scale is also graduated for tangent elevation and range for several types of ammunition.

Caliber	7.6 mm.
Length of bore	40 calibers.
Muzzle velocity	2,264 feet per second.
Maximum horizontal range	9,000 yards.
Maximum effective ceiling	15,750 feet.
Theoretical rate of fire	20 rounds per minute.
Practical rate of fire	15 rounds per minute.
Maximum elevation	20°.
Maximum depression	3°.
Elevation	3° to 80°.
Traverse	360°.
Weight of projectile	14.5 pounds.
Type of shell	HE or shrapnel.
Type of fuze	Mechanical time fuze.
Mount	Square pedestal.

c. 76/45 (2.99-inch) AA gun.

Caliber	76 mm.
Length of bore	45 calibers.
Muzzle velocity	2,463 feet per second.
Maximum horizontal range	10,900 yards.
Maximum effective ceiling	21,000 feet.
Weight of projectile	14.3 pounds.
Weight in draft	2.2 tons.
Traverse	360°.

d. 77/28 (3.01-inch) AA gun.

Caliber	77 mm.
Length of bore	27.1 calibers.
Muzzle velocity	1,700 feet per second.

RESTRICTED

ARMAMENT AND EQUIPMENT

Maximum horizontal range	7,700 yards.
Maximum effective ceiling	13,100 feet.
Weight of projectile	13.2 pounds.
Weight in action	2.47 tons.
Elevation	5° to 73°.
Traverse	360°.

e. 90/53 AA gun.—(1) *General.*—This is a new gun which should be useful for barrage fire against armored vehicles, dive-bombers, and aircraft at medium height. The range disks are calibrated for sharpnel as well as HE. The gun is towed by a tractor in a single load when on a mobile mount. The gun is electrically connected to the fire control station.

(2) *Characteristics.*

Caliber	90 mm.
Length of bore	57 calibers.
Total length of gun	5 meters (approximately).
Length of barrel	4.770 meters (53 calibers).
Maximum horizontal range	14.000 meters.
Maximum vertical range	10,000 meters.
Rate of fire	20 rounds per minute.
Weight of gun in battery, on a semifixed platform	6,200 kg (approximately).
Height of gun on mobile mount	8,300 kg (approximately).

(3) *Ammunition.*

Antiaircraft with smoke box and powder fuze.
Percussion.
Flashless (blue and white base) and smokeless (red base) charges.

Separate components of ammunition provided for making up on site.

f. 102/35 (4.016-inch) AA gun.—(1) *General.*—This gun (fig. 66) is listed also as a 4.02-inch. It is a dual-purpose: for antiaircraft and for coast defense. Electrical transmission is used to convey data from the predictor to the guns, which is an improvement on earlier Italian types where telephone transmission was employed. The 102/35 gun is also equipped with a telescopic sight, enabling the gun to work independently of the predictor in an emergency. It is possible to maintain an average rate of fire of 10 rounds per minute to 12 rounds per minute for barrage work, though after 30 to 40 rounds have been fired at this rate, the breeches tend to jam from overheating. The buffer and recuperation system is simple: a liquid buffer and two spring recuperators.

FIGURE 66.—102/35 (4.016) AA gun.

ARMAMENT AND EQUIPMENT

(2) *Characteristics.*

Caliber	102 mm.
Length of bore	35 calibers.
Muzzle velocity	2,477 feet per second.
Maximum horizontal range	14,425 yards.
Maximum vertical range	31,000 feet.
Maximum depression	10°.
Elevation	10° to 70°.
Recoil	Maximum, 14 inches; average, 12 inches.
Buffer capacity	7.875 pints.
Breech mechanism	Semiautomatic, sliding vertically.
Fuze setter	Mechanical.
Weight of projectile	29 pounds.
Practical rate of fire	10 to 12 rounds per minute.
Traverse	360°.

(3) *Ammunition.*—(a) *Types.*—The following three types of ammunition have been used: HE (time fuze), HE (percussion), and illuminant (flares) (time fuze). Ammunition marked "102/45" has been used with no appreciable effect on results.

(b) *Fuzes.*—There are three different types of fuzes: 160, 58, and 13 (these figures referring to the maximum setting possible). All are powder fuzes similar in principle to the British 199 fuze. Reference 160 fuze, the settings are in quarter seconds time of flight (under normal conditions). None of these fuzes is interchangeable, though the 13 fuze can be used in place of the percussion fuze.

(c) *Flares (illuminanti).*—Half of the normal charge is used with these shells. On bursting, a parachute flare is released, which illuminates a wide area for 35 seconds, dropping approximately 2,000 feet before extinguishing. There are two types of *illumi-*

RESTRICTED

nanti shells using the 58 and 13 fuzes, though the effect, allowing for the difference in setting, would appear to be familiar.

(d) *Dimensions of shells.—*

	Length		Weight
HE (fuze 160)	39.75 inches.	Cartridge (complete HE)	17 pounds.
HE (fuze 13)	38.6 inches.	Cartridge (complete *illuminanti*)	14 pounds, 8 ounces.
HE (percussion)	38.5 inches.	Projectile (HE)	29 pounds.
Illuminanti (fuze 13)	38.87 inches.	Projectile (*illuminanti*)	25 pounds.
Illuminanti (fuze 58)	39 inches.	Fuze 160	1 pound, 12 ounces.
		Fuze 58	8 ounces.
		Fuze 13	8 ounces.
		Total weight of HE shell with 160 fuze	48 pounds, 12 ounces.
		Total weight of *illuminanti* shell with 13 or 58 fuze	40 pounds.

(e) *Color markings on ammunition.*

Ammunition	Shell nose	Base of cartridge case	
		Band near base	Colored ring
HE	Red	None	180° red, 180° white.
HE (flashless)	Red	None	180° blue, 180° white.
HE (percussion)	Red	None	Red.
Illuminanti	Red	Green	180° green, 180° white.

g. 102/47 AA gun (4.02-inch) (Orlando) model 1929.

    Caliber _____ 102 mm.
    Length of bore _____ 47 calibers.
    Muzzle velocity _____ 2,950 feet per second.
    Maximum horizontal range ____ 16,500 yards.
    Maximum effective ceiling _____ 32,800 feet.
    Practical rate of fire _____ 8 to 10 rounds per minute.
    Weight of projectile _____ 33 pounds.
    Elevation _____ 80°.
    Depression _____ 0°.
    Traverse _____ 360°.

226. Intermediate small-caliber antiaircraft weapons.—Antiaircraft automatic rifles are issued to men serving the 75/46 antiaircraft guns. Other weapons issued to the antiaircraft units are the 8-mm Fiat machine gun and the 8-mm Breda machine gun (see 209, above).

227. Special communication equipment assigned to antiaircraft batteries and groups.—This equipment is assigned to batteries and groups as follows:

	Battery	Group
Optical telegraphs, 80 mm	2	4
Telephones, type G. A., model 31	6	6
Telephones for line guards	4	4
Kits for telephone operators and line guards	8	8
Switchboards, 6 lines	1	2
Telephone wire (km)	20	30
Safety belts	1	1
Foot hooks	2	2
Drums for wire	10	14
Forked poles	3	4
Signal flags	4	4
or		
Flashing flags	2	2

	Battery	Group
Lanterns	--	12
Megaphones	2	--
Radio stations, RF2	2	--
Radio sets, RA1	--	1
Signal panels for communication with aircraft	--	48

228. Antiaircraft fire control instruments *(Galileo)*.—*a. Goniometer.*—This is an angle-measuring instrument provided with two telescopes and means of transmitting the angle of sight and bearing electrically to the main plotting table. It is graduated in Italian measure (64 graduations to the circle).

b. Range-finder.—This is of the normal stereoscopic type, with either a 4-meter (157.48-inch) or 2.7 meter (106.3-inch) base length. The slant range is telephoned to the plotting table. Magnification is 14 or 28. The field of view is 3° or 1°30′. The range scale is graduated from 1,600 to 20,000 meters.

c. Plotting table.—This is a flat metal table, with open windows covering scales for recording the angle of sight, bearing, and slant range. It is operated by nine men. Prediction is advanced by a previously set drill time of 5 to 10 seconds. On the order FIRE a "hooter" starts, prediction is stopped, and exact readings are telephoned to the guns. When the drill time is over, the "hooter" stops, and the guns fire. Prediction is then restarted and FIRE ordered after a few seconds have been allowed for the gun dials to steady. Electrical transmission from the plotting table to the guns is employed with 102/35-mm AA gun, but with earlier equipment all transmission other than from the goniometer to the plotting table, is by telephone.

d. Transmission (Telefunken gear).—This is a system of telephone communication between the main plotting table and the gun positions, and consists of a main battery and connection box and a number of head and breast sets.

RESTRICTED

ARMAMENT AND EQUIPMENT

229. Searchlights.—*a. General.*—In use in the Italian Army for antiaircraft defense are 90-cm, 105-cm, 120-cm, 150-cm, and possibly 210-cm searchlights.

b. 90-cm (35.43-inch) searchlight (Galileo).

Weight of projector _____ 1,210 pounds.
Lamp (input) _____ 150 amperes; 70 volts.
Diameter of positive carbon _____ 16 mm (0.6299 inch).
Diameter of negative carbon _____ 11 mm (0.4331 inch).
Reflector (focal length) _____ 42 cm (16.8 inches).
Beam range _____ 7,100 yards.
Divergence _____ 2¼°.

c. 105-cm. (41.34-inch) searchlight (Galileo).

Weight of projector _____ 1,430 pounds.
Lamp (input) _____ 150 amperes; 70 volts.
Diameter of positive carbon _____ 19 mm (0.7480 inch).
Diameter of negative carbon _____ 14 mm (0.5512 inch).
Reflector (focal length) _____ 50 cm (19.69 inches).
Beam range _____ 7,600 yards.
Divergence _____ 2¼°.

d. 120-cm (47.24-inch) searchlight (Galileo).

Weight of projector _____ 1,430 pounds.
Lamp (input) _____ 180 amperes; 70 volts.
Diameter of positive carbon _____ 16 mm (0.6299 inch).
Diameter of negative carbon _____ 13 mm (0.5118 inch).
Reflector (focal length) _____ 55 cm (21.65 inches).
Beam range _____ 8,200 yards.
Divergence _____ 1°25′.

e. 150-cm (59.06-inch) searchlight (Galileo).

Weight of projector _____ 2,090 pounds.
Lamp (input) _____ 200 to 300 amperes.
Diameter of positive carbon _____ 17 mm (0.6693 inch).

RESTRICTED

Diameter of negative carbon _ _ _ _ _ _ _ 14 mm (0.5512 inch).
Reflector (focal length) _ _ _ _ _ _ _ _ _ _ _ 65 cm (25.59 inches).
Beam range _ 8,750 yards.
Divergence _ 1¼°.

f. 210-cm (82.68-inch) searchlight (Galileo).—A searchlight of this type with a beam range of 16,400 yards has been reported in production, but it is not known on what scale, if any, it is actually in service.

230. Sound locator *(Galileo)*.—This is an altazimuth locator with paraboloidal trumpets. The sound-lag corrector is of the graphical type, and is not automatic, requiring an operator. Corrections for wind and parallax are set by a second operator. The height can also be found, but, as it is based on a guessed air speed, it is not likely to be very reliable.

Diameter of trumpets _ _ _ _ _ _ _ _ _ _ _ _ _ 19.69 inches.
Traverse _ 360°.
Elevation _ 15° to 90°.
Range _ 13,000 to 16,000 yards.
Distance between sound locator and searchlight _ 220 yards.

SECTION IV

ARTILLERY

	Paragraph
General	231
Guns	232
Howitzers	233
Mortars	234

231. General.—All Italian artillery is distinguished by two numbers separated by an oblique stroke. The first number indicates the caliber in millimeters; the second number gives the length of the bore in calibers. Equipment is classified as follows:

ARMAMENT AND EQUIPMENT 221-32

   a. Gun (cannone).—Bore longer than 22 calibers.
   b. Howitzer (obice).—Bore between 12 and 22 calibers.
   c. Mortar (mortaio).—Bore shorter than 12 calibers.
   Note.—For the characteristics of artillery weapons, see the tabulation in figure 67.

   232. Guns.—*a. 57/30 fortress gun.*—This is a naval gun used in fortifications. It has a pedestal mount, fixed to a concrete foundation block.

      Caliber _____ 57 mm.
      Length of bore _____ 30 calibers.
      Muzzle velocity _____ 2,000 feet per second.
      Weight of shell _____ 6.38 pounds.
      Maximum range _____ 7,100 yards.
      Elevation _____ 15°.
      Depression _____ 10°.
      Traverse _____ 30°.
      Weight of gun, including pedestal _ 1,650 pounds.

   b. 57/43 gun.—It is possible that some of these guns are mounted on Rhodes and Leros for protecting mine fields, and they may also be used in fortifications defending the Brenner Pass and other passes through the Alps. Owing to the indicated limited traverse on a pedestal mount (on an outrigger platform), which should be 360°, it would appear that these guns are to be mounted in bombproof casemates or other types of bombproof construction. Both the 57/30-mm and the 57/43-mm guns fired fixed ammunition weighing approximately 11 pounds.

RESTRICTED

Weapon	Description	Arcs of fire		Maximum range	Weight of shell
		Vertical	Horizontal		
25/17	AT gun	−5° to +15°	60°	Penetrates 40 mm at 100 yd.	0.7 lb tracer AP.
37/35	AT gun	−8° to +25°	60°	Penetrates 38 mm at 30° at 400 yd.	1 lb 6 oz HE; 1 lb 8 oz AP.
47/32	AT gun (close-support).	−15° to +36°	62°	3,800 yd HE; 7,600 yd AP.	5.2 lb HE; 3.2 lb AP.
47/34	AT gun	−5° to +20°	40°	1,100 yd (effective).	3.4 lb AP; 7 lb HE.
65/17	Gun	−7° 30′ to +20°	8°	7,100 yd	9.15 lb HE; 9.3 lb AP.
75/13	How	−10° to +50°	7°	9,000 yd	13.9 lb
75/18 M 34, M 35	How	−10° to +65° Mod. −10° to +45° Mod.	50°	10,280 yd	14 lb
75/27 (Model 06)	Gun	−10° to +16°	7°	11,000 yd	14 lb
75/27 (Models 11 and 12).	Gun	−15° to +65°	52° 9′	9,000 yd	13.9 lb
75/34	Gun	?	?	13,500 yd	14 lb
77/28	Gun	−7° 30′ to +18°	8°	?	?
100/17 Model 14	How	−8° to +48°	5° 21′	10,000 yds	HE 28 lbs., shrapnel 25 lbs.
100/17 Model 16	Mtn How	−8° to +70°	5° 5′	10,000 yds	HE 28 lbs., shrapnel 25 lbs.
100/24	How	+8° to +42°	?	10,800 yds	32.2 lbs. HE
105/17	How	+6° to +50°	58°	11,200 yds	34.5 lbs. HE
105/28	Gun	−5° to +37°	14°	14,800 yds	35 lbs
105/32	Gun	−10° to +30°	6°	17,500 yds	?
149/12	How	3°30′ to 65°	5° 20′	7,200 yds	90 lbs
149/13	How	−5° to +70°	6°	9,000 yds	90 lbs
149/19	How	−5° to +62°	60°	16,000 yds	90 lbs

ARMAMENT AND EQUIPMENT

Transport	In issue to—	Remarks
H-Dr or Mtz (trailer can be manhandled or truck-borne).	Inf Units, 2d Line	Hotchkiss, model 1934; weight in action, 1,050 lb; MV, 3,000 f/s.
H-Dr or Mtz (can be manhandled or truck-borne).	Inf Units, 2d Line	German; MV, 2,500 f/s.
On Trk or 5-mule Pks (can be towed by truck or H-Dr).	Inf Regts	Standard close-support and AT weapon.
Trk or H-Dr or Mtz	Inf Regts, 2d Line	Belgian.
6 Pk loads or own wheels	Alpine and Colonial units.	Now being superseded by the 47/32 gun in Inf Divs.
7 Pk loads or own wheels	Inf and Alpine Inf	To be replaced by the 75/18 (in Inf).
8 Pk loads or H-Dr or Mtz.	Inf and Mtz Inf	To replace the 75/13 howitzer and the 75/27 gun (in Inf), and the 75/27 in Mtz. A self-propelled (*semovente*) version exists, in which the gun is mounted on the chassis of an M 13 tank.
H-Dr or Mtz or 2 loads for mountain transport.	Inf, *célere*, Armd, Mtz, and Trk-borne.	To be replaced by the 75/18 in -Inf, Mtz, and Trk-borne, and by the 75/34 in *célere* and Armd. A self propelled (*semovente*) version is believed to exist, in which the gun is mounted on a SPA tractor and fires over the hood.
H-Dr or Mtz		There is also an AA model of this gun. Not generally in issue; to replace the 75/27 in *célere* and Armd.
H-Dr or Mtz	Not known	There is also an AA model of this gun.
H-Dr or Mtz		Old Austrian design.
H-Dr (3 loads)	Inf	A modification for mountain warfare.
H.Dr and Mtz	Coast defense units and some corps Regts.	Skoda M 14/19 Czech (a large number lent by Germany to Italy).
Mtz	Corps Arty	French (105 C 1935 B).
Mtz	Corps	
Mtz	Corps	
Mtz	Not known	
Mtz (4 loads)	Corps	Will probably be replaced by the 149/19
Mtz (2 loads)	Corps	To replace 149/13.

Weapon	Description	Arcs of fire		Maximum range	Weight of shell
		Vertical	Horizontal		
149/28	How	1.30° to 45°	60°	14,630	95.7 lbs
149/35	Gun	−10° to +35°	?	19,100 yds	101 lbs
149/40	Gun	0° to 45°	60°	24,000 yds	112 lbs
152/13	How	0° to 45°	8°	10,300 yds	100 lbs
152/37	Gun	−6° to +45°	6°	23,800 yds	119 lbs

Caliber _____ 57 mm.
Length of bore _____ 43 calibers.
Length of gun _____ 2,729 mm.
Muzzle velocity _____ 1,997.75 feet per second.
Elevation _____ +15°.
Depression _____ −10°.
Traverse _____ 30°.
Weight of gun, including pedestal _____ 1,650 pounds.
Maximum range _____ 7,590 yards.
Weight of piercing shell with nose cap _____ 2,900 kg.
Weight of brass case containing type C_2 propellant powder _ 0.550 kg.

c. *75/27 gun, models 1906, 1911, 1912* (figs. 68 and 69).

Caliber _____ 75 mm.
Length of bore _____ 27 calibers.
Muzzle velocity _____ 1,730 feet per second.
Weight of projectile _____ 14 pounds.
Maximum range _____ 11,000 yards.
Rate of fire _____ 20 rounds per minute (with trained crew).

ARMAMENT AND EQUIPMENT

Transport	In issue to—	Remarks
Mtz	Corps	German Med How (S. F. H. 18); MV, 1,705 fs.
Mtz (1 load)	Army	Obsolescent; to be replaced by 149/40.
Mtz (2 loads)	Army	To replace 149/35; adapted for mountain warfare.
Mtz (1 heavy tractor)	Army	
Mtz (2 loads)	Army	Austrian design modernized by Ansaldo.

FIGURE 67.—Characteristics of artillery weapons.

Elevation:
  M 1906 _____ 16°.
  M 1911 _____ 65°.
  M 1912 _____ 65°.

FIGURE 68.—75/27 gun in traveling position.

Depression:
 M 1906_____ 10°.
 M 1911_____ 15°.
 M 1912_____ 15°.

FIGURE 69.—75/27 gun with shield raised.

Traverse (all three)_____ 52°.
Weight of gun in action_____ 1 ton.
Method of transport_____ Towed on own wheels.

d. 90/53 AA and coast defense gun.—This gun is electrically connected to the fire control station.

Caliber_____ 90 mm.
Length of bore_____ 53 calibers.
Total length of gun_____ 5 meters approximately.
Length of barrel_____ 4.770 meters (53 calibers).

ARMAMENT AND EQUIPMENT

Maximum horizontal range	14,000 meters.
Maximum vertical range	10,000 meters.
Rate of fire	20 rounds per minute.
Weight of gun in battery on semifixed platform	6,200 kg (approximately).
Weight of gun on mobile mount	8,300 kg.
Method of transport	Towed by a tractor, in one single load, when on mobile mount.

FIGURE 70.—90/53 AA and coast defense gun.

e. 102/45 naval AA and coast defense gun.

Caliber	102 mm.
Length of bore	45 calibers.
Traverse	360°.

RESTRICTED

f. 102/47 (4.02-inch) gun (Orlando) M 1929 (AA and coast defense).

Caliber	102 mm.
Length of bore	47 calibers.
Muzzle velocity	2,950 feet per second.
Maximum horizontal range	16,500 yards.
Maximum effective ceiling	32,800 feet.
Weight of projectile	33 pounds.
Practical rate of fire	8 rounds per minute.
Elevation	0° to 80°.
Traverse	360°.

g. 149/35 gun (fig. 71).

Caliber	149 mm.
Length of bore	35 calibers.
Muzzle velocity	2,200 feet per second.
Weight of shell	92 pounds
Maximum range	17,400 yards.
Rate of fire	2 rounds per minute.
Elevation	35°.
Depression	10°
Weight in action	8 tons

h. 381/40 railway gun (fig. 72).

Caliber	381 mm.
Length of bore	40 calibers.
Muzzle velocity	2,500 feet per second.
Weight of shell	1,925 pounds.
Maximum range	26,200 yards.
Rate of fire	1 round per 15 minutes.
Elevation	25°.
Traverse	38°.
Transport	(See par. 237.)

RESTRICTED

ARMAMENT AND EQUIPMENT

i. 400/30 gun.

    Caliber＿＿＿＿＿＿＿＿＿＿＿＿ 400 mm.
    Length of bore＿＿＿＿＿＿＿＿ 30 calibers.
    Weight of projectile＿＿＿＿＿ 2,020 pounds.

j. 120/21 gun.—This gun has three types of mount: fortress mount for battery with minimum loophole; fortress mount for armored turret; and fortress casement mount.

    Caliber＿＿＿＿＿＿＿＿＿＿＿＿ 120 mm.
    Length of bore＿＿＿＿＿＿＿＿ 21 calibers.
    Maximum range＿＿＿＿＿＿＿＿ 7,700 m.
    Elevation＿＿＿＿＿＿＿＿＿＿＿ +35°.
    Depression＿＿＿＿＿＿＿＿＿＿ −10°.
    Rate of fire
        Normal＿＿＿＿＿＿＿＿＿＿ 1 round per minute.
        Maximum＿＿＿＿＿＿＿＿＿ 4 rounds per minute.
    Propelling charge:
        Minimum weight＿＿＿＿＿ Ballistite.
        Maximum weight＿＿＿＿＿ 0.120 kg.
    Projectile: 1.100 kg.
        Weight of projectile＿＿＿＿＿
        Total weight＿＿＿＿＿＿＿ Siperite.
        Quality of powder＿＿＿＿＿ 2.100 kg.
        Fuzes＿＿＿＿＿＿＿＿＿＿＿ 16.400 kg.
        Bursting charge＿＿＿＿＿＿ Percussion, model 17.
        Initial velocity＿＿＿＿＿＿ 482 meters per second.
    Dispersion 50 percent zone:
        Width＿＿＿＿＿＿＿＿＿＿＿ 9.6 m.
        Depth＿＿＿＿＿＿＿＿＿＿＿ 169 m.

k. 305/50 gun.—This gun is on a rigid carriage.

    Caliber＿＿＿＿＿＿＿＿＿＿＿＿ 305 mm.
    Length of bore＿＿＿＿＿＿＿＿ 50 mm.
    Maximum range＿＿＿＿＿＿＿ 19,000 m.

RESTRICTED

FIGURE 71.—149/35 gun.

FIGURE 72.—381/40 railway gun.

Rate of fire:
    Normal _____ 1 per 10 minutes.
    Maximum _____ 1 per 5 minutes.
Propelling charge:
    Quality of powder_____ C_2.
    Maximum weight_____ 160 kg.
Projectile:
    Bursting charge_____ TNT.
    Weight_____ 5.455 kg.
    Total weight_____ 445 kg.
    Fuzes_____ Percussion, model 1911 (K. S. R.).
    Initial velocity_____ 805 meters per second.
Dispersion 50 percent zone:
    Width _____ 5.6 m.
    Depth_____ 88.4 m.

233. Howitzers.—*a. 420/12 howitzer.*

    Caliber_____ 420 mm.
    Length of bore_____ 12 calibers.
    Muzzle velocity_____ 2,500 feet per second.
    Weight of shell_____ 2,200 pounds.
    Maximum range_____ 16,000 yards.
    Weight in action_____ 113 tons.

b. 280/16 howitzer.—This howitzer has two types of installation: a rigid carriage and spring lower carriage (of the 280/9 mm mortar), and the carriage and lower carriage (of the 280/11-mm mortar).

    Caliber_____ 280 mm.
    Length of bore_____ 16 calibers.
    Maximum range_____ 12,760 yards.
    Elevation_____ +51°.
    Depression _____ −14°.

Rate of fire:
  Normal .... 1 per 10 minutes.
  Maximum .... 1 per 5 minutes.
Propelling charge:
  Quality of powder .... Ballistite.
  Minimum weight .... 3.600 kg.
  Maximum weight .... 12.800 kg.
Projectile:
  Bursting charge .... TNT.
  Weight .... 18.190 kg.
  Total weight .... 217.500 kg.
  Fuzes .... Percussion, model 1914.
  Initial velocity .... 460 meters per second.
  Dispersion 50 percent zone:
    Width .... 26 m.
    Depth .... 100 m.

c. 305/17 howitzer, model 1917.

  Caliber .... 305 mm.
  Length of bore .... 17 calibers.
  Muzzle of velocity .... 1,790 feet per second.
  Weight of projectile .... 772 pounds.
  Maximum range .... 19,200 yards.
  Rate of fire .... 1 round per 5 minutes.
  Elevation .... 65°.
  Depression .... 20°.
  Traverse .... 360°.
  Weight in action .... 33.75 tons.
  Weight in traveling position .... 47.7 tons.

234. Mortars.—*a. 280/9-mortar.*—This mortar has three types of pit installations: type A, type A. M., and type G.

  Caliber .... 280 mm.
  Length of bore .... 9 calibers.

ARMAMENT AND EQUIPMENT 234

Maximum range_____ 9,000 m.
Elevation_____ +6° to +75°.
Rate of fire:
    Normal_____ 1 per 10 minutes.
    Maximum_____ 1 per 5 minutes.
Propelling charge:
    Quality of powder_____ Ballistite.
    Minimum weight_____ 1.600 kg.
    Maximum weight_____ 9.000 kg.
Projectile:
    Bursting charge_____ TNT.
    Weight_____ 37.915 kg.
    Total weight_____ 199.500 kg.
    Fuzes_____ Percussion, model 1914.
    Initial velocity_____ 369 meters per second.
Dispersion 50 percent zone:
    Width_____ 26 m.
    Depth_____ 64 m.

    b. 280/10-mortar.—This mortar is set on a rigid mount and spring lower carriage.

Caliber_____ 280 mm.
Length of bore_____ 10 calibers.
Maximum range_____ 11,000 m.
Elevation_____ +60°.
Depression_____ −5°.
Traverse_____ 180°.
Propelling charge:
    Quality of powder_____ Ballistite.
    Minimum weight_____ 1.900 kg.
    Maximum weight_____ 12.200 kg.
Projectile (steel base-fuzed shell):
    Bursting charge_____ TNT.

Weight_____ 18.800 kg.
Total weight_____ 217.600 kg.
Fuzes_____ Percussion.
Initial velocity_____ 430 meters per second.
Dispersion 50 percent zone:
   Width_____ 19 m.
   Depth_____ 109 m.

c. 280/11 mortar.—This mortar is fixed on a rigid mount.

Caliber_____ 280 mm.
Length of bore_____ 11 calibers
Maximum range_____ 10,100 m.
Elevation_____ +5° to +45°.
Rate of fire:
   Normal_____ 1 per 10 minutes.
   Maximum_____ 1 per 5 minutes.

FIGURE 73.—305-mm howitzer.

ARMAMENT AND EQUIPMENT

Propelling charge:
    Quality of powder _____ Ballistite.
    Minimum weight _____ 1.700 kg.
    Maximum weight _____ 10.500 kg.
Projectile (base-fuzed shell):
    Bursting charge _____ TNT.
    Weight _____ 18.800 kg.
    Total weight _____ 217.600 kg.
    Fuzes _____ Percussion.
    Initial velocity _____ 410 meters per second.
Dispersion 50 percent zone:
    Width _____ 18 m.
    Depth _____ 19 m.

SECTION V

ARMORED VEHICLES

	Paragraph
Tanks	235
Armored cars	236
Armored trains	237
Other types of armored vehicles	238

235. Tanks.—*a. General.*—For detailed characteristics of Italian tanks, see figure 74.

b. L 3/35.—This tank (fig. 75), though highly ineffective, is a standard Italian armored vehicle, and may be used as a flamethrower or a bridge carrier. It has seven small, solid bogie wheels, one independent bogie being in the rear. The front six bogies are girder-connected. A spare bogie wheel is on the side behind the turret. Two 8-mm machine guns are mounted in a kind of "blister" in front of the turret. The rear idler wheel is very close to the ground but is not trailing. This tank used a great deal of water and has to stop every 10 miles to refill the radiator. It is able to

RESTRICTED

pass over a vertical obstacle of 2 feet high and it has a climbing ability to 45°.

c. Fiat-Ansaldo 3000 B (later model).—This tank (fig. 76) is a modern development. It has a boxlike superstructure surmounted by a many angled turret. Its 37-mm gun and light machine gun are mounted in a curved blister in the front of the turret. This suspension is distinctive because of the large swan-necked cantilever arms which connect the bogies to the hull. There are two track rollers at the top of the track. There are five bogie wheels, one an independently fixed bogie just forward of the rear idler wheel.

d. L 5–21/30.—This tank is an obsolete 1917 model of French (Renault) design. The manufacture of it stopped in 1930, though it may still be used by some second-line units.

e. L 6/40.—The suspension of this tank (see fig. 77) carries four rubber-tired bogie wheels mounted in pairs, each sprung by a curved cantilever arm and a torsion bar. The fifth bogie at the rear is of steel and acts both as a load carrier and to return the track. There are three return rollers. One 20-mm and one 8-mm machine gun are mounted coaxially in the revolving turret.

f. Carro d'assalto.—The suspension is completely obscured by skirting. The tank may have a liquid sprayer or a flame thrower.

g. Renault R35 (French).—This tank (fig. 78) has a cast turret, and a short, stubby 37-mm gun. On top of the turret is a small bowl-shaped cupola. The tank has five bogie wheels and five bogies. Two pairs are of the French scissor type; one is independent. The vision devices are in bulges. One 47-mm and one 8-mm machine gun are mounted coaxially in the hull, and one 8-mm machine gun is in reserve for antiaircraft. (The Germans had 450 of these shipped to Italy in April 1941.)

h. M11/39.—The turret of this tank (fig. 79), mounted offset to the left, amidships, is in the shape of a truncated cone mounted on a hull. It mounts a 37/40-mm gun in the right side of hull

Type	Light, C. V. 3 (33/35) or L 3/35	Light, Fiat-Ansaldo 3000 B (later mod)	Light, Fiat-Ansaldo 3000 B
Country of origin	Italy	Italy	Italy
Weight	3 to 3½ tons	5 tons	5 tons without tail
Crew	2 (driver, gunner)	2 to 3 (driver, gunner, commander).	2 to 3 (driver, 1 to 2 gunners).
Dimensions:			
Length	10 ft 6 in	11 ft 6 in	13 ft 10 in without tail.
Width	4 ft 7 in	5 ft 7 in	5 ft 6 in
Height	4 ft 3 in	6 ft 6 in	7 ft 7 in
Clearance	9 in	1 ft 11 in	1 ft 6 in
Armor basis (thickest plate known).	0.31 in (later model has 0.629 in).	0.629 in	0.709 in
Armament	Two 8-mm MG's coaxially mounted or one LMG and flame thrower.	One 37-mm gun one LMG	One 37-mm to 40-mm gun 1 LMG or 2 LMG's mounted.
Ammunition carried	2, 240 rounds	60 rounds for gun	60 rounds for gun
Engine	43-hp, 4-cylinder Fiat, water-cooled.	45-hp, 4-cylinder Fiat, water-cooled.	45-hp, Fiat, water-cooled.
Drive	Front sprocket	Front sprocket	Rear sprocket
Maximum speed on roads.	26 mph	20 mph	13 mph
Radius of action	55 to 60 miles	90 miles	60 miles
Suspension	7 small bogies; 1 independent bogie at rear.	5 bogies; 1 independent fixed bogie at rear; leaf springing and rocker.	4 bogies, obscured by large girder bearer; very large-spoked front idle wheel.
Performance:			
Spanning ability	4 ft 9 in	5 ft	5 ft
Vertical obstacle	2 ft	1 ft 8 in	1 ft 8 in
Fording ability	2 ft 2 in		2 ft 11 in
Climbing ability	45°	45°	45°
Intercommunication	Flag or Rad/Tg		
Remarks	Standard Galian Armd vehicle; large numbers in existence; designed from Cardon-Lloyd; may be used as bridge carrier which enables them to scale 22.9-ft obstacle; flame thrower, effective range 110 yd; high-16 ineffective tank.	Modern type of Italian light tank.	Obsolescent; a considerable number of these tanks may be in existence; carried on trailers or trucks.

Fugure 74. A - Characteristics of types of tanks.

Type	Light, L 5 21/30	Light, L 6/40	Light, Carro d'assalto
Country of origin	Italy	Italy	Italy
Weight	5.8 tons	6.5 tons	6 to 8 tons
Crew	2	2 (driver and gunner)	3 (driver, gunner, and commander).
Dimensions:			
Length	12 ft 3 in	12 ft 7½ in	12 ft 10 in
Width	5 ft 6 in	6 ft 1 in	6 ft
Height	7 ft 3 in	6 ft 10 in	6 ft 3 in
Clearance	1 ft 1 in	1 ft 2 in	1 ft 1 in
Armor basis (thickest plate known).		1.45 in	1.02 in
Armament	Two 8-mm coastal	One 20-mm and one 8-mm coaxial in turret or one 37-mm in turret.	One 20-mm HMG, one 8-mm LMG, or 2 8-mm.
Ammunition carried		280 rounds for 20-mm; 1,056 for 8-mm.	500 rounds for HMG; 2,000 rounds for LMG.
Engine	60 hp, gasoline	80 hp, gasoline, 4-cylinder, situated at the rear.	100 hp
Drive		Front sprocket	
Maximum speed on roads.	13 mph	26 mph	20 mph
Radius of action	5 hours	122 miles	124 miles
Suspension	4 bogies of 2 wheels semielliptic springs completely obscured by skirting.	4 rubber-tired bogie wheels mounted in pairs, each sprung by a curved cantilever and torsion bar. The fifth bogie at the rear is of steel and acts as a load carrier and to return the track. 3 return rollers.	Completely obscured by skirting.
Performance:			
Spanning ability	4 ft 11 in	5 ft 6 in	5 ft 10 in
Vertical obstacle	2 ft	2 ft 7 in	
Fording ability	2 ft 11½ in	3 ft 3 in	2 ft 6 in
Climbing ability	41°	40°	45°
Intercommunication	Flag or Rad for commander's tank.	Rad/Tp	Rad/Tg and Rad/Tp.
Remarks	1917 French Rennault design; obsolete; stopped manufacture in 1930.	Considered poor and primitive design.	300 of these were to be delivered in Feb. 1931.

Fugure 74. B - Characteristics of types of tanks.

Type	Light, Renault R 35	Light, M 11 39	Light, M. 13 (formerly M. 11)
Country of origin	France	Italy	Italy
Weight	11 tons	11 tons (approximately)	13 tons
Crew	2 (driver, gunner)	3	3 (driver, 2 gunners)
Dimensions:			
Length	13 ft 2 in	15 ft 5 in	16 ft 1 in
Width	6 ft	7 ft	7 ft 2 in
Height	8 ft 1 in	7 ft	6 ft 11 in
Clearance	1 ft 2 in	1 ft 2 in	1 ft 4 in
Armor basis (thickest plate known)	1.57 in	1.12 in	1.18 in
Armament	One 37-mm gun, one LMG, coaxially mounted.	One 37/40 gun in hull; two 8-mm MG's in.	One 37-mm gun in hull; two LMG's.
Ammunition carried	100 rounds for gun; 2,400 rounds for MG.	84 rounds for 37/40 gun; 1,440 for MG.	90 rounds for gun; 3,000 for MG.
Engine	83-hp 4-cylinder, water-cooled	105-hp Diesel water-cooled.	130-hp Diesel
Drive	Front Sprocket		Front sprocket
Maximum speed on roads	12½ mph	20 mph	20 to 22 mph
Radius of action	90 to 95 miles	125 miles	112 miles
Suspension	5 bogies, 2 pairs with scissor articulators, 1 independent.	2 double articulated bogies each with four 12-in diameter wheels. Each group independently sprung.	8 bogies, 2 bogies leaf springing.
Performance:			
Spanning ability	5 ft 3 in	6 ft 7 in	6 ft 6 in
Vertical obstacle	2 ft 11 in	2 ft 7½ in	2 ft 8 in
Fording ability	3 ft 7 in	3 ft 3¼ in	3 ft
Climbing ability	40°	40°	45°
Intercommunication	Radio Tn., Flag		Rad. Tg. only in commanders tank.
Remarks	A large number were in existence. May be fitted with tail to improve trench crossing performance. Can be easily mass produced.	Built in considerable numbers but owing to ordnance in hull is difficult to fire. Being replaced by M 13/40.	Identified in Libya and may exist in considerable numbers. Gun in hull is not so effective.

Fugure 74. C - Characteristics of types of tanks.

Type	Light, M. 13 40	Light, M. 14 14	Light, Carro di rottura
Country of origin	Italy	Italy	
Weight	13 tons	13.8 to 14.7 tons	14.75 tons
Crew	4	4	4 (driver, 2 gunners, radio operator, commander).
Dimensions:			
Length	16 ft 1 in		14 ft 8 in
Width	7 ft 3 in		7 ft
Height	7 ft 9 in		7 ft 3 in
Clearance	1 ft 2 in		1 ft 4 in
Armor basis (thickest plate known).	1.18 in		1.18 in
Armament	One 47-32 gun and one 8-mm coaxially in turret; two 8-mm MG coaxially mounted in hull; one 8-mm in reserve for AA.	One 47-32 gun; one 8-mm MG coaxially mounted; two 8-mm MG in hull.	One 47-mm gun; two 8-mm MG's.
Ammunition carried	104 rounds for gun; 3,048 for MG.		150 rounds for gun; 4,000 rounds for MG.
Engine	105-hp Diesel, water-cooled, 8-cylinder.	V8 Diesel, 125-hp	160-hp Diesel
Drive			
Maximum speed on roads.	19 mph	21.9 mph	25 mph
Radius of action	123 miles	122 miles	186 miles
Suspension	2 double articulated bogies each with four 14-in diameter twin wheels, each group independently sprung.		
Performance:			
Spanning ability	6 ft 11 in	6 ft 10 in	6 ft
Vertical obstacle	2 ft 6½ in	2 ft 11 in	1 ft 11 in
Fording ability	3 ft 3½ in	3 ft 3 in	2 ft 6 in
Climbing ability	45°		40°
Intercommunication	Rad. Tg		Rad. Tp-type R. F. C. A.
Remarks	Best of Italian tanks but lacks armor protection. AA mounting impracticable. Engine trouble in Middle East.	An improved model of the M13/40, being slightly heavier and fitted with a slightly larger engine. The performance is also improved.	First issued to units in 1939, possibly further 150 are already in service.

Fugure 74. D - Characteristics of types of tanks.

Type	Medium, Somua S. 35	Medium, "P25" Pesante
Country of origin	France	Italy.
Weight	18 tons	22 to 25 tons.
Crew	3, driver, gunner, commander.	Six.
Dimensions:		
Length	17 ft 6 in	25 ft.
Width	6 ft 8 in	8 ft 6 in.
Height	8 ft 10 in	9 ft.
Clearance	1 ft 4 in	
Armor basis (thickest plate known)	1.57 in	
Armament	One 47-mm; 1 LMG	One 47/32 gun in turret. 3 LMG's.
Ammunition carried	120 rounds for gun; 5,000 for LMG.	
Engine	190-hp V8 water-cooled.	
Drive	Rear sprocket	
Maximum speed on roads.	29 mph	20 mph.
Radius of action	140 miles	
Suspension	9 bogies, 4 bogies with leaf springing; 1 independent suspension protected by skirting.	
Performance:		
Spanning ability	7 ft 10 in	9 ft 10 in.
Vertical obstacle	2 ft 11 in	3 ft 6 in.
Fording ability	3 ft 3 in	3 ft 11 in.
Climbing ability	40°	
Intercommunication	Rad. Tg., Flag	
Remarks	Considerable numbers in existence.	Details unconfirmed indicate that a tank of the above specifications may be in advanced experimental stage.

Fugure 74. E - Characteristics of types of tanks.

ARMAMENT AND EQUIPMENT

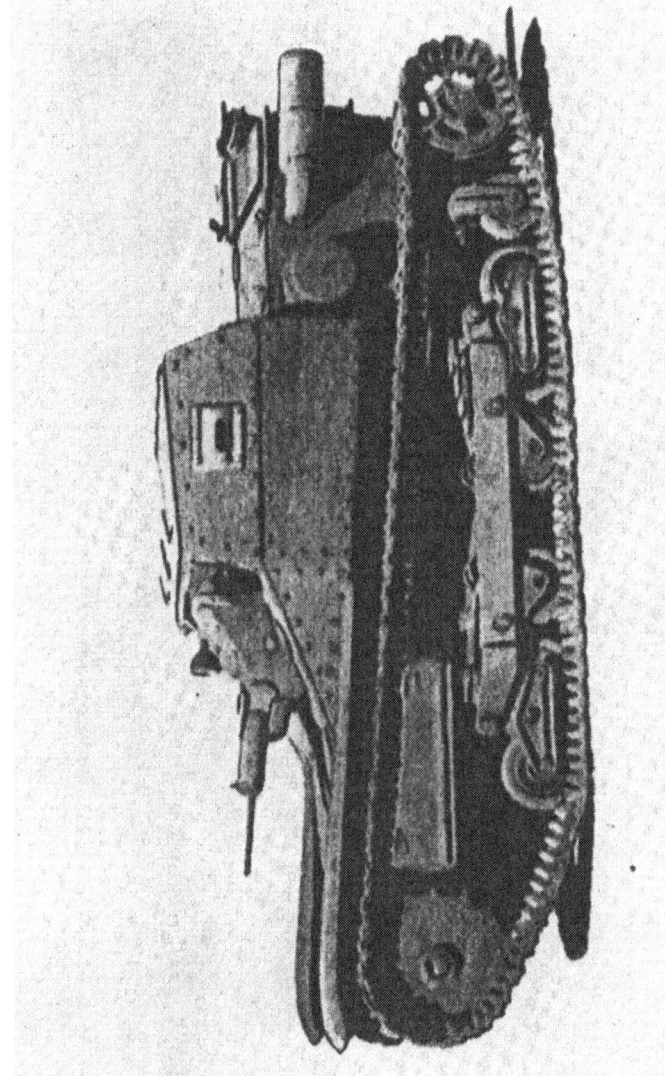

FIGURE 75.—L 3/35 tank.

FIGURE 76.—Fiat-Ansaldo 3000 B tank (old model).

ARMAMENT AND EQUIPMENT

Figure 77.—L 6/40 tank.

FIGURE 78.—Renault R 35 tank (French).

FIGURE 79.—M 11/39 tank.

FIGURE 80.—M13 (formerly M11) tank.

ARMAMENT AND EQUIPMENT 235

and two 8-mm machine guns in the turret. The suspension is based on the Cardon-Lloyd. There are two double articulated bogies, each with four small wheels. Each group is independently sprung. There is a front sprocket, as well as three track rollers, one hidden by step. There is a door in the left side of hull. Two

FIGURE 81.—M13/40 tank.

spare bogies are carried on the rear of the tank. This tank is being supplemented by the M 13/40.

i. M 13 (formerly M 11).—This tank (fig. 80) has the same suspension as the M 11/39 and the same general appearance except that the 37-mm gun has been moved into the turret, which

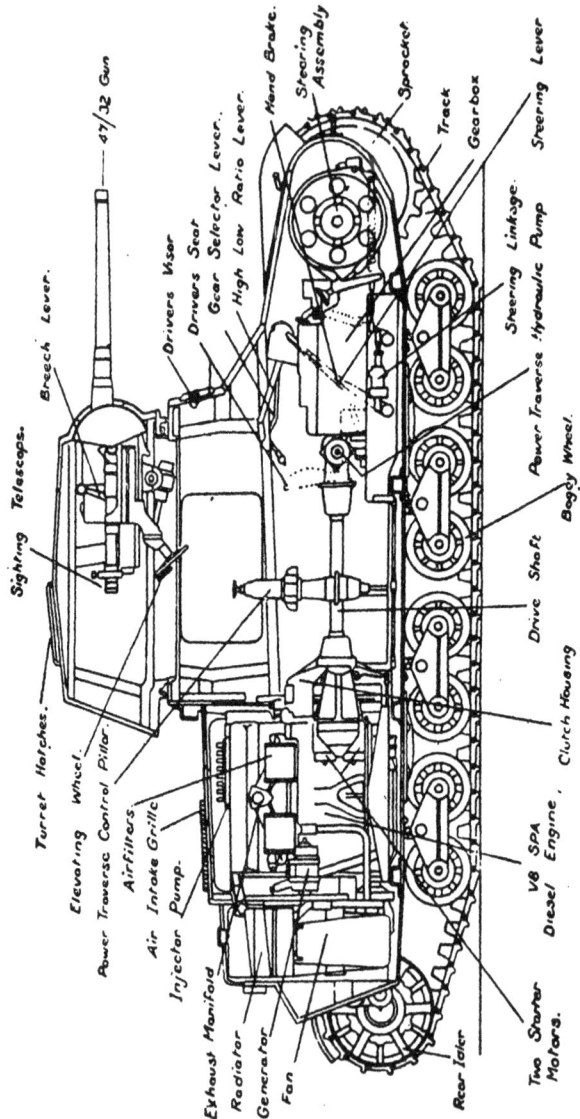

FIGURE 82.—Cross section of the M13/40 four-man tank.

has been centered over the hull. The two light machine guns have been lowered to the left front of the hull.

j. M 13/40.—This tank (figs. 81 and 82) is similar in general appearance to the M 13 (formerly M 11), with the exception that a cupola has been added to the turret and an 8-mm antiaircraft machine gun has been mounted therein. Fishpole antennae are on the right front of the main turret.

k. M 14/14.—This is an improved model of the M 13/40 tank, being slightly heavier and fitted with a slightly larger engine.

l. Carro di rottura.—This was first issued to units in 1939. It weighs 14.75 tons and has a crew of four. The armor basis is the same as that of the M 13/40. The armament consists of one 47-mm gun and two 8-mm machine guns.

m. S 35, Somua (French).—This is a very clean looking design (fig. 83). All surfaces are rounded and there are no sharp corners. There are nine bogie wheels and a rear sprocket drive, but the suspension is completely hidden by skirting. One track roller is visible in the center. There are three sizeable doors on each side, and square windows in the driver's compartment are unusually large. The hull overhangs the tracks. The turret and cupola are mounted forward and centered. The 47-mm gun is mounted in the right side of the turret.

236. Armored cars.—For detailed characteristics of Italian armored cars, see figure 84. The Autoblinda 40 (fig. 85) is a typical light model. There is also a medium 6-wheeled car and a heavy 10-wheeled.

237. Armored trains.—*a. General.*—Armored trains are a part of Italy's system of coast defense. There are about 30 types in all, with 4 to 6 guns of approximately 6-inch caliber with a range of approximately 20,000 to 24,000 yards. They are mounted on regular flat cars. The long stretches of unpopulated coasts make these railway batteries a most important addition to the fixed defenses located at strategic points where an invasion

FIGURE 83.—S 35, Somua (French) medium tank.

ARMAMENT AND EQUIPMENT

attempt might be made. A number of these trains are stationed at Reggio di Calabria for use on the western or eastern coastal areas. It will be noted that from Reggio di Calabria to Taranto a railway closely parallels the coast except for a short distance on the Crotone area. This railway commands the sea at practically all vital points.

	Light	Medium	Heavy
Type			
Name	Autoblinda 40	6-wheeler	10-wheeler
Weight	6 tons (approximately)	5½ to 6 tons	
Crew	4 (2 drivers and 2 gunners)	4 (2 drivers and 2 gunners)	
Dimensions:			
Length	17 ft 4 in	18 ft 4 in	
Width	6 ft 4 in	6 ft 6 in	
Height	7 ft 8 in	8 ft 5 in	
Armor basis (thickest plate known)	18 mm	0.39 inch	0.37 inch
Armament	One 20-mm Breda cannon; two 8-mm Breda MG	Three 20-mm MG's in turret; 1 in rear	
Number of wheels	4 (plus 2 spares for rough ground)	6	10
System of steering	4-wheel		
engine	Spa 6-cylinder, 85-hp, valves overhead, water and fan-cooled	122 B. side valve, 6-cylinder, 47-hp at 2,600 rpm; water-cooled	
Maximum speed on roads	50 mph (in sixth gear)	27 to 30 mph (engine governed at 2,600 rpm)	
Radius of action		200 miles	
Intercommunication	Radio in troop commander vehicles; internal communication by laryngaphone		
Remarks	May be driven from either end	Vulnerable amidships, particularly the gasoline tank in the center of the floor; tires not well protected	More robust but possibly more susceptible to frontal shots; tires have protection but are inadequate compared with body armoring

FIGURE 84.—Characteristics of armored cars.

b. *Organization.*—A typical armored train is composed of one combat section and one supply section. The combat section is made up of armored cars, two locomotives, one fire-control car, and one ammunition car. The supply section remains permanently attached to the headquarters of the armored train. It is composed of two cars for housing of officers and noncommissioned

FIGURE 85.—Autoblinda 40.

officers, four cars for housing sailors, one kitchen car, and one store car. It is not organized at stations where barracks are available.

c. *Armament.*—(1) *Combat section.*—The order of the cars is as follows: one locomotive, one car with two antiaircraft guns,

ARMAMENT AND EQUIPMENT

FIGURE 86.—Italian motorized divisions showing *autocarrette*.

two cars with one medium-caliber gun on each car, one fire-control car, two cars with one medium-caliber gun on each car, one ammunition car, one locomotive. The armored cars are built in such a way that the rails will bear the shock of the recoil of the gun when firing. Special devices are also installed on the cars in order to neutralize the tendency to overturning of the cars during the fire.

d. Employment.—The armored train is usually placed near the center of a section of a railway line about 25 miles long. One train is to be employed for each 10 to 15 miles of coast line.

e. Characteristics of armament.—A typical gun employed on armored trains is the 381/40-mm railway gun, the characteristics of which are as follows:

Caliber	381 mm.
Length of bore	40 calibers.
Muzzle velocity	2,500 feet per second.
Weight of shell	1,925 pounds.
Maximum range	26,200 yards.
Rate of fire	1 round per 15 minutes.
Elevation	25°.
Traverse	38°.

Other types of guns employed and their approximate dimensions are as follows:

Gun	Barrel	
	Length	Width
149/35-mm	5.21 m	0.6 m.
149/40-mm	5.96 m	0.6 m.
152/37-mm	5.60 m	0.7 m.
152/45-mm	6.08 m	0.7 m.

238. Other types of armored vehicles.—*a. Flame-thrower (lancia fiamme) tanks.*—The Italians use their L 3/35 tank as a flame-thrower carrier (fig. 75). When thus equipped, it carries one light gun in addition to the flame thrower. The flame chemical is carried in a wheeled trailer.

b. Bridging tank.—The bridging tank in use by the Italians is also a converted L 3/35. In this case the bridge is carried in a small two-wheeled trailer, apparently in knocked-down sections. It makes an awkward and bulky load. The tank itself carries a wire-braced superstructure consisting of a pair of masts wire-guyed all around. The bridge when put together is 22.9 feet in length and is designed to be carried in assembled position to the brink of the obstacle while suspended, after the manner of the boom of a derrick, from the bow of the tank. It is then lowered into position.

c. Autocaretta (four-wheeled truck).—The Italian General Staff has been experimenting for some time past with a light mechanical vehicle suitable for unit first-line transport. A type has now been evolved known in Italy as *autocaretta* (fig. 86) and it is understood that it has proved a great success. It is made by the Ansaldo Company for accompanying troops over rough mountainous country. These vehicles have been designed to carry a useful load of approximately 1 ton over narrow mountain roads and mule tracks. The gauge is therefore very narrow, being just over 3 feet, while the over-all width is 4 feet The engine is a four-cylinder 20 horsepower air-cooled type; it is mounted forward of the front axle and is very accessible. The steering and driving mechanism work on all four wheels, each of which is capable of considerable independent movement in a vertical plane. The vehicle has a turning circle of 23 feet radius. The tires are solid and can be fitted with steel tracks which have proved very effective. Experiments with pneumatic tires are being carried out. The maximum speed on the flat is about 15 miles per hour and the average gasoline consumption is about 7 miles per gallon. The machine can climb on a slope of 1 in 2½ fully loaded. The Italian General Staff hope that the *autocaretta* will be able not only to replace the limbered wagon but to travel in places inaccessible to that vehicle, and that it will also replace pack transport whenever some sort of track is available even if only 4 feet in width. While not designed especially for armored forces, it is issued to tank units as a cargo, and possibly as a personnel carrier. It is, so far as is known, unarmored, but may mount a machine gun.

 d. *S. P. A. Sahariano (Saharan) truck (Fiat).*—This truck (fig. 87) has been especially designed by the Fiat Company to

FIGURE 87.—S. P. A. Sahariano (Saharan) truck (Fiat).

operate in the desert, and in October 1940 was in quantity production. It has a very considerable radius of action, remarkable

ARMAMENT AND EQUIPMENT 238-239

speed, power of traction and load capacity, as compared to all other existing colonial trucks. For its design, the foot of the camel was scientifically investigated, and it was ascertained that it never sinks into the sand because it rests on the ground with a pressure of less than 2 pounds per square centimeter. Consequently in order to make it possible for the new truck to move on very soft ground without the danger of sinking into it, special tires of extremely large dimensions, very low pressure type, resting on the ground with a pressure identical to that of the camel's foot, were designed and built. The truck is four-wheeled drive and four-wheel steer. Each wheel is suspended independently of the others, which makes it possible for the truck to move over very irregular and broken terrain. The tires are of very large diameter and extremely wide section. While of high adhesion, they do not have the fault of biting into the sand which would result in their revolving without advancing. The maximum sinking into very soft sand never exceeds 6 cm (2.36 inches). The truck carries 132 gallons of gasoline and 105 gallons of water.

SECTION VI

ENGINEERS

	Paragraph
General	239
Bridges and bridging equipment	240
Demolitions in general	241
Igniters	242
Mines	243
Obstacles	244
Camouflage	245
Searchlights	246
Pioneer tools	247

239. General.—In the Italian Army, signal communications constitute an engineer function, but for convenience, signal equipment is discussed separately (see sec. VII).

240. Bridges and bridging equipment.—*a. General.*—For the many types of bridges and bridging equipment used by the Italian engineers, see figure 88.

Name of bridge	Type	Capacity (tons)	Remarks
Girder Bridge (*ponte metállico*), no. 1.	Herbert type. 1929	20 on 2 axles. 20 on 2 axles.	Made of soft steel. Made of silicon steel.
Girder bridge (*ponte metállico*), no. 2.	Cantilever-steel truss.	210 tons.	Maximum span 177 ft. Used for standard or narrow-gage railways.
Girder bridge (*ponte metállico*), no. 3.	Lattice girder.	210 tons.	Maximum span 336 ft. Used for standard or narrow-gage railways.
Footbridge (*passarella*), no. 1.	Floating footbridge.	67 lb per lineal ft.	Kapok; maximum 164 ft; weight of sections 123 lb.
Footbridge (*passarella*), no. 2.	Floating footbridge.	1 on 1 axle; 1.5 on 2 axles.	Normal length 171 ft.
Mountain footbridge (*passarella di montagna*).	Lattice girder, deck type.	202 lb per lineal ft.	Normal length 66 ft.
Ponton bridge, no. 0.	P & T.	3 tons on pontons; 5 tons on trestles.	Pontons covered with "Texco" light canvas.
Ponton bridge, no. 1.	P & T.	11 tons on 2 axles (reinforced).	Obsolete; ponton model, 1860/14.
Ponton bridge, no. 2.	P & T.	12 to 18.	Obsolete; pontons made up of half-pontons.
Ponton bridge, no. 3.	P & T.	672 lb per lineal ft.	Employs triangular, latticed-side beams of tubular steel; maximum span, 820 ft.
Raft (*záttera*) "K".	Raft.	6.	Made up of footbridge equipment; 24 by 13 ft; supported by 5 kapok floats.
Cableway, no. 1.	3-cable, shuttle.	606 lb.	14- to 18-hp motor; 32-ft towers.
Cableway, no. 2.	3-cable, semicontinuous.	441 lb.	25- to 35-hp motor; 26-ft towers.
Cableway, no. 3.	3-cable, semicontinuous.	551 lb.	15- to 18-hp motor; 12- to 36-ft towers.

FIGURE 88.—Tabulation of bridge equipment.

b. Girder bridge (*ponte metállico*) *no. 1.*—This is a steel truss bridge (fig. 89) using the Herbert type of truss, a type also used by

ARMAMENT AND EQUIPMENT 240

the Germans for the construction of heavy bridges. The Herbert type of truss as used in girder bridge no. 1 is made up of steel shapes, which are pin-connected. Therefore, the truss may be completely disassembled. Another type of Herbert truss is used with the heavy "Ponton Bridge no. 3" described below.

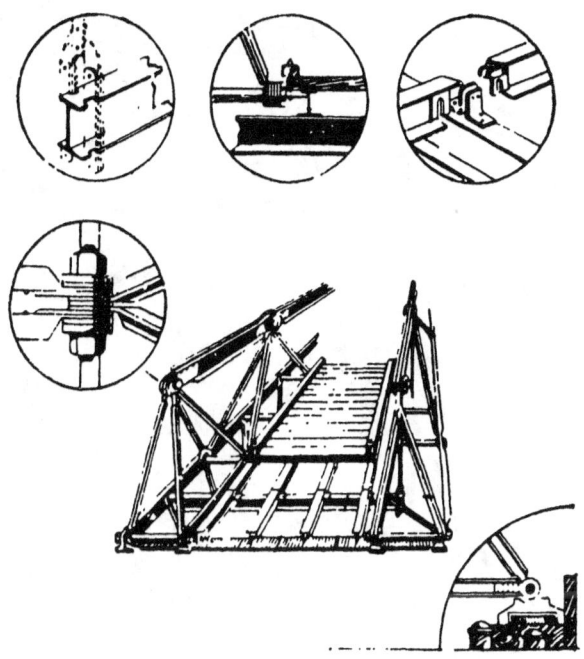

FIGURE 80.—Girder bridge (*ponte metállico*) no. 1.

c. Girder bridges nos. 2 and 3.—These are heavy-duty truss bridges which may be built to any capacity (up to 210 tons) by adding additional members. (The manner in which the bridges are strengthened by adding "stories" is indicated in figs. 90 and 91.) It appears that these bridges are designed primarily for railway use.

RESTRICTED

d. *Footbridges (passarella) nos. 1 and 2.*—Footbridges nos. 1 and 2 consist of duckboard superstructures supported on kapok-filled floats. The critical dimensions are as shown. It appears

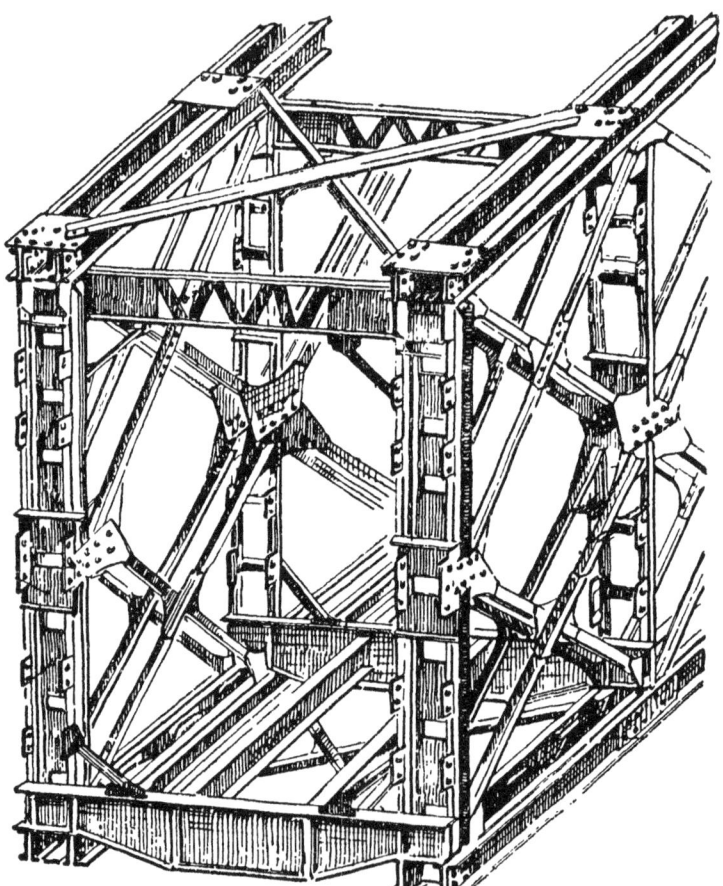

FIGURE 89.—Girder bridge (*ponte metállico*) no. 1.

that footbridge no. 2 could take very light vehicles and perhaps light artillery.

   e. *Mountain footbridge (passarella da montagna).*—This is a very light truss bridge (fig. 92) which apparently could take light

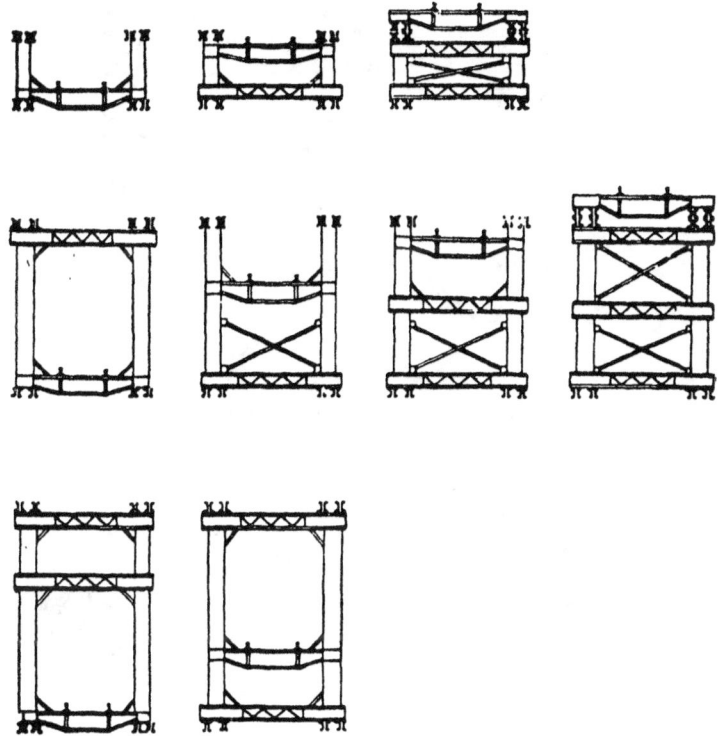

FIGURE 91.—Variations of girder bridge no. 2.

vehicles and light artillery over dry gaps with spans up to 66 feet.

   f. *Cableways.*—Since much of their training has been in mountainous areas, the Italian engineers have developed several types of cableways. These cableways are designed for transporting light loads, principally supplies, over dry gaps and up mountainous slopes. As indicated in the table, the cableways are suitable for loads up to about 600 pounds. (For a sketch of cableway no. 3, see fig. 93.)

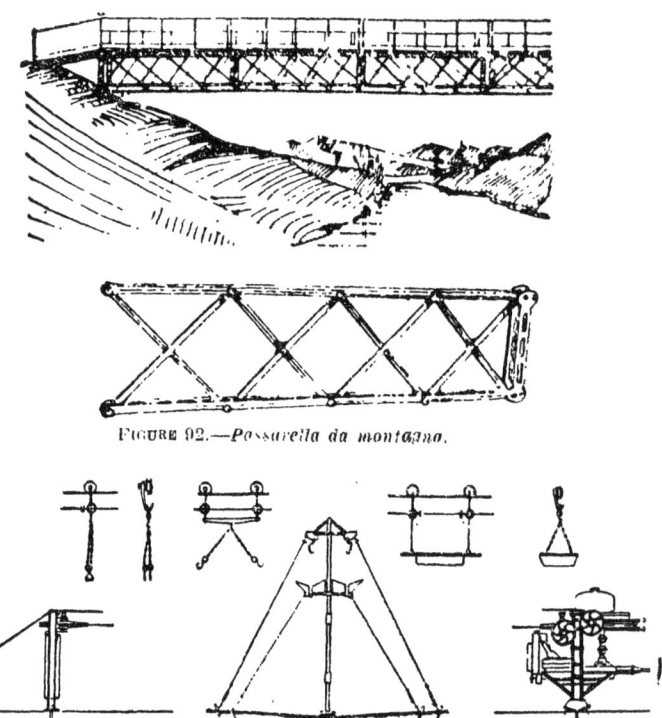

FIGURE 92.—*Passarella da montagna*.

FIGURE 93.—Cableway no. 3.

g. Ponton and trestle bridges.—The standard Italian ponton and trestle equipage is known as bridge equipment no. 3 (figs. 94 and 95). As indicated in the drawings, the piers are made up of half pontons, each of which weighs about 2,000 pounds. The superstructure for the bridge consists of Herbert trusses (see *b*

ARMAMENT AND EQUIPMENT   240

BRIDGE EQUIPAGE NO.3	19 half pontons, 8 trestles, 300 m of metal beams stamped out for lightness, material for deck units, etc., can build 150 m of bridge	The wooden deck and rests upon transverse balk, which, suspended of the two extremities, support the weight of the principal metal trusses (of prismatic design) supported upon pontons or trestles. In this Bridge alternate half pontons may be eliminated, the resulting upon of 20 m can support 10 tons
CAPACITY	1,000 kg per linear m, uniformly distributed. Twenty tons on two axles (20 m between vehicles). Trains of 30 tons (30 m between vehicles)	
SPAN	10 m for bridges on half pontons, 15 m for bridges on trestles and for deck units adjacent to abutments.	
WIDTH OF ROADWAY	2.28 m	
TRANSPORTATION REQUIRED	40 trucks with trailers.	
ASSEMBLY TIME	3 to 5 minutes per linear meter of bridge	

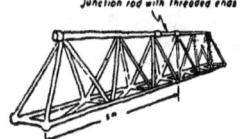
Junction rod with threaded ends

HALF-PONTON FOR BRIDGE No.3
Weight 920 kg

PONTON FOR BRIDGE No.3
(Produced by joining two half-pontons)
Transverse balk   Balk

PROCEDURE FOR ASSEMBLY OF THE BRIDGE. The ponton is moved out, with the balk and transverse balk in place, by using the beams of the wooden deck units. Using the deck unit as a bridge working surface, the prismatic metal trusses are brought into position by means of small maneuvering trucks, are placed so as to be supported upon the balk, and are fastened to the beam of the deck unit already mounted. The flooring is raised by means of jacks resting on the bottoms of the pontons.

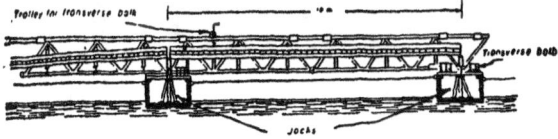
Trolley for transverse balk
Transverse balk
Jacks

The deck unit is raised on jacks and the transverse balk is attached to the trolley.

The transverse balk is now in position, hooked in suspension. The jacks are lowered, and the wooden deck unit rests upon the metal transverse balk suspended from the two prismatic trusses.

FIGURE 94.—Ponton and trestle bridges.

RESTRICTED

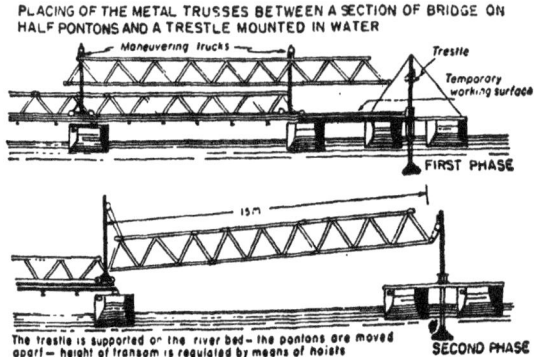
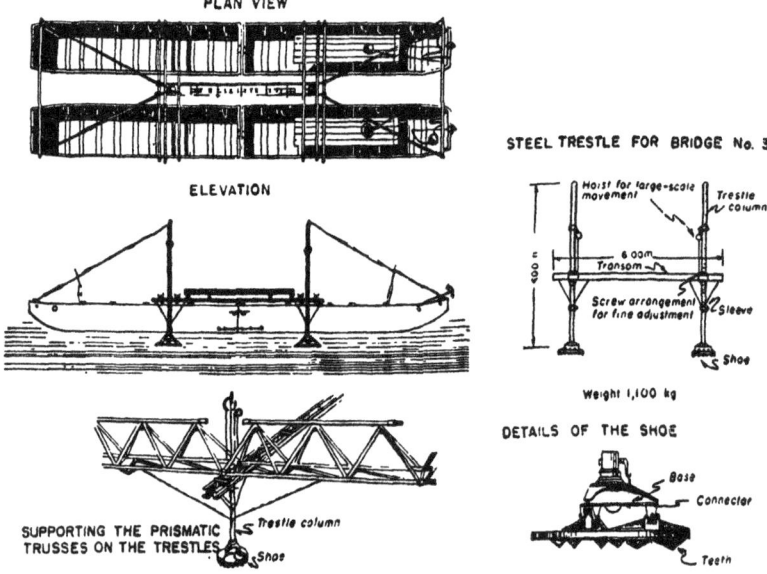

Figure 95.—Ponton and trestle bridges.

above), a steel I-beam balk, and wooden flooring. The Herbert trusses are issued in 16-foot lengths. The normal span between floats is 33 feet. The flooring system of the bridge may be assembled on the shore and guided into position by "maneuver trucks" which run along the top chords of the Herbert trusses. Details of this system are not available.

h. Special raft (záttera).—Raft "K" (fig. 96) is made up of five kapok floats and footbridge equipment, and will carry one regulation type of cart, three loaded mules, or the equivalent. The raft can be constructed in 20 minutes by five men; it is transported on four carts or one light truck. The maximum velocity of current admissible for use of the raft is approximately 3 feet per minute.

FIGURE 96.—Special raft *(Záttera)*.

241. Demolitions in general.—*a.* Italian methods of demolition, including calculation and preparation of charges, are conventional.

b. The standard-issue explosive in the Italian Army is TNT. This is issued in the following forms:

(1) Block no. 1, weighing 150 grams, 1 by 2 by 2½ inches.

(2) Block no. 2, weighing 200 grams, 1½ by 2 by 2½ inches.

(3) Block no. 3, weighing 500 grams, 4 by 2 by 2½ inches.

(4) Cartridge no. 4 (cylindrical), weighing 100 grams, 1⅛ inches in diameter and 4 inches long.

c. Other types of explosives used are as follows: gelatine, dynamite no. 1, ballistite, black powder, liquid oxygen, pentrite, T4 explosive, chlorate and perchlorate explosives, and ammonium nitrate explosives.

d. The Italian fuze is of two types; the safety fuze, which is white; and the instantaneous fuze, which is black. The safety fuze burns normally at the rate of about 2 feet per minute; but, much higher rates may be encountered.

e. The standard Italian electric detonator is pull- (rather than push-) operated.

f. On the tactical side, there is a tendency for the Italians to centralize control over the firing of demolitions. Sometimes they employ a system of passwords for giving the order to fire. The officer giving a fire order is held completely responsible for results and effects.

242. Igniters.—*a. General.*—The type of friction igniter shown in figure 97 is the only known Italian design. As com-

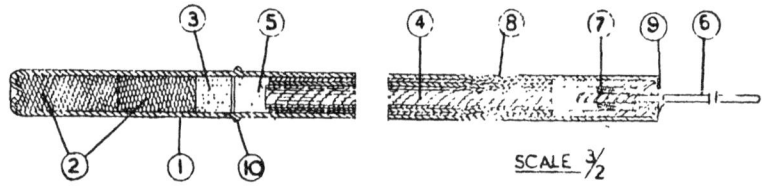

FIGURE 97.—Friction igniter (*miccia da 40*).

pared with the German types, this one is very simple in construction. The time-delay igniter shown in figure 98 is also of simple design and is made to screw into a demolition charge. This latter feature follows the well-established German practice; there are as yet, no details of the HE charges for which this igniter is intended.

b. Friction igniter (Miccia da 40).—The delay in this igniter (fig. 97) is 10 seconds. The assembly is enclosed in an aluminum tube (1), 3.7 inches long and 0.27 inches wide and 0.27 inches in diameter. It contains the main detonator filling (2), which consists of two distinct layers and is primed by a topping (3) of mixed lead azide and lead styphnate. The flash from the safety fuze (4) is reinforced by a pellet (5) consisting of a mixture of lead sulphocyanide and potassium chlorate. The safety fuze is retained in position by crimping the aluminum tube at (8). At the open end of the tube is the igniter, which consists of a length of galvanized iron wire (6) passing through a small block of match composition (7). The open end of the tube is closed round the wire (6) by a plastic seal (9). There are no identification marks. A sharp pull on the galvanized iron wire ignites the match composition which, in turn, initiates the safety fuze. The flange (10) is provided so as to retain the igniter firmly in the charge when the wire (6) is pulled.

c. Friction igniter (Miccia da 60).—This igniter is similar to the *Miccia da 40* except that it is 4.45 inches long with a safety-fuze delay of 15 seconds. There are no external identification marks. It is ¾ inch longer than the *Miccia da 40*.

d. Time delay igniter—(1) *Description*.—The igniter (fig. 98) comprises a striker (1), consisting of a hollow steel tube threaded externally at each end, projecting through one end of the igniter casing (2), which is of galvanized mild steel. Pressed into one end of the striker is a steel needle (3). The striker is surrounded by a spring (4) which presses at one end against a screwed flange (5) and at the other against the inside of the casing (2). Rotation of a galvanized steel nut (6) retracts the striker (1) and compresses the spring (4), the striker being prevented from turning by a setscrew (7) riding in a groove (8). The striker is provided with a flange which prevents withdrawal beyond a certain point; when this point is reached, a hole through the striker coincides with a hole in the casing thus permitting insertion of a 2-mm- ($\frac{5}{64}$-inch) diameter lead shear pin (9). The flange obviates the possibility of damage to the shear pin through overscrewing the milled nut (6). The latter is provided with a three-start thread, presumably for greater strength. To the other end of the igniter is screwed an aluminum adaptor (10) which is threaded externally for insertion into the charge. At (11) is a galvanized mild steel washer, which is pressed into a groove above the internally threaded portion of the adaptor, where is possessed a limited degree of lateral movement. A detonator (12) with a flanged percussion cap pressed into its open end is fitted into the

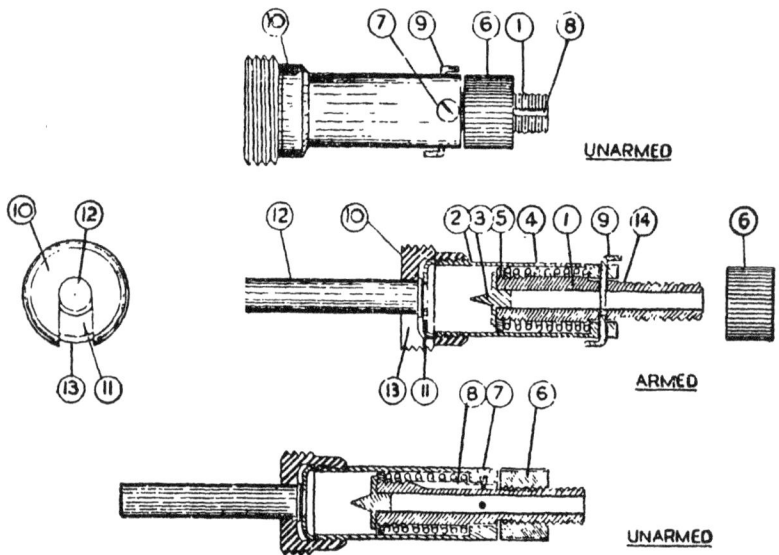

FIGURE 98.—Time-delay igniter.

adaptor (10), which for this purpose is unscrewed sufficiently to allow the flange of the cap to be inserted from the side via the slot (13) between the washer (11) and the head of the adaptor. The detonator and cap are then secured by screwing up the adaptor.

(2) *Operation.*—To arm the igniter, the milled nut (6) is unscrewed, leaving the lead shear pin (9) to retain the spring (4).

Under the pressure of the latter the shear pin eventually fails, allowing the striker (1) to fire the cap and detonator.

(3) *Time of delay.*—Four apparently identical specimens were tested in Middle East and gave the following results:

Number	Time
1	7 hours 16 minutes.
2	7½ minutes.
3	26 hours 47 minutes.
4	25 hours 45 minutes.

The discrepancy in these results may be due to possible tampering with the igniters before testing.

(4) *To neutralize.*—(*a*) Grip the striker at (14) with the cutting edges of a pair of wire-cutting pliers.

(*b*) Wire the plier jaws in position.

(5) *To disarm.*—(*a*) Unscrew the igniter from the charge, taking care not to dislodge the pliers.

(*b*) If the adaptor (10) remains in the charge, unscrew this also.

(*c*) Remove the detonator and percussion cap from the igniter.

(*d*) Release the pliers.

(*e*) Replace the milled nut (6) and take the strain off the lead shearpin (9).

(*f*) Remove the lead shearpin.

(*g*) Release the compression in the spring (4) by means of the milled nut (6).

243. Mines.—*a. Antipersonnel.*—(1) *General.*—(*a*) These mines, giving shrapnel effect, operate by means of a push-button or trip-wires. They are often difficult to detect, especially those operated by pressure in which only a portion of the cap and the push-button may appear above ground.

(*b*) The B 4 type is chiefly used as a hindrance against moving targets, and has considerable effect within a radius of 10 meters. It is easy to carry and manipulate, and is quickly put into position.

This trip-wire mine may be found in wire obstacles spaced at intervals of about 5 yards. The mines are commonly laid as close as 1 meter apart. (For details of improvised types, see par.
(2) *Antipersonnel mine, B4.*—(*a*) *Description.*—The weight of HE charge in this mine (fig. 99) is about a quarter of a pound and the total weight of the mine is 3 pounds. The mine consists of two cylinders (1) and (2), one inside the other. The space between the walls is filled with scrap metal (3). The outer cylinder (1) is flattened on one side (4), where there are six sharp projections (5) for attaching the mine to a tree or post. Two clips (6) are provided with fireproof cord for securing the mine by special rings (7).

The cylinders are held together at their common base (8) and by a cover (9) at the top. Into one end of the brass molding (10), screws a brass cap (11) carrying the striker (12) and the spring (13). Below this there is the percussion cap (14) in the holder (15) which is inserted from the side. The lower portion of the molding takes the detonator (16) and the charge (17). The open end of the molding is closed by the plug (18). The cavity between the brass molding and the inner cylinder is filled with powdered TNT.

The trip-release system consists of a trip key (19) having a ring (20) at one end to which the cords are attached. The key is held by the grooves (21) in the brass cap (11) so that it can move slightly in a direction parallel with the end of the mine. This allows the key to fit into the groove on the striker when in the armed position. A ring (22) guides the cords which are wound on bobbins (23), the latter being covered by a hinged flap (24) held closed by the pin (25). The pin (25) is used as the safety pin before setting the mine.

A special mechanism for detonating the mine, when a cord attached to the trip-release is cut, is shown in figures 100 and 101. It takes the form of a hammer (26) on the cover (9) which is set

ARMAMENT AND EQUIPMENT 243

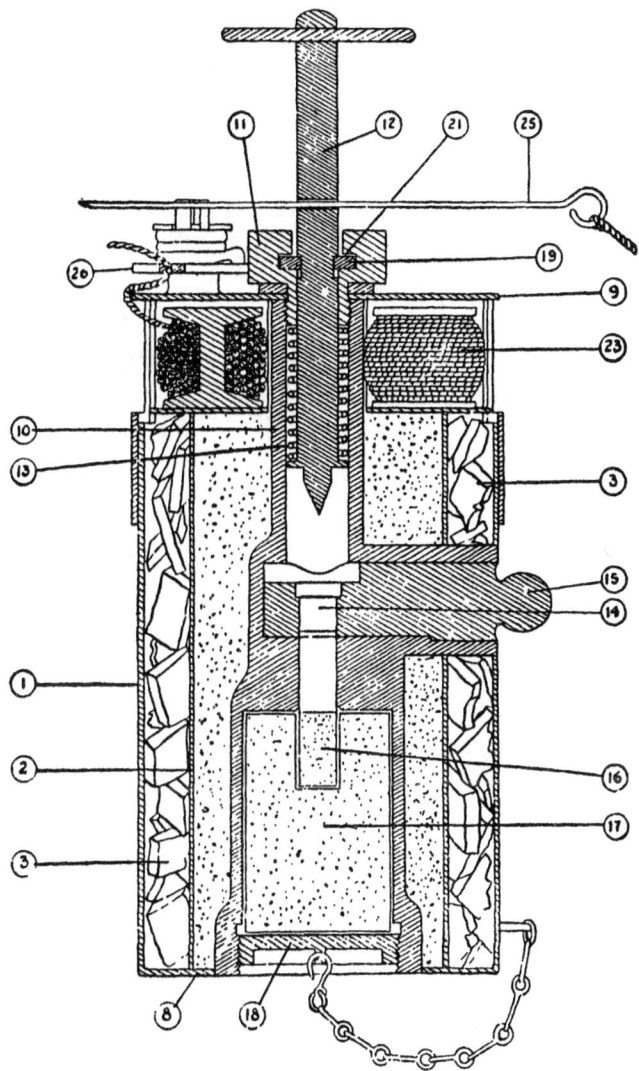

FIGURE 99.—Cross section of antipersonnel mine B4.

283 RESTRICTED

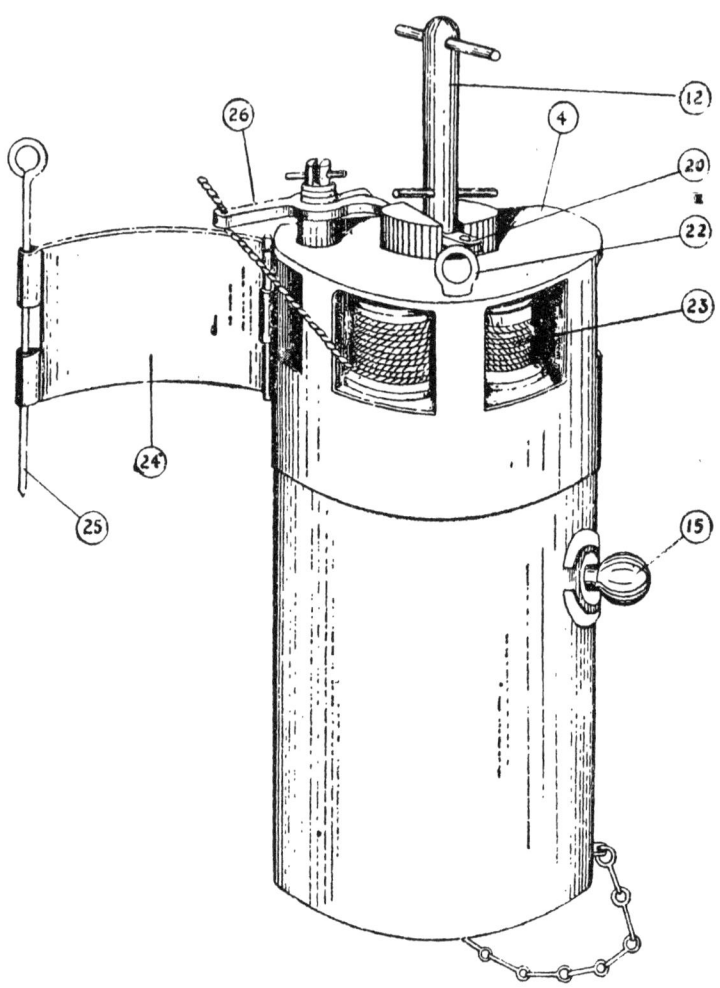

FIGURE 100.—Antipersonnel mine B4.

ARMAMENT AND EQUIPMENT 243

by attaching the thin cord to the eye and stretching it under sufficient tension to hold the hammer at least 4 mm from the end of the trip key (19). When the cord is cut, the hammer (26) drives the trip key forward and so releases the striker (12). This hammer is not provided on all B4 mines.

(*b*) *To neutralize.*—Insert a wire or nail in the safety pin hole in the striker.

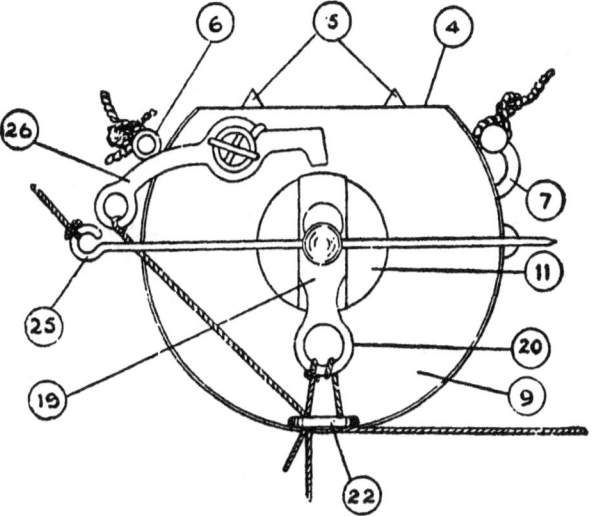

FIGURE 101.—Antipersonnel mine B4 (top view).

(*c*) *To disarm.*

  1. After inserting the wire in the striker, withdraw the cap holder (15) and take out the cap.
  2. Release the cords.

(3) *Antipersonnel bomb 4AR (thermos).*—(*a*) *Dimensions.*— The dimensions of this bomb are as follows:

Over-all length	12.3 inches.
Length of body	7.3 inches.
Diameter of body	2.7 inches.
Thickness of body	⅛ inch.
Weight of filling	1.3 pounds.
Total weight	8.5 pounds.
Color	Buff or Green.

(*b*) *Description.*—This bomb (fig. 102) included because it is designed to arm after it has come to rest on the ground. It is,

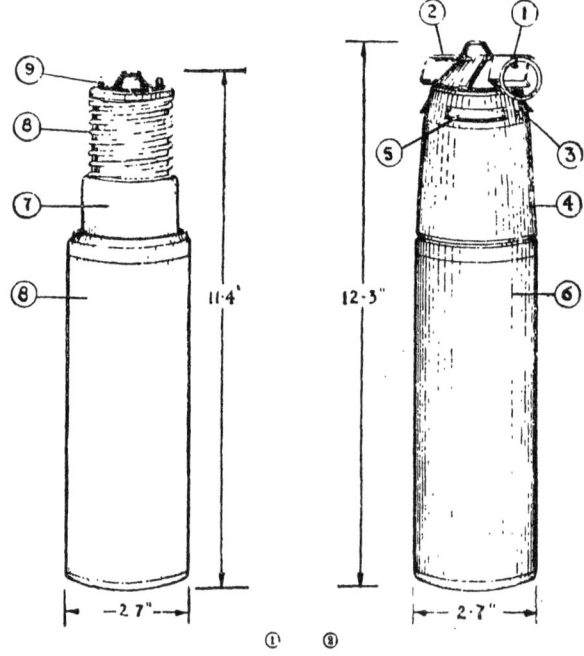

FIGURE 102.—Bomb 4AR.

therefore, in some respects an antipersonnel mine. It has been given the name of "thermos" because of its general resemblance, when complete, to a thermos bottle. The Manzolini fuze in this bomb is an anti-handling and anti-disturbance fuze which is sensitive to a jerk or a jolt.

The safety pin (1) passes through one of the vanes on the vaned cap (2) and into a slot (3) in the aluminum cup (4). This pin is removed before the bomb is dropped, thus allowing the vanes to rotate. The cup (4) has three projections (5) formed by cutting the metal and bending the tab outwards. These assist the removal of the cup when the vaned cap has become unscrewed and has fallen away during the fall of a bomb. The removal of the aluminum cup releases six clips which form the primary safety devices for the Manzolini fuze, and the bomb then has the appearance shown in figure 102①. In this condition the fuze is completely watertight and proof against the entry of grit which might impair its sensitiveness.

When the bomb strikes the ground the secondary safety devices are released and the arming of the fuze is completed after a delay period of a few seconds. This delay period enables the bomb to come to rest before the fuze becomes completely armed. Since this completion of the arming process takes place internally, figure 102② B shows the appearance of the bomb when found lying on the ground in a dangerous condition. It may be recognized by the following:

　1. The buff (or green) body—(6).
　2. The black steel collar—(7).
　3. The heavy steel spring—(8).
　4. The brass fuze cover—(9).

(*c*) *Handling.*—The bomb should de detonated as it lies by small-arms fire, by a 1-ounce guncotton primer, or by a stick of gelignite. Alternately, a loop placed loosely over the coils of the spring (8) can be used to give the bomb a sufficient jerk to detonate it. A few sandbags built up close to the bomb will give protection to the operator, who should use a coil of rope not less than 200 feet long and be in the prone position when he gives the necessary jerk.

The lethal area in the open, with the bomb on the surface is 100 feet. Complete immunity from fragments is obtained at 300 yards. When circumstances demand that the bomb should be moved, it must be remembered that the most dangerous position for the fuze is the vertical position with the nose pointing upward. Hence when moving the bomb (which will only be done in most exceptional circumstances), it should be carried horizontally, and in bringing it to this position the operator should avoid passing the fuze through the vertical. Great care must be exercised in lifting, carrying, and laying down the bomb to insure that there shall be no jolting or jerking. All movements must be slow and deliberate and excessive acceleration of the bomb must be avoided.

b. Antitank.—(1) *General.*—(*a*) There are three types of B2 mine. The design S. C. G. and the "hinged lid" type have, to a great extent, been abandoned in favor of the more recent design which has a heavier TNT charge. This mine is used in the gaps of antitank obstacles and on detours. The spacing between mines varies considerably but never more than three rows have yet been encountered. Usually they are laid on two rows, but sometimes in one row.

(*b*) A type of antitank mine which also has been used on a large scale in the Middle East is the N5. It is similar in shape to the B2 mine, the principal differences being the placing of the charge in the center of the box instead of at the two ends and the provision of initiators at each end instead of one at the center.

(*c*) A further type of standard mine is the D type, which is easily distinguished by the specially designed arming lever on the cover. This mine has not been encountered in large numbers.

ARMAMENT AND EQUIPMENT

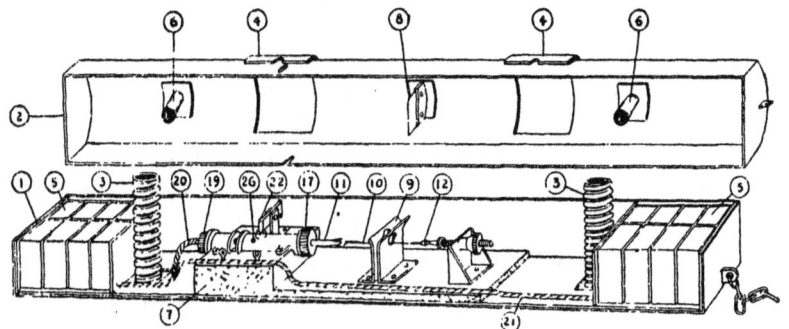

Figure 103.—Antitank mine B2.

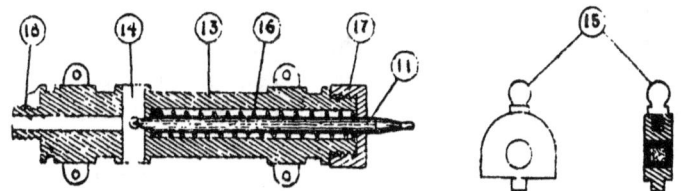

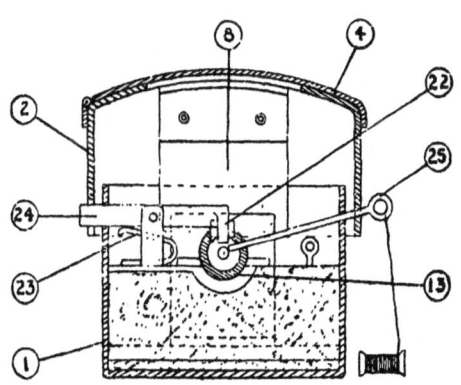

Figure 104.—Antitank mine B2 (cross section).

(2) *Antitank mine B2.*—(*a*) *Dimensions.*—The dimensions of this mine (figs. 103 and 104) are as follows:

Length	3 feet 6 inches.
Breadth	5 inches.
Height	4.7 inches.
Type of filling	TNT in 200-gm blocks.
Weight of filling	7 pounds approximately.
Total weight	33 pounds.
Firing pressure (on each spring)	220 pounds.

(*b*) *Description.*—This mine is the latest development of the older types of mine described in (3) and (4) below. It consists of a welded sheet metal box (1) with a metal lid (2) resting on two springs (3). The lid has two openings covered by hinged flaps (4), which correspond to the positions of the striker assembly and the wire-tensioning screw, respectively. At the ends of the box are the charges (5), each of eight 200-gram slabs of TNT.

On the under side of the lid are welded two short lengths of steel tube (6) which fit into the springs (3). Two similar lengths of tube are welded on the base of the box, and, together with those on the lid, serve to locate the springs. The explosive compartments and the foundation of the ignition mechanism are of wood (7). In the center of the lid is a knife (8) which is located directly above the guides (9). Through these guides passes a tension wire (10), which fastens the striker (11) to the brass adjustables hook (12).

The striker mechanism (fig. 104) consists of the body (13), which has a slot (14) for the percussion cap and holder (15), and for the striker (11) and its spring (16). The nut (17) retains one end of the spring and the thread (18) takes the nut (19) which retains the detonator (open end toward the percussion cap), the short length of instantaneous detonating fuze, (20) and

RESTRICTED

ARMAMENT AND EQUIPMENT 243

a long length of instantaneous detonating fuze, (21) which connects the detonator with the second charge. A detent (22) with spring (23) provides security against premature firing in the event of damage to the tension wire. It also insures that when the lid is depressed, the mine will function in the normal way by pressure on the lever (24), which releases the detent (22). This additional safety device is not found on all types. The safety pin (25) is placed on the hole (26) in the body of the striker and remains in this position until the mine is fully loaded, the hinged flaps (4) are closed, and the mine is covered with earth.

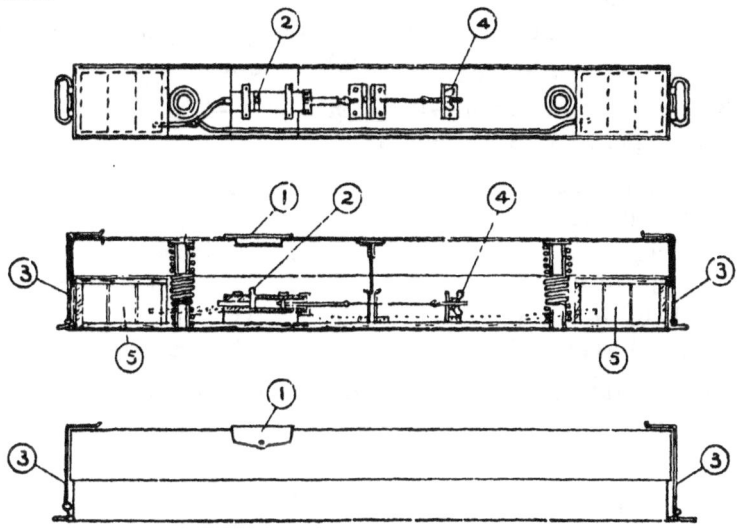

FIGURE 105.—Antitank mine B2 (S. C. G.).

The mine functions when pressure on the lid overcomes the resistance of the springs. The cutting blade will then descend and sever the wire holding the striker, the lid at the same time depressing the detent lever (24).

(c) *To neutralize.*—

    1. Open the hinged flaps (4) carefully, dusting away the loose earth.

    2. Insert the safety pin or a stout wire through the hole (26).

(d). *To disarm.*—

    1. Lift off the lid of the box and remove the cap holder and the cap (15).

    2. Unscrew the nut (19) and remove the detonator from the igniter.

    3. Release the tension of the striker spring (16) by turning the adjusting screw holding the hook (12).

(3) *B2 mine (S. C. G.).*—(a) *Dimensions.*—The dimensions of this mine (fig. 105) are as follows:

Length	3 feet 6½ inches.
Breadth	4¾ inches.
Height	6¼ inches.
Type of charge	TNT in 500-gm blocks.
Weight of charge	6.6 pounds.
Total weight of mine	30.75 pounds.

(b) *Description.*—This mine is the earliest type of steel-cased B2 mine and probably has been superseded by the mine described in (2) above.

    1. Externally, the mine shows the following differences when compared with a later model:

        (a) The lid of the mine has only one opening, with a cover (1). This opening is located above the percussion cap holder (2).

        (b) The attachment of the lid to the box is by means of two metal L-shaped pieces (3) instead of chains.

ARMAMENT AND EQUIPMENT 243

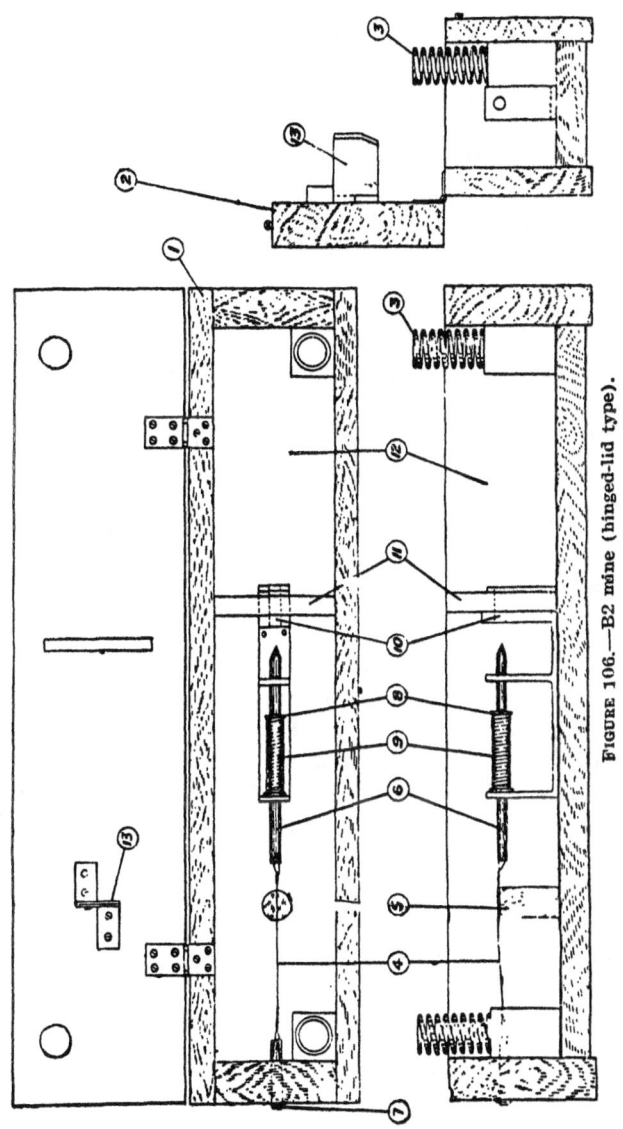

Figure 106.—B2 mine (hinged-lid type).

RESTRICTED

2. Internally, the main differences to be noted are as follows:
   (a) The absence of the detent.
   (b) A simpler striker mechanism.
   (c) The use of a butterfly nut (4) instead of the tensioning screw.
   (d) The charge (5) consists of six 500-gram blocks of TNT instead of sixteen 200-gram blocks.

(c) *To neutralize.*—The same method is used as for the B2 mine described in (2) (c) above.

(d) *To disarm.*—The same method is used as for the B2 mine described in (2) (d) above.

(4) *B2 mine (hinged-lid type).*—(a) *Dimensions.*—The dimensions of this mine (fig. 106) are as follows:

Length	2 feet 10½ inches.
Breadth	7½ inches.
Height (at hinges)	8½ inches.
Type of filling	TNT in 200-gm blocks.

(b) *Description.*—This is probably the earliest type of B2 antitank mine. It consists of a wooden box (1) with a hinged lid (2) resting on two springs (3). The springs hold the lid slightly open. As in other types of B2 mine, the method of firing depends upon the severing of a wire holding the striker. In this model the retaining wire (4) passes over the wood block (5) to the striker (6). The tension of the wire is adjusted by the screw (7). The flange (8) retains the spring (9) in compression. A cap and detonator (10) is mounted in the wooden dividing strip (11). A charge of TNT is held in the space (12). When sufficient pressure is applied to the lid of the mine, the knife (13) severs the wire (4), thus releasing the striker (6).

ARMAMENT AND EQUIPMENT

(*o*) *To neutralize.—*
  1. Carefully open the lid, which should move easily. Do not attempt to force it.
  2. Insert a strip of metal between the striker and the cap.

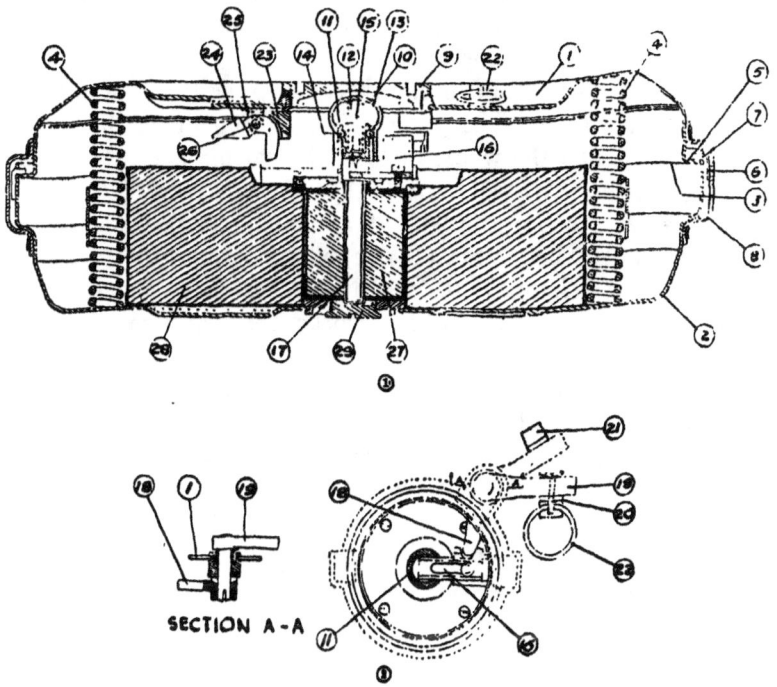

Figure 107.—Type D mine.

(*d*) *To disarm.*—Remove the cap and detonator (10).

(**5**) *Type D mine.*—(*a*) *Dimensions.*—The dimensions of this mine (fig. 107) are as follows:

  Diameter_____ 12 inches.
  Height_____ 3.6 inches.

(*b*) *Description*.—The body of this mine is made of steel and is in two sections, the cover (1) abutting the lower section (2) at (3). The cover is held in position by two strong steel springs (4), and in so doing a watertight joint is made by the lip of the cover (5), thus compressing a packing piece (6) which is placed in a slot (7) in the lower section of the mine. A circumferential pressed steel band (8) protects the joint.

In the center of the lid is the threaded plug (9), below which is the plunger (10). The plunger is a sliding fit on the striker housing (11), and the whole incloses the spring (12), the striker sleeve (13), the two steel balls (14), and the striker (15).

(The safety device consists of a channel-shaped piece (16) which masks the detonator (17) from the striker (15). Figure 107② shows the channel (16) which is operated by a toggle (18) coupled to an arm (19) which works between two stops (20 and 21).

When the mine is "safe," the arm is against the stop (20) and is fixed thereto by a split pin and ring (22). By moving the arm (19) to the stop (21), the toggle (18) slides back the channel (16) from the face of the detonator, and the mine is armed. Coupled with this safety device is the block (23), which engages a tumbler (24). The tumbler under the action of its spring (25) can rotate about its pivot (26), and when the arm (19) is moved to the stop (21), the block (23) moves toward the center, and returning the arm to the "safe" position is prevented by the new position of the tumbler (24).

When the pressure is applied to the cover (1), the plug (9) depresses the plunger (10), which descends until the steel balls (14) escape into the space in the head of the plunger. The striker (15) under the influence of the spring (12) strikes the detonator (17) firing the primary and main charges (27) and (28) respectively.

RESTRICTED

ARMAMENT AND EQUIPMENT

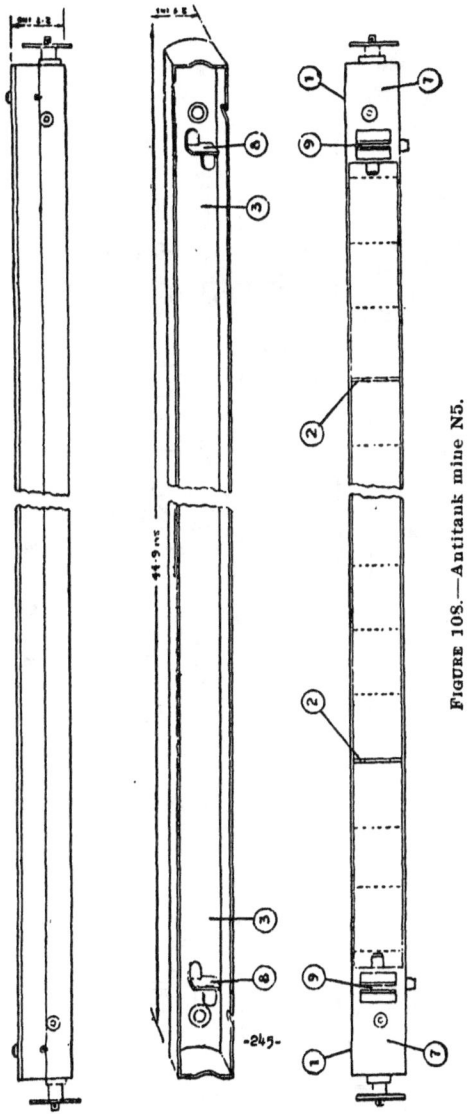

Figure 108.—Antitank mine N5.

243 HANDBOOK ON ITALIAN MILITARY FORCES

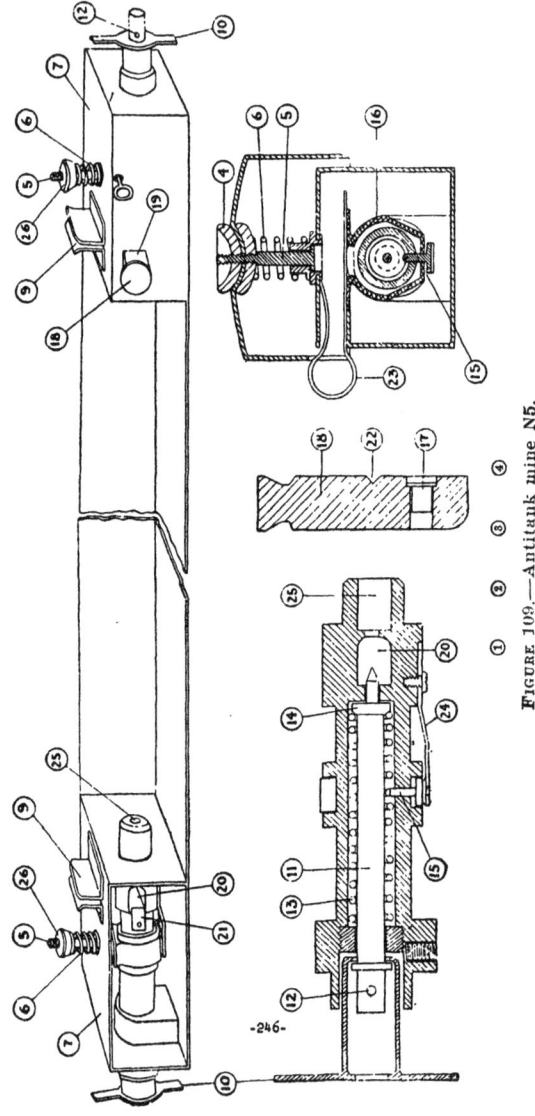

FIGURE 109.—Antitank mine N5.

RESTRICTED

ARMAMENT AND EQUIPMENT

(c) *To disarm.*—Unscrew the plug (29) and remove the detonator.

(6) *Antitank mine N5.*—(a) *Dimensions.*—The dimensions of this mine (figs. 108 and 109) are as follows:

Length	3 feet 8.9 inches.
Breadth	2.4 inches.
Height	2.7 inches.
Type of filling	TNT in 200 gm blocks.
Weight of filling	6 pounds (approximately).
Total weight of mine	17 pounds.

(b) *Description.*—According to an undated Italian document, with drawings, there appears to be two types of this mine, described as "V 3" and "V 5," respectively. The former is the type given here as the N5, and the latter is similar except that the mine is turned upside down; there are no reports that the "V 5" has been used.

The mine is made of sheet steel, the body (1) of which is strengthened by two partitions (2). The charge extends between the two firing mechanisms. The cover (3) is secured to the body by means of concave-headed nuts (4), engaging on the actuating bolts (5). The actuating bolts are retained in position by springs (6) which rest between the nut on the underside of the cover and the plate (7) covering the firing mechanism.

When the nuts (26) underneath the lid are screwed down, the springs (6) are compressed and the pressure required to operate the mine is increased. Unscrewing these nuts makes the mine far more sensitive to pressure, and with as little as 22 pounds, weight can be made to trip the striker. The under side of the cover is provided with two knives (8) which engage in the guides (9) which are provided to take copper pins. It is said that these pins offer resistance until the weight reaches 120 kg (264 pounds). At each end of the body are the cocking grips (10) (fig. 109①).

The grips are pulled to cock the strikers (11), and when these are returned to their former position, a hole (12) in the end of each striker is visible.

The striker mechanism is shown in figure 109 ②, ③ and ④. When the striker spring (13) is compressed, the flange (14) of the striker is held by the cotter (15) on the U-shaped spring clip (16). The percussion cap (17) is accommodated in the holder (18), and the latter is inserted in the hole (19) in the side of the mine. The holder (18) passes into the annular space (20) in the striker body and is held there by a blade retaining spring (21) engaging in the slot (22).

The actuating pin (23), which is also inserted through a hole in the side of the body, is the connection between the actuating bolt (5) and the U-shaped spring-clip (16) carrying the cotter (15).

When pressure is applied to the cover of the mine, the actuating bolt (5) is forced down against the spring (6) until it comes into contact with the actuating in (23). This causes the U-shaped spring clip (16) to be depressed against the retaining spring (24). The flange (14) thus freed allows the striker (11) to initiate the percussion cap (17) and fire the detonator at (25).

It is not known in what proportion of mines the copper pins, mentioned above, are fitted. As the operating pressure can be varied by manipulating the nuts (26), the use of copper pins may be ignored in the field.

(c) *To neutralize.*

1. Avoid all pressure on the lid.
2. Push a piece of stout wire or a nail through the hole (12) in the ends of each of the strikers (11). It may be necessary to manipulate the grips before these holes become visible.

ARMAMENT AND EQUIPMENT 243

3. Withdraw both actuating pins (23).

4. Remove both cap holders (18) and extract the caps, The cap holders may be a little difficult to remove if the springs (21) are very strong.

(*d*) To disarm.

1. After neutralizing as above, unscrew the nuts (4) and remove the lid of the mine.

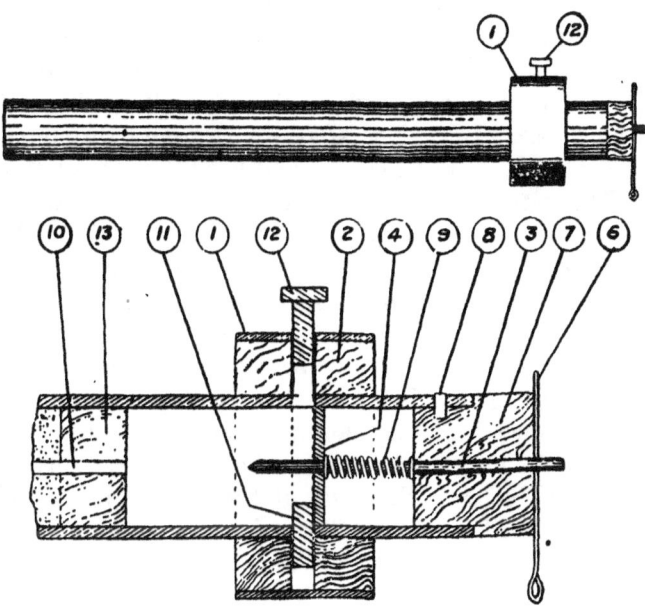

FIGURE 110.—Metal tube mine.

2. Remove the detonators from each of the end blocks of HE.

(7) *Metal-tube mine.*—(*a*) *Dimensions.*—The dimensions of this mine (fig. 110) are as follows:

Length	2 feet 2.3 inches.
Diameter	2.4 inches.
Thickness of tube	0.2 inches.
Weight of explosive	5.2 pounds.

(*b*) *Description.*—This mine has not been reported as having been used. The mine consists of a metal tube, plugged with wood, with the initiating mechanism at one end. An iron band (1) 2.6 inches wide by 4.4 inches in diameter is placed over the tube and secured by wood packing (2). This latter holds the striker-release mechanism. The striker (3) passes through the wood plug (7) in the end of the tube and has the guide plate (4) attached. The safety pin (6) passes through the striker and across the end face of the wood plug (7), the latter being held in position by a small wooden peg (8) passing through a hole in the tube. The striker (3) with its spring (9) is held away from the detonator (10) by the stop (11) which forms part of the pressure plate (12). The detonator passes through a hole bored in a wood plug (13) which retains the explosive filling. The tube is slotted diametrically to take the pressure plate which is 5 inches long and ¾ inch thick. When the head of the pressure plate is depressed, after withdrawal of the safety pin, the stop (11) moves downward and allows the strike to fire the detonator. The pressure plate is likely to be very sensitive to pressure.

(*c*) *To neutralize.*—Insert a wire in the safety-pin hole.

(*d*) *To disarm.*—

    1. Secure two pieces of wood ½ inch long under the head of the pressure plate.

    2. Take out the plug (7) complete with striker and safety pin.

ARMAMENT AND EQUIPMENT   243

3. Carefully tap out the detonators.
4. Replace the wood plug (7) without the striker.

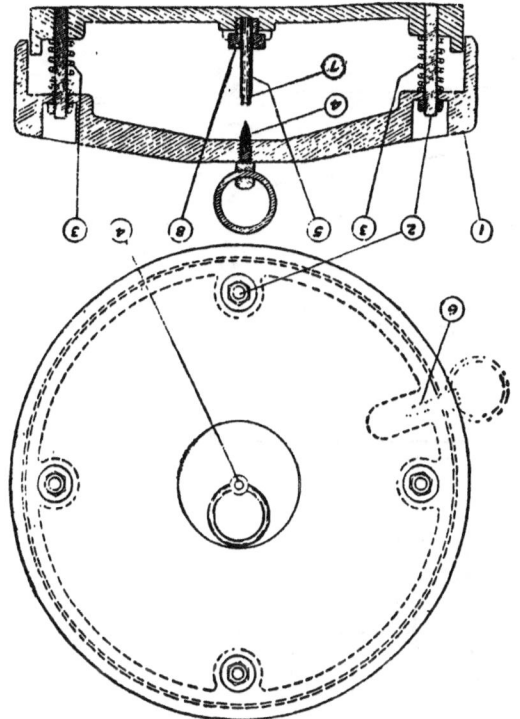

FIGURE 111.—Railway mine (old pattern).

c. Railway mines.—(1) *Old pattern.*—(*a*) *Dimensions.*—The dimensions of this mine (fig. 111) are as follows:

Diameter_____ 12 inches.
Height_____ 4 inches.
Type of filling_____ Gelignite or similar explosive.

(*b*) *Description.*—The mine is made of a light alloy. The lid (1) which is attached to the body by four bolts (2) is recessed to take the four hexagonal nuts. The lid (1) is supported on the four springs (3) and thus holds the striker (4) away from

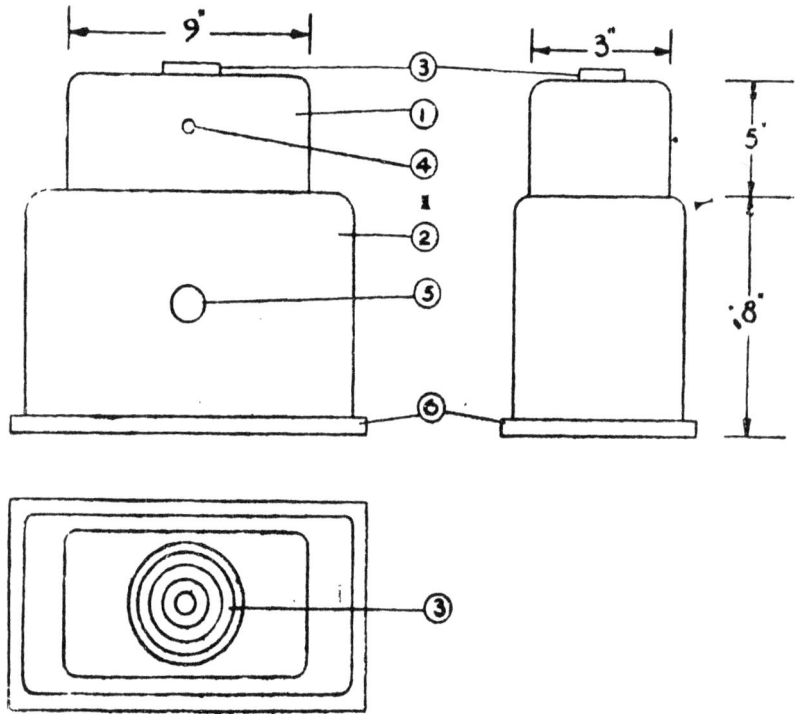

FIGURE 112.—Railway mine (new pattern).

the detonator (5). In the unarmed condition the striker with its ring is screwed into a recess in the side of the mine at (6). Below the striker is a detonator (5) with a percussion cap (7) held in position by the plug (8).

ARMAMENT AND EQUIPMENT 243

(c) *To neutralize.—*
   1. Unscrew the striker from the center of the lid.
   2. Screw the striker into the recess in the side of the mine.
(d) *To disarm.—*
   1. Unscrew the securing nuts and lift off the lid.
   2. Remove the gelignite surrounding the detonator.
   3. Unscrew the plug holding the detonator in the base of the mine.
   4. Replace the lid and replace the securing nuts.

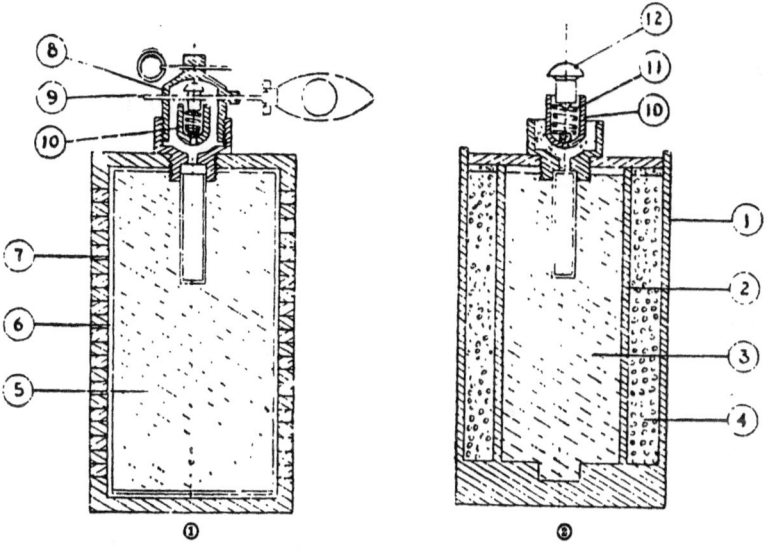

FIGURE 113.—Antipersonnel (2-kg) pressure mine.

(2) *New pattern.—*(a) *Description.—*Figure 112 gives a sketch of an Italian railway mine used by a raiding party. There are no further details than those given below, because the mine exploded during removal.

The body of the mine appears to be made in two parts (1) and (2), one above the other, with a circular metal pressure plate (3) on top. The portion (1) appears to be secured to the lower part (2) by steel springs, one on each side. In the specimen examined, a detonator (4), which had already been removed, had a length of instantaneous fuze attached. The lower part, which has rounded corners, appears to have a bakelite knob (5) in one side. The mine is mounted on a wooden base plate (6) having heavy leather straps, presumably for carrying, on each end.

(*b*) *Remarks.*—The detonator which was removed may have been the secondary means for firing. The bakelite knob (5) is probably coupled to some form of time-delay initiator.

d. Improvised mines.—(1) *Antipersonnel (2-kg) pressure mine.*—(*a*) *Dimensions.*—The dimensions of this mine are as follows:

Height_____ 4.5 inches.
Diameter_____ 2.8 inches.

(*b*) *Description.*—This mine is improvised from the 2-kg antipersonnel bomb dropped from aircraft. There are two types of this bomb shown in figure 113. One, Ⓐ figure 113①, consists of two concentric cylinders (1) and (2). The explosive charge (3) is contained in the cylinder (2) and the space (4) is filled with steel pellets embedded in concrete. The second type, figure 113② Ⓑ contains a slightly larger explosive charge (5) and the single container (6) is wound spirally on the outside with strip metal (7). The complete fuze is shown in figure 113②. For use in the mine, the top of the fuze (8) together with the safety rod (9) is unscrewed and removed. The cap holder (10) is placed centrally and cemented in position. The striker spring (11) and striker (12) are then placed in the cap holder as shown in ①. The mine is then set.

(*c*) *To neutralize.*—Lift out the striker.

(*d*) *To disarm.*—Unscrew the whole fuze from the lid of the mine and lift out complete with detonator.

(2) *Antipersonnel trip-mine, type 2.*—(*a*) *Description.*—No dimensions of this mine (fig. 114) are known. It is one of a type which the Italian Ministry of War suggests can be improvised in the field. An explosive charge (1) of about 2 kg is recommended, fitted with an electric detonator (2) which is fired by a 4.5-volt battery (3). The charge and mechanism are ap-

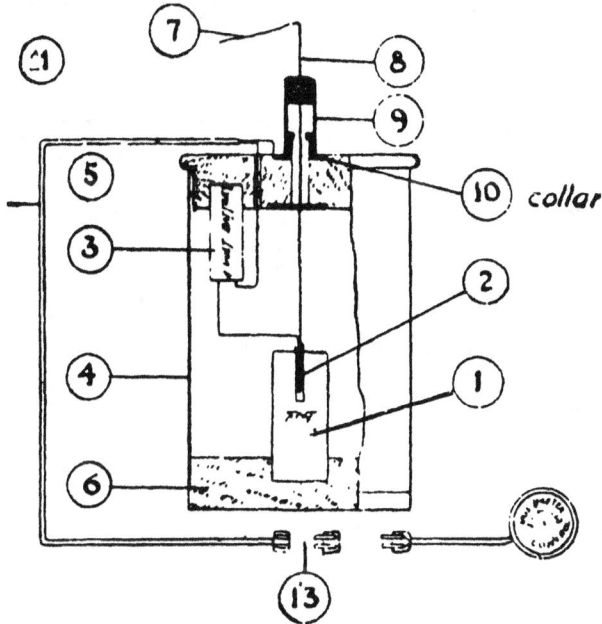

FIGURE 114.—Antipersonnel trip mine, type 2.

parently held in a metal cylinder (4) which is provided with wooden plugs (5) and (6). The switch for closing the circuit is operated by pull on the trip wire (7). The switch itself consists of a metal rod (8), one end of which connects to the detonator (2) and other to the trip wire. The rod is held in a short piece of rubber tube (9), and the movement of this tube causes the rod to make contact with the metal collar (10), thus completing the circuit. The device provides for two test wires (11) and (12) being brought out through the lid of the mine for continuity testing. These wires are bridged at (13) by means of a plug.

(*b*) *To neutralize and disarm.*—The layout of this type of mine can be considerably varied, though the underlying prin-

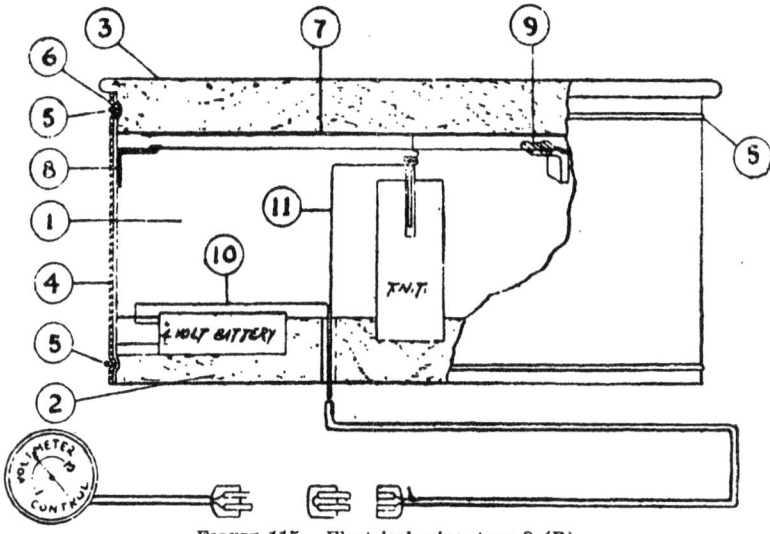

FIGURE 115.—Electrical mine, type 2 (B).

ciple will be the same. In all cases, a thorough examination of the mine externally is recommended before neutralizing is attempted.

(3) *Electrical mine, type 2.*—(*a*) *Description.*—This mine (fig. 115) consists of a circular metal drum (1) open at both ends, mounted on a wooden base (2) and covered by the wooden lid (3). A band of stout rubber (4) surrounds the circular body and is firmly attached to the lid and base by means of steel wires

ARMAMENT AND EQUIPMENT   243

(5) compressing the rubber into the grooves (6). The under side of the lid has a metal plate (7) attached. The top edge of the metal container has metal angle pieces (8), one of which is shown in perspective at (9). The rubber (4) holds the metal plate (7) away from the angle pieces (8). Test wires (10) and (11) may be found passing through a hole in the base or lid. The detonator, explosive charge, and battery are similar to those used in

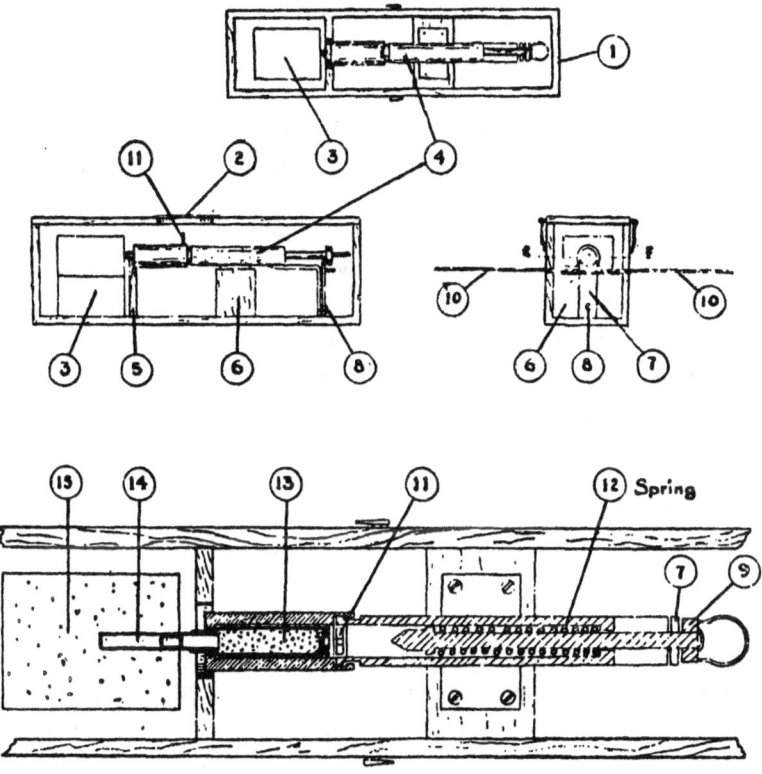

FIGURE 116.—Antipersonnel trip mine, type 9.

the antipersonnel trip mine described in (2) above, and illustrated in figure 114.

When pressure is applied to the lid (3), contact is made between the metal plate (7) and the angle pieces (8), and the electrical circuit is completed. The mine is then fired.

(b) *To neutralize.*

1. Examine the outside of the mine for test wires.
2. Cut the test wires, coil them apart, and insulate them with insulating tape.

(c) *To disarm.*

1. Cut or release the wires retaining the rubber and carefully raise the lid until the wire joining it to the detonator is seen.
2. Cut this wire and remove the lid.
3. Cut the second wire to the detonator and remove the latter.

(4) *Antipersonnel trip mine, type 9.*—(a) *Dimensions.*—The dimensions of this mine (fig. 116) are as follows:

   Length_____ 1 foot 1.2 inches.
   Breadth_____ 3.3 inches.
   Height_____ 4 inches.
   Type of filling_____ TNT.
   Weight of filling_____ 14 ounces (approximately).

(b) *Description.*—This mine consists of wooden box (1) having an access cover (2), a small charge (3), and a striker mechanism (4) supported on wood blocks (5) and (6). The striker mechanism is the same as that of the antitank mine described in (6) below, except the cranked arming lever is not used. The trip lever (7) is pivoted at (8) and its other end acts as a stop against the head of the striker (9). Trip wires (10) are run out from the trip lever, through the sides of the mine and fastened with

ARMAMENT AND EQUIPMENT

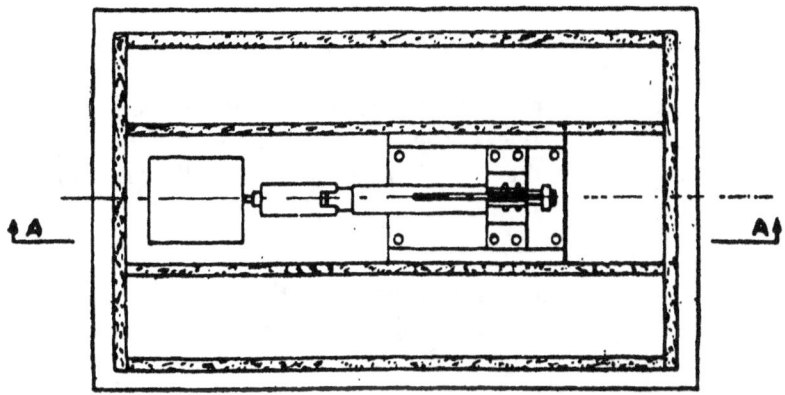

SECTION A-A

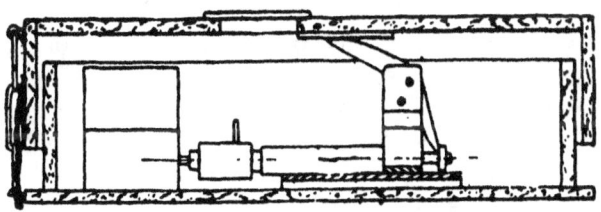

FIGURE 117.—Pressure mine, type 9.

very slight tension to pickets. After withdrawal of the safety strip (11) through the access cover (2), the mine is armed. Any pull on one of the trip wires (10) jerks the trip lever (7) to one side, and the striker (9) under the influence of its spring (12) detonates the cartridge (13) and fires the detonator and main charge (14) and (15), respectively.

(c) *To neutralize.*

1. Insert penknife or similar object in the safety slot at (11).
2. Cut the trip wires by scissors close up to the box.
3. Carefully release the tension in the spring. holding the ring at the end of the striker while the trip lever is removed.

(d) *To disarm.*

1. Unlock the striker tube from the cartridge holder by turning slightly, and then remove it.
2. Carefully extract the cartridge and detonator.
3. Replace the empty components.

(5) *Pressure mine, type 9.*—(*a*) *Dimensions.*—This mine (fig. 117) has the following dimensions:

Length	1 foot 3.6 inches
Height	4.7 inches
Type of filling	TNT in two blocks
Weight of filling	14 ounces (approximately).
Total weight	8 pounds (approximately).

(b) *Description.*—This mine is intended as an antipersonnel mine. The initiating mechanism is exactly similar to that described in (6) below. In this mine there is only one initiator.

(c) *To neutralize and disarm.*—See (6) (*c*) and (*d*) below.

(6) *Antitank mine, type 9.*—(*a*) *Dimensions.*—The dimensions of this mine (fig. 118) are as follows:

Length	3 feet 4.8 inches.
Breadth	6.6 inches.
Height	5.0 inches.
Type of filling	TNT in 8 blocks
Weight of filling	9 pounds (approximately).

RESTRICTED

ARMAMENT AND EQUIPMENT 243

(*b*) *Description.*—This pressure-operated mine consists of a wooden body (1) and lid (2) containing a charge (3) which is centrally placed and having two firing mechanisms (4). The details of each firing mechanism which is similar in all "type 9" mines, is shown in figure 118③. The lid (2) has two pivoted access covers (5).

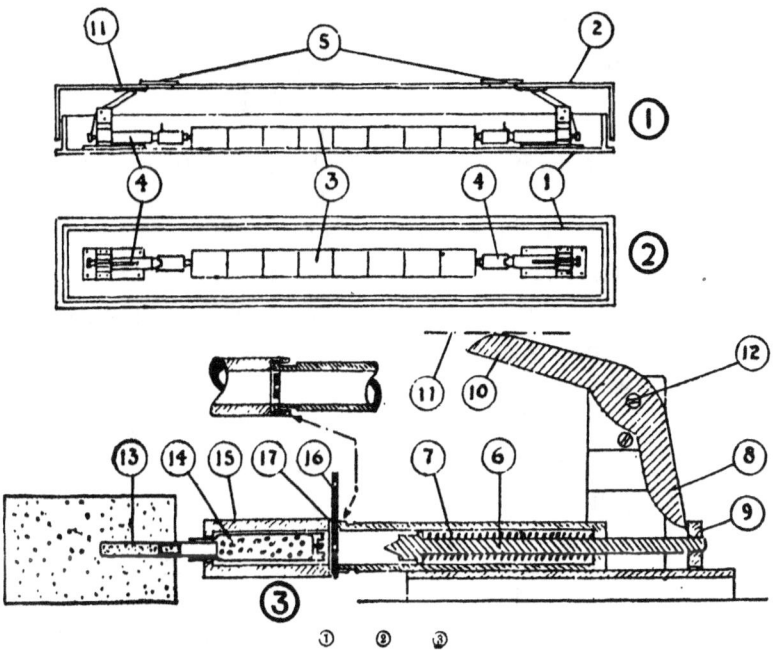

FIGURE 118.—Antitank mine, type 9.

When the striker (6) is cocked, the spring (7) is held in compression by the lower end of the cranked lever (8) bearing on the adjustable nut (9). The other end of the lever (10) presses against a small metal plate (11) on the underside of the lid. Pressure on the upper arm rotates the lever about its pivot (12),

RESTRICTED

and the lower end of the lever trips the striker (6). The detonating system consists of a No. 8 detonator (13) fitted in the open end of a cartridge (14) contained in the holder (15).

The safety device, which consists of a metal strip (16), is placed in the slot (17) between the striker tube and the end of the cartridge holder, and access to this is obtained through the access cover (5).

(c) *To neutralize.*
  1. Open the access cover (5). If this cover should be difficult to move, place some rough pieces of wood between the lid (2) and the base of the body (1) so as to prevent the lid from moving should undue pressure be exerted.
  2. Insert a penknife blade, or a strip of metal of similar size, in the safety slot (17).

(d) *To disarm.*
  1. Unlock the striker tube from the cartridge holder by turning slightly, and then remove it.
  2. Replace the empty components.

(7) *Mine, type N.*—(a) *Dimensions.*—The dimensions of this mine (fig. 119) are as follows:

Length	15.75 inches
Breadth	5.50 inches
Height	5.00 inches
Weight of filling	5 pounds
Type of filling	Gelignite.

(b) *Description.*—This antitank mine consists of a wooden box (1) bound with iron straps (2) and having a metal cover plate (3). The lid may be painted to blend with the surroundings, and the mine is provided with two carrying handles. The under side of the cover plate carries a wooden lining to which is attached the two steel pressure plates (4). The head of each striker (5) is held

ARMAMENT AND EQUIPMENT 243

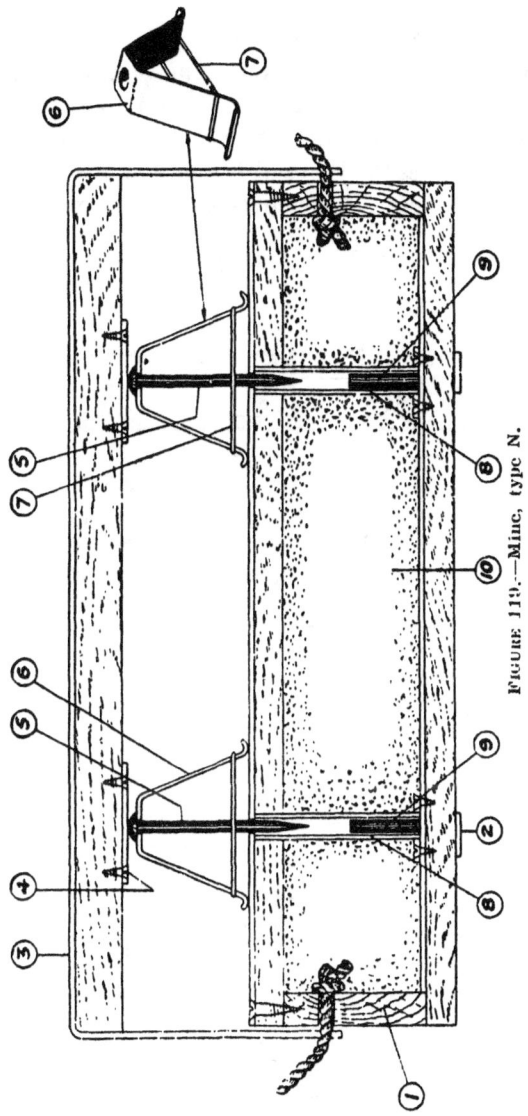

FIGURE 119.—Mine, type N.

against the pressure plate by means of an inverted U-shaped piece of steel (6), the limb of the latter being held in position by two strands of piano wire (7). Each striker is positioned in a steel tube (8) which holds the detonator (9). Pressure on the metal cover plate (3) forces the limbs of the steel strips (6) outward and breaks the piano wires (7). The strikers (6) are then free to move

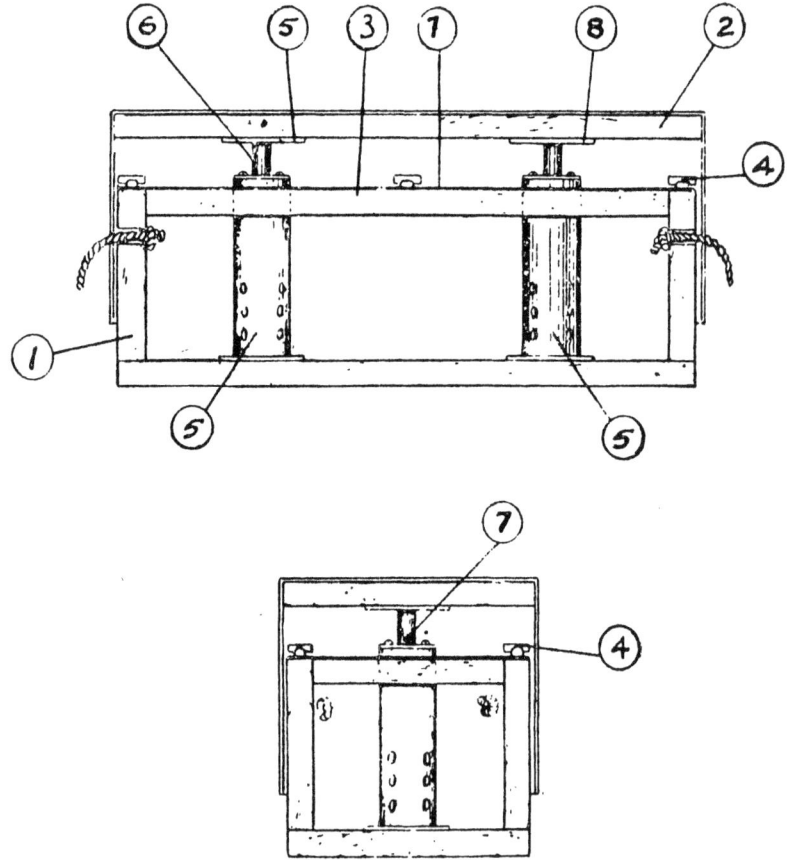

FIGURE 120.—Road and field mine.

ARMAMENT AND EQUIPMENT 243

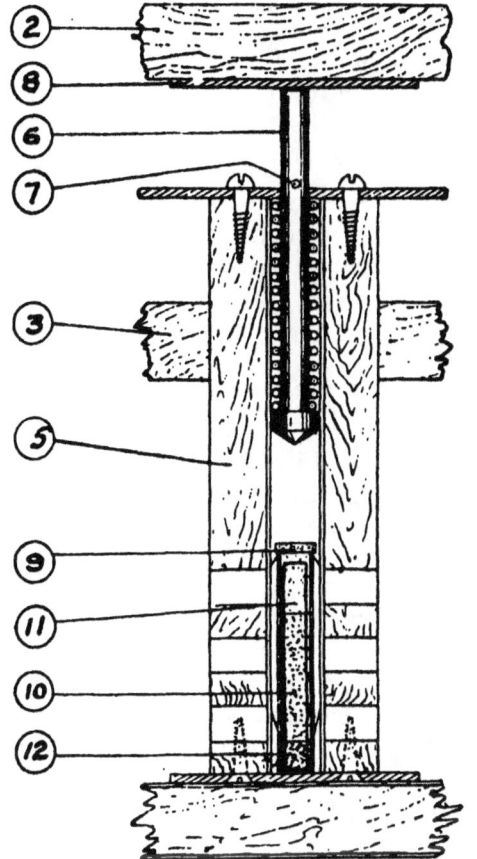

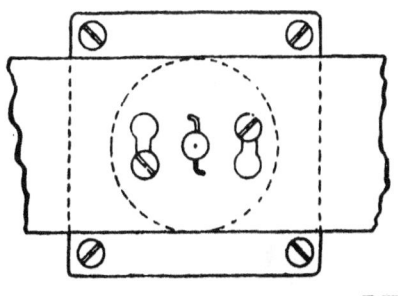

FIGURE 121.—Road and field mine (details).

downward under the applied load and initiates the detonators, thus firing the main charge (10). For transport the detonators are carried separately, and U-shaped steel strips are laid flat in order to make the mine more compact.

(c) *To neutralize.*

1. Lift off the lid after cutting any outside fastenings.
2. Remove the U-shaped strips and strikers.
3. Replace the lid.

(d) *To disarm.*

1. Take out the detonators.
2. Place the U-shaped steel strips on their side, close down the lid, and fasten it securely.

(8) *Road and field mine.*—(a) *Dimensions.*—The dimensions of this mine (figs. 120 and 121) are as follows:

Length _____ 1 foot 4 inches.
Breadth _____ 7 inches.
Height _____ 7 inches.
Type of filling _____ Gelignite cartridges.

(b) *Description.*—The box is made of wood, with the base covered inside and out by a thin metal sheet about 1-mm thick. The box (1) is provided with rope handles, and the metal sides of the lid (2) are slotted to permit downward movement. The inner lid (3), provided with holes for the exploders, is held in place by screws (4). Two exploders (5) are provided, and these may be of the percussion or chemical type. The remaining space in the box (1) is packed with cartridges of gelignite or similar explosive. The exploder (5) is contained in a cylinder 4.9 inches high and 1.5 inches in diameter. The striker (6) is retained in the armed position by a copper shear wire (7). For antipersonnel setting, the diameter of the shear wire is 1.4 mm; for use an an antitank mine, the shear wire is 2 mm. Above the

ARMAMENT AND EQUIPMENT

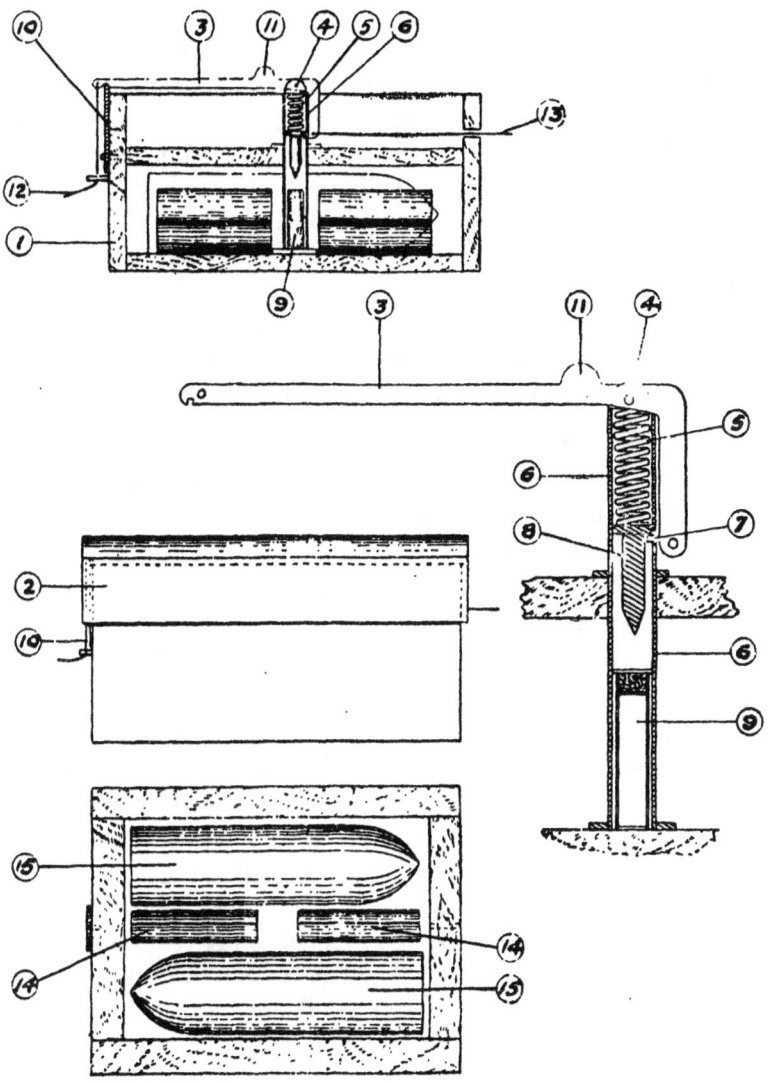

FIGURE 122.—Shell mine.

head of the striker and attached to the under side of the lid (2) is a metal pressure plate (8) 2.4 inches square.

In the base of the exploder is a model 1891 cartridge (9) from which the bullet and propellant have been removed. A detonator (10) is placed inside the cartridge case with its open end facing the cartridge cap. Black powder (11) is placed between the cap and the detonator, and the cartridge is closed with plaster and cotton wool pad (12) and varnished black. The cap end of the cartridge is painted red.

(c) *To neutralize.*

    1. Carefully remove the lid.

    2. Extract the strikers and the supporting plates together by turning the latter and lifting.

(d) *To disarm.*

    1. Unscrew the screws (4) and lift out the inner lid (3).

    2. Lift out the exploders.

    3. Replace the lid.

(9) *Shell mine.*—a *Dimensions.*—The dimensions of the mine (fig. 122) are as follows:

Length	11½ inches.
Breadth	8½ inches.
Height	6½ inches.
Type of filling	Two HE shells and four sticks of gelignite.

(b) *Description.*—This mine consists of a wooden box (1) with a thin sheet-metal lid (2). The lid is secured to the body by wires passing over the top and fastened to pegs in the side. The firing mechanism consists of a lever (3) pivoted at (4) retaining one end of the spring (5) in the tube (6). The lever is cranked to provide a stop (7) which retains the striker (8) and the lower end of the spring (5). The tube (6) passes through to the base of the mine

ARMAMENT AND EQUIPMENT 243

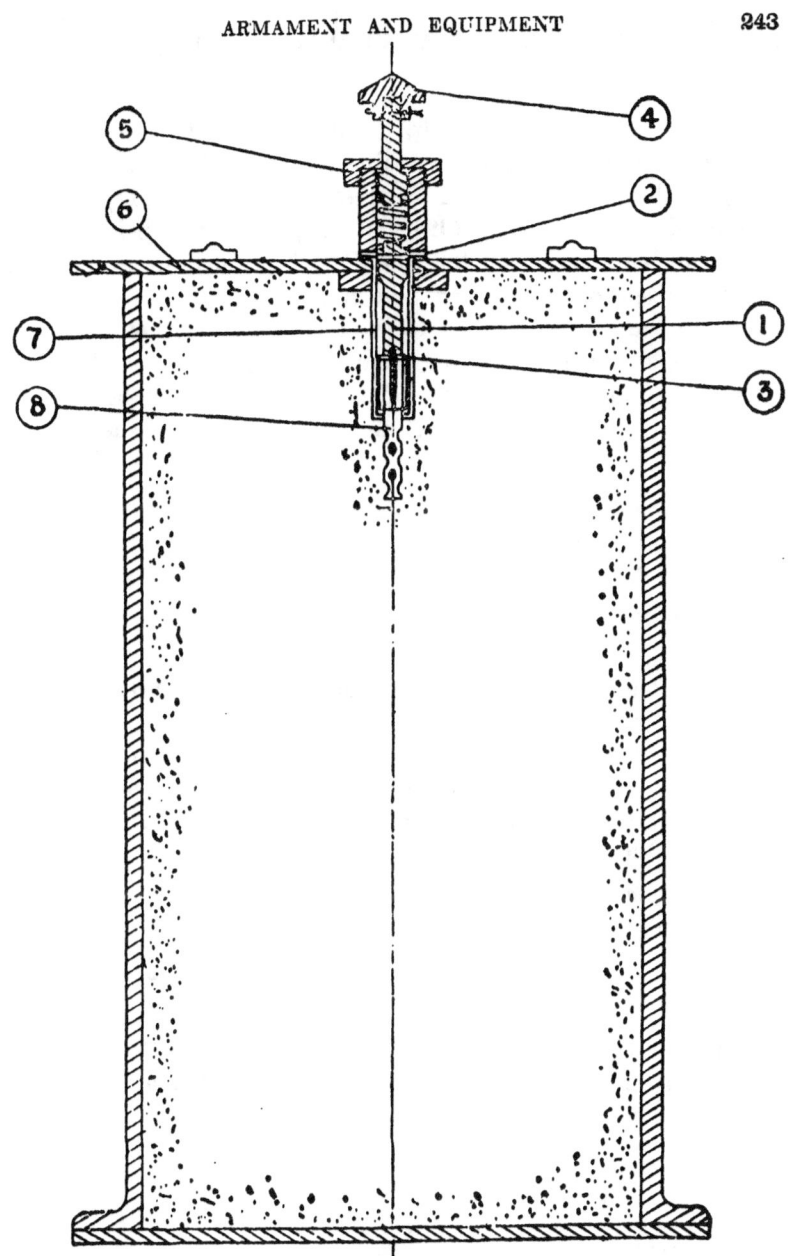

FIGURE 123.—Pressure mine with grenade exploder.

and contains the cap and detonator (9). The striker mechanism is held in the "safe" position by means of a cam (10) which supports the lever (3) and thus retains the stop (7) in place. The firing mechanism is operated by pressure on the lug (11) by way of the lid or by tripwires (12) and (13), the latter being 3 to 5 meters in length. When the cam (10) is rotated so as to allow free movement of the lever (3), the mine is armed.

On pressure being applied to the lever or tension on the tripwires, the stop (7) is removed from the flange on the striker (8). The striker, under the influence of the spring (5), fires the cap and detonator (9), the gelignite packing (14), and the two shells (15).

(c) *To neutralize.*

> 1. Rotate the cam (10) gently until it engages with the long arm of the lever (3).
> 2. Cut the trip wires.

(d) *To disarm.*

> 1. Remove the lid.
> 2. Remove the screws in the side of the box, retaining the lid of the explosive container.
> 3. Remove the false lid and the striker mechanism together.
> 4. Withdraw the tube holding the detonator, pulling the tube and at the same time giving it a slight rotating motion.

(10) *Pressure mine with grenade exploder.*—(a) *Dimensions.*—The dimensions of this mine (fig. 123) are as follows:

> Height _____ 10 inches.
> Diameter _____ 6 inches.

(b) *Description.*—This cylindrical mine may be fitted with the initiator from an ordinary hand grenade. The striker (1) is held in the safe position by a safety pin passing through the hole (2). On withdrawal of the pin, the striker moves downward until the shoulder rests on the lead washer (3). In this position it is not possible to reinsert the safety pin. Pressure on the hammer (4) causes the strike (1) to shear the washer and fire the mine.

(*c*) *To neutralize.*—Unscrew the cap (5) and remove the hammer, spring, and striker.

(*d*) *To disarm.*—Unscrew the cover plate (6) and withdraw the detonator holder (7) and detonator (8) together.

244. Obstacles.—On the tactical side, Italian doctrine as to use of obstacles is conventional. For example, Italian doctrine holds that obstacles must be susceptible of being easily bypassed; must be covered effectively by fire; and must not afford local material for rendering the obstacles passable.

245. Camouflage.—Italian camouflage equipment includes adjustable camouflage frames (tubular steel or wood) which may be used to support a canopy for machine guns or artillery emplacements, and sniper suits utilizing materials affording protective coloring. Road screens are employed, as well as dummy hay stacks and rock formations to conceal gun emplacements. Nitro-cellulose paints are used along with an electric driven spray gun. The usual flat tops and nets are employed. Certain items of camouflage equipment are illustrated in figure 124. (See also ch. 10.)

246. Searchlights.—Galileo searchlights are of many varieties, ranging from 60 to possibly 210 cm. The standard 120-cm searchlight unit is shown in figure 125. (See par. 229 for details of certain types of searchlights.)

247. Pioneer tools.—The usual picks, shovels, hammers, hand saws, etc., are to be found in Italian engineer equipment. Some portable and mobile power-driven equipment is also utilized. Among the latter are the Ingersoll-Rand type of air compressors

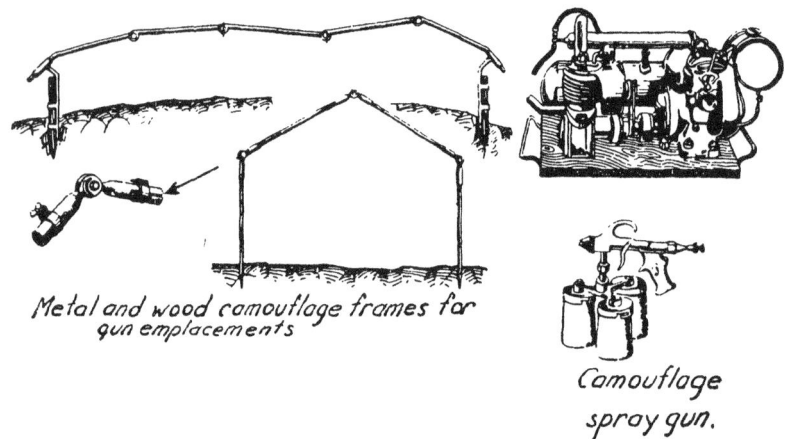

FIGURE 124.—Items of camouflage equipment.

FIGURE 125.—Searchlight unit (120-cm).

(mobile and portable) with attachments, a motorized pump, power-driven circular and band saws of German make, a portable mortiser, blacksmithing equipment, and mobile generators.

ARMAMENT AND EQUIPMENT 248-249

Section VII

SIGNAL COMMUNICATIONS

	Paragraph
General	248
Telephones	249
Telegraph	250
Special telephone and telegraph equipment	251
Teletype equipment	252
Optical equipment	253
Phototelephonic equipment	254
Radio equipment	255
Storage batteries	256
Pigeon equipment	257
Communication orders	258

248. General.—There is no "signal corps" as such in the Italian army, signal communications coming under the control of the engineers. The Italians have shown great ingenuity and skill in their signal equipment, of which the more commonly used types are described.

249. Telephones.—*a. Telephone sets.*—(1) *Standard field set, G. A. 31.*—(*a*) *Characteristics.*

Weight	8 kg.
Dimensions	31 by 14 by 24 cm.
Voltage	3 volts from 2 dry cells.

(*b*) *Description.*—This set (fig. 126) makes possible the testing of the set by depressing the white button and actuating the magneto generator (if the set is operating properly the bell should ring), and the testing of the line by depressing the red button and actuating the magneto generator after having disconnected the insulated line at its other end (the visual indicator will show the location of a short circuit if one exists). Referring to figure 126④, it is possible to connect set 1 at the end of line *b* to set 2 at the end of line *a* by means of a double plug. Either of the sets or both may be included in or excluded from the circuit, depending upon whether the connecting plug is inserted in the "set included" or the "set excluded" jack.

(2) Standard set for linemen.—(a) *Characteristics.*

Weight _____ 8 kg.
Dimensions _____ 25 by 21 by 12.5 cm.
Voltage _____ 3 volts from 2 dry cells.

(b) *Description.*—This set (fig. 126) is for testing the efficiency of lines and the continuity of wire on reels. It has two connections of a special type adapted to pierce the insulation of the wire and a lamp for use at night.

(3) *Set for selective telephony.*—This set (fig. 126) weighs 11 kg. A maximum of 20 of these sets may be connected to the line. It is possible to connect one set to all of the others or to connect one set with another without calling the rest. A call is made by means of a dial which operates to select a decentralized or a centralized system with or without secrecy (busy signal). It may also be used as an ordinary telephone.

b. *Switchboards.*—(1) *O. G. M. rotary key type for 10 lines.*—(a) *Characteristics.*

Weight _____ 15.2 kg.
Dimensions _____ 20.5 by 49 by 22.5 cm.

(b) *Description.*—This switchboard (fig. 127) permits the simultaneous connection of all incoming lines. It also permits—

1. As many separate connections as there are pairs of lines.
2. Interconnection of all lines among themselves or with the operator.
3. A combination of *1* and *2* above in any desired manner.

The switchboard has 20 spring binding posts and a microphone having an extensible arm and a built-in switch.

RESTRICTED

ARMAMENT AND EQUIPMENT 249

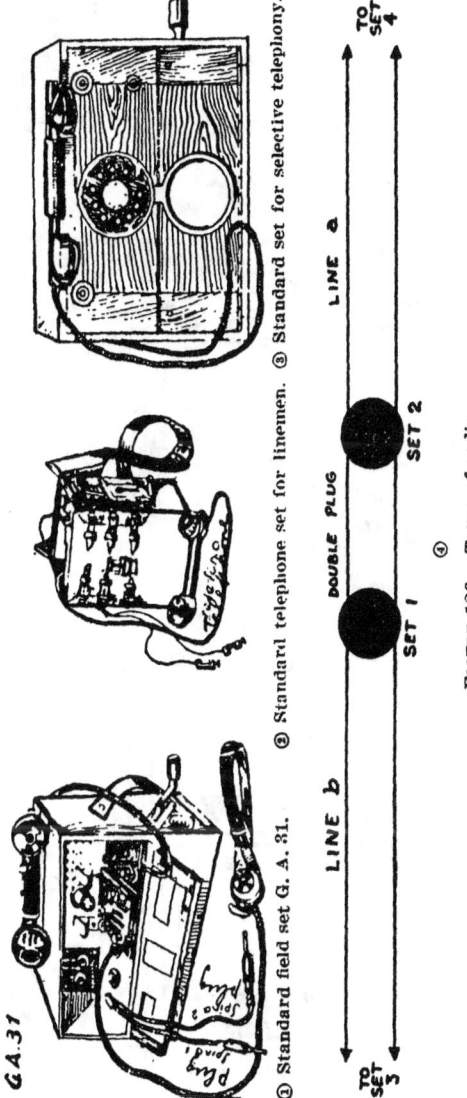

① Standard field set G. A. 31. ② Standard telephone set for linemen. ③ Standard set for selective telephony.

FIGURE 126.—Types of radio.

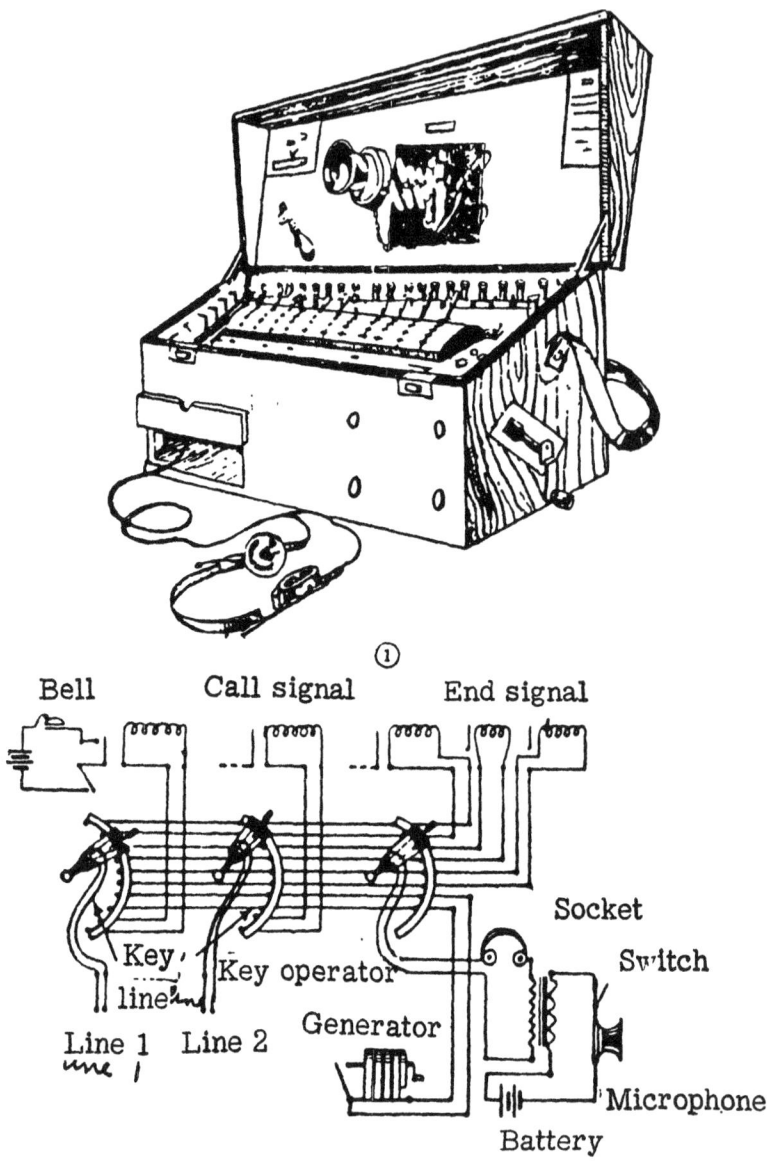

FIGURE 127.—Type O. G. M. rotary key telephone switchboard (with circuit diagram for 10 lines).

ARMAMENT AND EQUIPMENT

(2) *Plug type for 30 lines.*—(a) *Characteristics.*

Weight _____ 35.3 kg.
Dimensions _____ 24 by 60 by 46 cm.

(*h*) *Description.*—This switchboard permits the interconnection by pairs of all lines terminating in the board. An ordinary telephone set must be used with it.

(3) *Commutator type for 30 lines.*—(a) *Characteristics.*

Weight _____ 40 kg.
Dimensions _____ 56 by 32 by 44 cm.

Type of stranded telephone wire	Maximum effective 1 length (km)		Content of spools		Tensile strength	Resistance at 150 (ohms/km)	Insulation resistance (meg-ohms/km)	Composition
	Field line	With insulated supports	Meters	Kg				
5.2 mm (artillery)	40	80	500	19	65	12.5	1000 0.5	Wire: 7 strands of electrolytic copper. Insulation: Spiral of lacquered cotton; layer of rubber; spiral of rubberized cloth. Protection: Sheath of varnished cotton.
4 mm (artillery)	30	60	500	12	60	21.5	1000 0.5	Wire: 7 strands of electrolytic copper, tinned. Insulation and protection: Same as for 5.2-mm wire but without spiral of rubberized cloth.
2.5 mm (infantry)	6	15	500	5.25	40	55	------	Wire: 1 strand of electrolytic copper, tinned; 6 strands of phosphorbronze, tinned. Insulation: Spiral of lacquered cotton; layer of rubber. Protection: Sheath of varnished cotton.

FIGURE 128.—Characteristics of the various types of telephone wire.

RESTRICTED

(b) *Description.*—This switchboard has 31 circular commutators, 30 of which connect to the incoming lines and the other serving to connect the generator to the lines. There are 17 different positions for each commutator, 15 of which are for the connection of the lines with each other and 2 (lettered L and C) for the rest and call positions, respectively. A call is made by means of the magneto generator actuated by a lever. The board has 60 spring binding posts.

c. *Wire.*—In figure 128 are tabulated the characteristics of the various types of telephone wires in use.

250. Telegraph.—*a. Morse set.*—(1) *Characteristics.*

Transmission	Key.
Reception	Tape.
Weight:	
Box	18.0 kg.
Battery box	9.2 kg.
Stand	8.0 kg.
Tent	30.0 kg.
Folding stool	2.0 kg.
Total	67.2 kg.

Dimensions_____ 50 by 19 by 21 cm.
Operating range___ 40 km under best conditions; will operate for 25 days and 8 hours without servicing.

(2) *Description.*—For setting up the set connect the positive terminal of the battery to the small anterior anvil of key; the negative terminal of the battery to the output of the writing machine; the line wire to the vertical bars to the left of the commutator and the ground wire to the vertical bar to the right. For a line not over 20 cm in length, 16 to 18 battery cells are sufficient (the instrument employs 2 coils in series, has a resistance of 600 ohms, and requires 0.01 to 0.02 amperes to operate it).

ARMAMENT AND EQUIPMENT 250

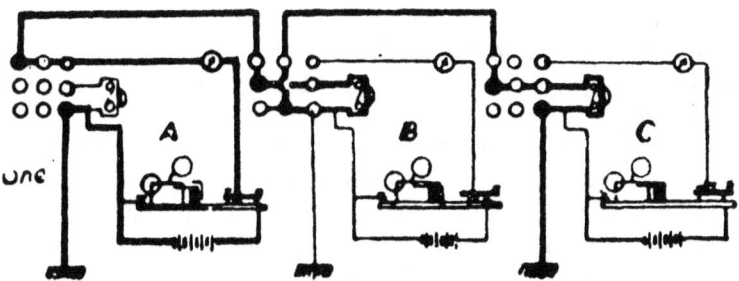

① Station A calling B and C.

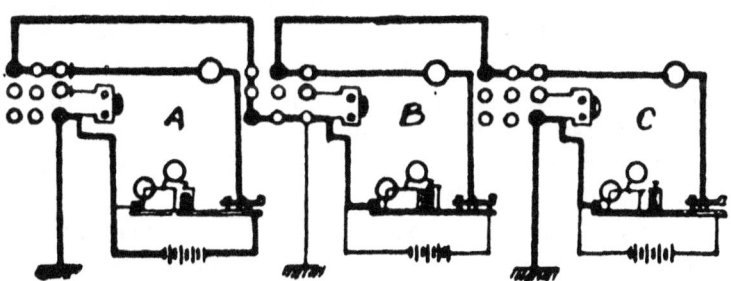

② Station A transmitting, B and C receiving.

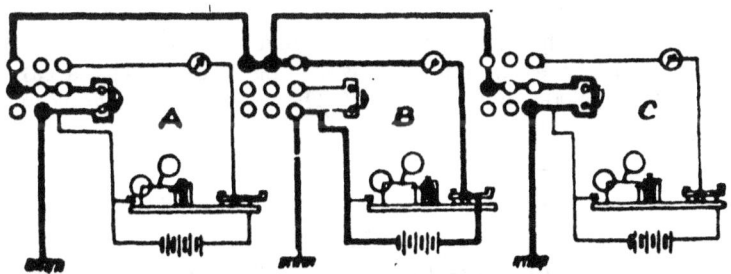

③ Station B calling A and C.

FIGURE 129.—Circuit diagrams of Morse telegraph set. (The black holes indicate the positions of the plugs.)

For grounding, an iron tube is buried in moist ground or placed in a stream of water or a well, and is connected to the set by a galvanized iron wire. If the tube is not available, a large iron spike or a copper plate may be used. Stations may be connected in various ways as illustrated in figure 129.

b. High-speed apparatus.— (1) *Wheetstone.* — Transmission with this equipment is normally automatic, a perforated tape being used. At times, however, a manual key is used. Specially trained personnel are needed for the preparation of the tape unless the Creed perforator is used. Morse groups are used, the signal consisting of two different amplitudes of positive current and spaces being represented by a negative current of given amplitude (dots and dashes). This system permits of a single transmission in a given direction and simultaneous transmission on different circuits. Reception is either by tape or aurally. The rate of transmission varies between 30 and 150 words per minute, and it is possible to send up to 1,150 words per hour with the Creed perforator. Synchronization is not necessary.

(2) *Hurghes.*—This apparatus is used in the field by the commands of large units. Transmission is manual by means of a key. Personnel need not be specialized but must be accustomed to harmonious sending. Signals are differentiated on the basis of elapsed time following an initial emission. The system permits a single transmission in one direction. Synchronization is necessary. The rate of transmission is 33 words per minute with a capacity of 1.500 to 1.800 words per hour. The received message is printed on a tape.

(3) *Bautot.*—With this type of equipment, manual transmission with a special keyboard is used, though at times the system is operated automatically. Experienced personnel are required. Five-letter groups are employed, the signals consisting of different combinations of emissions of positive and negative current. This system permits up to four transmissions simultaneously in the

same direction. Synchronization is required. The rate of transmission is 30 words a minute with a capacity of 1,800 words per hour. Tape reception with printed characters is employed.

251. Special telephone and telegraph equipment.—*a. Noninterceptible telegraph set, model 1931.*—(1) *Characteristics.*

Dimensions _____ 21 by 17 by 17 cm.
Weight _____ 3.9 kg.

(2) *Description.*—This set is similar to the now obsolete buzzerphone. Security is attained by means of filters which reduce the current aplitude and the slopes of wave fronts of the signal. The set is equipped with a vibrator by means of which the line current actuates the telephone.

b. Connector box for field telephone, type G. A. (1931).—(1) *Characteristics.*

Dimensions _____ 16.5 by 16 by 13.5 cm.
Weight _____ 1.35 kg.

(2) *Description.*—This device permits the use of the civil telephone system. Connection is made to the top of the G. A. 1931 set by a cord having two plugs. The receiver rests on the hook and the two line wires are connected to the terminals on the box. Calls are made by dialing the desired number.

c. Repeating coil field telephone, model O. G. M. 1928—(1) *Characteristics.*

Weight _____ 5.6 kg.
Dimensions _____ 23.5 by 15 by 16 cm.

(2) *Description.*—This telephone is used for phantoming telephone circuits. It must be balanced if lines are long. There are five pairs of terminals, two pairs for two incoming lines and three pairs for the three telephone sets. It is similar to but larger than the C-75 repeating coil.

d Repeating coil for simultaneous phantom telephony and simplex telegraphy, model O. G. M. (1928).—(1) *Characteristics.*

Weight _____ 8.5 kg.
Dimensions_____ 31.5 by 15 by 16.5 cm.

(2) *Description.*—This device (fig. 130) is connected to two metallic telephone circuits, one phantom telephone circuit, two simplex and one simplex phantom telegraph circuits.

e. Mobile telephone and telegraph trailer for corps headquarters.—(1) *Description.*—The trailer is of the Viberti type, compensated steering. It is 5 meters long, 2.07 meters wide, and 2.70 meters high, with a width between tracks of 1.70 meters. It weighs approximately 1,500 kg, and has a speed fully loaded of 25 kms per hour. Its steering device permits making a complete turn within a circle of a radius not greater than 5.5 meters.

(2) *Apparatus.*—(*a*) *Telephone.*—Two standard switchboards with listening keys and plugs (the capacity of 1 board is 110 lines, 100 with local battery and 10 with central battery); 1 main distribution frame in 2 sections, each with a capacity of 110 lines; 2 panel-telephone sets and 1 lineman's set; and 1 terminal repeater, type O. M. T.

(*b*) *Telegraph.*—Four teletype machines (Creed tape type); two Morse tables; two noninterceptible telegraph sets; and four repeating coils for multiple telephone (phantom circuits) and simultaneous telegraphy (simplex).

(3) *Power supply.*—(*a*) The storage battery is of 24 element ferro-nickel, with a 117 ampere-hour capacity.

(*b*) The rectifier is of the selenium oxide type for voltages from 30 to 60 and from 100 to 200.

(*c*) The generator set is of the gasoline-electric type, with a power output of 1.5 km. Its 3.5 horsepower engine develops a peak current of 35 amperes and 24 to 45 volts.

RESTRICTED

ARMAMENT AND EQUIPMENT   251-252

(4) *Cables.*—Cables are carried in rolls on the tractor truck and consist of 24 conductors arranged in 12 pairs. The cables weigh 370 kg per km.

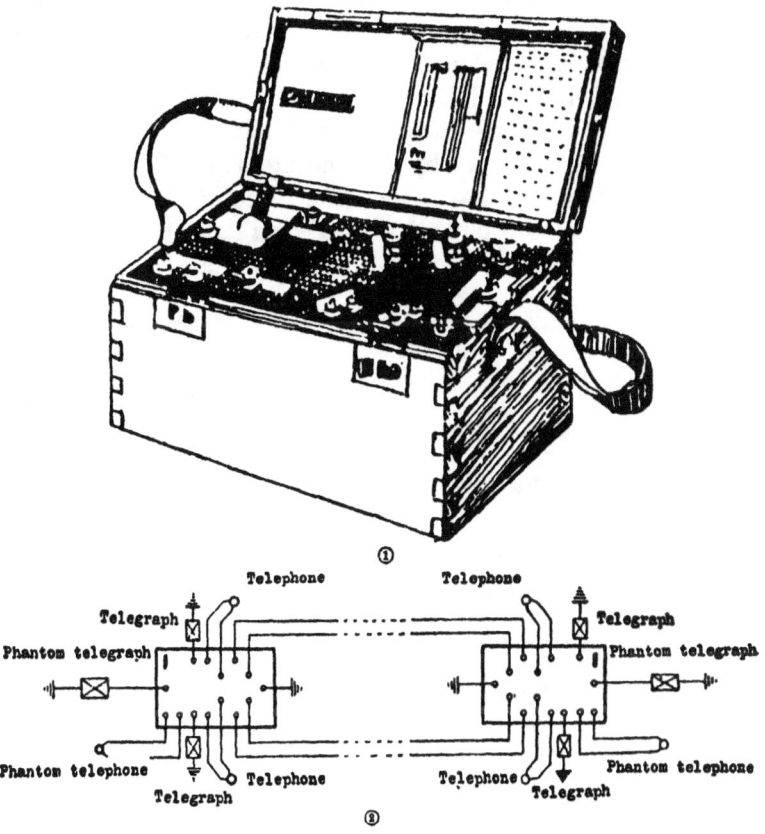

FIGURE 130.—Repeating coil for simultaneous phantom telephony and simplex telegraphy, model O. G. M. (1928) (with circuit diagram).

252. Teletype equipment.—*a. General.*—The standard teletype equipment is type O. M. T., model 36.

b. Characteristics.   *Weight*
    Instrument _____ 64 kg.
    Generator _____ 60 kg.

c. Description.—This apparatus is used in the field by the commands of large units. It is operated manually by means of a typewriter keyboard, but may be operated automatically if desired. It does not require specialized personnel. Five-letter groups are used. Signals comprise different combinations of positive and negative currents preceded by the sending of "start" and followed by "stop." Transmission in but one direction is possible. In reception, typed characters are printed on a tape or sheet of paper. Synchronization is not required. The unit is powered by dry

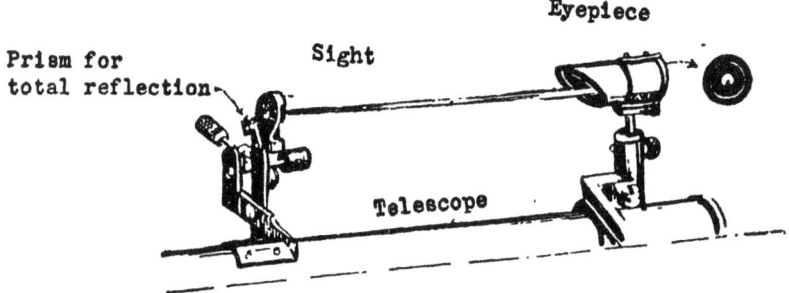

FIGURE 131.—Heliograph rectifier of 80-mm optical signaling apparatus.

batteries, by storage batteries, by dynomotor, or by commercial current suitably rectified. The approximate speed of transmission is 66 words a minute.

253. Optical equipment.—The 80-mm optical signaling apparatus is the standard equipment. This apparatus is used only by engineer units, which have 16 sets (4 of which are in reserve) per section. The equipment is transported in 3 boxes containing, respectively, the instrument, the tripod, and batteries and accessories or generator. The total weight is 25 kg. The apparatus has an 80-mm diopter, a 4-watt lamp, and a heliograph (fig. 131) with mirrors 7 by 7 cm. It is powered by a generator or by a battery of eight 1.5 volt cells, the voltage being regulated by a three-position potentiometer. The range in daytime with diopter is 10 km, with heliograph 22 km. When powered by dry cells, the apparatus is good for 200 hours of intermittent operation. The generator (fig. 132) is operated by a gear and crank arrangement

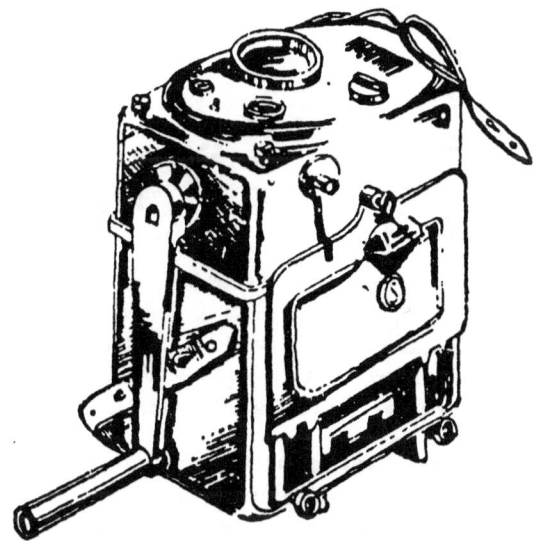

FIGURE 132.—Generator of 80-mm optical signaling apparatus.

and should be turned at such a rate as to keep the pointer of the voltmeter on a red mark corresponding to 8 volts.

254. Phototelephonic equipment.—*a. General.*—This apparatus, of two types, permits telephonic and telegraphic communication between two points, each of which is visible infrared radiation. The transmitting station transforms acoustic vibrations first into variations in an electric current and then into variations in intensity of a luminous beam. By means of a caesium photoelectric cell, the receiving station transforms the variations in an electric current and thence into acoustic vibrations. This

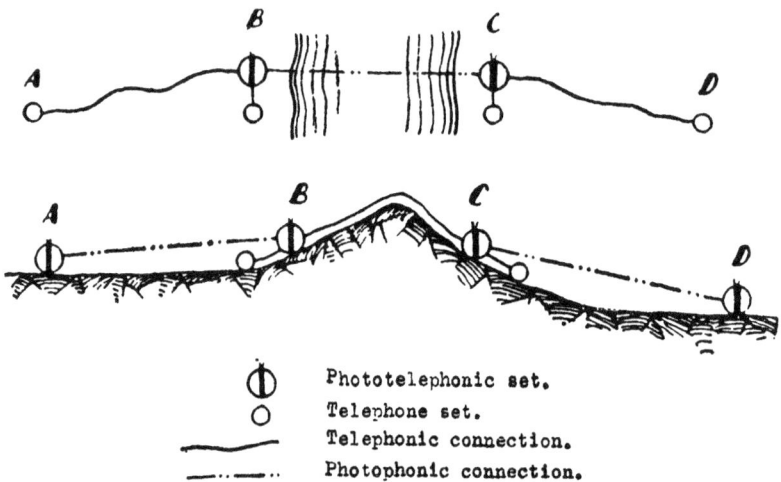

Ⓘ Phototelephonic set.
○ Telephone set.
——— Telephonic connection.
—··—·· Photophonic connection.

FIGURE 133.—Showing use of the converter of the 180-mm phototelephonic set.

equipment has the advantage over wire communication in that it obviates the laying of lines, and over radio communication in that it is not susceptible to interference and cannot readily be intercepted.

b. 15-mm set.

Number of packs _____ 3 (can be carried in knapsack).
Weight _____ 27 kg.
Range (in km):   Day   Night
    Telephonic _____ 1 to 5   Much greater
    Telegraphic _____ 15   30
Time without servicing ___ 120 hours.
Optical system _____ Dioptric.

c. 180-mm set.—(1) *Characteristics*.

Number of packs _____ 3 (can be carried in knapsack).
Weight _____ 38.6 kg.—72.0 with box and reserve accessories.
Range: Day   Night
    Telephonic _____ 1 to 10   Much greater.
    Telegraphic _____ 15 to 20 Much greater.
Time without servicing ___ Not known.
Optical system _____ Catoptric.

(2) *Converter*.—This part of the equipment of the 180-mm. set makes possible the connection of a distant telephone set to a phototelephone set. Thus it is possible to create a telephone circuit, part of which is metallic and part of which consists of a photophonic link. This is of value, for example, in crossing streams or in cases in which the line of sight between the points which it is desired to connect is obstructed as indicated in fig. 133.

255. **Radio equipment.**—*a. General.*

Type	Voltage	Capacity (ampere hours)	Weight (kg)	Application	Remarks
T 10	1.5	--------	0.300	Set G. A., 1931.	Each set uses two batteries in series.
T 40	1.5	--------	1.000	Telegraph set.	Each set uses eight batteries in series.
N3/0/60	3	--------	2.500	Phototelegraphic sets.	Each set uses three batteries and one in reserve.
63A5	60	3.5	5.250	Radio sets	⎫
63A3	60	1.66	3.000	Radio sets	⎪
63A2	60	1.00	2.000	Radio sets	⎬ Number of batteries used depends on type of set.
45A2	45	1.50	1.500	Radio sets	⎪
15A2	15	1.20	0.500	Radio sets	⎪
15C8	1.5	3.00	4.000	Radio sets	⎪
4.5C3	4.5	1.00	5.500	Radio sets	⎪
4.5C1	4.5	10.0	2.100	Radio sets	⎭
M 1 (single unit).	4.5	--------	--------	--------	--------
	128	--------	--------	--------	--------
	80	--------	--------	--------	--------
	9	--------	--------	--------	--------
M2	--------	--------	--------	--------	--------

FIGURE 135.—Types, numbers, characteristics, and applications of storage batteries.

b. Use in tanks.—At the beginning of the war Italian tanks were not fitted with radio. As the war progressed, the need for a tank radio was established, with the result that most command tanks were furnished with radios. Most Italian tanks are now fitted with radios, the latest of which is the **T. R. 7**, with a range

ARMAMENT AND EQUIPMENT 255–258

of about 3 to 4 miles. All Italian sets reflect a marked German influence with many components of German manufacture.

256. Storage batteries.—The type, numbers, characteristics, and applications of storage batteries are tabulated in figure 175.

257. Pigeon equipment.—*a. Mobile pigeon loft, model 1930.*—The loft is generally motor-drawn but may be horse-drawn. It is equipped with a folding cage which permits the pigeons to accustom themselves to their surroundings. (It must be kept in a locality for at least 5 days before homing of the pigeons is assured.) It is used by the headquarters of large units. It may be transported on a railway car without being dismounted.

```
Dimensions of chassis_____ 4.30 by 2.00 by 0.75 meters.
Gage (wheels)_____ 1.50 meters.
Axle spacing_____ 2.72 meters.
Capacity _____ 120 birds.
```

b. Antigas pigeon loft.—This trailer vehicle, holding 80 to 100 birds, has a radius of action of 25 to 30 km. The pigeon-containing chamber is lined with tinned zinc and may be rendered gastight. When this is done, a slight excess pressure is maintained in the chamber by means of a cylinder of compressed air.

c. Cloth pigeon knapsack.—This knapsack will carry two birds. It is provided with a "rest net," a drinking trough, an eating trough, and a sack of grain. It is used by liaison officers, by those assigned to assault troops, and by officers and men doing patrol and reconnaissance duty. Birds should not be left in the container longer than 4 hours.

d. Portable pigeon basket.—This basket is made of osier (similar to wicker). It may be carried on the back or in the hands. It is used in place of the knapsack for carrying birds from the lofts to places where they are kept in trenches.

258. Communication orders.—Orders for the organization and operation of communications include diagrams for radio, wire, and optical communication. (The diagrams shown in fig. 136 are merely exemplary.)

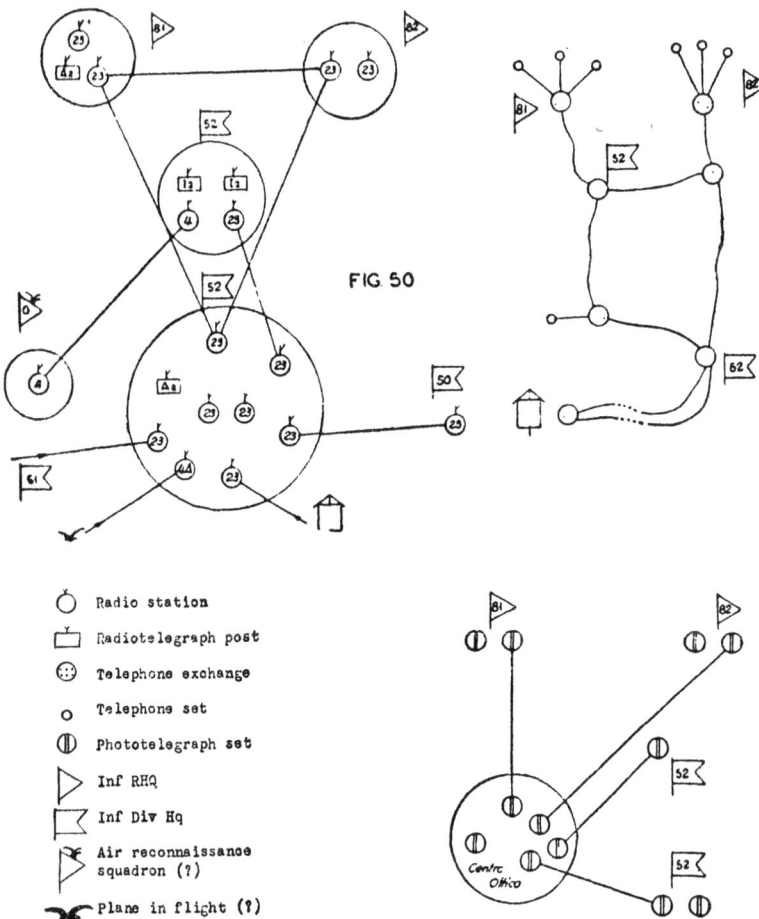

FIGURE 136.—Diagrams of communication nets.

ARMAMENT AND EQUIPMENT

Section VIII

CHEMICAL WARFARE

	Paragraphs
Manufacture and storage of toxic gases	259
Chemical agents	260
Ground weapons	261
Aerial weapons	262
Flame throwers	263
Gas masks and gas detectors	264
Protective clothing	265
Collective protection	266
Decontamination	267
Gas alarms	268
Civilian protection	269

259. Manufacture and storage of toxic gases.—*a.* The Italian chemical industry has developed to a considerable extent in recent years, and there is evidence of a number of factories in Italy for the manufacture of war gases. According to rough estimates the following maximum quantities of chemical agents could be produced:

Mustard gas (*iprite*)	5,000 to 10,000 tons per year.
Phosgene (*fosgene*)	5,000 to 10,000 tons per year.
Chloropicrin (*cloropicrina*)	1,000 to 2,000 tons per year.
Diphenylchlorarsine (*difenilclorarsina*).	1,000 tons per year.
Chloracetophenone (*cloroccetafenone*).	500 tons per year.
Lewisite	Very much limited.

NOTE.—The limiting factor for the above output would be the supply of chlorine.

b. In Italy there is a general shortage of coal, coal tar products, chlorine, arsenic, bromides, and fluorides, but this shortage could no doubt be met in part by supplies from Germany, Hungary, and other Axis powers.

c. While it is generally believed that Italy does not possess large stocks of war gases, at least six storage points have been definitely located and others are thought to exist.

260. **Chemical agents.**—*a. General.*—(1) Should Italy resort to gas warfare, it is believed that mustard gas, phosgene, chloropicrin, and arsenical smokes are the principal agents that would be used. Tear gases, it is also believed, would be used only to a limited extent and principally in combination with toxic gases.

(2) The following markings are used by the Italians to indicate the classification of their war gases:

Blister gases (vesicants)_____ Geneva Cross in green
Choking gases (lung irritants)__ Geneva Cross in White
Nose gases (toxic smokes)_____ Geneva Cross in black
Tear gases (lacrimators)_____ Geneva Cross in red

(3) It has been reliably reported that the Italians in the Abyssinian war of 1935–36 used many 10.5-cm artillery shells filled with DA (diphenylchlorarsine) and nearly 5,000 air-burst aircraft bombs filled with mustard gas. Among the chemical warfare stores found in Libya were drums of mustard gas, but none of the other gases mentioned above. The Greeks, however, reported the capture in December 1940 of drums of blister gas of which the composition was approximately equal parts by weight of mustard gas and phenyldichlorarsine.

(4) In a list of smoke and chemical shells for artillery, among the documents captured in Libya in January 1941, mention was made of shells filled with phosgene and also with a mixture of 80 percent chlorpicrin and 20 percent chloracetophenone. That the Italians regard chlorpicrin as a lacrimator as well as a lung irri-

tant is shown by the fact that containers of chlorpicrin are marked with both white and red crosses.

b. Peril No. 1.—Italian documents of undetermined date reveal that research and field trials in Libya had been made with "Peril No. 1—a new gas, very persistent and toxic; a blistering gas with an arsenic base causing painful and even mortal sores." The report continues: "A few centigrams are sufficient to kill a man." Responsible authorities discount the existence of such a new gas and believe that the document refers to lewisite, which reports indicate has been manufactured only in small quantities in Italy.

261. Ground weapons.—*a. 8.1-cm chemical mortar.*—The basic weapon of the Italian chemical troops is the 8.1-cm (3.19-inch) mortar. Model 35 is described as a smooth-bore, muzzle-loading, high-angle fire weapon of the Stokes-Brandt type[3], being similar to the British 3-inch mortar. Its total weight is only 129 pounds and it fires both chemical and HE shells at the rate of 18 to 20 rounds per minute. The chemical shells, of 2 types, weigh approximately 8½ pounds. A "short" type has a maximum range of 1,980 yards, whereas the range of the "long" type is said to be limited to 1,420 yards. No information is available concerning the nature of the chemical fillings of either type. Reports have been received to the effect that model 35 is being replaced by a new and improved model, with a heavier shell and an increased range.

b. Artillery.—Italian documents refer to gas shells of a wide variety of calibers as being standard in the Italian army. In addition to the fillings previously discussed, two types of smoke

---

[3] The Stokes mortar is a smooth-bore, muzzle-loading weapon firing a cylindrical projectile which is unstabilized in flight and which therefore requires an "always" fuze, that is, a fuze designed to function upon impact regardless of the manner in which the projectile strikes. The Stokes-Brandt mortar contains all the principles of the original Stokes, but fires a projectile that is stabilized in flight throughout its trajectory. This stabilization is accomplished through the design of a shell of a torped or dart shape with a fin tail. In flight the shell travels nose-on through the entire trajectory, thus eliminating the need for the "always" fuze required by the Stokes shell. Instead of the "always" fuze, a point-detonating type of fuze with bore-safe characteristics is used.

shells are reported in use by the artillery. One, called *fumógeno incendiário* (smoke incendiary), is filled with white phosphorus and the other, called *fumógeno* (smoke), with a smoke mixture, probably oleum and sulfur trioxide. Ammunition of both types is said to be provided for the 7.5-cm, 10-cm, and 10.5-cm guns.

c. Infantry.—In addition to a number of hand grenades and candles, the Italian infantry is provided with a short bomb-thrower weighing 2 kg (4.4 pounds), which projects all types of hand grenades a distance of 330 yards. In the many Italian documents available, no specific mention is made of the guns or howitzers employed by the infantry.

d. Candles and grenades—(1) *Toxic smoke candles.*—Italian toxic smoke candles are reported to be of the following types:

(*a*) *Small candle.*—This small candle (*candelotto*) contains 50 percent DA (diphenylchlorarsine), 25 percent kieselkguhr, and 25 percent nitrocellulose (and acetone), and weights 380 grams (13½ ounces). The weight of the filling is 220 grams (7¾ ounces). This candle is probably intended for use as a hand grenade.

(*b*) *2-kg candle.*—This candle (*candela*) has the same composition as that above, weighing 2.8 kg (6.16 pounds). This filling weighs 2.2 kg (4.8 pounds) and burns 2 minutes.

(*c*) *4-kg candle.*—This candle (*candela*) contains 54 percent DA (diphenylchlorarsine), 16 percent kieselguhr, and 30 percent T_4 (hexagene).

(*d*) *5-kg candle.*—This candle (*candela*), with the same composition as above, weighs 6.5 kg (14.3 pounds). The weight of the filling is 5.5 kg (12.1 pounds).

(2) *Lacrimatory candles.*—Lacrimatory candles are of the same sizes and weights as above. The small tear-gas generator, which also may be used as a hand grenade, and the 2-kg and 5-kg candles contain 50 percent CN (chloracetophenone). 50 percent nitrocellulose (and acetone). The small candle burns 1 minute, whereas the 2-kg candle burns 2 minutes.

(3) *Smoke candles.*—(a) *General.*—Smoke-screen generators or candles include the *candela fumógena* (smoke generator) and the *candelotto fumógeno* (smoke candle). Both have bodies of tin plate equipped with zinc igniter caps. They are filled with a Berger-type mixture,[4] consisting of approximately 50 percent carbon tetrachloride, 35 percent zinc powder, 5 percent zinc oxide, and 10 percent kieselguhr. The candles are painted dark green and have labels giving the name of the generator and directions for use, together with the marking "F/ZN."

(b) *Candela fumógena (smoke generator).*—This candle is $9\frac{3}{4}$ inches long by 3 inches in diameter, with a $\frac{9}{16}$-inch recess at the bottom housing the igniter pellet and striker and closed by a lid. The filling weighs 2 kg (4.4 pounds) and burns $3\frac{1}{4}$ minutes.

(c) *Candelotto fumógeno (smoke candle).*—This small candle is $3\frac{1}{2}$ inches long by $2\frac{1}{2}$ inches in diameter, with the ignited pellet housed in the cap. The filling weighs 450 grams (1 pound) and burns 1 minute.

(d) *Small smoke and incendiary grenade.*—This grenade weights 0.48 kg (1.05 pound and contains 0.3 kg ($\frac{2}{3}$ pound) of WP (white phosphorus), with a burster charge of 10 grams of black powder ignited by a Bickford fuze.[5]

e. *Bulk contamination.*—(1) *General.*—Italian spray apparatus appears to have been designed from the point of view of using toxic gas or smoke in all types of country.

(2) *Knapsack sprayer (irroratore spalleggiato).*—This apparatus, while adaptable for producing smoke, is primarily designed for spraying mustard gas. It consists of a 12-liter (3-gallon) container, with compressed-air bottle and discharge jet, all carried on the back by means of straps. When filled, it weighs 32 kg (70.4

---

[4] The "Berger mixture," a smoke agent named after its French inventor, had the following composition (by weight) in World War 1: 25 percent zinc dust, 50 percent carbon tetrachloride, 20 percent zinc oxide, 5 percent kieselguhr.

[5] A commercial type of powder-train fuze.

pounds). The time of emission is 5 minutes, and it may be completely refilled in 8 minutes.

(3) *Portable smoke generator (cloramma barellato).*—This spray apparatus, designed for producing smoke, consists of two containers and a compressed-air cylinder mounted on a hand barrow or carried by a stretcher. It is reported that one container was designed for chlorsulfonic acid and the other for ammonia, but both containers are now filled with two liters (6 gallons) each of chlorsulfonic acid. The time of emission with one nozzle is 50 minutes; with two nozzles, 25 minutes. Six minutes are required for refilling.

(4) *Mobile smoke generator (cloramma carrellato).*—This name is given to the above-described smoke apparatus when it is mounted on a two-wheeled handcart. There seems to be no reason why both types could not be used for spraying blister gas.

(5) *Six-wheeled cross-country mustard gas truck (autodovunque yperite* [6]*).*—A standard cross-country truck carries four drums containing 800 liters (211 gallons) of mustard gas, compressed-air cylinders, and perforated piping for ground contamination. The time of emission is 9 minutes and the drums may be refilled in 30 minutes. When used as a smoke weapon the vehicle is known as *autodovunque nube* (cross-country smoke truck). It then carries 500 liters (132 gallons) of chlorsulfonic acid in two drums. With two nozzles its time of emission is 100 minutes; with four nozzles, 50 minutes.

(6) *Four-wheeled mustard-gas truck (autocarretta yperite).*—This light truck carries two drums (400 liters) of mustard gas, a compressed air cylinder, and perforated piping for ground contamination. Its time of emission is 6 minutes and the drums may be refilled in 15 minutes. When used as a smoke weapon, the vehicle is known as *autocarretta nube* (four-wheeled smoke truck). It then carries one 250-liter (66-gallon) drum of smoke liquid

---

[6] *Yperite* is the French word for "mustard gas"; the Italian form is *iprite*.

ARMAMENT AND EQUIPMENT 261

(probably chlorsulfonic acid), with an emission time of 60 minutes from two noozles or 30 minutes from four nozzles.

(7) *Light tank with trailer (carro veloce con rimorchio).*—A light tank (Fiat-Ansaldo C. V. 3) draws a trailer with 240 liters (63 gallons) of mustard gas or smoke liquid in two containers. When mustard gas is to be used, the equipment includes a cylinder of compressed air and perforated piping, which disperses the contaminating agent in 5 minutes. With smoke acid as the agent, the time of emission is 17 minutes from four nozzles. Both types of agents require 30 minutes for refilling.

f. Miscellaneous.—A simple apparatus, which may be used either as a portable sprayer or as a chemical mine, consists of a tin-plate cylinder with a capacity of 6 liters (1.6 gallons) of mustard gas. It may be used like a garden watering can by screwing in a tube with a sprinkler at the end, or it may be burst by an explosive charge.

New designation	Old designation	Nature and weight of filling	Weight of complete bomb	Diameter of bomb body	Over-all length
Bomba	*Bomba*	*Kg*	*Kg*	*Inches*	*Inches*
500 C	C. 500 T.[1]	HE (?) Mustard 210	280 (or 298)	18.0	96.6
100 C	C. 100 P.[2]	HE 28.7 DA 14.3	101.9	10.7	50.2
40 C	C. 40 P	HE 13.0 DA 6.5	47.0	9.0	32.3
15 C	C. 15 P	HE 3.65 DA 1.7	16.0	4.7	31.0
4 C	Doppio Spezzone C.	HE 0.67 DA 0.33	2.8 (?)	2.7	12.2
2 C	Spezzone C.	HE 0.29 DA 0.14	1.55	2.7	6.1
	Furetto	Lacrimator 10	25	6.3	32.7

[1] *T.* probably is an abbreviation for *tempo* (time).
[2] *P.* probably is an abbreviation for *percussione* (percussion).

FIGURE 137.—List of gas bombs.

262. Aerial weapons.—*a. Spray.*—Reports regarding the use of vesicant gases by means of aerial sprays in the Abyssinian campaign are conflicting. There is no direct evidence that Italian land planes are equipped with spray apparatus, but Italian documents describe a spray apparatus, *irroratore B*, two of which are carried outside the fuselage of the seaplane Cantiere Z. 501. Each tank has a capacity of 180 liters (47.5 gallons) of mustard gas or smoke liquid, with a total emission time of 20 seconds. When used for producing smoke screens, the following results are claimed from a height of 30 meters (100 feet):

Initial thickness of cloud_____ 40 meters (44 yards).
Thickness after 15 minutes____ 80 meters (88 yards).
Length of curtain_____ 1,200 meters (1,300 yards).

b. Gas bombs.—(1) Gas-filled bombs, as listed in figure 137, have been identified from enemy documents and other reliable sources. According to a recent report these bombs are painted yellow with the usual Geneva Cross to indicate the filling (see par. 260 above). With the exception of type *500 C.* and the *bomba furetto*, these bombs are filed with DA (diphenylchlorarsine). They have a bursting charge approximately double the weight of the gas fillings and are fitted with percussion fuzes. The *500 C.* has a time fuze and a relatively small bursting charge, indicating that it is filled with blister gas and is designed for air bursting. The *bomba furetto* is obviously filled with tear gas and is described as a vaporizing percussion bomb.

(2) Other than in the case of the *500 C.* bomb, the weights of these bombs roughly correspond with their nomenclature. No doubt the *500 C.* is so named because it has the same external dimension as the 500-kg HE bomb and would fit the same bomb racks. Naturally, a gas-filled bomb of the same dimensions, having a thinner metal case, would be considerably lighter in weight.

(3) Not included in figure 137 is a smoke (*vento*) bomb having a body diameter of 5.2 inches and an over-all length of 17.3 inches. The nature and weight of the smoke mixture is not indicated.

c. Incendiary bombs.—The Italians are reported to have used incendiary bombs on relatively few occasions to date. Those known to exist are listed in figure 138.

New designation	Old designation	U. S. equivalent	Nature and weight of filling	Weight of complete bomb	Diameter of bomb body	Over-al length
				Kg	*Inches*	*Inches*
Bomba 100. S. P. I*[1]*.	*Bomba*	Bomb Combined antipersonnel and incendiary.	(See note)	89.1	10.7	53.2
70. I. P			Thermite 24.5	62.0	9.9	47.2
20. I	da *Kg.* 20. I	Incendiary	Thermite	19.4	6.3	34.0
Z. I	*Bombetta incendidria mista da Kg.*	Indendiary	Thermite/oil mixture.		2.7	12.2
1. I		Incendiary	Thermite		2.7	6.1

[1]Contains sixteen 2-kg or thirty-two 1-kg incendiary bombs.

FIGURE 138.—List of Italian incendiary bombs.

263. Flame throwers.—*a. General.*—It has been learned from a reliable source that the Italians have made extensive use of flame throwers on the Russian front as supporting weapons for infantry action. In practice they have considered it inadvisable to operate flame throwers in units smaller than the "group" which consists of one leader, one assistant, and six squads of two teams each, the latter being composed of one operator and one assistant. There are several known types of Italian flame throwers.

b. Portable, model 35.—(1) This apparatus (fig. 139) consists of two cylinders carried on the back of the operator, a length of flexible tubing, and a jet tube, which carries the trigger and ignition arrangement, the whole weighing 27 kg (59.4 pounds) when filled.

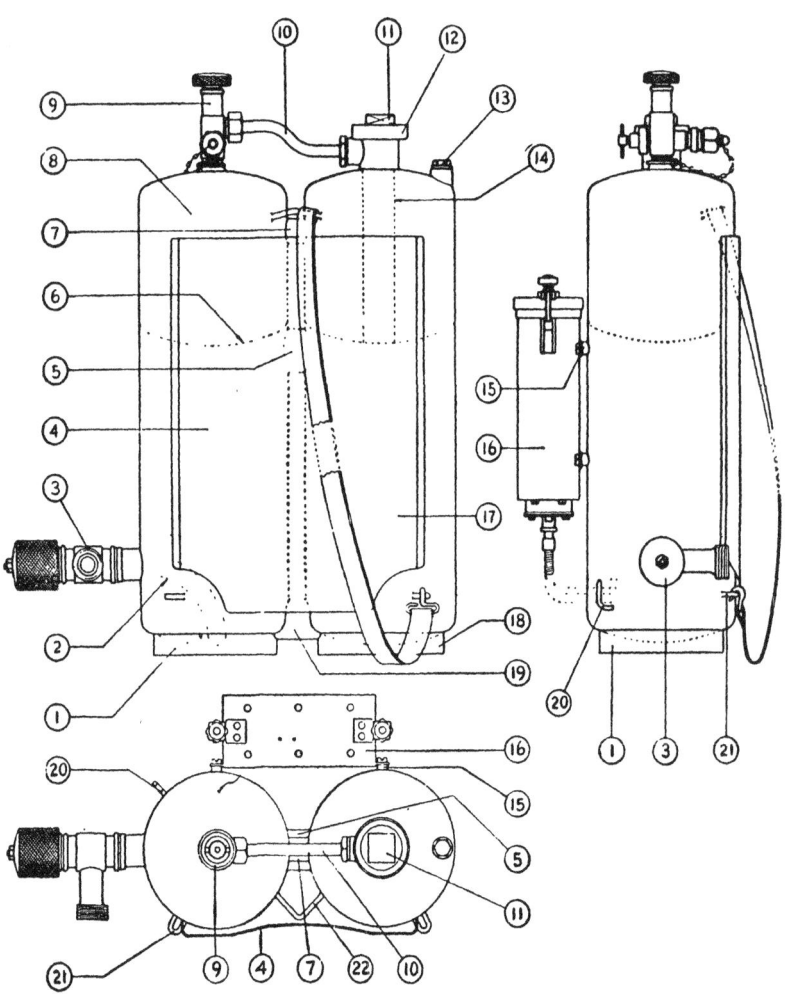

FIGURE 139.—Portable flame thrower, model 35.

ARMAMENT AND EQUIPMENT

1. Diaphragm.
2. Fuel take-off tube.
3. Main fuel control valve.
4. Elastic carrier.
5. Gas transfer tube.
6. Diaphragm.
7. Gas transfer tube.
8. Gas compartment.
9. Gas transfer valve.
10. Gas transfer tube.
11. Threaded plug.
12. Charging nipple.
13. Cylinder plug.
14. Charging tube.
15. Threaded lug.
16. Battery and transformer case.
17. Liquid fuel compartment.
18. Supporting ring.
19. Liquid transfer tube.
20. Securing hook.
21. Lower support stirrup.
22. Upper support stirrup.

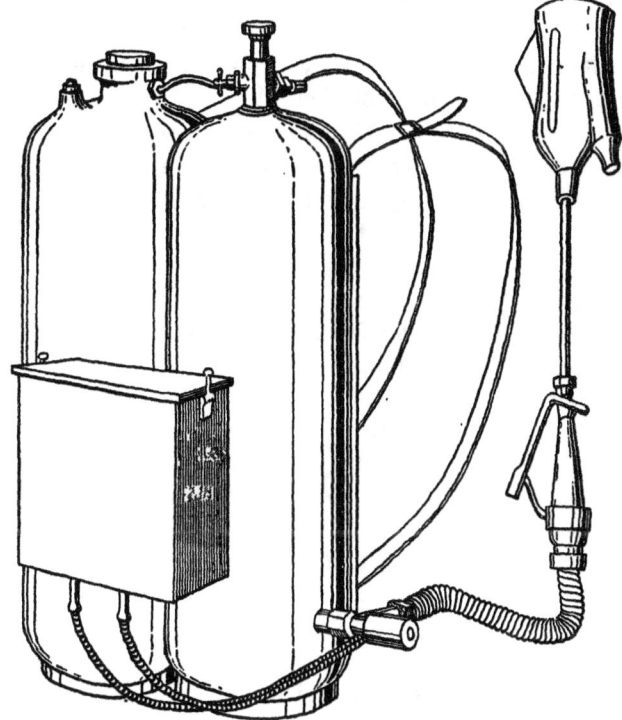

FIGURE 140.—Portable flame thrower, model 35, showing nozzle.

RESTRICTED

(2) The two cylinders are identical and each contains nitrogen under pressure and fuel oil, which is taken off the lower end through a connecting piece and valve. Ignition is effected by a battery coil and a spark gap with or without a wick, or on some models by means of a friction tube and wick, which burns for 2 minutes.

(3) The fuel is a mixture of benzene and light oil having a flash point of 10° C. The apparatus is capable of throwing a flame 25 yards and making untenable a zone of 35 yards long by 15 yards wide. It can produce 10 intermittent bursts of flame or one continuous jet of 20 seconds, and should not be used in a head wind of more than 12 miles per hour.

c. Portable, model 40.—(1) This apparatus (fig. 141) is similar in appearance to the model 35, differing mainly in the ignition system and in the insertion of a pressure gauge in the connecting tube between the heads of the two cylindrical containers. The fuel passes to the rubber hose and discharge piece through a small turbine driving a high-tension magneto for ignition purposes. Control of the fuel passing from the discharge piece to the nozzle is effected by a cone valve in the nozzle operated by a hand lever.

(2) After the fuel has passed the cone valve, a small proportion is diverted through two filters and atomizing sprays adjacent to the main jet. Both the main jet and the sprays discharge into the ignition chamber, where a standard automobile spark plug ignites the spray, which in turn ignites the main jet. The spark plug is actuated by the turbine-driven magneto. The fuel used in this flame thrower is a medium petroleum distillate containing about 15 percent gasoline.

(3) It is reported that while the impeller-driven magneto gives 100 percent positive ignition, the use of the impeller in the oil stream so disturbs it that the maximum range attainable is only 18 yards.

FIGURE 141.—Portable flame thrower, model 40.

d. Motorized.—It is also reported, but not confirmed, that the Italians have a motorized flame thrower for which a maximum range of 75 yards is claimed. Fuel for this apparatus is carried in a separate armored trailer. No other details of this weapon are available. (See fig. 142 for an illustration of a flame-thrower tank.)

FIGURE 142.—Italian flame-thrower tank, L 3/35, with trailer.

264. Gas masks and gas detectors.—*a. Gas masks.*—Italian service gas masks are of two general types. Group A is like the U. S. Army service mask, with separate canister and corrugated rubber connecting tube; group B is similar in appearance to the U. S. training mask, with a tdrum canister attached directly to the facepiece.

(1) *Facepieces of group A.*—(a) *General.*—Facepieces of group A are of the separate canister type.

(b) *P (Penna.).*[7]—This facepiece is an obsolete model still in use and is made in three sizes of green press moulded rubber, with

---

[7] This mask is undoubtedly named after Col. L. Penna, the first chief of the Italian Military Chemical Service.

inlet and outlet valves contained in a holder of aluminum alloy fastened to the chin part of the mask. A rubber baffle just below the eyepiece is intended to prevent exhaled breath from reaching the eyepieces. The latter are of splinterless glass and are held in place by crimping rims.

(c) *M (M. 31 and M. 33)*.—This facepiece is similar to the earlier model, but is gray or brown in color (fig. 143). Instead

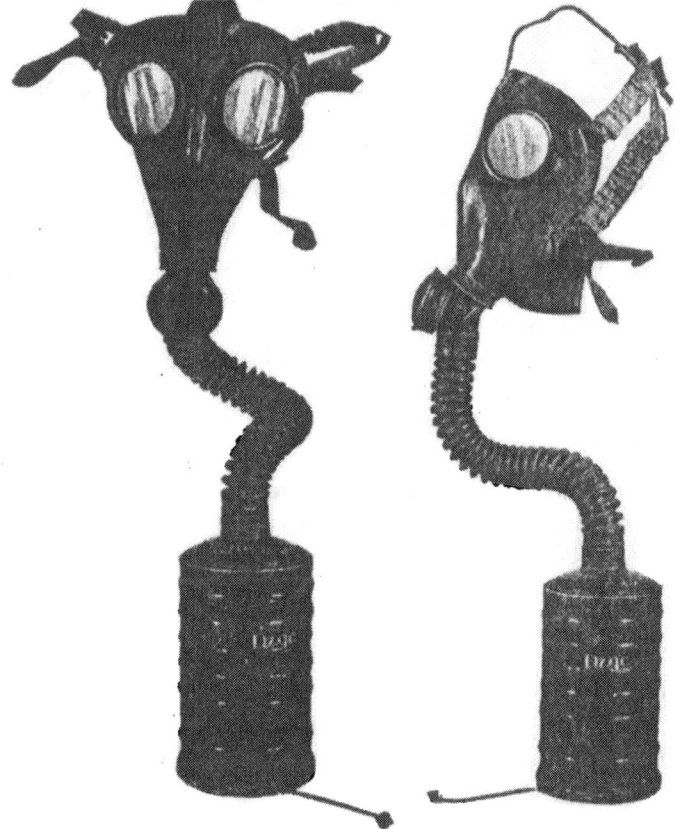

FIGURE 143.—Military gas mask, M31. The separate type canister is attached)

of the rubber baffle, this type has an inner secondary mask of black rubber wired to the valve holder. A considerable improvement over model P is effected by a change in position of the eyepieces so as to give a better field of vision.

(d) *Naval* (*R. M.* and *R. M. F.*).—This differs from model M chiefly in that the facepiece does not have an inner secondary mask. Prevention of dimming is sought by providing a forked rubber tube to lead incoming air over the eyepieces. This model is designated *R. M. F.* (*Regia Marina, fónica*—Royal Navy, phonic type) when provided with a special outlet valve carrying a short trumpet-shaped attachment, consisting of three concentrated horns on the outside. This attachment improves the speech characteristics of the mask.

The haversacks for the *R. M.* (*Régia Marina, Royal Navy*) type are of rubberized fabric, with two external pockets carrying a spare outlet valve and a tube of anti-dimming soap. They may be carried either on the chest or at the side in the manner customary for naval personnel.

(2) *Facepieces of group B.*—(a) *General.*—Facepieces of group B are of the attached canister type.

(b) *T. 35*[8].—This facepiece (plate IV, following p.   ) is made of moulded rubber in four sizes. The outlet valve is opposite the mouth, and the inlet valve is contained in the adaptor, in which the canister is screwed, below the outlet valve.

(c) *F. T. 35* [9].—This facepiece is the Navy version of T. 35. It is provided with a voice-amplifying device similar to that attached to the *R. M. F.* type.

(3) *Canisters.*—(a) The separate type canister (originally flat in shape) consists of a cylindrical container made of an aluminum

---

[8] *T. 35, tipo 35* (type 35).
[9] *F. T. 35, fonica tipo. 35* (phonic type 35).

alloy, approximately 8 inches long and 4 inches in diameter. It is filled with a thick central layer of activated charcoal, a layer of granules of zinc carbonate intimately mixed with charcoal fines, and a filter pad of wool and viscose rayon impregnated with resin. In late models the filter pad (particulate filter) is contained in a separate metal holder. Tests indicate that this canister will afford adequate protection against all of the common types of war gases.

(*b*) The attached drum canister, $3\frac{1}{2}$ inches in height (excluding the neck) and $4\frac{1}{2}$ inches in diameter, is likewise made of aluminum alloy. The filling is the same as that contained in the larger cylindrical container, but possibly the charcoal used is of a higher grade. Tests indicate that this type canister affords protection over considerably shorter periods than does the larger type.

b. Gas detectors.—The only gas detector mentioned in Italian documents is the "Alfa Detector," issued to the Air Force to determine whether decontamination of aircraft is complete. A cherry red liquid, contained in a bottle is packed with a number of strips of absorbent cardboard. The test is carried out by pouring three or four drops of the liquid on one of these strips and placing it on the object to be tested. If the strip turns pale blue, or is decolorized, blister gas is still present and further decontamination is necessary. It is not known if army units are equipped with this detector.

265. Protective clothing.—*a.* Among stores captured in Libya were a number of antigas suits made of a rubberized fabric, probably Pirelli cloth, type C, which consists of two lightweight fabrics proofed with a green rubber composition and cemented together with a gluelike adhesive. When tested, this fabric resisted liquid mustard for more than 2 days and lewisite for more than 7 hours.

b. A decontamination suit (*S. C. M.*[10] *36*) made of Pirelli cloth, type D, likewise has been reported. This material is lighter in weight than the type C fabric, and upon test resisted liquid mustard over 24 hours and lewisite over 7 hours. This garment may be decontaminated by immersion in boiling water for 30 minutes.

c. An Italian naval manual describes the protective clothing used in the Navy. A one-piece outfit in the form of a diving suit, with separate hood and gloves, and the heavy combination suit of apron, overshoes, hood, rubber gloves, and oversleeves, are made of rubberized fabric, probably Pirelli cloth, type C. Also described is an over-all suit, made of a thick cotton impregnated fabric, with hood, socks, rubber shoes, and heavy rubber gloves. Wearing of the one-piece and heavy combination suits would be limited to 15 to 20 minutes in hot weather or 1 hour in cold weather; the over-all suit could be worn for somewhat longer period.

d. An Italian document listing antigas equipment issued to units reveals that 10 complete antigas suits, each consisting of an over-all suit with hood, gloves, and overshoes, were issued to the headquarters of artillery battalions, but none were issued to other units. This document also shows the issue of a limited number of antigas gloves to various units. It is assumed that the Army would have protective clothing for decontamination squads similar to that described for the Navy, and this assumption appears justified upon careful scrutiny of the protective clothing worn by Italian chemical warfare units, as shown in figure 144.

e. Pre-war reports mentioned that cellophane garments for crossing contaminated ground, to be destroyed after use, were

---

[10] *S. C. M., Servizio Chimico Militare* (Military Chemical Service).

ARMAMENT AND EQUIPMENT

FIGURE 144.—Protective clothing.

being considered by the Italians. Likewise, it was reported that antigas clothing was being made of an impregnated silk, a complete suit weighing not more than 1¾ pounds. Neither type of garment, however, has been seen to date.

266. Collective protection.—*a.* An Italian document (*Manual for the Infantry Officer*, July 1940) describes various types of shelters to provide protection, against chemical agents, for a number of persons in such places as command posts, telephone exchanges, and dressing stations.

b. Airtight shelters are provided with curtains, preferably attached to a frame in an inclined position. These curtains are to be kept dampened continuously during a gas attack. The number of hours this type of shelter may be used without change of air is calculated by means of the formula $T=\dfrac{G}{N}$ where G represents the cubic content (in meters) of the shelter and N represents the number of persons sheltered.

c. The air-filtered type of shelter must be installed by technical troops. Purified air is admitted by means of a collective filter apparatus contained in five crates and weighing 270 kg (600 pounds). Normally, the quantity of air necessary is that which allows 1 cubic meter per person per hour, but in exceptional cases and in periods lasting not over 1 hour, the air may be reduced by 50 percent. The infantry shelter of this type is designed for 30 men at rest.

d. A box of chloride of lime is always placed before the entrance of the shelter for decontaminating shoes that may have come into contact with mustard gas.

267. Decontamination.—*a. Personal decontamination.*—(1) Pre-war literature on the subject of individual protective measures recommended that parts of the skin touched by liquid mustard gas,

ARMAMENT AND EQUIPMENT 267

after removal of the liquid be covered with calcium chloride, sodium bicarbonate, or any other absorbent powder with which the soldier might be provided. China clay, talc, and *magnesia alba*, particularly the latter, were also mentioned as being satisfactory. The use of ashes or dried earth was recommended as a makeshift.

(2) An Army pamphlet (*First Aid for Gas Casualties*, 1934) mentions the removal of liquid mustard gas from the skin by means of absorbent blotting paper contained in the first-aid "packet," or by washing with gasoline for 3 to 5 minutes, followed by application of a special "decontaminating powder" also contained in the packet. This powder was to be renewed two or three times at a few minutes' interval. For a complete personal decontamination, bathing in a warm solution of 0.4-percent solution of potassium permanganate and washing the eyes, mouth, and throat with sodium bicarbonate solution are prescribed.

(3) The decontaminating powder mentioned above may be "Mixture M," a white powder contained in a soldered tin box, which upon analysis was found to consist of chloramine T (8.6 percent), magnesium carbonate (70.3 percent), alkaline salts (14.4 percent), and undetermined matter (6.7 percent).

(4) An item of Italian decontamination equipment recently examined by the British consisted of sealed glass ampoules, each containing 7½ to 8 cc of a solution of chlorine in carbon tetrachloride containing 2.7 percent free chlorine.

b. Ground decontamination.—(1) Ground decontamination is effected by means of standard Army trucks fitted with a hopper at the back from which chloride of lime may be distributed on the ground. They are of two types, the heavy 6-wheeled cross-country truck (*autodovunque*), and the light four-wheeled truck (*autocarreta*). The trucks carry drums of bleaching powder from

RESTRICTED

which the hoppers are filled. Details of these trucks and their equipment are as follows:

	Heavy truck	Light truck
Capacity of hopper	1,100 pounds	440 pounds.
Number of drums of bleaching powder	24	14.
Weight of bleaching powder	2,640 pounds	1,540 pounds.
Weight of apparatus without drums	660 pounds	220 pounds.
Time required to empty hopper, traveling at 2 miles per hour	1 minute	1 minute.

The heavy truck distributes its hopper content over an area approximately 5 yards wide and 55 yards long, at the rate of (roughly 3⅔ pounds per square yard. The light truck presumably distributes its hopper content over an area of approximately 100 square yards at the same rate.

(2) A handcart apparatus, weighing 230 kg (500 pounds) when filled, is also provided for decontamination purposes. It consists of a container holding 60 kg (132 pounds) of chloride of lime, which is ejected through a nozzle by compressed air during a period of 2 minutes. Thirty minutes are required to recharge the compressed air cylinder (20 liters at a pressure of 150 atmospheres) which is said to be able to discharge six containers of bleaching powder. It is not stated whether the bleaching powder is dry or in solution.

c. Decontamination of personnel.—No recent information is available regarding the facilities provided for decontamination of personnel. An official Army manual (*Defense against Gas*, 1930) describes the *formazione automóbile di bonifica truppa* (motorized unit for the decontamination of personnel), consisting of 1 *autobagno* (mobile bathing unit) carrying a tank approximately 530 gallons capacity, a pump for filling this in 15 minutes, and a boiler; a second truck carrying 2 tents; and a third with clothes and equipment. For use the two tents are set up, one at each side of the *autobagno;* personnel undress in the first tent, pass under the 12 showers of the *autobagno*, and put on fresh clothing in the second tent.

d. Decontamination of clothing.—(1) The above-mentioned Army manual did not mention field laundries for decontamination of clothing. It merely stated that "articles of clothing, if very heavily contaminated (that is, if they have been splashed with mustard gas) must be destroyed (burnt or buried). If they are slightly contaminated, they may be washed with soap and water, well rinsed, and wiped. In every case it is necessary to have changes of clothing."

(2) An Army pamphlet on decontamination, published in 1934, describes very clearly the usual methods of decontamination of clothing by washing with soap and water, but does not imply that special laundries would be provided for that purpose. Nor does it mention the use of steam for decontaminating clothing.

(3) A Naval manual, published in 1939, also makes no mention of special laundries for decontaminating clothing except by implication. It states that if protective clothing becomes contaminated, the use of soap and water will not be sufficient to cleanse it, it being necessary to send it to a gas protective center where special means are provided for doing the work.

268. Gas alarms.—Gas alarms to be employed in the event of gas attack consist of sirens or klaxons, sounding three short notes and one long note, repeatedly.

269. Civilian protection.—*a.* The UNPA (*L'Unione Nazionale per la Protezione anti-Aérea*) corresponding to the Air Protection League of Germany, undertook the matter of assisting air defense organizations, disseminating information, and cooperating in the execution of air defense measures. In some cases, especially in the larger Italian cities, good results were obtained, but from prisoners of war it has been learned that the smaller towns had practically no air defense organization. Children in particular were trained in air raid conduct. Air raid warning sectors were established, wardens appointed, and blackouts held, but apparently interest lagged.

b. From a commercial source, it is learned that only about 1 million gas masks have been sold to the public. The Pirelli company, which has a government franchise to manufacture masks, is said to have about 2½ million unsold. It is assumed that recent raids on Genoa, Milan, Naples, and other centers have stimulated the public's desire to own and carry gas masks.

Chapter 7
AIR FORCE

	Paragraph
Brief history	270
High command	271
Operational units	272
Strength in personnel	273
Strength report as of 24 April 1943	274
Air bases and landing fields	275
Procurement of supplies	276
Equipment	277
Training	278
Camouflage of airdromes and aircraft	279

270. Brief history.—*a. World War I.*—When Italy entered World War I in May 1915, the air forces, consisting of 382 planes, formed a part of the Army and the Navy and were under the direction of the Ministries of War and Navy. In May 1916, the rapid development of aviation and submarines as war weapons necessitated the formation of an Inspectorate of Submarines and Aviation, under the Ministry of the Navy, for the purpose of organizing properly the new arms for defense. For the same purpose, in July 1917, the Director General of Aeronautics, under the Ministry of War, was transferred to the Ministry of Arms and became the Commissariat of Aeronautics.

b. Period 1918–23.—In the period immediately following the war, the program in the course of execution for the favorable development of the new arms was interrupted. The Inspectorate of Submarines and Aviation in the Navy became the Inspectorate of Aeronautics, on 24 September 1918, in the Office of the Chief of Staff, Ministry of the Navy. When the Ministry of Arms was abolished, the Commissariat of Aeronautics became the Under Secretariat for Aeronautics. On 30 June 1919, the Under Secre-

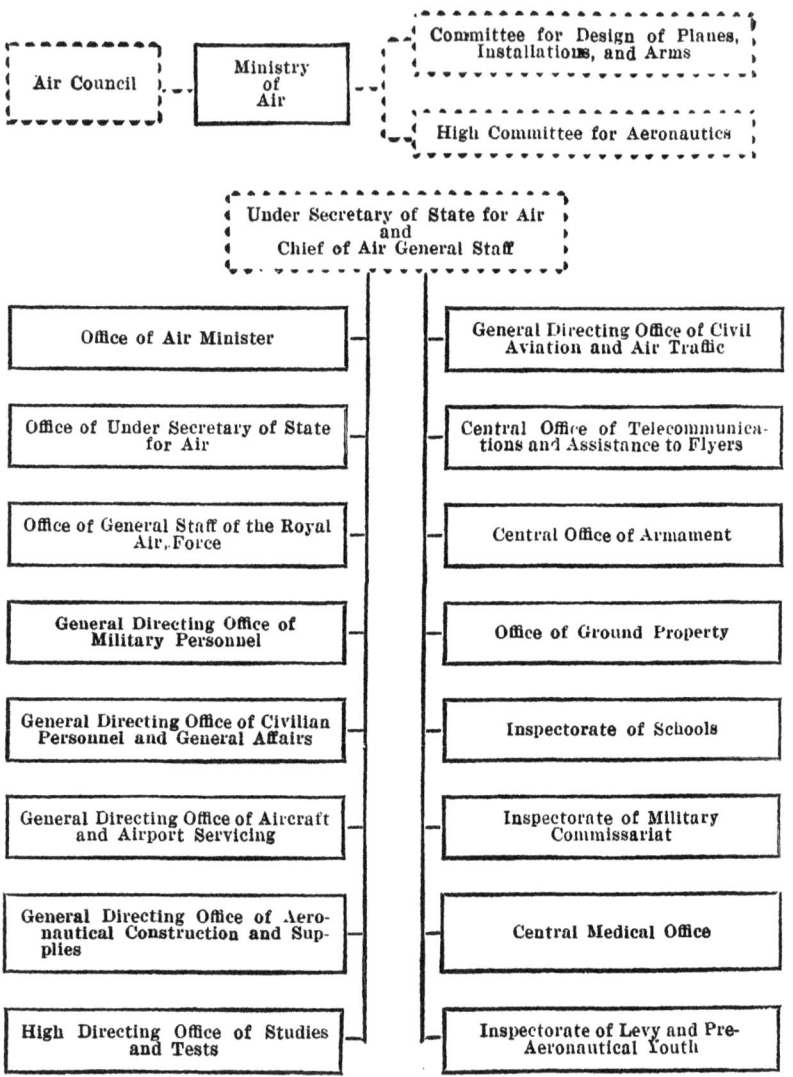

Figure 145.—Organization of the Air Ministry.

tariat for Aeronautics became again the Director General of Aeronautics, attached first to the Ministry of Transport and later to the Ministry of Industry.

Meanwhile, in January 1920, following the disbanding of the Command of Aeronautics, which was attached to the High Command, there was established an Inspectorate of Aeronautics in the Army, analogous to the Inspectorate of Naval Aviation. On the basis of this arrangement the Director General of Aeronautics was charged with all matters concerning technical and judicial questions in regard to aeronautics, while all questions relating to tne strictly military organization remained under the jurisdiction of the Inspectorates of Aeronautics of the Army and Navy.

c. Separate establishment.—By 1923, the need for separating the air forces from the Army and Navy was felt, and the remainder of the demobilized air forces was organized as an independent arm on 24 January 1923. On 30 August 1925, the Air Ministry was established.

271. High command.—*a. Commander in Chief.*—The King has delegated his authority as Commander in Chief to the Minister of Air.

b. Air ministry.—The Air Ministry (see fig. 145) controls both the Royal Air Force (*Régia Aeronáutica*) and civil aviation. It is actually administered by the Under Secretary of State for Air. For unity of direction, the offices of the Under Secretary of State and of the Chief of the Air General Staff have been consolidated. The Air Ministry includes the following offices:

(1) Office of the Air Minister.

(2) Office of the Under Secretary of State for Air.

(3) Office of the General Staff of the Royal Air Force.

(4) General Directing Office of Military Personnel.

(5) General Directing Office of Civil Personnel and General Affairs.

(6) General Directing Office of Aircraft and Airport Servicing.

(7) General Directing Office of Aeronautical Construction and Supplies.

(8) High Directing Office of Studies and Tests.
(9) General Directing Office of Civil Aviation and Air Traffic.
(10) Central Office of Telecommunications and Assistance to Flyers.
(11) Central Office of Armament.
(12) Office of Ground Property.
(13) Inspectorate of Schools.
(14) Inspectorate of Levy and Records of Pre-Aeronautical Youth.

c. Councils for air defense.—(1) *Supreme Council for National Defense.*—The Chief of Staff for Air is a member of the Supreme Council for National Defense.

(2) *Air Council.*—The Air Council is a consultant to the Air Ministry on the more important questions concerning military and civil aviation. It is convened and presided over by the Minister for Air and consists of the Minister, Under Secretary of State for Air, Chief of Staff, general officers of the Air Army and Air Fleet, and, by invitation of the Air Minister, certain persons from other ministries, scientific or industrial organizations who possess special knowledge. The Air Council is a peacetime organization and at mobilization ceases to functon for the duration of the war.

(3) *High Committee for Aeronautics.*—The High Committee for Aeronautics is a consultative organ of the Air Ministry for more detailed questions concerning organization, personnel, construction, general and technical expenditures, and contracts. It is presided over by a general of the Air Force and consists of six general officers and colonels and one member of the Central Administration Office for Civil Aviation. Other individuals with expert knowledge may be invited to attend by the president.

(4) *Committee for Design of Planes, Installations, and Arms.*— The Committee for Design of Planes, Installations, and Arms is consulted by the Air Ministry on technical matters concerning aviation equipment and armament. The president is a general

RESTRICTED

of an Air Fleet, with a general of the Construction Corps as vice president, and six other high-ranking Air Force officers from technical departments as additional members.

272. Operational units.—*a. Component arms.*—The Air Force consists of the following components:

(1) *Aeronautical Arm*, consisting of the Navigation Branch (flying); Ground Service Branch (airdrome duty); Specialist Branch (mechanics, riggers, armorers, etc.), is divided into the following:

(*a*) Aerial Army, consisting of all air forces designed to carry out aerial warfare, including air defenses of the kingdom or any territory under the sovereignty of the State.

(*b*) Air Force for the Army, consisting of air units assigned to the Army to furnish air observation, communications, and fire support to the Army. Equipment and pilots are supplied by the Air Force, and observers are specially trained officers of the Army.

(*c*) Air Force for the Navy, consisting of all units assigned to furnish air observation, communications, and fire support to the Navy. Equipment and pilots are furnished by the Air Force, and observers are specially trained officers of the Navy.

(*d*) Air Forces for Colonial Garrisons, consisting of those Air Units stationed in the colonies which carry out garrison duties exclusively.

(2) *Aeronautical Engineering Corps*, consisting of technical personnel charged with the supervision of design, construction, testing, and production of equipment, installations, and landing fields. It operates the research center at Guidonia and experimental fields at Montecelio, Vigna di Valle, and Furbarra.

(3) *Aeronautical Commissariat Corps.*

(4) *Aeronautical Medical Corps.*

(5) *Military Schools of the Royal Air Force.*

272   HANDBOOK ON ITALIAN MILITARY FORCES

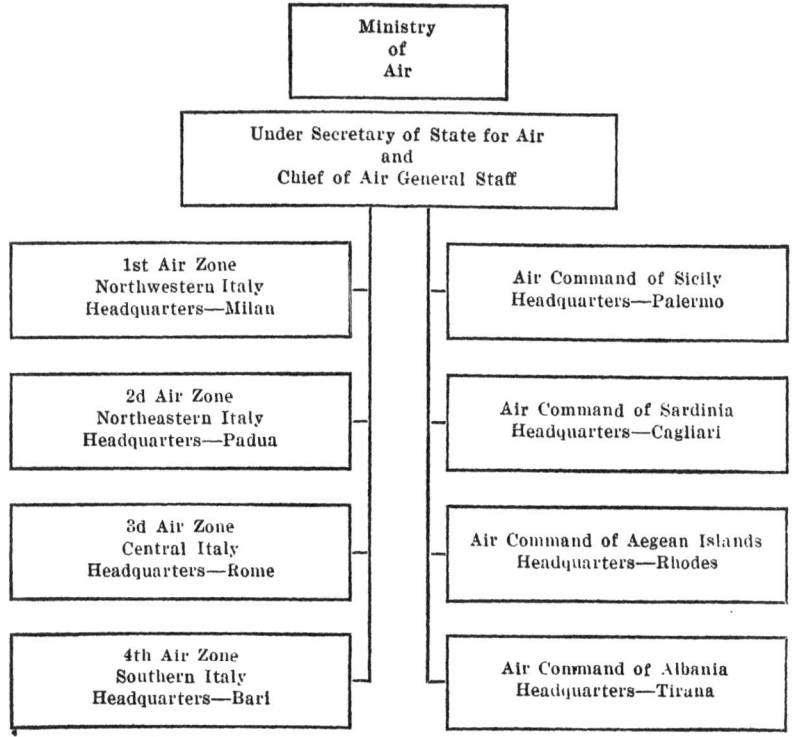

FIGURE 146.—Territorial Organization of the Air Force.

b. Territorial organization.—Italy is divided into four territorial air zones and four territorial air commands, each under the command of a general officer, as follows (see fig. 146):

1st Air Zone	Milan	Northwestern Italy.
2d Air Zone	Padua	Northeastern Italy.
3d Air Zone	Rome	Central Italy.
4th Air Zone	Bari	Southern Italy.
Air Command of Sicily	Palermo	Sicily.
Air Command of Sardinia	Cágliari	Sardinia.
Air Command of Aegean Islands	Rhodes	Dodecanese Islands.
Air Command of Albania	Tirana	Albania.

RESTRICTED   372

c. Tactical units.—(1) The Aerial Army includes all combat elements in the Mediterranean area. It consists of two Air Fleets organized into divisions, brigades, wings, groups, and squadrons. Additional wings are organized in the Dodecanese Islands, Albania, Sicily, and Sardinia (see fig. 147).

(2) An Air Fleet consists of two or more homogeneous Fighter or Bomber Air Divisions.

(3) An Air Division consists of two or more Air Brigades.

(4) An Air Brigade consists of two or more Wings.

(5) An Air Wing consists of two or more Groups.

(6) An Air Group consists of two or more Squadrons.

(7) A Bomber Squadron consists of six initial and three reserve aircraft.

(8) All other squadrons consist of nine initial and three reserve aircraft.

273. Strength in Personnel.—Estimated strength in personnel of the Air Force is as follows:

Pilots	12,000
Nonflying officers	6,100
Enlisted men	185,000
Total	203,100
Parachute troops	5,000
Total	208,100

274. Strength report as of 24 April 1943.—Depot reserves of aircraft are practically nonexistent. The total number of Italian combat aircraft is estimated to be 3,500, which includes aircraft in combat squadrons, schools, undergoing repair, staff, etc. It is doubted that the strength of the Italian Air Force is being increased.

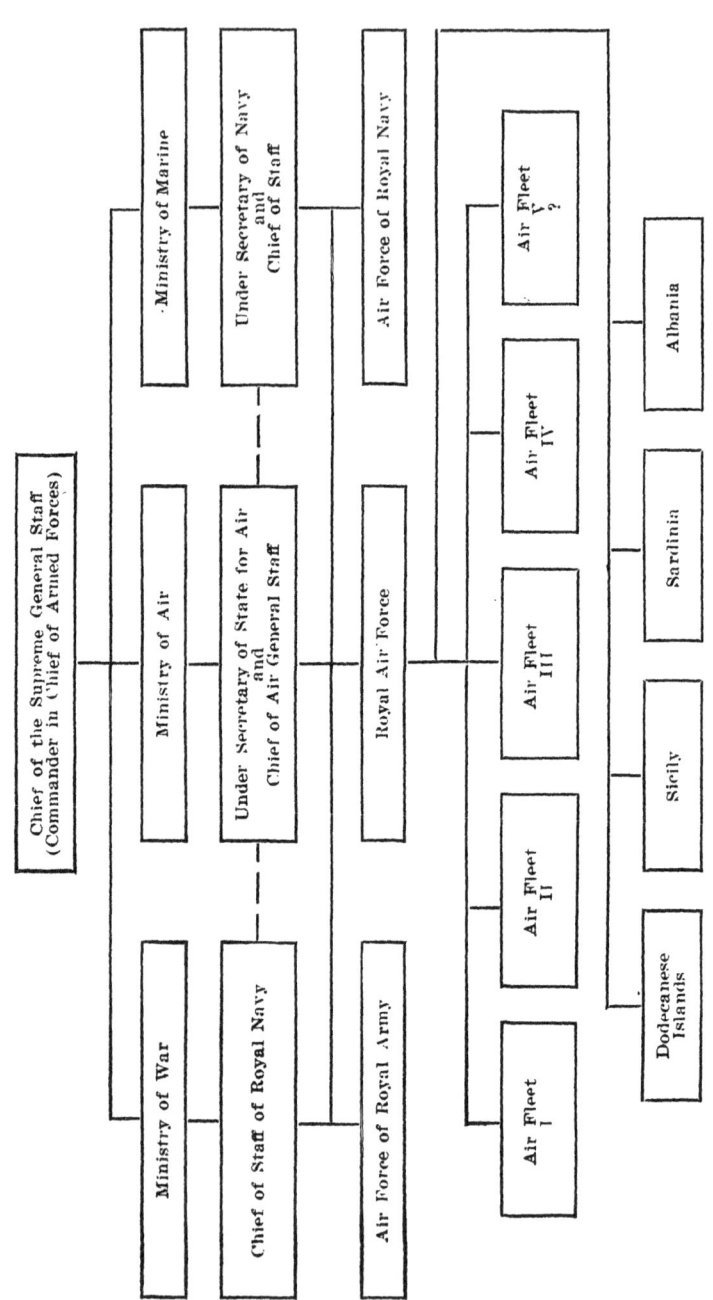

FIGURE 147.—Tactical organization of the Air Force.

Area	Bomber-reconnaissance	Torpedo bomber	Single-engine fighter	Army cooperation	Seaplane	Total
Sicily, Sardinia, Italy, and Southern France	170	110	510	85	190	1,065
Balkans, Aegean, and Rhodes	60	60	95	70	40	285
Total operational	230	170	605	155	230	1,350
Nonoperational in Italy	45	30	100	100		275
Grand total	275	200	705	255	230	1,625

FIGURE 148.—Strength report of the Italian Air Force, April 1943.

275. Air bases and landing fields.—*a.* Prior to the war, Italy had organized and was operating land and seaplane bases as follows:

    In Italy _____ 52 landplane and 18 seaplane bases.
    In the Dodecanese
        Islands _____ 1 landplane and 1 seaplane base.

The number of available air bases in Italy, plus 110 emergency fields, gave Italy a wide selection of bases for operational use. (There were also 82 emergency fields in East Africa and 20 in Libya.)

Name	Popular name	Manufacturer
Long range bomber:		
P-108		Piaggio.
Medium bombers:		
Cant. Z-1007 Bis	Alcione (Kingfisher)	Cantiere Riuniti.
BR-20	Cicogna (Stork)	Fiat.
SM-79	Sparviero (Hawk)	Savoia-Marchetti.
SM-84		Savoia-Marchetti.
Bomber reconnaissance:		
CA-310	Libeccio (Southwest Wind).	Caproni.
CA-311		Caproni.
CA-312 Bis		Caproni.

HANDBOOK ON ITALIAN MILITARY FORCES

Name	Popular name	Manufacturer
Army cooperation:		
RO-44		Meridionale.
RO-37 Bis		Meridionale.
CA-311		Caproni.
CA-313		Caproni.
CA-314		Caproni.
CA-133		Caproni.
Transport:		
SM-81	Pipistrello (Bat)	Savoia-Marchetti.
SM-82	Canguru (Kangaroo)	Savoia-Marchetti.
G-12		Fiat.
Torpedo bombers:		
SM-79	Sparviero (Hawk)	Savoia-Marchetti.
SM-84		Savoia-Marchetti.
Dive bombers:		
Ju-87 (built under license).		Junkers.
SM-85		Savoia-Marchetti.
SM-86		Savoia-Marchetti.
Fighter bomber:		
G-50	Falco (Falcon)	Fiat.
MC-200	Saetta (Thunderbolt)	Macchi.
Fighter:		
CR-42	Freccia (Arrow)	Fiat.
MC-200	Saetta (Thunderbolt)	Macchi.
MC-202	Saetta II (Thunderbolt)	Macchi.
MC-205		Macchi.
RE-2000	Falco I (Falcon)	Reggiane (Caproni).
RE-2001	Falco II (Falcon)	Reggiane (Caproni).
RE-2002		Reggiane.
RO-44 (floatplane)		Meridionale.
Flying boat:		
RS-14		Fiat.
Cant. Z-501		Cantiere Riuniti.
Cant. Z-506-B	Airione (Heron)	Cantiere Riuniti.

FIGURE 149.—Aircraft in operational use.

RESTRICTED

FIGURE 150.—SM-82 transport planes in flight.

b. In 1942, Italy had 46 major airdromes, 37 landing fields, and numerous emergency landing fields. Sicily had 9 airdromes and 8 emergency landing fields; Sardinia has 6 airdromes and 4 emergency landing fields; Corsica has 7 airfields and 7 emergency landing fields; Rhodes and the Dodecanese Islands have 3 airdromes and 3 landing fields.

276. Procurement of supplies.—*a. Aircraft industry.*—(1) *General.*—Italian factories are mainly engaged in the manufacture of aircraft parts, which are sent to Germany for assembly. This materially decreases Italian plane production. Completed planes, mainly Junkers 87 dive bombers, and engines have been received in Italy as payment for parts sent to Germany. The numbers are not known.

(2) *Production.*—Italian production has been estimated variously at from 150 to 200 planes per month. A recent, though unconfirmed, report (March 1943) estimates production at about 200 aircraft per month. When Italy entered the war, production was estimated at 350 planes per month. Even though present production shows a substantial increase, it is insufficient to meet expansion requirements and to replace current losses. Production is being concentrated on the following types:

(*a*) Re. 2002_____ Fighter.
(*b*) MC. 202 and 205_____ Fighter.
(*c*) Cant. Z 1007 Bis_____ Three-engine bomber.
(*d*) Cant. Z 506 Bis_____ Three-engine bomber, seaplane.
(*e*) CA. 313_____ Torpedo bomber and reconnaissance.
(*f*) SM. 82_____ Transport.

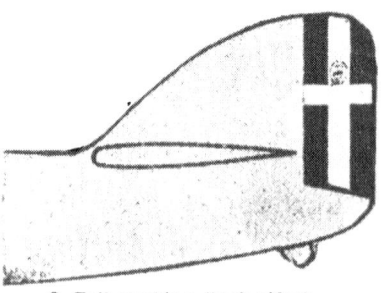 

① Tail marking (both sides).   ② Wing marking (upper and lower surfaces).
FIGURE 151.—Markings of Italian aircraft.

FIGURE 152.—P-108, long range bomber.

Performance:
　Maximum speed: 270 miles per hour.
　Range: 1,550 miles.
　Service ceiling: 23,000 feet.
Offensive and defensive equipment:
　Bombs: 7,700 pounds.
　Armament: Six 12.7 mm. machine guns (flexible).
　　Two 7.7-mm. machine guns.
Power plant: Four 1,300-horsepower engines (Piaggio PX11 RC35).

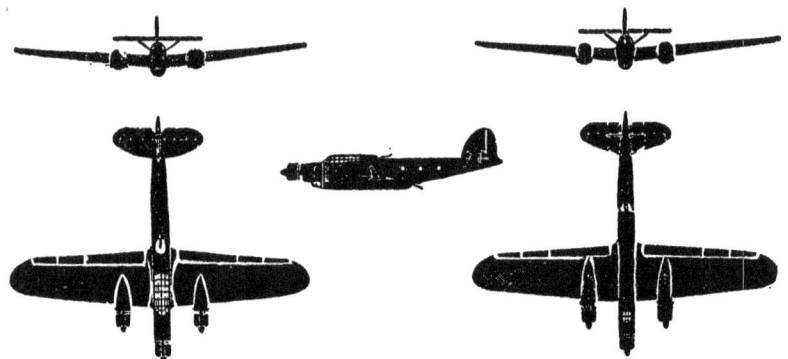

Figure 153.—Cant. Z-1007, Bis, *Alcione* (Kingfisher), medium bomber.

Performance:
- High speed: 280 miles per hour at 13,100 feet.
- Range: 930 miles at 195 miles per hour (2,640 pounds of bombs and 700 gallons of fuel).
- Climb: 13,100 feet within 10.5 minutes.
- Service ceiling: 26,500 feet.

Offensive and defensive equipment:
- Bombs: 2,640 pounds (normal); 4,850 pounds (maximum).
- Armament: One 12.7 mm. machine gun (flexible; top).
  One 12.7-mm machine gun (flexible; bottom).
  Two 7.7-mm. machine guns.

Power plant: Three 1,000-horsepower, 14-cylinder air-cooled engines (Piaggio PXI RC 40).

Characteristics.
- Span: 81 feet 4 inches.
- Length: 60 feet 4 inches.
- Wing area: 703 square feet.
- Construction: All wood.
- Empty weight: 19,000 pounds.
- Gross weight: 29,630 pounds.
- Maximum fuel: 1,170 gallons.

Status: Italy's best bomber in squadron service.

AIR FORCE 276

FIGURE 154.—BR-20, *Cicogna* (Stork), medium bomber.

Performance:
  Maximum speed: 268 miles per hour at 16,400 feet.
  Range: 1,863 miles at 13,100 feet (maximum).
  Climb: 16,400 feet within 18 minutes.
  Service ceiling: 25,000 feet.
Offensive and defensive equipment:
  Bombs: 2,200 pounds (normal); 3,500 pounds (maximum).
  Armament: One 7.7-mm machine gun (flexible; nose).
    One 7.7-mm machine gun (flexible; rear; bottom).
    One 12.7-mm machine gun (power turret; rear top).
  Armor: Leakproof tanks; armor protection for crew on some models.
  Power plant: Two 1,000-horsepower, 18-cylinder, air-cooled engines (Fiat A80 RC 41).
Characteristics:
  Span: 70 feet 6 inches.
  Length: 52 feet 10 inches.
  Wing area: 796 square feet.
  Construction: Metal structure; mixed metal and fabric covering.
  Empty weight: 14,332 pounds.
  Gross weight: 22,220 pounds.
  Maximum weight: 967 gallons.
Status: Standard Italian bomber; used in many of their raids.

RESTRICTED

FIGURE 155.—SM-79, *Sparviero* (Hawk), medium bomber.

Performance:
    Maximum speed: 295 miles per hour at 16,400 feet.
    Range: 2.175 miles (maximum).
    Climb: 16,400 feet within 14.5 minutes.
    Service ceiling: 23,000 feet.
Offensive and defensive equipment:
    Bombs: 1,760 pounds (normal; either one or two torpedoes).
    Armament: One 12.7-mm machine gun (fixed; forward).
    One 12.7-mm machine gun (flexible; top rear).
    One 12.7-mm machine gun (flexible; bottom).
    Two 7.7-mm machine guns (one on each beam).

Armor: Leakproof tanks; armor for crew.
Power plant: Three 1,000-horsepower, 14-cylinder, air-cooled engines (Piaggio P XI RC 40).

Characteristics:
Span: 69 feet 3 inches.
Length: 58 feet 7 inches.
Wing area: 656.5 square feet.
Construction: Mixed metal and plywood.
Empty weight: 16,750 pounds.
Gross weight: 27,700 pounds.
Maximum fuel: 2,134 gallons.

Status: This is a standard Italian bomber and has wide use.

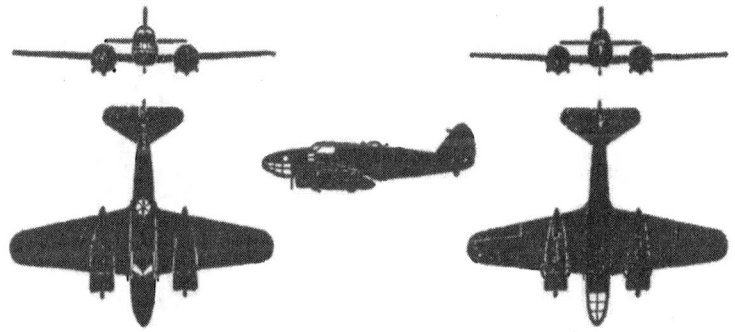

FIGURE 156.—CA-310, *Libéccio* (Southwest Wind), reconnaissance bomber.

Performance:
Maximum speed: 230 miles per hour at 13,120 feet.
Range: 1,100 miles at 196 miles per hour.
Climb: 1,000 feet per minute (initial).
Service ceiling: 25,000 feet.

RESTRICTED

Offensive and defensive equipment:
  Bombs: 880 pounds.
  Armament: Five 7.7-mm machine guns.
Power plant: Two 460-horsepower, 7-cylinder, air-cooled engines (Piaggio P VII C35).

Characteristics:
  Span: 53 feet 2 inches.
  Length: 40 feet.
  Wing area: 416 square feet.
  Construction: Wood wings; steel tube; fuselage fabric covered.
  Empty weight: 6,730 pounds.
  Gross weight: 10,250 pounds.
  Status: Used in Libya.

FIGURE 157.—CA-311, reconnaissance bomber.

Performance:
  Maximum speed: 258 miles per hour.
  Range: 1,240 miles at 218 miles per hour.
  Service ceiling: 27,300 feet.

Offensive and defensive equipment:
  Bomb load: ?
  Armament: One 7.7-machine gun (fixed).
  Two 7.7-machine guns (flexible).
Power plant: Two 650-horsepower engines (Piaggio P XIV).
Characteristics:
  Empty weight: 7,550 pounds.
  Gross weight: 12,390 pounds.

FIGURE 158.—SM-82, *Canguru* (Kangaroo), transport.

Performance:
  Maximum speed: 230 miles per hour at 8,200 feet.
  Range: 1,350 miles at 143 miles per hour (1,000 pounds of bombs).
  Climb: 650 feet per minute.
  Service ceiling: 17,000 feet.
Offensive and defensive equipment:
  Bombs: 6,600 pounds (maximum).
  Armament: One 12.7-mm machine gun (power turret).
  Three 7.7-mm machine guns (top).
Power plant: Three 860-horsepower, 9-cylinder air-cooled engines (Alfa-Romeo 128 RC 21).

Characteristics:
 Span: 97 feet 6 inches.
 Length: 73 feet 6 inches.
 Wing area: 1,276 square feet.
 Construction: Wood wings; fabric covered metal fuselage.
 Empty weight: 22,000 pounds.
 Gross weight: 39,700 pounds.
 Maximum fuel: 1,470 gallons.
 Status: Longest range Italian airplane; used extensively for transport service.

FIGURE 159.—SM-85, dive bomber.

Performance:
 Maximum speed: 317 miles per hour.
 Range: ?
 Service ceiling: ?

Offensive and defensive equipment:
 Armament: One 12.7-mm machine gun (fixed).

Power plant: Two 1,000-horsepower engines (Piaggio P X RC 40).

AIR FORCE   276

FIGURE 160.—Cant. Z–506B, *Airone* (Heron), flying boat.

Performance:
    Maximum speed: 236 miles per hour at 13,120 feet.
    Range: 1,240 miles at 199 miles per hour.
    Climb: 13,120 feet within 13 minutes.
    Service ceiling: 24,500 feet.
Offensive and defensive equipment:
    Bombs: Bombs or torpedo.
    Armament: One 12.7-mm machine gun (power turret).
        Three 7.7-mm machine guns (bottom).
Power plant: Three 750-horsepower, 9-cylinder air-cooled engines (Alfa-Romeo 126 RC 34).
Characteristics:
    Span: 87 feet 1 inch.
    Length: 62 feet.
    Wing area: 936 square feet.
    Construction: All wood except for metal floats.
    Empty weight: 18,300 pounds.
    Gross weight: 26,750 pounds.
    Maximum fuel: 1,100 gallons.
Status: In use over the Mediterranean.

RESTRICTED

Figure 161.—Cant. Z-501, flying boat.

Performance:
    Maximum speed: 171 miles per hour at 8,200 feet.
    Range: 1.500 miles at 150 miles per hour.
    Climb: 650 feet per minute (initial).
    Service ceiling: 16,000 feet.

Offensive and defensive equipment:
    Armament: Two 7.7-mm machine guns (flexible; nacelle).
    One 7.7-mm machine gun (flexible; nose).
    One 7.7-mm machine gun (flexible top).

Power plant: One 970-horsepower, 12-cylinder liquid-cooled engine (Isotta; Fraschini Asso XIRC).

Characteristics:
- Span: 73 feet 10 inches.
- Length: 46 feet 9 inches.
- Wing area: 667 square feet.
- Construction: Wood frame; fabric and wood covered.
- Empty weight: 8,500 pounds.
- Gross weight: 12,500 pounds.
- Maximum fuel: 900 gallons.
- Status: A standard naval reconnaissance airplane.

FIGURE 162.—RE-2001, *Falco II* (Falcon), fighter.

Performance:
- Maximum speed: 360 miles per hour (estimate).
- Service ceiling: 34,000 feet.

Offensive and defensive equipment:
- Armament: Two 12.7-mm machine guns (wing). Two 7.7-mm machine guns.

Power plant: One 1,150-horsepower, 12-cylinder liquid-cooled engine (Daimler Benz DB 601A).

Characteristics:
- Construction: All metal.
- Comment: A variation of the "RE 2000."
- Status: Newest Italian fighter.

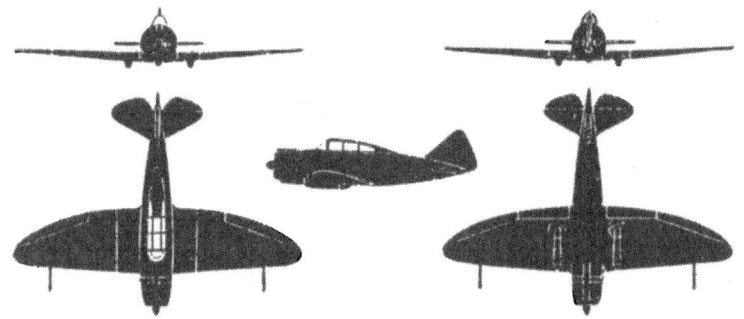

FIGURE 163.—RE-2000, *Falco I* (Falcon), fighter.

Performance:
  Maximum speed: 329 miles per hour at 13,120 feet.
  Range: 620 miles at 299 miles per hour.
  Climb: 2,750 feet per minute (initial).
  Service ceiling: 32,000 feet.

Offensive and defensive equipment: One 1,000-horsepower, 14-cylinder, air-cooled engine (Piaggio PXIRC 40).

Characteristics:
  Span: 36 feet 9 inches.
  Length: 26 feet
  Wing area: 235 square feet.
  Construction: All metal.
  Empty weight: 4,400 pounds.
  Gross weight: 5,800 pounds.

Status: This plane and Re 2001 have been reputed to be Italy's best.

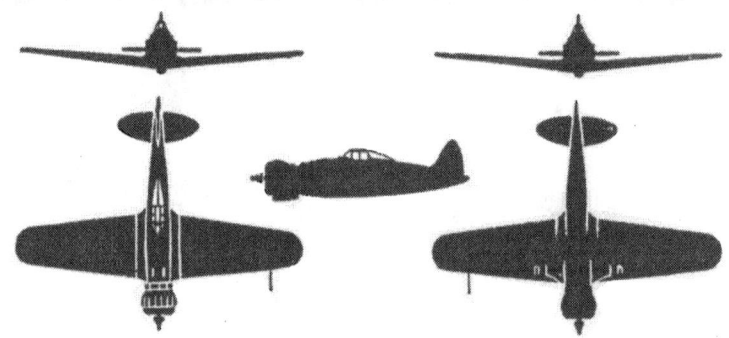

FIGURE 164.—MC-200, *Saetta* (Thunderbolt), fighter.

Performance:
  Maximum speed: 313 miles per hour at 15,760 feet.
  Range: 435 miles at 280 miles per hour.
  Climb: 3,100 feet per minute.
  Service ceiling: 33,000 feet.

Offensive and defensive equipment:
  Armament: Two 12.7-mm machine guns (synchronized).

Power plant: One 840-horsepower, 14-cylinder, air-cooled engine (Fiat A74 RC 38).

Characteristics:
  Span: 34 feet 8 inches.
  Length: 26 feet 10 inches.
  Wing area: 180 square feet.
  Construction: All metal.
  Empty weight: 3,910 pounds.
  Gross weight: 5,440 pounds.
  Maximum fuel: 163 gallons.

Status: Standard, being used to a great extent.

RESTRICTED

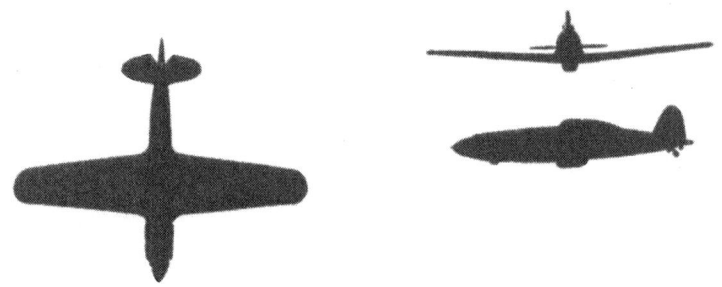

FIGURE 165.—MC-202, *Saetta II* (Thunderbolt), fighter.

Performance:
  Maximum speed: 360 miles per hour (estimated).
  Range: 425 miles.
  Service ceiling: 35,000 feet.

Offensive and defensive equipment:
  Bombs: Two 200-pound bombs.
  Armament: Two 12.7-mm machine guns (fixed).
    Four 7.7-mm machine guns.
    One 23-mm cannon or
    Two 7.7-mm machine guns.

Power plant: One engine, Daimler Benz 601A.A.

FIGURE 166.—MC-205, fighter. (This fighter resembles the MC-202 in appearance.)

b. Supply system.—(1) At the time Italy joined the Axis, there were 12 central supply depots organized throughout Italy at which were stored and issued reserve aircraft, engines, and parts for all types of service aircraft. These depots were located at Ghadi, Malpensa, Parma, Sesti Calendo, Taliedo, Lonate Pozzolo, Bologna, Montecelio, Naples, Bari, Palermo, and Cagliari. In addition, there was one central depot at Tripoli, supplying all units stationed in Libya, and six central depots in East Africa, supplying units stationed in that Territory.

(2) Also, supply activities were located as follows:

Central depot for fuel and lubricant	Ciampino (Rome)
Special flight equipment depot	Ciampino (Rome)
Miscellaneous supplies such as tools, fabrics, etc.	Poggio Renático
Photographic supply depot	Montecelio (Rome)
Armament depot	Acquasanta (Rome)
Meteorological supply depot	Centocelle (Rome)
Airplane and automobile spare depot	Ciampino (Rome)
Experimental store depot	Montecelio (Rome)
Construction material depot	Rome
School supply depot	Caserta
Radio supply depot	Rome

(3) Further local storehouses were organized at available fields in Italy, and magazines at seaplane bases were established. In addition, there was a large number of underground depots for the storage of fuel and bombs. Repair shops for the overhaul of airplanes and engines existed at the more important air bases.

277. Equipment.—*a. Aircraft.*—Figures 152 to 165, inclusive, illustrate and describe briefly some of the aircraft assigned to combat units in the Italian Air Force. For all the aircraft in operational use see fig. 149.

b. Armament.—(1) *Guns.*—Fire power has been increased only in the case of new four-engined bombers and on some standard torpedo planes which have had additional guns installed. It is believed that no guns larger that .50 caliber are carried. Information has been received, however, that cannon are installed on the Brada Ba-88 and Fabricci 5. On the four-engined bombers, automatically-operated wing guns firing to the rear and capable of cross-fire are used, but this method must inevitably produce certain blind spots in the control section arc.

(2) *Bombs.*—(*a*) *Common types.*—Fighter and attack planes carry 4.4 bombs. Army cooperation planes have provision for 77-pound and 33-pound bombs. In heavy bombardment a variable load is carried which in most instances comprise: 10 each, 220-pound; 4 each, 1,100-pound; one each, 1,760-pound; or one each, 2,200-pound bomb. Italy is reported to be experimenting with a 3,300-pound bomb.

(*b*) *4.5-kg. (10-lb.) thermos bomb.*—This bomb, or hand grenade, 13.5 inches long and 3.5 inches in diameter, resembles a thermos bottle. It is filled with TNT, and is painted black and khaki and has two brass rings around its nose. The bomb is fitted with a very sensitive fuze which becomes operative about 30 seconds after impact and will then be discharged by a vibration or disturbance. It is intended primarily for use on airdromes. The method of clearance is by means of a heavy cable or chain dragged between two suitably protected vehicles; it can also be destroyed by small-arms fire from a minimum range of 50 yards.

(3) *Fuzes.*—The standard fuze for HE bombs appears to be of the inertia type with needle strikers to pierce small detonators, which in turn operate the main detonator and exploder. Fuzing is usually in the tail only, but the 160-kg antisubmarine bomb appears to have both nose and tail fuzing. Arming vanes are fitted. A feature of the standard fuze is the provision of two strikers and two small detonators, apparently to give a double assurance of functioning.

(4) *Sights.*—Bomb sights have not been brought up to date. The Italian pilot relies on dropping a stick of medium or small bombs, hoping in this manner to make hits. He does not attempt more accurate bombing with heavier bombs.

(5) *Turrets.*—The majority of observation, bombardment, attack, and multiple-engined fighters are equipped with hydraulically operated turrets, or tourelles. The Italians assert that the "lag" which was a difficulty in older hydraulic types, has been eliminated in the new equipment. No attempt has been made to install power turrets in the tail of bombardment aircraft.

(6) *Technical development.*—The Italians apparently prefer to produce types already in service, for which plants are tooled, rather than to attempt new designs requiring planning and retooling. Some modifications on standard types have been made to meet war demands, but these changes have not materially increased the defensive characteristics of the planes. Because of lack of steel, little thought has been given to armor protection for crews, which exists only in a few models of service aircraft. There have been increases in fighter and bomber speeds, bomb loads, and, in some cases, fire power, but there has been nothing to indicate that the Italians have been able to produce airplanes which can compare with those employed by the British. The fastest Italian airplane is said to be 95 to 125 miles per hour slower than United States, British, or German types.

278. Training.—*a. Preaeronautical training.*—Every Italian child between the ages of 6 and 20, inclusive, is compelled by law to belong to the *Gioventù Italiana del Littório*, or *G. I. L.* Preaeronautical training begins in the elementary schools and includes model airplane construction; flying model construction; elementary courses in aviation; glider instruction; training and instruction in the mechanical trades; and flying instruction leading to a brevet as a tourist plane pilot.

b. Training of regular officers.—Regular officers are obtained from graduates of the Royal Aeronautical Academy, to which cadets are admitted at the age of 19 by competitive examination. The course extends over a period of 3 years, during which students receive 100 hours of flight training. The cadets are awarded brevets as military pilots on graduation, and before the war, were posted to the Advanced Aeronautical School at Florence for another year, where 50 additional hours were flown. The Advanced School at Florence has been closed for the duration of the war and second lieutenants now go directly to tactical units from the academy.

c. Training of reserve officers, noncommissioned officers, and enlisted men.—(1) When the *Gióvani Fascisti*, or *G. F.*, advanced group of the *G. I. L.*, are called up for active military service (at the age of 21 years), a selection of complementary, or reserve, officers, noncommissioned officers, and enlisted men is made from those who have had preaeronautical training.

(2) Reserve officer pilots are obtained from those *G. F.* who have been granted a license in gliding or have qualified as a tourist plane pilot and who have at least a high-school education. Those with less than a high-school education are appointed noncommissioned officers. Specialization courses lead to a noncommissioned specialist rating, while those who pursued only the general training course become enlisted men.

(3) Boys who pursue courses in glider training but who do not receive a brevet as a tourist pilot are assigned on a selective basis to one of the primary flying schools where a 3-month course and 50 hours in the air leads to a brevet as an airplane pilot.

(4) After another 3 months at an advanced flying school with an additional 50 hours in the air, a brevet as military pilot is granted. At the conclusion of the latter course, an examination is given and on the basis of the grade he achieves, the candidate receives either a commission as second lieutenant or a rating as a noncommissioned officer.

(5) Those who secure brevets as tourist pilots are assigned directly to an advanced flying school, after which a period of 18 months' duty in a tactical unit is served. At the end of this tour, those who have not been transferred to the regular officers' list return home and become reserves, subject to annual refresher courses.

(6) Noncommissioned personnel follow the same course, except that they enlist for 4 years, at the end of which they may reenlist or return to civil life, participating in annual refresher courses.

(7) Nonflying specialists are called to duty as noncommissioned officers at the age of 21. They take advanced courses and on graduation enlist for 30 months. At the end of the period, they may reenlist or return to civil life on reserve status, with annual refresher courses. Those who reenlist may, by promotion, reach the rank of captain in the Specialist Branch.

d. Schools.—(1) Prepilot courses are given at Punticello and S. Caterina.

(2) Primary Flying Schools are located at Como, Lido di Roma-Cantù, Parma, Taiedo, Falconara, Rímini, Centocelle, Pisa, Foligno, Firenze, Grosseto, Arezzo, Lucca, Siena, Naples, Bari, Pescara, and Elmas.

(3) Advanced Flying Schools are located at Portorose, Cameri, Aviano, Malpensa, Orvieto, Novara, Fóggia, Grottáglie, and Castiglion del Lago.

(4) The Royal Aeronautical Academy has flying schools at Caserta and Cápua.

(5) The Advanced Aeronautical School is at Florence.

(6) The School of Aerial Warfare is at Rome.

(7) Pursuit Schools are at Foligno, Passignano, and Castiglión del Lago.

(8) The Air Bombing and Gunnery Schools are at Malpensa, Mestre, Perúgia, Aviano, and Augusta.

(9) Observation Schools for Army and Navy officers are at Cervetéri and Táranto.

(10) The Blind and Night Flying School is at Littória.

(11) The Parachute School is at Viterbo.

(12) The Torpedo School is at Spézia.

(13) Specialist Schools for mechanics, riggers, etc., are at Cápua, Naples, and Bologna.

e. Unit training.—Training of combat units is conducted by directive to wing commanders. A shortage of aviation gasoline has been evident for some time and has curtailed both combat and training activities.

f. System of promotion for officers.—Promotion is by arm and corps for each branch and category. Promotion to first lieutenant is by seniority; from first lieutenant to lieutenant colonel, inclusive, by selection and seniority; and above the grade of lieutenant colonel, by selection. Either the regular or the special course at the School of Aerial Warfare is a requirement for promotion above the grade of captain. (For a chart showing the ranks of Air Force officers and their approximate equivalents, see fig. 35.)

g. Flying pay.—Flying personnel of the armed forces receive additional flight pay. For officer pilots, the rate of pay is 900 lire per month, which increases to 1,000 lire per month after 15 years of flying duty, and to 1,100 lire per month after 20 years of flying duty. In addition, the Air Ministry issues insurance for permanent disability or death as a result of flying accidents in the line of duty. Pensions, depending upon the degree of disability and rank of the person injured, are also provided by law.

279. Camouflage of airdromes and aircraft.—*a. Satellite airdromes.*—Wide use of satellite airdromes has been made by the Italians to conceal the strength and position of operational bases. These are constructed in the vicinity of the main airdrome. At stations subject to air attack, squadron personnel fly their aircraft to the satellite airdromes in the early morning and remain there until evening. All precautions against detection are taken, including the covering of boundary marks and aircraft with brush, scrub, and camouflage netting.

b. Dummy aircraft.—Aerial photographs have revealed the use of dummy aircraft on Italian airdromes to lure the enemy into expending bombs and ammunition and to conceal the fact that the airdromes have been evacuated.

c. Airdrome buildings.—The standard method of camouflage is the application of matte green and red paint to the buildings in a large pattern with no sharp edges.

d. Dummy fires.—The Italians light bundles of hay or ignite a powder called *Volpi*, which produces clouds of dense smoke, to give the impression of a successful air raid.

e. Bomb and fuel dumps.—In concealing bomb and fuel dumps, use is made of natural camouflage. Fuel is stored in camouflaged drums and further camouflaged to resemble thickets. Though it is difficult to detect the dumps, detection is not impossible, if it is remembered that they are usually square in plan and that at each corner is usually a small tower for guards.

Chapter 8
TACTICS

	Paragraphs
SECTION I. Doctrine	280–284
II. Principles of employment	285–288

SECTION I
DOCTRINE

	Paragraph
General	280
Combined action	281
Security	282
Meeting engagements	283
Attack and pursuit	284

280. General.—*a. "War of Rapid Decision."*—During the past 20 years, the Italian Army has been developing a new military doctrine, which is called by its General Staff the "War of Rapid Decision." Its chief features are—

(1) Fast-moving divisions, designed for exploitation and reconnaissance.

(2) Tank brigades, designed for penetration, encirclement, and exploitation.

(3) Motorized divisions, designed for rapid maneuver over a wide range and for the reinforcement of mechanized or fast-moving units. This new doctrine emphasizes that surprise, speed, intensity, sustained action, and flexibility of plan allowing for unforeseen contingencies are the basic factors for a successful action.[1]

b. Main policies.—In an effort to obtain the requirements for

---
[1] Italian staff studies and war plans have apparently laid no stress upon the defensive, the assumption being that offensive action against Italian troops was a remote possibility. Recent Italian military history demonstrates the inadequacy of a purely offensive war machine.

victory, the Italian combat effort has become predicated upon the following policies:

(1) Enormously increased fire power.

(2) Opposition to hostile fire by combined fire and movement.

(3) Direction of fire mass against the sector of least resistance to achieve rapid penetration and to permit subsequent flanking movement.

(4) Simultaneous fire and movement with supporting artillery fire to neutralize enemy effort.

(5) Substantially independent exercise of command except as regards reserve employment and artillery support.

c. Comparison of doctrines.—Italian tactical and strategic doctrine is not materially different from that of any other modern army. There has been an obvious effort to pattern the Italian strategy and tactics after those of Germany but this has proved only partially successful. Discussion in this chapter is mainly confined to Italian enunciation of strategic and tactical principles which differ more or less from those common to all military students.

281. Combined action.—A primary element of the Italian doctrine is the combined employment of various arms, particularly infantry and artillery.[2] Italian infantry is designed to be used in small, flexible, highly maneuverable units of great fire power. Each forward echelon, upon achieving a break-through, is followed by reinforcements for purposes of exploitation. Mobility and maneuverability comprise the fundamental characteristics of Italian artillery. Closely allied to the artillery's mission to support the infantry is the secondary mission of engaging in counterbattery firing. Cavalry maneuver is mounted, but combat may be mounted or dismounted. Mechanization of the cavalry has resulted in increased mobility and fire power. This has added, for the first time, the element of fire mass to the common cavalry

---

[2] Little consideration was given by the Italians to the possibility of employing aircraft as a substitute for artillery. Even now the unsuitability of Italian aircraft for such missions prevents its full utilization as a supporting arm.

missions of reconnaissance and exploitation. Italian engineers, although armed, are more concerned with normal engineer functions and less concerned with combat than in other modern armies.

282. Security.—Basing their policy upon the German principle that "action is the first protection," the Italians aim at security through offense and penetration. Intelligence, camouflage, and similar means of attaining security are regarded as preliminaries to offensive penetration. Security measures are not merely supposed to guard against surprise by the enemy, but are also supposed to be so planned as to enable the Italian commander to inflict on the enemy a surprise of his own. Italian leaders are urged not to let security measures betray them into undue caution, which might slow up the forward drive of an action. On the contrary, daring is thought to be quite as important as security. Major Umberto Mascia observes: "It is not sufficient to avoid surprise; a complete freedom of action must also be guaranteed." Nevertheless the Italians keep a somewhat greater distance between the advance guard and main body than the Germans do.

283. Meeting engagements.—*a. General.*—Meeting engagements, as distinct from mere preliminary engagements or patrol actions to test the enemy's strength and determine his weak points, are regarded by the Italians as a matter of rapid, aggressive action. It is believed such engagements will occur only in the case of relatively small forces, for Italian military theory denies the possibility of surprise in modern warfare, at least on any considerable scale. As Major Mascia remarks, the Italians "do not admit that a sudden and unplanned clash can occur between sizable forces." In other words, proper reconnaissance must always reveal the presence of large enemy units.[3]

b. Doctrine.—The Italians believe that their system successfully combines the best features of both French and German tactics. It is supposed to provide for "both conceptions—planned collision

---

[3] In view of the complete surprise of General Wavell's first attack on Marshall Graziani, it is obvious that the Italian Army, like other armies, finds its main difficulty in applying theories rather than in evolving them.

and swift and precise intervention with decidedly aggressive behavior." The commander is urged to "take the initiative in operations and attack with decision, seeking victory in swiftness of movements, in direction, in immediacy and power of impact." Actually, the Italians have rarely succeeded in doing anything of the sort, though a military historian might conceivably assert that Graziani's initial advance into Egypt owed its success to application of these principles.

284. **Attack and pursuit.**—Italian ideas of attack and pursuit are much like those of any other modern army, though the emphasis placed on the offensive almost recalls the pre-1914 doctrines of the French Colonel de Grandmaison. The 1940 Italian doctrine provided that the attack was to be recklessly pressed, was never to halt, and was to "overcome the resistance with continuity of effort." But the almost hysterical appeals for initiative, violence, and audacity on the part of Italian troops have not enabled them to approach German effectiveness in attack and pursuit. As for "continuity of effort," one Greek tactical authority with much experience in the Albanian campaign against Italy declares that an obvious characteristic of all Italian attacks was their extreme brevity and the failure of officers rather than men to "follow through." It became almost a proverb in the Greek Army that an Italian attack was certain to flag after the first 20 minutes. A Greek unit which had successfully sustained an attack for that length of time, usually felt that it had for all practical purposes already won. This was not, of course, what the Italian tacticians had taught. "The Italian military doctrine of the present," wrote Major Umberto Mascia in 1939, "reaffirms the reasoning which was Caesar's and Machiavelli's: the offensive, because only the offensive can bring victory. There is a return to the Roman concept, to the Latin and Italian spirit, because those qualities which bring success—a sense of responsibility and the willingness to meet danger—are peculiarly Italian, manly in courage and daring in spirit, ready to overcome difficulties. To

take the offensive means to attack, to go forward, to force one's will on the enemy, and in this direction the mental, moral, and material preparation of all is turned toward an ever greater formation of the offensive consciousness." The actual performance of the Italian Army in the present war has, of course, often fallen short of this high standard.

Section II

PRINCIPLES OF EMPLOYMENT

	Paragraph
Resistance	285
Infantry	286
Artillery	287
Armored forces in offensive operations	288

285. Resistance.—*a.* The German belief that a concentration of force against the enemy's main defensive position is unnecessary is not wholly shared by the Italians. The Italian teaching is that a commander should concentrate his fire power on such a position whenever it is encountered. It is the Italian view that such action imposes on the commander merely a temporary pause in a "position of arrest"—a mere lull in his sustained offensive movement. Otherwise, Italian tactics discourage any assumption of a static position.

b. When the Italians are compelled to assume the defensive in a position of resistance, they hope to resume the offensive at the earliest possible moment—a doctrine common to most armies. "Defense does not mean giving up the resumption of movement as soon as possible." The main line of resistance is removed as far as possible from the enemy's artillery fire, and the Italians endeavor to establish a "zone of security" with a depth ranging from 2,000 to 3,500 yards. In this area, utilizing all footholds that the terrain may offer, they organize holding positions. These deliver long-range fire, especially along the easiest routes of penetration, with a view to wearing the enemy down before coming to grips with him.

286. Infantry.—*a. General.*—The Italian ideal of the employment of infantry presupposes the possibility of an attack undivided into principal and auxiliary actions. Supposedly sufficient elasticity may be maintained to direct the effort to those points where success appears best assured upon initial contact.

b. Infantry division.—The infantry division is the basic large combat unit and is designed particularly for impact and penetration. It has a fixed table of organization and is considered to be an indivisible unit. Whenever its strength must be made more adequate for accomplishing its mission, superior commands are expected to assign the required additional equipment and personnel.

287. Artillery.—*a. General.*—It is planned that Italian artillery shall be divided into echelons: the first to operate in direct support of the infantry battalions of the first echelon; the second to act generally as a reserve for the purpose of lateral extension of the line or depth. Depth in echelon is sought for the purpose of increasing shock and penetration, almost to the point of risking the maintenance of a sufficiently strong front.

b. Division artillery.—The division artillery commander regulates the employment of artillery except in counterbattery and interdiction. Decentralization of command for these functions is designed to expedite rapid and effective action, and thus contribute to the desired war of movement.

In defensive situations roving pieces are sent far forward of the main defense area in order to force the enemy to deploy and to execute counterbattery fire.

288. Armored forces in offensive operations.—*a. General.*—The Italian mechanized divisions are modeled after the German panzer divisions. They are designed, by virtue of their speed and power, to break through to the enemy rear, or to arrive first at critical terrain features. As a result of their experience in Spain, both the Italians and the Germans have recognized the need of motorized infantry and ordinary infantry to follow the

TACTICS   288

tanks and consolidate conquered ground. There are two types of
mechanized divisions in the Italian army, the fast-moving, or
light motorized division (*célere*), and the armored division
(*corazzata*).

  b. Mobile (cavalry) division (divisione célere).—In general,
the *célere* division fulfills the mission formerly assigned to cavalry,
that is, reconnaissance and covering missions. In addition, it
has the mission of seizure of certain terrain features of strategical
importance.

  c. Armored division (divisione corazzata).—The armored division has the primary mission of break-through and is only
slightly adaptable to other uses. In this division, artillery is
echeloned in great depth, with patrols projected far forward.

  d. Tank units.—Tank units of the Italian Army are designed
to serve primarily as a basic shock element and in support of the
infantry arm. In this respect, reconnaissance missions may be
assigned as a particular task for light tanks.

Chapter 9
PERMANENT FORTIFICATIONS

	Paragraph
General principles	289
General description of Alpine Line	290
Po—Ádige—Tagliamento Line	291
Frontier Guard (*Guárdia alla Frontiera*, or *G. a. F.*)	292
Army, Navy and Air Force responsibilities	293
Coast defense installations	294

289. General principles.—*a.* By territorial acquisition following World War I, and by frontier fortification, Italy has sought to bar the traditional roads of invasion from the north and northwest. The fixed fortifications of the northern frontiers were intended to give insular security. The sea frontiers were to be protected by strong naval and air power in addition to coastal defenses.

b. Following the principle of organization of terrain in depth to the greatest extent practicable, extensive use is made of obstacles, and the covering of obstacles and terrain with fire. The Italian fortifications differ from the German and Russian defenses in depth because of their rugged mountainous environment, which in many cases necessitates expensive excavations and roads. Individual positions, although more costly and difficult in preparation, tend to be relatively stronger because of greater topographic prominence and command over rugged natural barriers.

290. General description of Alpine Line.—*a.* The fortifications known as *Il Vallo Alpino del Littorio* (the Alpine Fortifications of the Lictor) may be referred to simply as the Alpine Line. The complete system follows a great semicircle through the Alps from the Mediterranean Sea near Ventimiglia to the Adriatic Sea near Fiume. Fortifications face the German frontier as well as the French, Swiss, and Yugoslav borders. Construction began over 10 years ago and was evidently continued as recently as the spring of 1942. At that time—possibly because of Hitler's protests—work ceased on the section facing Austria, and it is probable that work on the sectors facing Switzerland and France has not been continued at full speed. The presence of Italian troops in French Savoy decreases the importance of the sector of fortifications in this area.

b. Italy's land frontier totals 1,851 km: namely, French, 487 km; Swiss, 724 km; German, 420 km; and Yugoslav, 220 km.

(1) *French-Italian frontier.*—Along the French-Italian frontier the topographical advantages favor the French. Because the mountains were, before the present war, almost entirely in the possession of the French and because the frontier describes an arc, the general direction of the road net converges toward the plains of Lombardy and diverges from the Rhone River. Because of the narrowness of the mountain strip within Italy, Italian fortifications are practically all located on one line.

(2) *Swiss-Italian frontier.*—The Swiss-Italian frontier extends along the high crest of the Alps, but on the Swiss side there is a greater depth of mountains and more dominating positions. Elaborate stone and cement "cowsheds" have been constructed by the Italian Government and are actually leased to cowherders. These are said to be suitable for use as barracks, in both summer and winter.

(3) *German-Italian frontier.*—Italy's 1914 Austrian frontier was about 674 km long. From a military point of view it was extremely unfavorable to Italy because the Austrians held practically all the passes and dominating positions. The present frontier with Germany is only 420 km long, and Italy holds most of the key points. Italian defenses are said to be especially strong in the vicinity of Brenner Pass where four lines exist, the fourth being in the vicinity of Trento, 100 km south of Brenner Pass. The most recent Italian fortification construction, ap-

parently still in progress in 1941-42, has been along the Swiss and German borders, and the line is jocularly referred to as the "we-have-no-faith-line."

(4) *Yugoslav-Italian frontier.*—On the Yugoslav-Italian frontier the mountains do not constitute a series barrier, and the topographical advantages and disadvantages are about the same for both nations. In the Tarvisio sector near the junction point of Yugoslav, German, and Italian borders, the defense works are constructed in a triple zone.

c. The arrangement of elements in the Alpine Line is irregular, taking advantage of local topographic and geologic features of terrain. The elements are constructed of thick, reinforced concrete, and house several heavy guns, as well as machine guns and antiaircraft guns. Bunkers above the ground as so situated as to utilize protection afforded by natural rock masses of the mountains. The forts, though camouflaged, are often distinguishable because of the mule paths leading to them. In addition to low forts with artillery emplacements covering the main passes, systems of land mines have been established. It is reported that entire mountains have been mined. Barbed-wire entanglements, covered by machine-gun pillboxes, have been constructed at passes. Along the Swiss and German borders, the fortifications have been excavated from solid rock. When several fortifications are located in the same mountain, they are connected by passageways through the solid rock.

291. *Po—Ádige—Tagliamento Line.*—In January 1943, a report was received of a new system of fortifications facing south. Some of the Brenner works are being transferred to serve as a reserve line for this new system, but the main line is said to be from Genoa down the Trébbia Valley to the Po, thence along the North bank of the Po to the Ostiglia. Thence the line runs overland to Legnano on the Ádige, and along the Ádige to the sea. The barrier islands off the coast from Chióggia to Carole are a part of this line also, including Venice's Lido Beach. The line then runs up the Tagliamento into the mountains. Such a line is of considerable military strength, but whether it is politically feasible to hold any line after giving up three-quarters of Italy is questionable.

292. Frontier Guard (*Guárdia alla Frontiera*, or G. a. F.).—*a.* Frontier Guards are responsible for fórtress duties previously carried out by the army corps stationed in the frontier districts. In 1939 Frontier Guards were formed into a special corps. Their tasks remained the defense of frontier districts; but whereas they were formerly only fortress artillery, the new organization gave them supporting arms, independence of action, and the primary task of acting as a covering force.

b. Frontier Guard headquarters attached to the headquarters of 11 army corps, are allotted a certain length of frontier divided into subsectors containing a varying number of fortified positions (*caposaldi*).

c. Personnel is provided mainly by the army corps, but infantry are also drawn from the Frontier Guard infantry regiment. The regiments and *raggruppamenti*, of Frontier Guard artillery are under the command of army corps Frontier Guard headquarters and reinforce, as required, the artillery units permanently allotted to sectors and subsectors.

d. A large part of the Frontier Guards in Northern Italy have been taken from frontier defense for coast defense in Southern Italy and the Mediterranean Islands. Others are employed on garrison duties in occupied territories in the Balkans.

293. Army, Navy, and Air Force responsibilities.—The coast defense of Italy is the responsibility of the Army, except in certain zones which are considered to be primarily of naval interest.

a. Naval jurisdiction in coast defense.—The following are the special zones and organizations:

(1) Navy yards or important naval bases (*piazze militari maríttime*):

(a) La Spezia.
(b) La Maddalena.
(c) Táranto.
(d) Bríndisi.
(e) Venice.
(f) Pola.

These installations are of relatively limited area. The Navy is in command and is completely responsible for defense.

(2) Naval defense zones (*zone militari maríttime*):
(a) Italian Aegean Islands.
(b) Tuscan Archipelago.
(c) Island of Saseno (off the Albanian coast).
(d) Island of Lagosta Cazza, etc. (off the Dalmatian coast).

These zones are almost entirely composed of groups of islands. The Navy is in command and is responsible for their defense. The armed forces assigned to the territorial defense of these zones are controlled during war by the flag officers and commandants of the zones themselves.

(3) Naval coastal sectors (*settori militari maríttime*):
(a) Cágliari (Sardinia).
(b) Trápani.
(c) Augusta Bay (Sicily).
(d) Messina Naval Station (Sicily).

These are important operating bases of the Navy serving as home and fueling stations. The Navy is completely responsible for their organization and administration. The Navy is also in charge of the close-in coast artillery, antiaircraft batteries, and the defense of the anchorages and plants of the bases themselves. They are under the direct command of the naval commanding officer. However, as they are situated on islands where there is a higher Army command, they come under this command in the event of a major coastal attack.

b. Army jurisdiction in coast defense.—(1) The Army is responsible for the defense of all coasts outside the areas specifically assigned to the Navy, including Italy proper, Sardinia, and Sicily. The Army furnishes, mans, and controls portable railway batteries of large caliber (8-inch mortars, 8-, 12-, and 15-inch guns). The Army furnishes, mans, and controls certain heavy permanent batteries within the limits of the areas assigned to the Navy. Such batteries are under the naval high command in the area. The Army mans and controls the Fortress of Messina located on both sides of the Straits of Messina.

(2) *Coast defense units.*—(*a*) Coastal troops are responsible for the defense of the Italian coast, the Mediterranean islands, and occupied territories. Identification has thus far been made of 17 divisions, 9 brigades, 72 to 75 regiments, and 575 to 590 battalions. The battalion, which is the basic unit in Italian coast defense, contains an estimated 600 to 800 men.

(*b*) The coastal divisions, which at first appeared to be administrative groupings of coastal and territorial battalions have now assumed a more definite establishment and more closely approach the organization of an ordinary field division. Machine-gun, mortar, antitank, and coast defense artillery units have been allotted to them, together with motor transport, engineers, and signal personnel sufficient to make them independent operational formations.

(*c*) Coast defense units are composed generally of low-category troops—men of low medical grade, men of older classes, and men who have served for long periods abroad. Recently, some attempt has been made to raise the standard of training and personnel in the coastal divisions in order that they might be better suited for the task of taking the initial shock of any invasion. Although much improved, they remain inferior in all respects to the first-line divisions.

c. Air Force in coast defense.—The Air Force contributes to coast defense by building, equipping, and manning seaplane observation group stations, which support the important naval bases of La Spézia, Táranto, Livorno (Leghorn), Venice, Pola,

Augusta Bay, Naples, and Cagliari. Also of potential support in coast defenses are the heavy seaplane bombing group stations at La Spezia, Orbetello, Trapani, Brindisi, Pola, and Rodi.

294. **Coast defense installations.**—*a. Calábria.*—The Calabrian coast from Amantea to Catanzaro has been fortified with medium caliber and machine-gun nests. Machine guns have been placed to control vital road junctions.

b. Naples.—(1) Entry through the mine fields to the Port of Naples is marked by green lights, the ship channel by red lights, and ship anchorages in white. The north coast is fully mined, and entrance is made south of the Island of Capri (1941).

(2) In 1935 a shore battery of three ships' turret guns (280-mm, or 11-inch) were installed at Naples on a shelf cut in Caijola Point directly behind and above Caijola Island. It is on a direct line ashore from the Cavallera shoal light buoy. One hundred feet above the battery a range-finder is located.

c. Génoa.—Batteries of 381-mm guns are located at Monte Morro, and of 6-inch guns at Monte Fascio and at Monte Righi.

d. Capo San Marco and Isola Mal di Ventre.—At these places (north of the Gulf of Oristano) there are installed naval coastal guns and 90-mm antiaircraft battery.

e. Capo Marrargiu.—Batteries of 90-mm antiaircraft guns have been installed.

f. Capo Pécora.—Batteries of 90-mm antiaircraft guns have been installed.

g. Because of a lack of 90-mm antiaircraft guns in Italy, 76-mm antiaircraft guns have been installed at the following centers:

(1) Capo Falcone.
(2) Capo di Frasca.
(3) Capo Teulada.
(4) Capo Cáccia.
(5) Isola di San Pietro.
(6) Capo Mannu.
(7) Isola di San Antíoco.

PERMANENT FORTIFICATIONS

h. West coast.—Italy has shown great concern about the fortification of the West Coast and the Tirso basin. Electrical installations of major importance have been made. The batteries of the Tirso zone are placed in the following localities:

(1) Macomer.
(2) Ponte Arata.
(3) Ghilarza.
(4) Colle del Tirso.
(5) Atzara.

The listening sound stations function efficiently (1941).

i. Sardinia.—A large quantity of motorized artillery of 152 mm is located in Sardinia.

j. Sicily (Mondello).—Guns of large caliber (6- or 8-inch) with very short barrel and apparently mounted in a revolving turret were sited approximately 200 feet above sea level. They were camouflaged by green and brown paint, with foundations of rocks that give appearance of ordinary stone walls.

k. Sicily (Palermo).—In 1939 there was a battery of four guns of 210-mm. In 1935 two batteries of 75-mm Ansaldo and 76-mm Armstrong guns were mounted on the north mole in Palermo harbor, just south of the lighthouse along the eastern side of the sea wall.

l. Sicily (Monte San Giuliano near Trápani).—Several large batteries of the largest caliber coast defense rifles (estimated at 16-inch). Air raid shelters are provided for the garrison.

m. Sicily (Augusta Submarine Base).—The base is defended by heavy guns of extreme range. Fortifications are on Monte Tauro, Peninsula Magnini, and Capo S. Panagni, north of Siracuso.

n. Sicily (Monte Pellegrino, near Palermo).—Naval guns of about 10-inch caliber are sited on a solid rock mountain (606 meters above sea level).

o. Brindisi.—In 1934 coast defenses consisted of four 381-mm guns, two in position north of the harbor and two in position south.

RESTRICTED

Also twenty-four 152-mm guns were placed in batteries of 4, plus two 102-mm antiaircraft guns for each battery (or a total of 16 antiaircraft guns). Ammunition storage was about 300 yards behind each 381-mm battery (underground). The barracks for gun crews were about 80 feet in rear of battery.

p. Trieste (at the fort of Krekich).—Naval guns of heavy caliber are installed.

q. Trieste (at Monte Spaccato).—Naval guns of heavy caliber are sited at an elevation of 405 meters directly overlooking Trieste.

r. Trieste—Monfalcone.—Floating guns are stationed in the Gulf of Panzano and motorized long range guns utilize the motor road.

s. Straits of Messina.—The Straits are well fortified on both sides; about 30 guns of 305-mm, or greater caliber are in position.

t. Bari.—Fortified by (12- to 15-inch) guns.

u. Anzio.—Guns from 8- to 12-inch caliber are installed.

v. There are also fortifications important but of unknown extent, in the following places:
  (1) Cape Paffas, Greece (at entrance to Gulf of Corinth).
  (2) At entrance to Saronic Gulf, on the north shore.
  (3) On Rhodes Island, principally near the town of Rhodes.
  (4) On Leros Island, principally facing the Turkish mainland.

Chapter 10
CAMOUFLAGE

	Paragraph
General	295
Field camouflage	296
Individual nets	297
Metal net supports	298
Dummy strawstack to hide machine-gunners and riflemen	299
Simulative cloaks	300
Lookouts concealed in dummy bales of straw	301
Exposure and camouflage of observation posts	302
Telegraph and telephone lines	303
Machine-gun camouflage	304
Barbed-wire entanglements	305

295. General.—The Italians place great emphasis on artificial camouflage and installations garnished with natural materials and tied into the natural surroundings.

296. Field camouflage.—*a.* In Italian field camouflage, canvas, raffia, shavings, and similar materials are colored with a spray gun, which is both quick and convenient as compared with the usual paintbrush method. This field spraying is done with compressed air in a special blower. The compressed air may be furnished from a shoulder-portable compressor or from compressed air tanks, periodically filled.

b. Machine guns are camouflaged by being covered with wire netting stretched over a frame of iron rods. The weight of material to camouflage a machine-gun position is given as follows:

5 by 5 m garnished net	3.8 kg.
3 metal frames	6.75 kg.
Wire	0.5 kg.
Total	11.05 kg.

Bunches of hay are fastened to the netting with twine.

297. **Individual nets.**—Individual camouflage nets are 1 to 80 m square, with reinforced edges furnished with buttons and garnished with strips of sisal (hemp) material colored with three shades of green and two of maroon.

298. **Metal net supports.**—The metal frames for overhead cover are made in two sizes, with spans of 1.50 meters or 4 to 5 meters. The smaller frame is made of flat metal and weighs 2.2 kg. The larger is made of tubular metal and weighs 2.25 kg. Both sizes consist of collapsible span sections and two end pickets. The pickets of the smaller type are fixed to the outside span section. Those of the larger type are mounted on a tubular collar which slides on the outside section, giving a variable span. Both types collapse into compact bundles.

299. **Dummy strawstack to hide machine-gunners and riflemen.**—*a.* The dummy strawstack consists of a frame of wooden poles, joined at their upper extremity around a central post like the ribs of an umbrella. On this frame is wrapped a spiral strip of jute fabric 25 meters long with bunches of hay or straw sewn on. This strip is fastened to the poles with large-headed tacks. In the lower part of the strawstack an opening is left as an entrance for the men.

b. The Italians contemplate the use of these simulations in meadows or grain fields where it is natural to find haystacks, shocks of cut grain, etc. The strawstack, as illustrated, can conceal 15 men and can be moved short distances without attracting the enemy's attention. The Italians state that 10 trained men can build this strawstack in 1 hour. It is made of the following materials: 8 poles, 1 post of greater length, 25 meters of jute fabric, half a hundredweight of hay or straw, and tacks, string, and iron wire.

300. **Simulative cloaks.**—*a.* The simulative cloak is used by the Italian Army as an aid for the combatant who must remain on observation duty or must advance under the eye of the adversary. A man disguised by such a cloak becomes invisible, even

on barren ground, and so can accomplish his mission unmolested, even at a short distance from the enemy. The cloak is easily made by the Italian soldier and has been produced even with improvised materials by the combatant himself. It consists of a rectangular piece of burlap (jute fabric) 1.80 meters long and 1.50 meters wide. The rectangle is folded along a line and sewn along the upper edge to form a hood easily worn by the soldier, without hindering his freedom of movement.

b. To blend readily with the surroundings, the cloak is covered with hay, grass, straw, etc., depending on what is available in the particular region, and on what background is to be imitated. This cloak may be used to conceal telegraph-line guards, men stationed near roads, liaison men, etc.

301. Lookouts concealed in dummy bales of straw.—*a.* Each bale of straw consists of a wooden framework, made of two frames fastened together by strong slats so as to obtain a rectangular parallelopiped 60 by 60 by 160 cm. Over this frame, jute fabric is stretched, on which straw is carefully sewn. The entrance is in the front end and has a loophole to permit observation. Wire bindings make the imitation truer to the model.

b. This simulation is used near dairies, farm houses, and other places where its presence is likely to seem natural. The necessary materials are as follows: two boards, 3 cm thick, from which the slats for the frame are cut; four meter square piece of jute fabric; six kg of straw; eight meters of iron wire; and nails and twine. Four men can construct this simulation in 1 hour.

302. Exposure and camouflage of observation posts.—*a.* According to Italian theory, the great importance of observation posts makes their concealment essential, since on their existence the effectiveness of artillery fire largely depends. The Italians also believe that although the "lay of the land" may help in picking out enemy observation posts, only aerial photography can reveal them with any degree of certainty. The most revealing clues to their location are beaten tracks, approaches, entrances, protective walls, excavated dirt, contrasts with the terrain, and increase in the lines of communication.

b. To conceal their own observation posts, the Italians believe that it is necessary to disguise the most revealing features and to discipline the movement of personnel around them. The greatest attention has been paid to imitation of natural screening formations, and the Italians have at times gone so far as to set up completely false observation posts at points characteristically adopted to them.

303. Telegraph and telephone lines.—*a. How detected.*—Telephone and telegraph lines are not difficult to find on good large-scale photographs. The clues are the shadows of poles, even the shadows of wires if projected against a light background, tracks left by the line guards from pole to pole, and round spots indicating the poles.

b. How concealed.—For concealment, the line should be planned so as to throw the fewest shadows, or have them concealed under trees. It should also make use of natural and preexisting supports instead of poles, avoid wearing trails, comouflage the disturbance of ground at the base of the poles, and, if possible, camouflage the poles and wires also.

304. Machine-gun camouflage.—The methods of camouflaging heavy machine-gun emplacements with imitative netting in the Italian Army follow conventional practices for flat tops, shadow breaking and blending in the shrubbery.

305. Barbed-wire entanglements.—*a. How detected.*—On unaltered and rocky terrain barbed-wire entanglements appear as more or less dark lines varying from gray to black according to how recently they have been set up and according to the materials used (wooden or iron posts, chevaux de frise, etc.). Usually they are very obvious and follow the lines of the trenches with frequent jutting and reentrant angles. In ground without snow, and therefore dark in the photograph, a careful examination reveals the heads of the posts like so many white dots, geometrically placed. Barbed-wire entangelements on snow, when not covered, show as pale grey streaks. The appearance of a single line of entanglement almost always indicates the excavation of a new trench.

b. How camouflaged.—The line of the entanglements should be such that the guns, while able to sweep in front and behind the entanglement itself, lie in a staggered line. Near the trench, the Italians combine the main entanglement with various simulated entanglements. These are blended in such a way that it is hard to tell real from simulated entanglements. It is, of course, necessary to conceal the characteristic gloss and shadow projection of wire entanglements. To accomplish this, the entanglements are spotted with variegations and covered with light vegetation, which may be either natural or artificial. It is particularly important to conceal posts and stakes.

Chapter 11
ABBREVIATIONS

	Paragraph
General	306
Principles of formation	307
How to find	308
Military abbreviations	309
Telegraphic addresses	310

306. **General.**—The Italian armed forces use military abbreviations on maps, charts, tables of organization, field orders, and other papers. The abbreviations are sometimes used in conjunction with signs and symbols, and are often a key to the specific interpretation of a general sign. Because many words are abbreviated in more than one manner, and because abbreviations are frequently improvised, it is impossible to have all Italian abbreviations listed. Only the standard and most frequently used are listed here. No hard and fast rule can be followed in analyzing the formation of abbreviations. It has been observed, however, that in forming abbreviations the Italians tend to follow certain principles.

307. **Principles of formation.**—*a.* Where one word is to be abbreviated (not a compound word), several methods are used. Either the first letter of the word, or the first letter and another letter (usually at the beginning of a new syllable), of the word, or the first two or three letters of the word are combined to form the abbreviation. Examples are as follows:

Armata _____ *A.*
bombarde _____ *bb.*
Alpini _____ *al.* or *alp.*

b. When a compound word is abbreviated, usually the first letter of each individual word within the compound word forms the abbreviation. Examples are as follows:

autobotti .... *ab.*
anticarro .... *ac.*

c. When a group of words is abbreviated, the first letter of every important word in the group usually forms the abbreviation. Examples are as follows:

Alto Comando del Régio Esercito .... *A. C. R. E.*
autogruppo leggiero .... *Agl.*

d. It appears that little importance is attached to the avoidance of duplication or ambiguity in military abbreviations: for example—*ca.* can denote *careggio, controaérei, carro d'assalto,* and, in certain cases, *corpo d'armata.*

In cases of ambiguity, therefore, the deciding factor must be the relative positions of the components in any group, as well as the context of the group as a whole. Examples are as follows:

ca. rgt. b. .... careggio di reggimento bersaglieri.
pl. p. *ca.* .... plotone pezzi controaerei.
btg. *ca.* .... battaglione carri d'assalto.
cp. g. *ca.* .... compagnia genio di corpo d'armata.

308. How to find.—The abbreviations are listed alphabetically. Thus *A* .... *armata* is the first item. If a combination of abbreviations is not listed, look under the proper portion of the alphabetically listed abbreviations for each part of the abbreviation.

309. Military abbreviations.—The list of abbreviations which follows has been prepared from various Italian documents.

A

Abbreviation	Italian	Translation
A	armata	army
a	acciáio	steel
a	arresti	arrests
a	autoportato, autotrasportábile	motor-transported
a	artieri	mechanics
a	autocarrette	autocarrettes (small trucks)
a	artiglieria	artillery
A A	arma aeronáutica	air force arm
a a	arma aérea	air force
a, acc, aec	armi d'accompagnamento	support arms
a, al, alp	alpini	Alpine troops
a alp	artiglieria alpina	Alpine artillery
a, ar, art	artiglieria	artillery
ab	autobotti	water-tank trucks
a c	controaérei auto-campale	mobile antiaircraft artillery
ac	anticarro	antitank
a C A	artiglieria di corpo d'armata	corps artillery
aca	autocarréggio	motortransport
acc	accompagnamento	accompanying (arms)
acad	autocarrette divisionali	divisional autocarrettes (small trucks)
aca rgt b	autocarreggio di reggimento Bersaglieri	Bersaglieri regiment motor-transport
A C R E	Alto Comando del Regio Esército	high command of the Royal Army
a D	artiglieria di divisione	divisional artillery
a d cr	artiglieria di divisione corazzata	armored divisional artillery

Abbreviation	Italian	Translation
a d f	artiglieria di divisione fanteria	divisional artillery
aer	aerológica	aereorological
aer	aerostieri	balloonists
A F	arresti in fortezza	fortress arrests
Afl	ambulanza fluviale	river ambulance
Ag	autogruppo	motor group
Agb	autogruppo autobus	motor bus group
Agca	autogruppo di autocarrette	motor group of autocarrettes (small trucks)
Agg	autogruppo autocarri "giganti"	extra heavy motor truck group
Agl	autogruppo leggiero	light motor group
Agp	autogruppo pesante	heavy motor group
A M	auitante maggiore	adjutant major
Am	Americano	American
am	autoblindo mitragliatrice	armored car with mounted machine gun
a m	artiglieria motorizzata	motorized artillery
amc	automobilístico e materie di consumo	motor car and fuel
a od	ambulanza odontoiátrica	field dental dispensary (ambulance)
A O I	África Orientale Italiana	Italian East Africa
A R	arresti di rigore	close arrest
Ar	autoreparto	motor detachment
Ar	artiglieria	artillery
Arb	autoreparto autobus	motor bus detachment
Arca	autoreparto di autocarrette	motor detachment of autocarrettes (small trucks)
a rd	ambulanza radiológica	field X-ray laboratory (ambulance)

Abbreviation	Italian	Translation
Arg	autoreparto autocarri "giganti"	extra heavy motor detachment
A Rg A	autoraggruppamento di armata	army motor groupment
A Rgm	autoraggruppamento di manovra	motor-maneuver groupment
Arl	autoreparto leggiero	light motor detachment
Arm	autoreparto misto	mixed motor detachment
Arp	autoreparto pesante	heavy motor detachment
A R Q	aspettativa per riduzione di quadri	temporary dismissal for reduction of personnel
art	artiglieria	artillery
art	artiere	mechanic (of engineers)
art c a	artiglieria controaérei	antiaircraft artillery
art camp	artiglieria da campagna	field artillery
art c o	artiglieria da costa	coastal artillery
art mont	artiglieria da montagna	mountain artillery
art p f	artiglieria su ferrovia	railroad artillery
art p p	artiglieria di grande pontenza e gittata	artillery of heavy caliber and range
art pes	artiglieria pesante	heavy artillery
art pes c	artiglieria pesante campale	heavy field artillery
A S	arresti semplici	open arrests
As	autosezione	motor section
Asb	autosezione autobus	motor section of motorbusses
Asca	autosezione di autocarrette	motor section of autocarrettes (small trucks)
Asf	autosezione frigoríferi	motor section of refrigerator cars
Asg	autosezione autocarri "giganti"	extra heavy motor section
Asl	autosezione leggiera	light motor section
Asm	autosezione mista	mixed motor section

Abbreviation	Italian	Translation
Asp	autosezione pesante	heavy motor section
Asp Rb mot	autosezione pesante con rimorchi biga per divisione motorizzata	heavy motor section with two-wheel trailers, motorized division
a str	artieri stradali	road engineers
at	autotrasportábile	motortransport
av	aviazione	aviation
av A	aviazione d'armata	army aviation
aviot	aviotrasporto, aviotrasportábile	air-borne

B

B	bronzo	bronze
b	bicicletta	bicycle
b (bers)	Bersaglieri	Bersaglieri (sharpshooters)
b a	batteria antiaérea	antiaircraft battery
ba (bb)	banda	band
ba cm	banda camellata	camel band
ba irr	banda irregolare	irregular band
ba r/c	banda regolare a cavallo	regular mounted band
ba r/p	banda regolare a piedi	regular band on foot
bb	bombarde	trench mortars
bes (b)	Bersaglieri	Bersaglieri (sharpshooters)
b g (bog)	bonífica per gassati	antigas first aid
bm	bandature e mascálcia	harness and horseshoeing equipment (farriery)
bog (bg)	bonífica per gassati	antigas first aid
brg	brigata	brigade
btg	battaglione	battalion
btg b a	battaglione Bersaglieri autoportato	battalion of motor transported Bersaglieri (sharpshooters)
btg cr p	battaglione carri pesanti	heavy tank battalion

Abbreviation	Italian	Translation
btg g m	battaglione misto génio	mixed engineer battalion
btg K	battaglione truppe chímiche	chemical warfare battalion
btg m	battaglione mortáio	mortar battalion
btr	batteria	battery
btr bb	batteria bombarde	battery of trench mortars
btr c ca	batteria cannoni controaérei	antiaircraft gun battery
btr f	batteria cannoni per fanteria	infantry gun battery
btr f	batteria su ferrovia	railroad gun battery
btr f o cp 47/32	batteria cannoni per fanteria o compagni da 47/32 someggiata	battery of infantry guns or company of 47/32 pack artillery
btr/m	batteria óbici piccolo cálibro motorizzata	motorized battery of small caliber howitzers
btr p ca	batteria cannoni centro aérei	battery of antiaircraft guns
btr pp	batteria cannoni di grande potenza e gittata	battery of heavy caliber long-range guns
B U	Bollettino Ufficiale	official report

C

C	commissariato	commissariat
C	comando	command; headquarters
C	campo	field
C	centro	central
C	collegamento	connection, communications
c	centro	center
c	comando	command
c	collegamenti	connection communications
c	carro	tank
c	cannone	gun

ABBREVIATIONS

Abbreviation	Italian	Translation
c (cav)	cavallo, cavalleria	horse, cavalry
C A	corpo d'armata	army corps
ca	carreggio	animal transport
c a	contro aérei	antiaircraft
C A cr	Corpo d'Armata corazzato	armored corps
ca/Afr	cannonieri África	African cannoneers
c ac	cannone anticarro	antitank gun
ca/col	cannonieri coloniali	colonial cannoneers
CAFO	Comando Aeronáutico Fronte Orientale	Air command of East Africa.
cal	cálibro	caliber
cap	capitano	captain
c Arl	comando autoreparto leggiero	command of light motor detachment
carm	carri armati	tanks
c Arm	comando autoreparto misto	command of mixed motor detachment
c aut	centro automobilístico	motor car park
cav	cavallo, cavalleria	horse, cavalry
cav	cavaliere	knight (grade of an order of chivalry)
cav uff	Cavaliere Ufficiale	Officer Knight (grade of an order of chivalry)
C B	comando di base	base command
C btg sh	comando battaglione sahariano	Saharan battalion headquarters
cbm	carréggio, bardature, mascalcia	wagon, harness, and horseshoeing equipment.
C c	campo contumaciale	isolation camp
c c	controcarro	antitank
C C N N	Camície Nere	Black Shirts
cc nn	camície nere	Black Shirts
C C R R	Carabinieri Reali	Royal Carabineers

Abbreviation	Italian	Translation
cc rr	Carabinieri Reali	Royal Carabineers
c dicat	comando difesa contro aérei territoriale	territorial antiaircraft defense command
cdo	comando	command, headquarters
C F	centro di fuoco	center of fire
cg (coll)	collegamento	liaison, connection, communication
c g s	centímetro-grammo-secondo	centimeter-gram-second
ch	chirúrgico, chirurgo	surgical, surgeon
cl	célere	celere troops (cavalry)
cl	colonna	column
clb m	colombáia móbile	mobile pigeon loft
cl gs	colonna gas	gas column
cl sm al	colonna salmerie per divisione alpina	pack train column for Alpine division
Cms (C m s)	comando militare stazione	military command station
C mot	commissariato del movimento	transportation commissariat
c n (usually cc nn)	camície nere	Black Shirts
col	collegamento	liaison, communications, connection
col, coll	colonnello	colonel
com (cdo)	comando	command or headquarters
comm	commendatore	commander (grade of order of chivalry)
conc	concentramento	concentration (center)
conv	convalescenziário	convalescent station
conv/q	convalescenziário per quadrupedi	convalescent station for animals

RESTRICTED

Abbreviation	Italian	Translation
C O R V	centrale osservazione e rilevamento vampa	center of observation and flash ranging company
cp	compagnia	company
cp	compagnia fucilieri	rifle company
cp c	comando compagnia	company headquarters
Cp ca Afr	compagnia cannonieri África	African cannoneer company
cp ca/Afr	compagnia cannonieri África	African cannoneer company
cp ca/col	compagnia cannonieri coloniali	company of colonial cannoneers
cp cc	compagnia armi di accompagnamento	support company
cp c rgt	compagnia comando reggimento fanteria	headquarters company of infantry regiment
cp cr M	compagnia carri medi	medium tank company
C P F	comando di piazzaforte	fortified town or place
cp fe a	compagnia fotoelettricisti artiglieria	artillery searchlight company
cp g	compagnia genio	engineers company
cp K	compagnia truppe chimiche	chemical company
cp m 81	compagnia mortai da 81	81-mm mortar company
cp pr	compagnia presidiária	garrison company
C R	centro raccolta	collection center
C R C	comando régio corpo	Royal corps command
C R E M	Corpo Reali Equipaggi di Marina	Royal Corps of Navy Crews
C R I	Croce Rossa Internazionale	International Red Cross
cr L	carro L (leggiero)	light tank
cr L 1	carro L (leggiero) lanciafiamme	light tank flame thrower
cr M	carro M (medio)	medium tank
C R N	centro raccolta notízie	message center

HANDBOOK ON ITALIAN MILITARY FORCES

Abbreviation	Italian	Translation
cr P	carro P (pesante)	heavy tank
C R R	cerchiato, rigato, retrocárico (art)	hooped, rifled, breech-loading (artillery)
C R ve	centro raccolta vestiário-equipaggiamento	collection center for clothing and equipment
cs	caposaldo	reference point
cs	carréggio-salmerie	animal transport and pack train
C s	comando di settore	sector command
C S	comando superiore	high command
C S F F AA	comando superiore forze armate	high command of the armed forces
C s/gr bb	comando sottogruppo bande	command of subgroup of bands
C sh/L	comando del Sahara líbico	command of Libyan Sahara
C smt	centro di smistamento	clearing station (sanitary service)
C s/s	comando di sottosettore	subsection command
C str mb	commissariato stradale móbile	mobile road commissariat services
C sz	commissariato di sezione	commissariat section
C s/z	comando di sottozona	subzone command
C T	comando di tappa	base (halting place) HQ
ct	centúria	company of the militia
c t	centrale telegráfica	telegraph central
c tef (tel)	centralino telefonico	telephone central
ct M d s	centúria milízia forestale	forest militia company
ct M N F	centúria milízia forestale	forest militia company
cv	caverna	dugout
C vb	compartimento della viabilità	road maintenance department
c z	comando di zona	zone command

RESTRICTED

Abbreviation	Italian	Translation
c v	cavallo vapore	horsepower
cr	corazzato	armored
c r	carri armati	tanks

D

Abbreviation	Italian	Translation
D (Div)	divisione	divisions
D at	divisione autotrasportábile	semimotorized division
Dc	depósito centrale	central depot
Dca	depósito centrale automobilístico	central motor depot
Dc Ar A	depósito centrale di artiglieria di armata	central army artillery depot
D cl	divisione célere	mobile division
Dc m k	deposito centrale materiale chímico	central depot for chemical material
D cr	divisione corazzata	armored division
Dc s v	depósito centrale di sanità e di veterinária	central depot for medical and veterinary units
D f	divisione fanteria	infantry division
dfm	divisione motorizzata fanteria	motorized infantry division
dicat	difesa, controérea territoriale	territorial antiaircraft defense
dif	difesa	defense
dig	digestore	sterilizer
Div (D)	divisione	division
D L	Decreto luogotenenziale	Lieutenant's order
D mot	Divisione motorizzata	motorized division
dp	depósito	depot
dp mu	depósito munizione a terra	ammunition depot
dra	drappello automobilístico	motorcar unit (party) or detachment
D S T A M	delegazione servízio técnico armi e munizioni	technical commission for arms and ammunition

Abbreviation	Italian	Translation
D T M	delegazione trasporti militare	military transportation commission

E

E	eritrei	Eritreans
E	est	East
e	esplorazione	reconnaissance
ecc	eccétera	etc.
el	elettricità	electricity
espl	esploratori	scouts (reconnaissance)

F

f (fant, ftr)	fanteria	infantry
f (fer, ferr)	ferrovia	railroad
f	fiume	river
f/F	forestale	forest (adjective)
f	frazione	section, part
f/Ar A	frazione di magazzino di artiglieria di armata	branch of army artillery storehouse (depot)
f carr	fanteria carrista	tank troops
fe	fotoelettricisti	searchlight operators
	fotoeléttrica	searchlight
fe a	fotoeléttrica artiglieri	artillery searchlight
fer/f	ferrovieri (génio)	railroad engineers
ferr/f	ferrovie	railroads
ff	fototelefónica	phototelephone
f.f	facente funzione	performing function
f /F p l	frazione di magazzino fieno, páglia e legna	branch of hay, straw, and wood store
F F A A	forze armate	armed forces
fir, firm	firmato	signed
fm	fanteria motorizzata	motorized infantry
f m	fucile mitragliatore	automatic rifle
fo fto	firmato	signed

Abbreviation	Italian	Translation
fo	fotografia	photograph
fo	fortino	small fort, blockhouse
F O	fuori organico	nonorganic
F o	forte	fort
font	fonotelemétrico	sound-ranging
f/Paa A	frazione di parco automobilístico di armata	branch of army automobile park
F P L	fieno, páglia, legno	hay, straw, wood
f/q c b	frazione di parco quadrupedi, carréggio e bardature	branch of animal carts and harness park
ft (fotel)	fototelegráfica	phototelegraph
ftr	fanteria	infantry
f/Sa	frazione di magazzino di sanità	branch of medical storehouse (depot)
f/V A	frazione di magazzino víveri d'armata	branch of army ration storehouse (depot)
f/V E	frazione di magazzino vestiário ed equipaggiamento	branch of clothing and equipment storehouse (depot)
f/Vm	frazione di magazzino di veterinária e mascalcia	branch of veterinary and horseshoeing equipment storehouse (depot)

G

G	ghisa	cast iron
g	giorno	day
g (ge)	génio	engineers
G a F	Guárdia alla frontiera	frontier guard
G C	Gran Croce, Gran Cordone	Grand Cross, Grand Cordon (grades of orders of chivalry)
g c	génio civile	civil engineer
g c	grosso cálibro	large caliber

Abbreviation	Italian	Translation
ge	génio	engineers
gen	generale	general
gen	geniere	engineer
g f	Reale guárdia di finanza	royal finance guard
G I L	Gioventù Italiana del Littório	Fascist youth organization
G I L E	Gioventù Italiana del Littório all'estero	Fascist youth organization outside Italy
G M	Giornale Militare	Military newspaper
G N	Génio Navale	naval engineer
g p	gruppo pesante	heavy artillery
gr	granata	grenade
gr	grande	large
gr	gruppe	group
gra (gran)	granatieri	grenadier
gr a dfm	gruppo artiglieria divisione fanteria motorizzata	motorized divisional infantry artillery group
gr av O	gruppo d'aviazione da osservazione	aviation observation group
gr c	gruppo squadroni	squadron cavalry group
grt	granatieri	grenadiers
gr tt	gruppo trattrici	group of tractors
G U	Grandi Unità	large units

H

hec	Orário Europa Centrale	central European time
hr	ora, orário	hour, schedule

I

I	intendenza	intendant (quartermaster)
i	ídrici	water supply troops
IA	intendenza d'armata	army intendant (quartermaster)
I G	intendenza generale	intendant (quartermaster) general

ABBREVIATIONS

Abbreviation	Italian	Translation
i g s	incárico grado superiore	temporary rank
inf	informazione militare	military intelligence
inf T	infermeria temporánea	emergency infirmary
int	zone interiore	zone of the interior
iq	infermeria quadrupedi	infirmary for animals
I s lg	ispettorato servízio legnami	wood service inspectorate
It	Italiano	Italian
itq	infermeria temporànea quadrupedi	temporary infirmary for animals

J

J T	intercezione radio o telefónica	radio or telephone intercept
J T O	servízio segreto messaggieri operanti	secret messenger service of operating troops

K

K	truppe chímiche	chemical warfare troops
Kg	chilogrammo	kilogram
Km	chilómetro	kilometer

L

L	Líbici	Libyan
L	laboratório	laboratory
l	leggiero	light
l	lungo	long
Lab K c	laboratório chímico da campo	field chemical laboratory
lav	làvoratori	workers
lav	lavori	works, labor
lf	lanciafiamme	flame thrower
L g c	laboratório del génio civile	civil engineer laboratory
L K	laboratório chímico da campo	field chemical laboratory
L kbt	laboratório chímico, batteriológico, tossicalógico	chemical, bacteriological and toxilogical laboratory

Abbreviation	Italian	Translation
LL MM	Loro maestà	their majesties
L R	línea di resistenza	main line of resistance
L S	línea di sicurezza	outpost line of resistance
L str	laboratório stradale	road laboratory
lung	lunghezza	length, wave lengths

M

Abbreviation	Italian	Translation
M	magazzino	storehouse, depot
M	monte	hill or mountain
m	materiale	material
m	médio	medium
m	metro	meter
m	minatori (génio)	miners, sappers (engineers)
m	misto	mixed
m	mitragliatrice	machine gun
m	móbile	mobile
m	montagna	mountain
m	mortáio	mortar
m	morto	casualty
m	motorizzata	motorized
m	munizioni	ammunition
m 81	mortáio da 81	81-mm mortars
m a 45	mortáio 45 d'assalto	45-mm mortars
M A C (MACA)	Milízia artiglieria contro-aérei	antiaircraft artillery militia
M A M	milízia Artigleria Maríttima	Maritime Artillery Militia
M Ar A	magazzino di artiglieria d'armata	army artillery storehouse (depot)
M Ar bm	magazzino speciale artiglieria, bardature e mascálcia	special depot for artillery harness and horseshoeing equipment
M A S	motoscafo antisommergíbile	Italian mosquito boat

Abbreviation	Italian	Translation
mas	mascheratori	camouflage engineers
mb	móbile	mobile
m c	médio cálibro	medium calibre
m c	matérie consumo e vari	fuel and motor supplies
mcg	marcónigram	radio (wireless) message
M D A C O S	Milízia Defesa Coste	Coast Defense Militia
m d s	milízia delle strade	road militia
me	meccánici elettricisti	electrician mechanic
M F	milízia ferroviária	railroad militia
M F P L	magazzino fieno, paglia e legna	hay, straw, and wood depot
mg	montagna	mountain
mil	militare	military, soldier
mitr	mitragliatrice	machine gun
M K	magazzino materiale chímico	chemical storage depot
mm	millímetro	millimeter
m M N F	manípolo milízia forestale	subunit (maniple) of forest militia
mn	munizioni	ammunition
M N F	milízia nazionale forestale	forest militia
mod	modello	model
mont	montagna	mountain
M O T (mot)	motorizzata	motorized
mp	manípolo	fascist subunit (maniple)
mp M d S	manípolo milízia della strada	subunit of road militia
M Str A	magazzino strade d'armata	road-building maintenance army storehouse
M T	móbile, territoriale	mobile, territorial
mtr	mitraglieri	machine-gunners
mtr	mitragliatrice leggiera	light machine gun

RESTRICTED

Abbreviation	Italian	Translation
mtrp	mitrigliatrice pesante	heavy machine gun
mu	munizoni	ammunition
mv	munizioni, víveri	ammunition and food
M V A	magazzino víveri avena	depot for rations and forage
M V E	maggazzino vestiário ed equipaggiamento	depot for clothing and equipment
M V S N	Milízia Volontária per la Sicurezza Nazionale	Voluntary Militia for National Security (Facist Militia)

N

N	nord	North
N (n)	núcleo	small party or group
N	número	number
n	notízie	messages
n ch	núcleo chirúrgico	surgeon's party
n e	núcleo d'esplorazione	reconnaissance party
N E C	núcleo esplorante célere	reconnaissance party (fast)
n i b	núcleo inquadramento boscaiuoli	party of deforestation planning
n /ma	nucleo movimento stradale e assistenza automobilística	road traffic and motor aid party
N O	nave ospedale	hospital ship

O

O	osservatório	observation post
O	osservatório in caverna o in casamatta	observation post in a dugout or fortified position
O	ovest	west
O	ora, l'ora	the hour, zero hour
o	óbice	howitzer
O A	osservazione di artiglieria	artillery observation post
o a	osservazione aérea	aerial observation

ABBREVIATIONS

Abbreviation	Italian	Translation
ob	óbice	howitzer
O C (o c)	Osservazione e collegamento	observation and communications
o c	onde corte	short wave
o c	ospedale da campo	field hospital
O d g	órdine del giorno	order of the day
Of	officina	workshop
Of cg	officina autocarreggiata	mobile workshop
o m	onde médie	middle waves
O M S	Órdine Militare di Savóia	Military Order of Savoy
O N B	Ópera Nazionale Balilla	National Balilla organization
O N D	Ópera Nazionale Dopolavoro	Worker's recreation organization
org	orgánico	organization
orv	osservazione e rilevamento vampa	observation and flash ranging
osp	ospedale	hospital
oss	osservazione	reconnaissance
ost	osteria	tavern or inn
O V R A	Ópera Vigilanza Ripressione Antifascista	Vigilance Organization for the Repression of Antifascism

P

P	partenza	start
P	pesante	heavy
P	posizione	position
P	protocollo	protocol
p	personale	personnel
p	piano	level
p	píccolo	small, little
p	pezzo	piece
p	pistola	pistol

441   **RESTRICTED**

Abbreviation	Italian	Translation
p	pontiere (génio)	bridge-building (engineer)
p	porto	port
p	posto	post
P A	posizioni di arresto	combat outpost line of resistance
Pa	parco	park
pa	panettieri	field bakery
Paa	parco automobilístico	motor park
pac	panettieri con forni carreggiábili (modello 1897)	field bakery with animal drawn ovens (model 1897)
p aer	posto aerológico	aerological post
p a g	posto di avviamento materiali del génio	supply depot for engineers
p a m	posto avviamento munizioni	ammunition distributing station
p a q	posto abbeverata	watering post for animals
par	paracadutisti	parachutists
p a s	panettieri con forni someggiabili 1897	field bakery with transportable ovens
paw	panettieri con forni rotabili (modello Weiss)	field bakery with rolling ovens (Weiss model)
p B, p Bn	posto di blocco	roadblocking station
p c	píccolo cálibro	small caliber
p c	posto di corrispondenza	message center
p ca	cannone controaérei	antiaircraft guns
p c c	per cópia conforme	confirmed statement
p d	posto distribuzione	distribution point
p d a m	posto distribuzione ed avviamento munizione	distribution and ammunition supply post

Abbreviation	Italian	Translation
p d / N Sual	posto distribuzione di núcleo di sussistenza per reggimento alpino	rations party's distributing point for alpine regiment
p d m c	posto distribuzione matérie consumo e vari	distribution post for motor and fuel supplies
p d Su	posto distribuzione sussistenza	rations distribution point
p d / s z Sual	posto distribuzione di sezione sussistenza per divisione alpina	supply section distributing point for alpine division
P F	polizía forestale	forest police
pf	piazzaforte	fortified town or place
pf	portaferiti	stretcher
pg, ptg	pattúglia	patròl
pg Oc	pattuglia di osservazione e collegamento	observation and liaison patrol
pic	píccolo	little
pl, plat	plotone	platoon
pl c	plotone cavalieri	cavalry platoon
pl c ac	plotone cannoni anticarro	antitank gun platoon
pl c mtr	plotone cavalieri mitraglieri	cavalry machine-gun platoon
pl cr L	plotone carri leggieri	light tank platoon
pl m 81	plotone mortái da 81	81-mm mortar platoon
pl pf Saal	plotone portaferiti di sezione sanità alpini	stretcher bearer platoon of sanitary section for Alpini
pl p o pl 47/32	plotone pezzi o da 47/32	platoon of guns or platoon of 47/32's
pl sh	plotone sahariano	Sahara platoon
P M	Púbblico Ministero	Public Minister
pm	pompieri	fire fighters

Abbreviation	Italian	Translation
p m	posta militare	field post office
p me	posto medicazione	dressing station
P N F	Partito Nazionale Fascista	National Fascist **Party**
P O	protocollo ordinário	ordinary protocol
pont	pontieri (génio)	bridge builders (engineers)
pp	grande potenza e gittata	power and long range
P R	protocollo riservato	reserved protocol
pr	presidiário	garrison
p r f	posto raccolta feriti	medical collecting center
p rt	posto radiotelegráfico	radiotelegraph station
P S	Púbblica Sicurezza	Public Safety
p s	posto soccorso	aid station
p s a	posto di segnalazione con aérei	aerial signal post
p s b	posto segnalazione con bandiere	flag signal post
p s f	posto segnalazione con fari	flare signal post
p s f	posto di sosta feriti	dressing station
p s fr	posto di soccorso ferroviário	railroad aid station
P so	passo	pass
p S, p Sn	posto di segnalazione	signal post
p s r	posto segnalazione con razzi	rocket signal post
pte	ponte	bridge
ptg, **pg**	pattúglia	patrol
p u	peso útile	working load
p v	posto vettovagliamento	reprovisioning (food) point
p v ca	posto vedetta della rete d'avvistamento contro-aérei	antiaircraft warning net observation post

Q

Abbreviation	Italian	Translation
q	quadrato	square
q	quadrupedi	animals
q	quota	spot height
qch	quadrupedi, carreggio, bardature	animals, wagons, harnesses
Q G (qg)	quartiere generale	General Headquarters (Personnel)
quadr	quadrupedi	pack animals

R

Abbreviation	Italian	Translation
r	razza	rocket, Very, light
r	reggimento	regiment
R A	Régia aeronáutica	Royal Air Force
rag	raggruppamento	special groupment
R C T C	Régio corpo truppe coloniali	Royal corps of colonial troops
R D	Régio Decreto	Royal Decree
rd	radiologica	radio (adj.)
R E	Régio Esército	Royal Army
r e g g, reggto	reggimento	regiment
rep	reparto	unit
rep s Saal	reparto someggiato di sezione sanità per alpini	pack animal unit of Alpine sanitary section
rp	radiotelefónica	radiotelephone
r f	reggimento fanteria	infantry regiment
R G	Régia Guárdia	Royal Guard
R G F	Régia Guárdia di Finanza	Royal Customs Guards
rgp	raggruppamento	special groupment
rgr	raggruppamento	special groupment
rgt	raggruppamento trattrici	special tractors group
rgt	reggimento	regiment

Abbreviation	Italian	Translation
rgt a D mot	reggimento artiglieria di divisione motorizzata	artillery regiment of motorized division
rgt c	reggimento cavalleria	cavalry regiment
R I	radio intercetto	intercept (radio) apparatus
ris	riservato	secret
ris	riserva	reserve
R M	Régia Marina	Royal Navy
R N	Régia Nave	Royal Ship
R N	Riserva Navale	Naval Reserve
R P	riservato personale	reserved personnel
rp	reparto	detachment, unit
rp /Ar A	reparto di magazzino	Army artillery depot detachment
rp a	reparto autocarrato	motor car detachment
rp ca Sz Sa	reparto carreggiato di sezione sanità	mobile detachment of medical section
rp/Do Ar A	reparto deposito centrale di artiglieria d'armata	central army artillery depot detachment
rp/Ge	reparto di magazzino del génio	engineers depot detachment
rp lav	reparti do lavoro	labor detachment
re m re	reparto munizioni e víveri	ammunitions and rations detachment
rp pf	reparto portaferiti	stretcher-bearers detachment
rp toca	reparto topocartográfico	cartographical detachment
trp/ne	reparto di magazzino vestiário ed equipaggiamento	clothing and equipmen depot detachment
R S	Ruolo Speciale	special roster

S

Abbreviation	Italian	Translation
S	Somali	Somali
S	Sud	South
s	segreto	secret
s	staffetta	messenger
s	someggiata	pack-carried
Sa	sanità	sanitary, medical
Sab	sezione autobotti	water-tank truck section
san	sanità, sanitário	medical
S A R	Sua Altezza Reale	His Royal Majesty
Sa V	sanità e veterinária	medical and veterinary
s b	staffetta in bicicletta	bicycle messenger
s c	staffetta a cavallo	messenger on horseback
sc	scaglione	echelon
sc mu	scaglione munizione	munitions echelons
sett	settore	sector
sett	settentrionale	northern
sez (sz)	sezione	section
sez aer	sezione aerológica	aerological section
sez font	sezione fonotelemétrica	sound detector section
s/gr	sottogruppo	subgroup
sh	Sahariana	Sahara
sh/L	Sahara Líbica	Libyan Sahara
S I A	Servízio Informazione Aeronáutica	Air Force Intelligence Service
S I M	Servízio Informazione Militare	Military Intelligence Service
S I N	Servízio Informazione Navale	Naval Intelligence Service
S M	Stato Maggiore	Staff
SM	Sua Maestà	His Majesty
Sm	salmeria	pack train
sm ca	salmeria e carreggio	animal transport
s mo	staffetta in motociclo	motorcycle messenger

Abbreviation	Italian	Translation
S M O M	Sua Maestà Officina Medica	His Majesty's medical commission
smt	smistamento	clearing
S O	sud-ovest	Southwest
S O M	Sovrano Órdine di Malta	Sovereign Order of Malta
som	someggiato	pack transport
Sott uff	sottufficiale	noncommissioned officer
S P	Sala di Punizione	place of punishment
sp	speciale	special
s p	staffetta a piedi	messenger on foot
s p e	servízio permanente effettivo	permanent effective service (regular army officer)
sq	squadra	squad
sq	squadrone	squadrone
sq al	squadra alpina	Alpine squad
sq c	squadra cavalieri	cavalry squadron
sqd	squadrone	squadron
sqd	squadrone cavalieri	cavalry squadron
sqg	squadríglia	flotilla (marine) squadron (av)
sqg O	squadríglia da osservazione	observation squadron (air)
sq i b	squadra inquadramento boscaiuoli	squad of deforestation planning
sq mtr ca	squadra mitraglieri controaérei	antiaircraft machine-gun squad
sq pas	squadra panettieri con forni someggiábili (modello 1897)	field bakery squad with portable ovens (1897 type)
sq pam	squadra panettieri con forni rotábili (modello Weiss)	bakery squad with rolling ovens (Weiss model)

RESTRICTED

ABBREVIATIONS

Abbreviation	Italian	Translation
sq T/Cr	squadra tráino per carro armato	tow squad for tanks
sq toca	squadra topocartográfica	cartographic squad
sq tocafrg	squadra topocartográfica-fotogrammétrica	cartographic and photogrammetric squad
s s	servízio di sanità	medical service
s/s	sottosettore	subsector
S T	servízio técnico	technical service
st	stazione	station
st aer	stazione aereológica	aerological station
st fe	stazione fotoeléttrica	searchlight station
st fe a	stazione fotoeléttrica artiglieria	artillery searchlight station
st ff	stazione fototelofónica	phototelephone station
st font	stazione fonotelemétrica	sound-ranging station
st ft	stazione fototelegráfica	phototelegraphic station
st orv	stazione osservazione e rilevamento vampa	observation and flash ranging station
str	strada	road
st rt (rv)	stazione radiotelefònica	radiotelegraph or radiotelephone station
st t	stazione telegráfica	telegraph station
S U	Stati Uniti	United States
S u	sussistenza	supply
S V	sanità veterinária	medical and veterinary
sz	sezione	section
s/z	sottozona	subzone
sz acad	sezione autocarrette divisionale	divisional light trucks section
sz b g	sezione bonífica per gassati	gas aid section
sz bog	sezione bonífica per gassati	gas aid section
sz cc rr b	sezione Reali Carabinieri in bicicletta	section of Royal Carabinieri bicyclists

Abbreviation	Italian	Translation
sz cc rr c	sezione Reali Carabinieri a cavallo	section of mounted Royal Carabinieri
sz cc rr	sezione Reali Carabinieri per divisione corazzata	section of Royal Carabinieri for armored division
sz cc rr mg	sezione Reali Carabinieri da montagna	section of mountain Royal Carabinieri
sz d	sezione disinfezione	disinfection section
sz f	sezione ferroviária	railroad section
sz fc	sezione fotoelettricisti	searchlight section
sz ff	sezione fototelefónica	phototelephone section
sz font	sezione fonotelemétrica	sound ranging section
sz ft	sezione fototelegráfica	phototelegraphic section
sz g c	sezione del génio	section of engineers
sz mv	sezione di reparto munizioni e víveri	munitions and rations section
sz av o	sezione d'aviazione da osservazione	air observation section
sz pa	sezione panettieri senza forni móbili	field bakery section without mobile ovens
sz pac	sezione panettieri con forni carreggiabili (modello 1897)	field bakery section with horse-drawn ovens (model 1897)
sz p ca	sezione cannoni centro aérei	antiaircraft gun section
sz su	sezione sussistenza	supply section
sz to	sezione topográfica per l'artiglieria	artillery topographic section
sz toca	sezione topocartográfica	cartographical section
sz vb	sezione della viabilità	road maintenance section
sz zt	sezione záptie	section of Eritrean carabineers

RESTRICTED

T

Abbreviation	Italian	Translation
T	territoriali	territorials
T	tonnellata	ton
t	telegráfico o telegrafisti	telegrafic or telegraphers (engineers)
tatt	táttico	tactics
T C	torretta di carro	tank turret (map)
t/cr	trattore per carro armato	tank tractor
telefer (tf)	teleferisti	cable car (engineers)
telfot	telefotografista	telephoto operator
tf (telefer)	teleferisti	cable car (engineers)
t m	tráino meccánico	mechanically drawn
tmec	tempo europeo centrale	middle European time
to	topográfica	topographical
toca	topocartográfica	cartographical
tocafog	topocartográfica fotogrammática	cartographic photogrammetric
tre	torretta	turret (map)
tr O	treno ospedale	hospital train
tt	trattrici	tractor

U

Abbreviation	Italian	Translation
U	unità	unit
U C P	ufficio censura postale	postal censorship office
uff	ufficiale o ufficio	officer or office, function
umis	ufficio militare imbarchi e sbarchi	military embarkation and debarkation headquarters
unfoc	unità di fuoco	Day's fire unit
U P	ufficio postale	post office
U P C	ufficio postale di concentramento	central post office
urg	urgento	urgent
urgmo	urgentíssimo	most urgent

RESTRICTED

Abbreviation	Italian	Translation
U T	ufficio permanente di tappa	permanent base headquarters
U T C	ufficio telegráfico di concentramento	central telegraph office

V

V	valle	valley (map)
v	vettovagliamento	rations (victuals)
V A	víveri, avena	rations and oats
vb	viabilità	road maintenance
ve or vel	velocità	velocity, speed
V E	vestiário, equipaggiamento	clothing and equipment
vel or ve	velocità	velocity, speed
V F P L	víveri, fieno, páglia e legna	rations, hay, straw, and wood
vest	vestiário	clothing
vet	veterianário	veterinary
vett	vettovagliamento	supplies
viv	víveri	provisions
V m	víveri munizione	rations and ammunition

Z

Z	zona	zone
Z A	zona d'armata	Army Zone
zap (zapp, zp)	zappatori	sappers
zm	zappatori-miratori zaptie	sappers-miners Eritrean Carabineers

310. **Telegraphic addresses.**—The following information has been obtained from a captured document. The document was published by the "Minister for War" and is titled *Indirizzi Convenzionali Telegráfici* (Conventional Telegraphic Addresses). Before the outbreak of war these addresses were used frequently in the addressing of messages. A number of the abbreviations published in the following list are still being used.

ABBREVIATIONS

Abbreviation	Translation
Accademiles	Artillery and engineer school
Accademiles	Infantry and cavalry school
Accascuolmiles	Artillery and engineer training school headquarters
accascuolmiles	Infantry and cavalry school
Alpini	Alpine regimental headquarters and headquarters of the detachment: battalion
Approautomiles	Separate headquarters for the supply of mobile units
Armatamiles	Acting army headquarters
Armificimiles	Small-arms factory
Arremiles	Army arsenal
Arteprecimiles	Army laboratory for precision instruments
Artesperimiles	Artillery proving grounds
Artialpina	Headquarters of alpine artillery regiment and headquarters of the battalion
Articelere	Headquarters of artillery of a *célere* division and headquarters of the detachment: battalion
Articorparmata	Headquarters of corps artillery regiment and headquarters of the detachment: battalion
Articosta	Headquarters of coast artillery group and headquarters of the detachment: battalion
Artidarmata	Headquarters of army artillery regiment and headquarters of the detachment: battalion
Artifante	Headquarters of infantry division artillery regiment and headquarters of the detachment: battalion.
Autocentromiles	Headquarters of a motor pool and headquarters of a detachment
Avvocamiles	Judge Advocate
Balnearimiles	Thermal baths
Battevetermiles	Military laboratory for veterinary bacteriology

Abbreviation	Translation
Bersaglieri	Bersaglieri regimental headquarters and headquarters of the detachment: battalion
Bibiartimiles	Artillery and engineer library
Bibliomiles	Central military library
Bibliomiles	Garrison library
Brigacelere	*Célere* brigade headquarters
Brigatafante	Divisional infantry brigade headquarters
Brigramatieri	Sardinian Grenadier brigade headquarters
Carabinieri	Headquarters of a detached carabineer unit
Carbanieri	Carabineer territorial headquarters
Carbanieri allievi	Headquarters of Carabiniere cadet unit and headquarters of battalion and company cadets
Carabinieri Comando Generale	Carabineer general headquarters
Carabinieri Ispettorato	Carabineer zone inspectorate
Carabinieri Legione	Headquarters of Carabineer territorial legion
Carabinieri Legione Lazio	Carabineer headquarters for Lazio
Carabinieri scuola	Central Carabineer academy
Carcemiles	Central military prison
Carcefrevemiles	Military prison for minor offenses
Carnemiles	Army canned goods factory
Carrarmati	Tank regimental headquarters and headquarters of the detachment: battalion
Casanatomiles	Army sanatorium
Caseromiles	Barracks supply depot
Cavalleria	Cavalry regimental headquarters and headquarters of the detachment: battalion

ABBREVIATIONS

Abbreviation	Translation
Chimiles	Chemical warfare regimental headquarters
Chimibromiles	Army food laboratory
Codicat	Headquarters of territorial antiaircraft defense
Colombamiles	Military pigeon loft
Coloniamiles	Central depot for Colonial Troops
Comagenimiles	Corps engineer headquarters
Comartimiles	Corps artillery headquarters
Comascuomiles	Central military school headquarters
Comcarmilitare	Military commission for supply of frozen meat
Comiantiaerea	Central interministerial board for antiaircraft defense
Comozonamiles	Zone headquarters
Comosamiles	Medical company headquarters
Contraerei	Regimental antiaircraft artillery command and headquarters of separate battalion
Corazzieri Roma	King's body-guard (carabineers)
Corpamiles	Corps headquarters
Costamiles	Post headquarters
Construgenimiles	Army engineer construction workshop
Dechimiles	Central chemical warfare headquarters
Depalpino	Depot headquarters for an alpine regiment
Departialpina	Depot headquarters for an alpine artillery regiment
Departicelere	Depot headqdarters for a *célere* division artillery regiment
Departicorparmata	Depot headquarters for a corps artillery regiment
Departidarmata	Depot headquarters for an army artillery regiment

455   **RESTRICTED**

Abbreviation	Translation
Departifante	Depot headquarters for an infantry division artillery regiment
Depobersaglieri	Depot headquarters for a bersaglieri regiment.
Depocarrarmati	Depot headquarters for a tank regiment
Depocavalleria	Depot headquarters for a cavalry regiment
Depocontraerei	Depot headquarters for an antiaircraft regiment
Depocosta	Depot headquarters for a separate coast artillery battalion
Depofanteria	Depot headquarters for an infantry regiment
Depogenio	Depot headquarters for an engineer regiment
Depogenieferri	Depot headquarters for a railroad engineer regiment
Depogeniomina	Depot headquarters for an engineer mining regiment
Depogenioponti	Depot headquarters for a bridging engineer regiment
Depogranatieri	Depot headquarters for the Sardinian Grenadier regiment
Detramiles	Military transportation delegation
Difesatermiles	Territorial defense headquarters
Dirartimiles	Office of artillery
Direcommiles	Office of the chief of corps administrative service
Dirsamiles	Office of the chief of corps medical service
Disciplinamiles	Penal company
Distremiles	Military district
Divifantemiles	Infantry division headquarters

RESTRICTED

ABBREVIATIONS

Abbreviation	Translation
Divimotomiles	Motorized division headquarters
Divisioalpina	Alpine Division headquarters
Divisiocelere	Celere division headquarters
Fanteria	Headquarters of infantry regiment and headquarters of the detachment battalion
Framachimiles	Pharmaceutical chemical institute
Foracombumiles	Fuel and food depot
Forgifimiles	Army engineer works office
Frigorimiles	Refrigerator
Gallettimiles	Baker
Genio	Headquarters of engineer regiment and detached battalion headquarters
Genioferri	Headquarters of railroad engineer regiment
Geniomina	Headquarters of engineer mining regiment
Genipponti	Regimental headquarters and headquarters of detached bridging engineer battalion
Geniostudimiles	Engineer central academy
Geomiles	Military geographic institute
Granatieri	Headquarters of Sardinian Grenadier regiment
Guerra Alpini	Alpine troops inspectorate
Guerra Amministrativo	Office of the chief of administrative service
Guerra artiglieria	Office of the chief of artillery
Guerra Celere	Celere troops inspectorate
Guerra Chimico	Office of the chief of chemical warfare service
Guerra commissari	Commissariat service inspectorate
Guerra diter	Office of his excellency deputy chief of staff for territorial defense

457   **RESTRICTED**

Abbreviation	Translation
Guerra fanteria	Infantry inspectorate
Guerra Gabinetto	Cabinet of the ministry of war
Guerra Genio	Office of the chief of engineers
Guerra Ippico	Veterinary service
Guerra Ispartiglieria	Artillery inspectorate
Guerra Ispegenio	Engineer inspectorate
Guerra Leva	General inspectorate of recruiting of noncommissioned officers and men
Guerra logistici	Office of the chief of logistics
Guerra milizia	Liaison office for the Faceist Militia
Guerra Motori	Motorization inspectorate
Guerra Personali civili	Office of the chief of public relations
Guerra Ragioneria	Central accounting army office
Guerra sanità	Office of the chief of medical service
Guerra Stamaggiore	Headquarters of the general staff corps
Guerra Ufficiali	Office of the chief of officer personnel
Infermiles	Permanent infirmary
Ispecommilitare	Inspectorate of military commissary zone
Ispedicat	Inspectorate of the territorial antiaircraft defense
Isposamiles	Medical inspectorate of a zone
Labocamiles	Shell loading laboratory
Lachimiles	Headquarters of central chemical warfare service laboratory at Scam ano Belfieri
Levamiles	Draft office
Magasamiles	Medical supply depot
Mangimimiles	Concentrated food factory
Memiles	Military district of Rome personnel
Molimiles	Mill
Munimiles	Collecting office for war ammunition supplies
Offautemiles	Automotive repair shop

ABBREVIATIONS

Abbreviation	Translation
Omiles	Army factory
Ordinamiles	Office of the chief of chaplains
Ordisupermiles	Service unit for army war college
Panemiles	Bread bakery
Pervamiles	Administrative office for military personnel
Piromiles	Pyrotechnic section
Portomiles	Army office for embarkation and debarkation
Presidimiles	Garrison headquarters
Proiettimiles	Shell factory (Genoa)
Quadrmiles	Remount station
Radioffimiles	Army radio broadcasting station in Rome
Radiostimiles	Army radio broadcasting institute
Reastamiles	Army staff unit in Rome
Reclaprimiles	Main penal camp
Reclusuccumiles	Subordinate penal camp
Revimiles	Corps finance office
Salmemiles	Office of the combined chiefs of staff service unit
Salemiles	Office of the combined chiefs of staff
Sasomiles	Noncommissioned officer's school
Saumiles	Reserve officer's training school
Scuolafamiles	Central infantry school
Scuolamiles	Central engineer school
Scuolapimiles	Central Alpine school
Scuolamiles	Military school
Scuolamiles	Central school of gunnery
Scuolaplimiles	Cavalry training school
Scuolaplimiles	Infantry training school
Scuolaplimiles	Quinto Cavalry training school detachment

RESTRICTED

Abbreviation	Translation
Scuolaplimiles	Training school for artillery and engineers
Scuolartimiles	Central artillery school
Scuolcelemiles	Central school for *célere* units
Segemiles	Engineer works office detached section
Siemiles	International service at Rome
Semiles	Rifle club bureau
Sespomiles	Fuse factory section
Sezartimiles	Artillery section
Sezicommiles	Detached commissary section
Sierantitemiles	Antitetanus serum laboratory
Spemiles	Army hospital
Spolettimiles	Fuse factory
Squaremomiles	Headquarters of remount squadron
Stabipenamiles	Headquarters of military penal establishment
Supergeniomiles	Headquarters of the engineer studies and testing services
Supermiles	Army war college
Supertigliemiles	Office of the chief of arms and munitions
Sussimiles	Supply company headquarters
Tatiromiles	Firing table section
Tribunamiles	Territorial military tribunal
Trisumiles	Supreme military tribunal
Uffartimiles	Detached artillery office
Ufficicommiles	Military commissary local office at Genoa
Uffigomiles	Permanently detached office of the office of engineer works
Vestequimiles	Central clothing depot
Viverimiles	Rations depot

Chapter 12

MISCELLANEOUS

	Paragraph
SECTION I. Road spaces	311–313
II. Flags and insignia of certain units.	
III. Coinage, weights, and measures	314–319

SECTION I
ROAD SPACES

	Paragraph
Movement by road	311
Movement by rail	312
Movement by sea	313

311. Movement by road.—*a. Speed of march.*—(1) *Rates of march.*—Two rates of march are recognized: ordinary (*márcie ordinárie*) and rapid (*márcie céleri*).

Unit	Ordinary (miles per hour)	Rapid (miles per hour)
Infantry, Alpini, Pack artillery, Pack transport } including halts	2½	3 to 3½
Cyclists	7½	11 to 12½
Cavalry and horse artillery	5	6¼
Motorized artillery	15½	
Light tanks	15½	
Other motorized units	15½	
Medium tanks	9½	

(2) *Distances per day.*—In a forced march the length and not the pace of the march is increased.

461 RESTRICTED

Arm	Ordinary (miles)	Forced (miles)
Infantry	15	20 to 30
Cyclists	40	75
Artillery	22	44
Cavalry	28	56
Pack transport	18½	28
Motor transport	50 to 75	75 to 100

b. Length of columns.—The length of columns given for the following units allows for intervals between march groups:

(1) *Infantry division.*—(*a*) For nonmotorized elements (foot, pack, and horse-drawn): 14 miles long on wide roads, and 17½ miles long on narrow roads—when halted or when moving at 2½ miles per hour. On wide roads 4 men march abreast and 2 men beside each pack animal. On narrow roads 3 men march abreast and 1 man beside each pack animal.

(*b*) For motorized elements: 1 mile long when halted, and 2½ miles long when moving at 15½ miles per hour.

(2) *Motorized division.*—11⅕ miles long when halted, if using light motor transport; 9½ miles long when halted, if using heavy motor transport; 46 miles long when moving at 15½ miles per hour, if using light motor transport; and 38 miles long when moving at 15½ miles per hour, if using heavy motor transport.

(3) *Mobile (Cavalry) division (divisione célere).*—(*a*) For mounted and horse-drawn elements: 1⁹⁄₁₀ miles long when halted or when moving at 5 miles per hour.

(*b*) For bicycle elements: 3½ miles long when halted or when moving at 7½ miles per hour.

(*c*) For motorcycle elements: ⅐ mile long when halted, and ½ mile long when moving at 15½ to 25 miles per hour.

(*d*) For motorized elements (including light tanks): 6½ miles long when halted and 26 miles long when moving at 15½ miles per hour.

MISCELLANEOUS

c. Order of march.—Italian manuals state that the order of march depends on circumstances. The following points are for guidance:

(1) Over long distances the order of march should be altered from time to time.

(2) Whenever circumstances permit, pack and transport should move with the units to which they belong.

(3) In a long column, weapon and ammunition transport should be collected into one echelon, marching at the tail of the column, except when the enemy is likely to be encountered; in this case, weapons should move with their units.

312. Movement by rail.—*a. Number of trains for units.*

Complete infantry division	46
Mobile division	35
Motorized or armored	48

b. Particulars of military trains.—(1) The normal composition of a military train is 40 wagons loaded or 50 unloaded.

(2) The normal speed of a troop train under favorable circumstances is 25 miles per hour.

(3) The normal capacity of a military train is one infantry battalion (less one company, or one squadron, or one troop).

(4) The following examples indicate the number of wagons and trucks required for units:

Infantry battalion	51
Alpine battalion	92
Black Shirt battalion	33
100/17-mm battery	79
75/27-mm battery	94
Mixed engineer battalion	51

RESTRICTED

c. *Times for loading and unloading a military train.*

Unit	Time (hours)	
	Entrainment	Detrainment
Infantry with animal transport	1½	¾
Cavalry, artillery, horse-drawn, pack, or armored units	2	1
Motor transport units	2½	1½
Heavy artillery and engineer park	3½	1½

313. Movement by sea.—As a basis for calculation, it can be assumed that an Italian division requires 60,000 tons of shipping, or 12 ships of 5,000 tons each.

Section II

FLAGS AND INSIGNIA OF CERTAIN UNITS

Flag or insignia of—	Size and shape	Colors and stripes	Inscription [1]
Supreme Command	1.10 by 0.75 m rectangular.	3 silk stripes green, white, and red (left to right). Flag is lined with white silk.	In center of white stripe, small national coat of arms embroidered with white silk.
Supreme Command Headquarters (detached from its commanding officer).	do	3 stripes, green, white, and red (left to right). No lining.	No coat of arms, name of headquarters shown.
Army Headquarters	do	Blue woolen	In center is word "Armata."
Headquarters detached from commanding officer.	do	Blue woolen with center vertical stripe of white woolen.	Name of headquarters shown.
Artillery Headquarters	0.75 by 0.75 m square.	2 vertical stripes blue and yellow (left to right).	Comando D'Artiglieria dell' ... Armata (three lines).
Engineers Headquarters	do	2 vertical stripes, blue and red (left to right).	Comando del Genio dell' ... Armata (three lines).
Aeronautical Headquarters	do	2 vertical stripes, light blue and dark blue (left to right).	Comando di Aeronautica dell' ... Armata (three lines).
Artillery Central Depot (used for all units of the services).	do	All orange	Deposito Centrale d'Artiglieria dell' ... Armata (four lines).
Engineer Depot (all units)	do	All red	Magazzino del Genio dell' ... Armata (three lines).

[1] Letters are of the same size, 120 mm high in rectangular flags and 80 mm high in square flags.

HANDBOOK ON ITALIAN MILITARY FORCES

Flag or insignia of—	Size and shape	Colors and stripes	Inscription [1]
Veterinary and Blacksmith Depot (all units).	0.75 by 0.75 m square.	White with blue diagonal stripe 10 cm wide from upper left to lower right corner.	Magazzino di veterinaria e di mascalcia dell' . . . Armata (four lines).
Animals, carts, and harness park (all units).	do	White with orange diagonal stripe 10 cm wide from upper left to lower right corner.	Parco Quadrupedi carreggio e Bardature dell' . . . Armata (four lines).
Motor transport (all units)	do	Same, but with green diagonal stripe.	Autoraggruppo dell' . . . Armata.
Corps Headquarters	1.10 by 0.75 m rectangular.	Green woolen cloth	. . . Corpo d'Armata (three lines).
Corps Artillery Headquarters.	0.75 by 0.75 m square.	2 vertical stripes, green and yellow (left to right).	Comando d'Artiglieria del . . . Corpo d'Armata (three lines).
Corps Engineer Headquarters.	do	2 vertical stripes, green and red (left to right).	Comando del Genio del . . . Corpo d'Armata (three lines).
Army Corps Aeronautical Headquarters.	do	2 vertical stripes, green and yellow (left to right).	Comando di Aeronautica del . . . Corpo d'Armata (three lines).
Corps Medical Headquarters (all units).	do	White woolen cloth, red cross 10 cm wide and sign in center.	Direzione Commissariato del . . . Corpo d'Armata (two lines).
Corps Quartermaster Headquarters (all units).	do	All violet	Direzione Commissariato del . . . Corpo d'Armata (three lines).

RESTRICTED

MISCELLANEOUS

Division Headquarters	1.10 by 0.75 m rectangular.	All red	... Divisione (two lines).
Mobile Troops (Corpo Celere).	...do...	Red with diagonal white stripe, 10 cm wide from upper left to lower right corner.	... Corpo Celere (three lines).
Infantry Brigades [2]	...do...	All white woolen cloth	... Brigata di Fanteria (three lines).
Mobile Group	...do...	White with diagonal red stripe 10 cm from upper left to lower right corner.	... Raggruppamento Celere (three lines).
Infantry Regiments [3]	0.75 by 0.75 m square.	2 vertical stripes, red and white (left to right).	... Reggimento Fanteria (three lines).
Cavalry Regiments	...do...	2 triangles lower red and upper white.	Reggimento ... (two lines).
Field Artillery [4] Regiment	...do...	2 vertical stripes yellow and white (left to right).	... Regimento Artiglieria da Campagna.

[2] Will be used by all infantry specialties for cavalry and eventually for tanks and Carabinieri.
[3] Will be used by all infantry specialties, tanks, and Carabinieri.
[4] Will be used by all artillery specialties, regiments or groups.

Source: M. A., Italy, No. 12,301, Jan. 5, 1931.

Section III

COINAGE, WEIGHTS, AND MEASURES

	Paragraph
Metric table	314
Coinage	315
Weights	316
Measures	317
Common Italian gun calibers	318
Convenient approximate conversions	319

314. Metric table.—The metric system is employed in Italy. The metric units are formed by combining the words meter (metro), gram (gramma), and liter (litro), with the six numerical prefixes as in the following table:

Italian	Prefix	Meaning		Units
Milli-	Milli-	1/1000	0.001	Meter for length; gram for weight or mass; liter for capacity.
Centi-	Centi-	1/100	.01	
Deci-	Deci-	1/10	.1	
Deca-	Deka-	10	10.	
Etto-	Hecto-	100	100.	
Chilo-	Kilo-	1000	1000.	

RESTRICTED

MISCELLANEOUS

315. Coinage.—Italy's currency is based upon the decimal system, the basic unit being the lira ($0.0526). There are approximately 19 lire to the American dollar.

Italian	Form	American equivalent (approximate)
Soldo (5 centesimi)	Coin	¼ cent.
Quattrosoldi (20 centesimi)	Coin	1 cent.
Mezzolira (50 centesimi)	Coin ceased to be legal tender 1 January 1941.	2½ cents.
Lira (100 centesimi)	Recently replaced by paper notes and some substitute coins.	5 cents.
2 lire	Formerly coin, now paper notes	10 cents.
5 lire	Formerly coin, now paper notes	25 cents.
10 lire	Coin has been entirely replaced by paper notes.	50 cents.
50 lire	Paper notes	$2.50.
100 lire	Paper notes	$5.00.
500 lire, etc.	Paper notes	$25.00.

316. Weights.

COMPARISON OF WEIGHTS

Long ton	Metric ton	Short ton	Hundred-weight (short)	Kilo-gram	Avoirdu-pois pound	Ounce	Gram
1	1.016	1.12					
0.984	1	1.1	22.04	1000			
0.907	0.89	1	20	907	2,000		
			1	45.3	100		
				1	2.2	35.2	1,000
				0.45	1	16	453.6
						1	28.3
						0.035	1

RESTRICTED

317. Measures.—*a. Linear.*

COMPARISON OF MEASURES OF LENGTH

Mile	Kilo-meter	Rod	Meter	Yard	Foot	Inch	Centi-meter	Milli-meter
1	1. 609	320	1, 609. 3	1, 760	5, 280			
. 62137	1	198. 8	1, 000	1, 093. 6				
		1	5. 02	5. 5	16. 5	198		
			1	1. 09	3. 3	39. 37	100	1,000
			0. 914	1	3	36	91. 4	
					1	12	30. 48	
						1	2. 54	25. 4
						. 3937	1	10
							. 1	1

b. *Area.*

COMPARISON OF MEASURES OF AREA

Square miles	Square kilometer	Hectare	Acre	Square rod	Square meter	Square yard	Square feet	Square inches	Square centimeter
1	2.59	258.9	640						
386	1	100							
		1	2.47	395.3					
		0.404	1	160					
				1	25.3	30.2			
					1	1.196	10.7		
					0.836	1	9		
							1	144	929
								1	6.45
								0.155	1

RESTRICTED

c. *Liquid.*

COMPARISON OF LIQUID MEASURE

Barrel	Gallon [1]	Liter	Quart	Pint	Ounce	Dram	Milliliter
1	42	158.8	168				
	1	3.785	4	8	128		
		1	1.056	2.113	33.8	270.5	1,000
		0.9463	1	2	32		
				0.5	1	16	
					1	8	29.5
						1	3.696
						0.033	1

[1] American gallon, 231 cubic inches; British gallon approximately 20 percent larger.

d. *Dry.*

COMPARISON OF DRY MEASURE

Hectoliter	Bushel [1]	Dekaliter	Peck	Quart	Liter
1	2.84	10			
	1	3.5	4	35.2	32
		1	1.13	10	9.08
			1	8.8	8
				1	1.1
				0.09	1

[1] American bushel. British bushel 3 percent larger.

318. Common Italian gun calibers.

1.0 mm = 0.0393	inches.	81 mm =	3.16	inches.
6.5 mm = 0.0256	inches	88 mm =	3.46	inches.
8 mm = 0.315	inches	100 mm =	3.93	inches.
9 mm = 0.354	inches.	102 mm =	4.01	inches.
20 mm = 0.79	inches.	105 mm =	4.14	inches.
25 mm = 0.98	inches.	120 mm =	4.72	inches.
37 mm = 1.45	inches.	149 mm =	5.86	inches.
40 mm = 1.57	inches.	152 mm =	5.98	inches.
45 mm = 1.77	inches.	210 mm =	8.26	inches.
47 mm = 1.85	inches.	260 mm =	10.23	inches.
57 mm = 2.24	inches.	280 mm =	11.02	inches.
65 mm = 2.55	inches.	305 mm =	11.99	inches.
70 mm = 2.61	inches.	350 mm =	13.75	inches.
75 mm = 2.95	inches.	380 mm =	14.93	inches.
76 mm = 2.99	inches.	420 mm =	16.5	inches.
77 mm = 3.03	inches.			

319. **Convenient approximate conversions.**—*a. Centimeters to inches.*—Multiply by 4 and divide product by 10.

b. Meters to yards.—Add 10 percent to the number of meters. 1 meter equals 1.09 yards; 1 kilometer equals 1093.6 yards.

c. Kilometers to miles.—Divide the number of kilometers by 8 and multiply the result by 5.

d. Kilograms to pounds.—Double and add $\frac{1}{10}$ of the figure arrived at.

INDEX

	Paragraph	Page
Abbreviations	306–310	422
Administration	45, 46	44
Administrative Service	157	132
Advisory councils	44	43
Air Force	3, 178, 270–279, 293	1, 158, 367, 411
Allotment	38	38
Alpine division (divisione alpina)	57	52
Alpine Line	290	408
Alpine regiment	71	66
Alpini	10	6
Antiaircraft and antitank	112, 222–230	98, 212
Antiaircraft artillery	98–100	88
Antigas units	137	111
Antitank company	110	97
Antitank units	97	87
Armament and equipment	204–269	179
Armored division (divisione corazzata)	59, 106	54, 94
Armored troops	103–117	92
Armored vehicles	235–238	251
Army corps (corpo d'armata)	49	46
Army General Staff (Stato Maggiore dell'Esército)	43	43
Army tank battalions	116	99
Artillery equipment	231–234	236
Artillery regiment	111	97
Artillery Service	158	132
Assault and landing division (divisione d'assalto e da sbarco)	52, 67	49, 63
Attack and pursuit	284	404
Automobile Corps and Service	139, 140, 156	112, 130
Awards	195–203	175
Bersaglieri	9	6
Bersaglieri regiment	72–74, 77, 109	68, 71, 97

INDEX

	Paragraph	Page
Black Shirts	25, 75–77	24, 71
Branches, distinctive	6–11	5
Cadre, professional	28–30	28
Camouflage	295–305	417
Cavalry	58, 78–82, 214–221	53, 71, 210
Changes, suggested	5	2
Chaplains' Service	163	142
Chemical Service	160	135
Chemical troops	133–137	109
Chemical Warfare	259–269	343
Chief of Army General Staff (Stato Maggiore dell' Esercito)	42	43
Citizens, training	32	30
Civil police forces	18	16
Classification of tanks	105	93
Clothing. (See Uniforms.)		
Coast artillery	101, 102	91
Coast defense installations	294	414
Costal division	61	56
Coinage	315	469
Colonial troops	25	24
Combined action	281	402
Command and staff	39–44	39
Commissariat Service	153	123
Communication Service	155	130
Communications battalion	113	98
Communications, signal	121–132	103
Conscription, system	20–27	18
Corps or army tank battalions	116	99
Corps headquarters (comando di corpo d'armata)	50	47
Councils, advisory	44	43
Creation of units	24	21
Decorations, medals, and awards	195–203	175
Designations of units	24	21
Doctrine	280–284	401
Efficiency	34	35
Emoluments	36–38	37
Employment	81	73

INDEX

	Paragraph	Page
Engineer	118-120, 239-247	99, 269
Engineer and communications, battalion, mixed	113	98
Engineer Service	159	135
Equipment	204-269, 277	179, 394
Errors, reporting	5	2
Exemptions	21	19
Expansion of existing units	23	21
Fascist Militia (Milizia Volontaria per la Sicurezza Nazionale, or M. V. S. N.)	13, 25, 65, 177	9, 24, 59, 158
Fascists organizations	13, 19	9, 17
Field artillery	87-97	76
Flags and insignia	313	465
Fortifications, permanent	289-294	408
General Staffs	41-43	42
Geographical Service	164	143
Glossary	306-310	422
Grenadiers of Sardinia	8	6
High Command	39, 271	39, 45, 369
Higher units	47-62	45
Highways	172	153
History, Air Force	270	367
Horses, Cavalry	82	74
Identification:		
Plate	194	171
Units	80	73
Infantry	63-77, 204-213, 286	57, 179, 406
Infantry division (divisione fanteria)	51, 53, 86	48, 50, 75
Insignia	180-194, 313	159, 465
Inspectorates (Ispettorati)	46, 142	45, 114
Intendance	141	114
Judge Advocate's Service	169	145
Land reconnaissance units	83-86	74
Light tank battalion	114, 115	98
Limitations	2	1

477

INDEX

	Paragraph	Page
Manpower	26, 27	26, 27
Measures	317-319	471
Medals	195-203	175
Medical Service	161	135
Merchant Marine Service	19	17
Metric table	314	468
Military Police	17	15
Military-Political Fascist Organization	19	17
Militias, special	14	11
Miscellaneous tank units	117	99
Mixed engineer and communications battalion	113	98
Mobile (cavalry) division	58, 84, 114	53, 74, 98
Mobilization	20-38	18
Morale	35	37
Motor transport agencies	138-140	112
Motorized division	56, 85	52, 75
Motorized infantry regiment	70	66
Motorized units	64	58
Mountain infantry division	55	51
Navy	179, 293	159, 411
Normal type, infantry, regiment	66	59
North African type Regiment	91	83
Officer:		
Professional	28-30	28
Rank	174, 175	157
Officer candidates	176	158
Offices, administrative	45	44
Operational units	272	371
Organization	39-140	39
Parachute division	60	56
Pay	36-38	37
Peacetime organization	134	109
Period of service	20	18
Permanent fortifications	289-294	408
Photographic company	132	108
Pioneer battalion	120	102
Po-Adige-Tagliamento Line	291	410

INDEX

	Paragraph	Page
Police:		
Civil, forces	18	16
Military	17	15
Secret, forces	18	16
Postal Service	168	144
Procurement	144	115
Professional cadre and officers	28–30	28
Pronunciation	4	1
Public security, Special Division	16	15
Purpose	1	1
Radiotelegraph battalion and company	122, 123, 126, 129	103–107
Rail, movement	312	463
Railroads	171	146
Rank	174–179	157
Recruitment and mobilization	20–38	18
Regiments	11, 89–96, 135, 137	7, 81, 110, 111
Resistance	285	405
Road spaces	311–313	461
Road and Water Service	165	143
Royal Carabinieri (Carabinieri Reali, or CC. RR.)	7, 12	6, 8
Royal Finance Guard (Regia Guàrdia di Finanza)	15, 25	14, 24
San Marco Marine Regiment	11	7
Scope	2	1
Sea, movement	313	464
Secret police forces	18	16
Security	16, 282	15, 403
Semicombat elements	25	24
Semimilitary Forces	12–19	7
Services, supply, and transportation	141–173	114
Signal communications	121–132, 248–258	103, 325
Soldiers, training	33	33
Special Division of Public Security (Divisione Speciale Pubblica Sicurezza)	16	15
Specialties	6–11	5
Spiritual assistance	163	142
Supply	141–173, 276	114, 378

INDEX

	Paragraph	Page
Supreme Commander	40	42
Supreme General Staff (Stato Maggiore Generale)	41	42
Tactics	280-288	401
Tank battalions	108, 116	96, 99
Tank regiment	107	96
Tanks, classification	105	93
Telegraphic addresses	310	452
Telephone, telegraph, phototelegraph units	131	108
Terminology	4	1
Territorial and field administration	143	115
Timber Service	167	144
Training	31-33, 278	30, 33, 396
Transport agencies, motor	138-140	112
Transport Service	154	127
Transportation	170-173	145
Troops, armored	103-117	92
Troops, chemical	133-137	109
Truck-borne infantry:		
Division	54	51
Regiment	68	
Units:		
Higher	47-62	45
Identification	80	73
Land reconnaissance	83-86	74
Uniforms and insignia	180-194	159
Veterinary Service	162	141
Volunteers	25	26
Warning system	100	91
Water Service	165, 166	143
Water transportation	173	155
Weights	316	470
Young Fascists	19	17

www.ingramcontent.com/pod-product-compliance
Lightning Source LLC
Chambersburg PA
CBHW052040220426
43663CB00012B/2387